Discovering the Footsteps of Time

Edinburgh Critical Studies in Romanticism
Series Editors: Ian Duncan and Penny Fielding

Available Titles
A Feminine Enlightenment: British Women Writers and the Philosophy of Progress, 1759–1820
JoEllen DeLucia
Reinventing Liberty: Nation, Commerce and the Historical Novel from Walpole to Scott
Fiona Price
The Politics of Romanticism: The Social Contract and Literature
Zoe Beenstock
Radical Romantics: Prophets, Pirates, and the Space Beyond Nation
Talissa J. Ford
Literature and Medicine in the Nineteenth-Century Periodical Press: Blackwood's Edinburgh Magazine, *1817–1858*
Megan Coyer
Discovering the Footsteps of Time: Geological Travel Writing about Scotland, 1700–1820
Tom Furniss

Forthcoming Titles
Peterloo and the Violence of Romanticism: Reflections on the Bicentenary of the 1819 Massacre of Reformers in Manchester
Michael Demson and Regina Hewitt

Visit our website at: www.edinburghuniversitypress.com/series/ecsr

Discovering the Footsteps of Time

Geological Travel Writing about Scotland, 1700–1820

Tom Furniss

EDINBURGH
University Press

Edinburgh University Press is one of the leading university presses in the UK. We publish academic books and journals in our selected subject areas across the humanities and social sciences, combining cutting-edge scholarship with high editorial and production values to produce academic works of lasting importance. For more information visit our website: edinburghuniversitypress.com

Edinburgh University Press Ltd
The Tun – Holyrood Road, 12(2f) Jackson's Entry, Edinburgh EH8 8PJ

Typeset in 11/14 Adobe Sabon by
IDSUK (DataConnection) Ltd, and
printed and bound in Great Britain by
CPI Group (UK) Ltd, Croydon CR0 4YY

A CIP record for this book is available from the British Library

ISBN 978 1 4744 1001 4 (hardback)
ISBN 978 1 4744 1002 1 (webready PDF)
ISBN 978 1 4744 1003 8 (epub)

Contents

List of Illustrations   vi

Preface   viii

Abbreviations   xi

1. Introduction: Tourism, Aesthetics and the Discovery
   of Scotland   1

2. Natural History, Travel and Early Explorations of
   Scotland's Natural History   31

3. John Walker's 'Report on the Hebrides' (1764–1771)   63

4. A Country Torn and Convulsed: Pioneering Geological
   Observations in Thomas Pennant's Tours of Scotland
   (1769, 1772)   97

5. Astonishing Productions of Volcanic Combustion:
   Barthélemy Faujas de Saint-Fond's *Travels in England,
   Scotland, and the Hebrides* (1784, 1799)   127

6. James Hutton's Geological Tours of Scotland (1764–1788)   155

7. Natural History among the Mountains of a Wild Country:
   Robert Jameson on Arran, 1797 and 1799   197

8. The End of Romantic Geology in Scotland?
   John MacCulloch's *A Description of the Western
   Islands of Scotland* (1819)   229

Bibliography   265

Index   298

List of Illustrations

Figure 2.1   Herman Moll, 'A New Map of the Western Isles
              of Scotland', in Martin Martin, *A Description
              of the Western Islands of Scotland* (1703),
              between pp. 18 and 19.   51
Figure 2.2   Martin Martin, 'Map of St Kilda', in *A Late
              Voyage to St. Kilda* (1698).   51
Figure 3.1   Margaret M. McKay, 'The Hebrides in
              Relation to Mainland Scotland', in McKay
              (ed.), *The Rev. Dr. John Walker's Report on
              the Hebrides of 1764 and 1771*, p. 34.   75
Figure 4.1   J. Bayly, 'A Map of Scotland, the Hebrides
              and Part of England adapted to Mr Pennant's
              Tours' (London: B. White, 1777) (detail).   105
Figure 4.2   Moses Griffith, 'an accurate view' of Staffa's
              'Eastern side' (detail), in Thomas Pennant,
              A Tour in Scotland, MDCCLXXII, I, between
              pp. 300 and 301.   115
Figure 4.3   Plate based on James Miller's drawing of
              Fingal's Cave, in Thomas Pennant, *A Tour
              in Scotland, MDCCLXXII*, I, between
              pp. 302 and 303.   116
Figure 5.1   J. Bayly, 'A Map of Scotland, the Hebrides
              and Part of England adapted to Mr Pennant's
              Tours' (detail).   128
Figure 6.1   Map of places visited on Hutton's geological
              tours of Scotland, from G. Y. Craig (ed.), *James
              Hutton's Theory of the Earth: The Lost
              Drawings*, p. 25.   164
Figure 6.2   J. Bayly, 'A Map of Scotland, the Hebrides and
              Part of England adapted to Mr Pennant's Tours'
              (detail).   167

Figure 6.3   John Clerk of Eldin, Boulder from Glen Tarff
              (1785), in G. Y. Craig (ed.), *James Hutton's
              Theory of the Earth: The Lost Drawings*, p. 30.   170

Figure 6.4   J. Bayly, 'A Map of Scotland, the Hebrides and
              Part of England adapted to Mr Pennant's Tours'
              (detail).   172

Figure 6.5   John Clerk of Eldin, Granite veins exposed on
              Cairnsmore of Fleet, in G. Y. Craig (ed.), *James
              Hutton's Theory of the Earth: The Lost
              Drawings*, p. 50.   173

Figure 6.6   Geological sketch map of the island of Arran,
              from James Hutton, *Theory of the Earth, with
              Proofs and Illustrations*, III, p. 203.   181

Figure 6.7   John Clerk of Eldin, Unconformity at Jedburgh:
              original drawing of the engraving for plate III
              of Hutton's *Theory of the Earth*, I (1787), from
              G. Y. Craig (ed.), *James Hutton's Theory of the
              Earth: The Lost Drawings*, p. 57.   187

Figure 6.8   'Siccar Point', by Dave Souza (2008), Wikimedia
              Commons © Dave Souza.   189

Figure 7.1   Map of Arran in Robert Jameson, *An Outline
              of the Mineralogy of . . . Arran* (between pp. 49
              and 50), with additions by Nicholas and Pearson,
              'Robert Jameson on the Isle of Arran'.   207

Figure 8.1   William Daniell, 'Loch Coruisg near Loch Scavig',
              from *A Voyage Round Great Britain* (1814–26).   247

Figure 8.2   J. M. W. Turner, *Loch Coruisk, Skye* (1831),
              National Galleries of Scotland.   248

Figure 8.3   John MacCulloch, 'View of the Scuir of Egg',
              in *A Description of the Western Islands of
              Scotland* (1819), III, plate v.   254

Figure 8.4   J. M. W. Turner, *Staffa, Fingal's Cave* (1832).   257

Preface

This book – about geological travel writing in Scotland in the long eighteenth century – attempts to pull together various aspects of my experience of living and working in Scotland since I was appointed as a lecturer in English Studies at the University of Strathclyde in 1987. My love of Scotland's landscape began in that first snowy winter and I explored the Highlands and Islands over the following decades principally in order to climb mountains. In my professional life I completed a book on Edmund Burke's politics and aesthetics and taught various classes that allowed me to develop my understanding of the Enlightenment and Romanticism and the interface between them. My experience of Scotland's mountains and love of Wordsworth's poetry mutually influenced one another, but private and professional passions really began to come together when I first read Dorothy Wordsworth's *Recollections of a Tour Made in Scotland* and followed her – and William's and Coleridge's – footsteps around the Loch Lomond and the Trossachs National Park. One of the consequences of this was the development of a masters class on 'The Discovery of Scotland' which focused on travel writing, novels and poetry about Scotland in the Enlightenment and Romantic periods. Dorothy Wordsworth's reference to a pamphlet guidebook to the Trossachs led me to the parish reports about the Trossachs in the first *Statistical Account of Scotland* and they, in turn, revealed that the representation of Scotland's mountain terrain in the period was imbued with geological controversy. My discovery of James Hutton's geological writings resulted in published essays and the impulse to retrace his footsteps over one glorious long weekend in Glen Tilt. The discovery that Hutton was not the only geologist to have traversed and written about Scotland in the period eventually led to the present book, which brings together my interests in literature, travel writing, aesthetics and science and my passion for the Highlands and Islands.

This book is written by a literary scholar with no academic or professional expertise in geology who has spent the last thirty years teaching and writing about the literature and philosophy of the eighteenth and early nineteenth centuries. As a consequence, the book is at least as much concerned with the literary techniques of the travel accounts it discusses, and the way they represent the terrain and the traveller, as it is with the geology. It is my contention that the literary strategies of this geological travel writing are as interesting as the geological theories and discoveries and, indeed, that there are mutually constitutive relationships between them. As a consequence, each chapter presents an extended close reading of one or two examples of geological travel writing in which I use the core techniques (quotation and textual analysis) of literary interpretation. The chapters examine a sequence of geological tours in chronological order in order to trace the way successive geological travel writers visit, revisit and reinterpret particular areas or places in Scotland, particularly in the Highlands and Islands. This chronological structure also allows me to locate each tour within various kinds of context – geological, literary, aesthetic – and to trace the way developments and controversies in all these contexts through the long eighteenth century impact upon each travel account. The book thus attempts to weave together histories of geology, literature, aesthetics, travel and representations of Scotland in ways that give the book a larger narrative and suggest how these different histories were always already interwoven. Although the book correlates the geological travel writing it examines with geological developments and controversies in Britain and Europe, I am not primarily concerned with whether a particular author's geological interpretations or conclusions were correct or prescient. Informed by current work in the history of science, the book focuses instead on the dynamics of geological controversy and the way they shape particular texts and overlay the terrains of the Highlands and Islands with stratum upon stratum of geological and aesthetic representations. The book is confined to geological travel writing in Scotland because of Scotland's special place in the history of geology in the period and because of the way it correlates with the proliferation of travel writing and literature that made Scotland a must-visit place in the later eighteenth century.

I want to thank Kenneth McNeil for unflagging support throughout this project; Michael Bath and Nigel Leask for their comments on the typescript; Nigel Fabb, for a key insight about Hutton's writing; EUP's two anonymous reviewers; Ian Duncan for an enthusiastic editor's report on the submitted text that helped me cut it down to size; Cathy Falconer for eagle-eyed copy-editing; and my wife, Hooi Ling Eng, for endless help with computer problems. Donald Fraser often hiked with me when I first came to Scotland and taught me how to use an ice-axe. I am also grateful to the Leverhulme Trust for granting me a Research Fellowship, which enabled me to carry out the bulk of the research for this book in the academic year 2013–14. I am grateful, too, to my colleagues in the School of Humanities at the University of Strathclyde for covering my teaching and administrative duties during a sabbatical in the autumn semester of 2014–15.

Abbreviations

ODNB	*Oxford Dictionary of National Biography*
PTRS	*Philosophical Transactions of the Royal Society*
TGSL	*Transactions of the Geological Society of London*
TRSE	*Transactions of the Royal Society of Edinburgh*

*To my wife, Hooi Ling Eng, and to Kenneth McNeil, companions
who have often walked with me in Scotland's mountains, following
the footsteps of time. My future is dedicated to my son, Aidan,
who began following the footsteps by climbing Conic Hill on the
Highland Boundary Fault when he was three.*

These lessons, which the geologist is taught in flat and open countries, become more striking, by the study of those Alpine tracts, where the surface of the earth attains its greatest elevation. If we suppose him placed for the first time in the midst of such a scene, as soon as he has recovered from the impression made by the novelty and magnificence of the spectacle before him, he begins to discover the footsteps of time . . .

John Playfair, *Illustrations of the Huttonian Theory of the Earth* (1802)

Chapter 1

Introduction: Tourism, Aesthetics and the Discovery of Scotland

In this book I explore a somewhat neglected element of the story of the early formation of geology as a discipline – geological travel writing about the Highlands and Islands of Scotland in what scholars refer to as the long eighteenth century.[1] This geological travel writing can be seen as a sub-genre of the travel writing about Scotland that increased so remarkably in the period and contributed to what Alastair J. Durie has called 'the discovery of Scotland' (*Scotland for the Holidays*, pp. 21–43).[2] While accounts of only a handful of tours of Scotland were published in the first sixty years of the eighteenth century, there were significant increases from the 1770s onwards, with the number rising to over fifty in the second decade of the nineteenth century.[3] Samuel Johnson's *A Journey to the Western Islands of Scotland* (undertaken in 1773 and published in 1775) was perhaps the most influential tour of Scotland in the period, partly because his largely negative views of Scotland's terrain needed to be refuted. For Johnson, the model tour of Scotland was Thomas Pennant's *A Tour in Scotland and Voyage to the Hebrides* (1772), whose geological observations will be examined in Chapter 4. For T. C. Smout, however, the tour that had the biggest impact on travel in Scotland was William Gilpin's *Observations, Relative Chiefly to Picturesque Beauty, Made in the Year 1776, On several Parts of Great Britain; Particularly the High-Lands of Scotland* (1789), which reveals that the mountainous scenery he encountered in the Highlands challenged the picturesque aesthetics he had begun developing in the 1760s.[4]

A number of factors helped to make Scotland a fashionable destination for travellers in the period. The Union of Parliaments of 1707 provoked new interest in Scotland south of the border. Daniel Defoe's *A Tour through the Whole Island of Great Britain* (1724–6) ends with 'An Account and Description of Scotland' which focuses mainly on the economic impact of the Union and the potential for Scotland to benefit from improved ways of exploiting its natural resources. Defoe looks at nature, as Robinson Crusoe does, solely in terms of its use-value. Although he celebrates the hospitality of some of the people of the Highlands, the Jacobite rebellion of 1715 reinforced Defoe's view of the Highland terrain as useless and terrifying:

> From this river or water of Abre, all that mountainous barren and frightful country, which lies south is called Loquabre. It is indeed a frightful country full of hideous desert mountains and unpassable, except to the Highlanders who possess the precipices. Here in spite of the most vigorous pursuit, the Highland robbers, such as the famous Rob Roy in the late disturbances, find such retreats as none can pretend to follow them into, nor could he be ever taken. (*A Tour through the Whole Island of Great Britain*, p. 672)

After the repression of the Jacobite rebellions of 1715 and 1745, the British state's military occupation, surveying and road building in the Highlands began to make travelling easier and helped to transform Scotland's brand image from 'a home to barbaric and hostile inhabitants' into 'both a respectable and safe destination' (Durie, *Scotland for the Holidays*, p. 35). The increasing wealth and leisure of the British upper and middle classes allowed them to acquire 'a taste for travel to look at scenery, enquire into antiquities and ruins, and pursue interests in botany, geology and natural history' (p. 37). Boosts to Scottish tourism also came from the Seven Years' War (1756–63), the American and French Revolutions, and the extended war between Britain and revolutionary France (1793–1815), which made traditional patterns of travel, such as the Grand Tour, difficult or sometimes impossible.

Another crucial factor in the transformation in attitudes towards the Scottish Highlands, as we will see in more detail below, was the fashion for the natural sublime stimulated by publications such as Edmund Burke's *Philosophical Enquiry into the Origin of our Ideas of the Sublime and Beautiful* (1757/1759). Almost simultaneously, the natural philosophers and natural historians of the Enlightenment began to see mountains as sources of evidence about the nature and origins of the world and as vast natural laboratories where experiments could be conducted. In the second half of the eighteenth century,

Scotland's mountainous terrain became a crucial testing ground for competing accounts of the origins of the earth and the physical forces that had shaped its geomorphology.[5]

Perhaps the most decisive cultural event that put the Highlands and Islands of Scotland on the tourist map was the publication of James Macpherson's *Fragments of Ancient Poetry* (1760), *Fingal* (1765) and *Temora* (1765).[6] As Durie points out, 'The search for Ossian preoc-cupied many an early visitor to Scotland from the 1760s onwards . . . The net effect was to put places such as Staffa, with its Fingal's Cave, firmly on the itinerary of serious tourists' (*Scotland for the Holidays*, p. 39). 'Whatever side one took in the controversy over their authentic-ity,' Malcolm Andrews writes, 'these poems accompanied nearly every Picturesque tourist into the Highlands, and provoked rapturous recita-tions by the sides of waterfalls, or on the mountain tops' (*The Search for the Picturesque*, p. 202).[7] Importantly for what follows, the cult of Ossian was not antithetical to scientific interest in the geology of the Highlands and Islands. Instead, as Ann MacLeod suggests,

> Macpherson's Ossianic imagery, with its emphasis on natural violence, fragmentation and decay, was in some ways the ideal imaginative coun-terpart to early geology. Both shared a relish for magnitudes beyond the measure of man and, in particular, for scenery in which humanity was minimised or excluded. (*From an Antique Land*, p. 143)

In 1875, Peter Hately Waddell claimed that Ossian's poetry con-tains precise observations of the way Scotland's terrain 'has been the creation of volcanic forces, enriched, harmonized and clothed by deluges of aquatic deposits, far beyond the memory of man' (*Ossian and the Clyde*, p. 9):

> In the course of [these] poems, . . . We trace the operation of earthquakes, with much subterranean disturbance, the moving of mountains, the fall of rocks, the frequent and often terrible discharge of electricity, the formation of new water-courses inland and the violent agitation of the sea outward. (pp. 300–31)[8]

The Ossian poems, then, reimagined the Highland landscape of the remote past as a scene of Romantic heroism and active geological processes.

The extent of this cultural revolution can be measured by contrasting Defoe's response to the Highlands with Sarah Murray's *A Companion, and Useful Guide to the Beauties of Scotland* (1799), which represents Scotland's mountainous terrain as a theatre of sublime geomorphology for the display of her own fortitude and delight. The following passage, which describes her approach to Loch Katrine along the road from Callander, is typical:

> The awfulness, the solemnity, and the sublimity, of the scene at the ford, and by Loch-a-chravy's side, towards the entrance to the foot of Loch Catherine, is beyond, far beyond description, either of pen or pencil! Nothing but the eye can convey to the mind such scenery ... When I quitted the narrow road under the rocks, by the side of Loch-a-chravy, it became amazingly jumbling and winding, amongst various shaped rocks and crags, covered with wood; and rent chasms, deep and dark on everyside; no trace of man, or living thing to be seen; every sound reverberated from rock to rock, flying through the gloomy labyrinth, to announce the approach of unhallowed steps. My heart was raised to heaven in awful silence; whilst that of my poor man was depressed to the dread of hell. (p. 149)

Here, the pass through the Trossachs to Loch Katrine, eleven years before Walter Scott's *The Lady of the Lake* (1810), generates religious awe in the traveller attuned to the sublime. The difference in aesthetic response between the middle-class Englishwoman, whose 'heart was raised to heaven in awful silence', and that of her 'poor man', a working-class guide from Scotland whose heart 'was depressed to the dread of hell', indicates that the new aesthetic response to mountain sublimity was not universally shared but served as a marker of class difference and taste.

By the Romantic period, the lure of Highland Scotland had become all-powerful, with Highland tours being undertaken by major cultural figures such as Coleridge and the Wordsworths in 1803, Walter Scott (1810 and 1814), John Keats (1818), Felix Mendelssohn (1829), J. M. W. Turner (1831) and many others. Nonetheless, we need to bear in mind that the number of visitors to Highland Scotland prior to the publication of *The Lady of the Lake* was relatively low by today's standards. Smout estimates that in the early nineteenth century there were only 'scores' of travellers to the Highlands ('Tours in the Scottish Highlands', p. 120).

Scotland's Geology and Geological Travel in Scotland

D. R. Oldroyd and B. M. Hamilton claim that Scotland was 'one of the countries that contributed most to the foundation of geological science, and provided some of its most notable founders, both in the field and as theoreticians' ('Themes in the Early History of Scottish Geology', p. 43). They also suggest that it was the geological fabric of Scotland itself – given that 'It is a small country, but one that is geologically both interesting and perplexing' – that allowed geologists in Scotland to contribute so significantly to geological science. As Charlotte Klonk notes,

> Scotland . . . displayed a far greater range of geological phenomena than any other part of Great Britain, from sedimentary formations of different ages in the Lowlands to stratified and unstratified formations and volcanic rock in the Highlands and Western Isles region. In no other region can one find so many illustrations of the same locations by different naturalist travellers as in Scotland – most other parts of Great Britain were not illustrated in any detail by more than one geologist. (*Science and the Perception of Nature*, p. 70)[9]

The fact that so many naturalists and geologists travelled to, illustrated and wrote about particularly interesting geological locations and formations across Scotland in the long eighteenth century meant that its spectacular terrain became a colossal geological text that was read and interpreted in support of a range of competing geological theories. Fredrik Albritton Jonsson has suggested that 'the Scottish Highlands offered a laboratory for rival hypotheses' (*Enlightenment's Frontier*, p. 71) about climate change in the eighteenth century; the same might be said for geological theories. Published tours made the Scottish landscape, especially that of the Highlands and Islands, into a core location for the geological history of the earth and the history of geology at one and the same time.

A conventional and convenient shorthand way of describing the geological controversies that shaped debate in the second half of the eighteenth century is to say that they took place between Neptunists, Vulcanists and Plutonists.[10] Although such labels can oversimplify the debate, some of the protagonists of the period represented themselves and each other in precisely these ways. Robert

Jameson, for example, used these terms in 1798 in order to distinguish his reading of Arran's geomorphology from James Hutton's,
claiming that they were coined by the Irish mineralogist Richard
Kirwan, whom he had recently visited.[11] Neptunism, which Martin
Rudwick identifies as the 'standard model' in the period, assumed
that most of the earth's geomorphology had been formed by or
within one or more primeval oceans that had supposedly covered
the entire surface of the planet at an early stage of its existence.[12]
The Vulcanism that gained prominence in the second half of the
eighteenth century argued that much more of the earth's surface
had been shaped by volcanic activity than had previously been
realised. Plutonism, usually associated with Hutton, was distinct
from Vulcanism in assuming that most of the earth's rocks and geomorphology, not just those associated with volcanoes, had been
formed by subterraneous heat and pressure. In what follows, I am
not concerned with whether the geological interpretations and theories developed in the various geological tours of Scotland in the
period were correct or prescient, but with the way they inscribe the
terrain with geological narratives that gradually accumulated significance stratum by stratum and added new aesthetic dimensions
to landscapes that were already conceived of in aesthetic terms.[13]

The way this succession of geological tours made the Highlands of
Scotland into 'classic ground' for geology can be compared with the
historical formation of other key geological locations. In the second
half of the eighteenth century the Auvergne region in south-central
France was visited by a large number of travellers in search of evidence about the contribution of ancient volcanoes to the earth's geomorphology. K. L. Taylor's essay 'Geological Travellers in Auvergne,
1751–1800' constitutes a blueprint for the kind of study that I am
developing here. As Taylor suggests, 'The transformation of particular localities like Auvergne into "iconic places" is a cultural process within the science that . . . has not yet been subjected to close
examination' (p. 74). Taylor admits that his essay 'simply gathers
the outlines of historical information about the first half-century of
Auvergne's geological exploration' as a prelude to further research
(p. 74). These preparatory outlines include a chronological inventory
of all the travellers to the region in the period who can be said to
have contributed to the geological exploration and description of the
Auvergne (pp. 82–8). Although the present book does not assemble a

chronological inventory of all the geological travellers to the Scottish Highlands in the period, it goes beyond Taylor's study by developing detailed close readings of the key geological tours to the region in roughly chronological order.

Scientific Revolutions: From Natural History to Geology

The long eighteenth century can be stretched back to encompass the scientific revolution of the seventeenth century, which is usually said to have its origins in Francis Bacon's promotion of a collective, all-encompassing scientific project based on the empirical method.[14] The establishment of the Royal Society of London for Improving Natural Knowledge in 1660 institutionalised the Baconian scientific revolution.[15] The dominant aims that governed the Royal Society's natural history project were initially set by Bacon's statement in *The Advancement of Learning* (1605) that 'natural history describeth the variety of things; physic the causes, but variable or respective causes; and metaphysic the fixed and constant causes' (p. 97). For Bacon, then, natural history should be confined to describing the variety of natural things, leaving questions of causation to natural philosophy and theology. Natural history involved collecting, describing and classifying specimens from the three 'kingdoms' of nature. It attempted to place the earth's natural objects, plants and animals within a taxonomic system that precluded the possibility that they might be features of a dynamic and developing geosystem or biosphere. Natural history was given a more precise scientific agenda by the publication in 1735 of the first edition of Carl Linnaeus's *Systema Naturae*, which 'established a classificatory system that could seemingly be used to catalogue the whole of the natural world' and initiated a 'taxonomic project [that] was eagerly taken up in the latter half of the eighteenth century' (Thompson, *Travel Writing*, p. 46). As Arthur O. Lovejoy has shown, the theoretical paradigm of the Great Chain of Being helped set the agenda for eighteenth-century natural history by asserting that natural objects and life-forms, from minerals to mankind, were organised in a continuous and coherent system, thus encouraging natural historians to seek out and name the missing links.[16]

Carl Thompson points out that 'Travel as an information-gathering exercise was regarded as [a] crucial arm of the New Science of the late seventeenth century, and to this end the Royal Society . . . did much to promote travel and coordinate the activities of travellers' (*Travel Writing*, pp. 45–6). The protocols of natural history governed what travellers should observe and collect and how they should write about it. Several influential figures, from Bacon to Robert Boyle, wrote guidelines to help travellers make useful observations and write about them in ways that would maintain 'epistemological decorum' (*Travel Writing*, p. 75).[17] The Royal Society's guidelines to scientific travellers influenced travel writing throughout the eighteenth century, especially via popular examples such as William Dampier's *New Voyage Round the World* (1697). Writers were advised, for example, to avoid using metaphors in scientific discourse, and the emphasis on empirical observation, description and classification meant that scientific travel writing tended to exclude the traveller's personal experience and speculative hypotheses about causal and historical origins.[18]

Chapters 2 to 4 of the present book examine natural history tours of Scotland that were wholly committed to the Royal Society's natural history project. Joseph Banks and his team of naturalists, for example, undertook their tour of the Hebrides and Iceland shortly after participating in Cook's first voyage to the Pacific Ocean (1768–71), which was commissioned by the Admiralty and the Royal Society in order to observe the transit of Venus on Tahiti and to discover and claim for Britain the postulated continent of *Terra Australis*. The imperial and scientific exploration of new worlds on the other side of the globe was thus intimately linked to the 'discovery' of Scotland that was undertaken by military surveyors, artists, writers and travellers in the period. The geological tours of Scotland examined in Chapters 5 to 9, by contrast, reveal the impact of what some historians of science have called the 'second scientific revolution'. Jan Golinski suggests that

> Thomas S. Kuhn seems to have been the first historian of science to label the period from about 1780 to 1830 the 'second scientific revolution.' This was the era when such new scientific disciplines as geology, biology, and physiology, were founded and existing ones, especially physics and chemistry, dramatically reconfigured. In general, disciplines became more central to the production of knowledge, embodied in the constitution of university departments and institutes, in specialized scientific societies, and in new journals. This was not simply a matter of specialization or the progressively finer division of a stable domain

of knowledge. Rather, entirely new fields were marked out and came to shape how scientific knowledge was made. ('Humphry Davy: The Experimental Self', p. 15)[19]

Kuhn's notion of the second scientific revolution, articulated in *The Essential Tension: Selected Studies in Scientific Tradition and Change* (1977), may well have been influenced by Michel Foucault's argument in *Les Mots et les choses* (1966), translated as *The Order of Things* in 1970, that the natural history of the Enlightenment or 'classical period' was displaced in the final years of the eighteenth century by an epistemic revolution that saw the emergence, primarily in the work of Georges Cuvier, of biology and botany. While natural history was concerned with the taxonomic classification of minerals, plants and animals based on empirical observation and description of visible structure, biology was concerned with investigating the 'internal laws of the organism', seeing animals and plants as living things that interact in dynamic ways with the outside world and change through time as the ecosystem undergoes geological revolutions.[20] Natural history, then, was displaced by a scientific outlook that saw nature and natural organisms as intrinsically historical. For Foucault, the fact that 'the opposition between organic and inorganic' was fundamental to biology meant that rocks and minerals were excluded from the new science of life (*The Order of Things*, p. 251). Yet the contemporaneous emergence of geology, which viewed rocks and minerals as elements within a dynamic, temporally changing earth system, can be seen as another expression, alongside biology, of the new order of things that emerged at the end of the eighteenth century.

Richard Holmes follows a number of recent scholars in associating the second scientific revolution with Romanticism, Romantic science or Romantic-period science.[21] For many critics, Romantic science is not merely a backdrop to Romantic literature but part of a much more extensive Romantic cultural formation that has more continuities with the Enlightenment project than is usually recognised. Romantic science is often said to have rejected the mechanism of Bacon and Newton in order to see nature as a complex system of subtle dynamic forces and powers – gravity, electricity, magnetism, chemical activity – that constitute nature's intrinsic self-animating vitality.[22] As with the first scientific revolution, travel and travel writing remained crucial. Holmes locates what he calls the 'Age of

Wonder' 'roughly, and certainly symbolically, between . . . Cook's first round-the-world expedition aboard the *Endeavour*, begun in 1768, and Charles Darwin's voyage to the Galapagos islands aboard the *Beagle*, begun in 1831' (*The Age of Wonder*, p. xvi).[23]

As suggested, the shift from mineralogy to geology towards the end of the eighteenth century can be seen as one of the manifestations of the paradigm shift that constituted the second scientific revolution.[24] According to Rachel Laudan and Roy Porter, mineralogy's mode of static description was displaced by geological analysis of the earth's dynamic history and formative processes. In his 'Geological Letters Addressed to Prof. Blumenbach', published in the *British Critic* in the early 1790s, Jean André de Luc noted that '*Geology* is principally distinguished from *Natural History*, which confines itself to the description and classification of the phenomena presented by our globe in the three kingdoms of Nature, insomuch as its office is to connect those phenomena with their causes' (pp. 231–2). In addition to its concern with causality, geological investigation entailed 'abandoning the natural history framework of expectations, which realized particular objects against a universal grid of Nature, and . . . developing a dynamic, relational, understanding of objects and processes within a view of the integrated development of the Earth' (Porter, *The Making of Geology*, p. 157). Romantic-period geology assumed that the earth was a dynamic, complex system of forces and materials that had undergone massive transformations and revolutions over vast timescales and that some of these processes were ongoing.[25]

Foucault's and Kuhn's claims that the second scientific revolution entirely reconfigured disciplines and knowledge are not entirely convincing. Porter stresses that geology was made possible by the mass of fieldwork observations accumulated by mineralogy, allowing mineralogy to be 'comprehended within geology, as the static within the dynamic, the building bricks within the fabric. In 1799, in an image which was to become commonplace, Richard Kirwan called mineralogy the letters of nature, which, written up into words, became geology' (*The Making of Geology*, pp. 157–8).[26] Nor can we say that Romantic-period geology wholly replaced natural history – as James Secord notes, 'natural history . . . seems to have come to an end so often'.[27] John Walker, Professor of Natural History at the University of Edinburgh from 1779 to his death in 1803, used his lectures and writings to stress the need to focus on description, classification and use rather than theoretical speculation and he rejected claims that the earth was subject to ongoing active forces such as volcanism.[28] In addition, as we will see below, the suggestion that natural history and geology appeared in a straightforward historical sequence is further complicated by the fact that a spate of competing geological theories of the earth appeared in late seventeenth-century Britain that anticipated at least some of the characteristics of Romantic-period geology.

Despite these caveats, it remains the case that Romantic-period geology was distinct from natural history and earlier geological speculation and was intimately connected with the emergence of Romanticism. Marjorie Hope Nicolson's *Mountain Gloom and Mountain Glory* (1959) was the first study to alert us to the interplay between geological speculation and the aesthetic experience and theory of the sublime in the long eighteenth century and to the interface in the Romantic period between literature, aesthetic theory and the earth sciences. Since then, a number of scholars have explored a variety of ways in which Romantic-period writers can be seen to have been influenced by, or to have influenced, the geological theories and controversies that were contemporary with their fashioning of Romantic literature and aesthetic theory.[29] Noah Heringman has argued that Romantic literature and geology were mutually constitutive discourses that emerged out of a shared cultural environment, which included topographical poetry, earth science, landscape aesthetics, travel writing, garden design and so on.[30] His coinage of the term 'aesthetic geology' registers the fact that geology was originally an intrinsic part of the common literary culture of the early Romantic period prior to the formation of geology and literature as mutually exclusive discourses and disciplines in the early nineteenth century.

If Enlightenment mineralogy attempted to locate the geological features and materials of specific places within general taxonomies of the kind produced by Linnaeus, Romantic-period geology exhibited what Taylor refers to as 'the "place-specificity" that was to characterize [geological science] during its nineteenth-century maturation' ('Geological Travellers in Auvergne', p. 74). As we will see, 'place specificity', which parallels the focus on place in Romantic literature, is a dominant feature of geological travel writing in Scotland in the Romantic period. Geological tourism was also influenced by the emergence of Romantic travel writing towards the end of the eighteenth century, marked by a switch in focus from objective description of the natural world to an emphasis on the traveller's physical and mental experience of reaching remote places and encountering natural wonders.[31] One of the key markers of Romantic-era scientific travel, according to Golinski, is

> the emergence of the 'scientific hero,' whose contributions to knowledge were stamped by their origin in strenuous physical exertion. The scientific hero had its archetype in the figure of Alexander von Humboldt, a man whose wanderings and bodily sufferings were widely viewed as exemplary for the seeker after knowledge in such fields as geology and natural history. The appeal of Humboldt's writings, however, was evidently connected with a Romantic sensibility toward the natural world, which licensed men's expression of emotional responses to its grandeur and wonders. ('Humphry Davy's Sexual Chemistry', pp. 18–19)

Humboldt's extensive accounts of his travels in South America appeared in the early decades of the nineteenth century.[32] But the first Romantic geological tour of Scotland – that of Barthélemy Faujas de Saint-Fond – took place in 1784 and was published in 1797 (in French) and 1799 (in English). As we will see in Chapter 5, Faujas characteristically foregrounds the dangers and difficulties of venturing off the beaten track in order to discover wild places that induce powerful subjective and aesthetic experiences and reveal awe-inspiring geological wonders at one and the same time.

Reading Science and/as Literature

If geological travel writing can be seen as a hybrid between 'science' and 'literature', we need to remember, as Tim Fulford, Debbie Lee and Peter J. Kitson remind us, that these terms had very different meanings at the end of the eighteenth century and that 'scientific' discourses – natural history and natural philosophy – were as much part of 'polite literature' as poetry.[33] Yet, as Ralph O'Connor points out, most studies of the relationship between science and literature – even those which recognise that modern disciplinary designations did not apply in the eighteenth and early nineteenth centuries – tend to reinforce the distinction by yoking them together with the conjunction 'and'.[34] By contrast, O'Connor examines 'science *as* literature, rather than science *and* literature', thus restoring scientific writing to the broader notion of literature that prevailed at the time and bringing it within the remit of modern literary critics (*The Earth on Show*, p. 15). O'Connor explores the way geological writing of the first half of the nineteenth century employed various kinds of literary strategy in order to gain cultural prestige and persuade readers to accept its extraordinary visions of the earth's past.

Golinski has identified the way the 'constructivist' history of science that has emerged in the last twenty years or so seeks to demonstrate that knowledge of the natural world is partly 'made' through the deployment of literary techniques and conventions – narrative strategies, genre conventions, figurative language, authorial self-fashioning, the manipulation of aesthetic categories, and so on.[35] But O'Connor stresses that reading 'scientific' texts as literature does not necessarily set out to 'expose scientific truth claims as illusory, or to assert that science can be somehow "explained" in purely literary or narrative terms' (*The Earth on Show*, p. 15). Nor does such a reading imply that there were no perceived distinctions between the literary genres of natural philosophy or natural history and what we now call 'imaginative literature'. As noted above, in the second half of the seventeenth century, the Royal Society attempted to distinguish scientific writing from other discourses by seeking to exclude unnecessary rhetoric and figurative language. John Locke's attempt to establish an absolute difference between philosophical language, whose aim was to 'speak of things as they are', and the deceptive use of figurative language in rhetoric and poetry remained influential throughout the eighteenth century.[36] O'Connor points out that 'The pejorative use of words like "poetry", "fiction", "romance", "dream", and "imagination" to denunciate the truth-values of rival theories was a standard part of the rhetorical armoury of Enlightenment science' (*The Earth on Show*, pp. 449–50). Yet elements of all these literary genres and modes 'were also used paradoxically to raise geology's public profile and claims to cultural authority' (p. 450). Given that their claims 'rested not on experimental demonstration, but on reconstructing the past from fragmentary evidence and developing plausible scenarios', geological writers of the period 'found it necessary to use stories to think about and communicate their ideas'.

As a consequence, 'The . . . tension between the repudiation and the cultivation of the poetic imagination can be traced right through geology's literary history' (p. 450).

The Literary Strategies of Geological Travel Writing

In *Bursting the Limits of Time*, Rudwick points out that written accounts of geological travel became especially important in the late eighteenth century as savants attempted to persuade readers to accept their theoretical claims by giving them a sense of contact with geological evidence that could not be brought back to museums:

> The more the importance of firsthand field observation was emphasised, the more pressing was the problem of making that experience real and convincing to those who had *not* in fact witnessed what was being described. . . . The real witness of certain features had to recount his experience in such a way as to make others '*virtual witnesses*' of it; he had to convince them that it was *as if* they too had seen it, so that they might also be persuaded to accept the interpretation or explanation offered for it. (pp. 74–5)[37]

Travelling geologists developed various 'literary technologies' for carrying their readers along with them and often made use of illustrations or 'proxy pictures' (*Bursting the Limits of Time*, pp. 75–80). O'Connor develops Rudwick's suggestion by showing how geological writings of the first half of the nineteenth century employed literary techniques and visual reconstructions in order to give readers a sense of being 'virtual tourists' who imaginatively shared geologists' field trips into the landscapes of deep time. In doing so, geological travellers were following a more general tendency in memoirs of scientific exploration. As Fulford, Lee and Kitson show, scientific travel writing such as Cook's and Mungo Park's enabled readers to experience an 'imaginative participation' in the journeys they read about, thereby becoming Romantic 'mental travellers' (*Literature, Science and Exploration in the Romantic Era*, pp. 18, 90–107).

Golinski explores the way that some contributions to the constructivist history of science have used the literary genre theory of Northrop Frye to highlight the literariness of scientific writing

(*Making Natural Knowledge*, pp. 192–4). As we will see in subsequent chapters, some of the key mineralogical and geological tours of Scotland in the eighteenth century can be read in terms of Frye's account of the myth of quest romance.[38] These tours foreground the naturalist-explorer's excited and arduous search for crucial evidence in the 'wilds' of Scotland's mountainous landscape and deploy the narrative dynamics of expectation, disappointment and eventual success.[39] The geologist-traveller figures as a heroic male adventurer in pursuit of the secrets of nature (in the form of buried treasure), battles against negative antagonists (other natural historians who hold contrary views about the natural world), overcomes difficulties to arrive at truth through a series of natural epiphanies, and brings back precious objects (rock samples and drawings of geological features) found on the quest.[40] Metaphors of desire, hunting and the uncovering of nature's inner secrets give particular resonance to common geological terms such as 'exposures' (places where geological features are exposed to, or by, the geologist).

In an essay titled 'Geological Travel and Theoretical Innovation' (1996), Rudwick offers another, related narrative model for understanding the geological quest – that of pilgrimage. He suggests that groundbreaking geological field trips typically fulfil certain conditions: the geologist leaves behind the familiar intellectual and geological environment of 'home' by undertaking an arduous journey to an unfamiliar 'liminal' place where he or she encounters new kinds of geological features in a context free from contact with other geologists who might reduce new findings to pre-existing paradigms. Such transformative journeys are analogous to pilgrimages in that the physical and mental experience of travelling to places outside everyday experience can dispose the traveller to new spiritual or intellectual insight.[41] Some of the geological travel accounts that are examined below foreground the way that the savant leaves behind an intellectual and social milieu that is not wholly sympathetic to his geological theory by venturing, sometimes with supportive companions, into fairly remote Scottish landscapes where the discovery of striking geological features enables him to develop his theory in innovative ways.

In this book I attempt to read eighteenth-century and Romantic-period geological travel writing about Scotland as a set of texts that use various literary techniques to convey the excitement and wonder of scientific discovery and to give readers the sense of being virtual tourists and virtual witnesses of the geological formations in the field and of the stupendous processes that are conjured up to explain them.[42] These literary techniques, I argue, are not optional strategies but intrinsic to the style of natural history or geology being articulated.

Mountains, Geology and the Sublime

The literary analysis of the natural history and geological tours developed in the present book will focus, among other things, on the way they either avoid or emphasise the aesthetic impact of Scotland's mountain wilderness and the geology that produced it. The most striking feature of British aesthetic theory in the eighteenth century is the rise to dominance of the sublime, a notion which had been current in literary criticism since Longinus's account in *Peri Hypsous* in the first or third century CE of how poetry may exhibit or arouse 'greatness of mind'.[43] Translations of Longinus in the seventeenth and eighteenth centuries impacted on literary criticism and aesthetics in Britain, where the trend, as Samuel H. Monk has argued, was to transform Longinus's account of the impact of powerful writing into an analysis of the effect of the greatness and power of nature on the perceiving mind.

Nicolson argues in *Mountain Gloom and Mountain Glory* that the emergence of the aesthetic experience and theory of the sublime in the long eighteenth century grew out of encounters with the Alps and was intimately connected with geological speculation about the origins of mountains. As we will see in Chapter 2, Thomas Burnet's *The Theory of the Earth* (1684) attempted to account for the disorientating shock of the Alps in theological, geological and aesthetic terms. While Burnet was appalled by mountains and saw them as the ruins of a once perfect world, he was also capable of experiencing their sublime grandeur.[44] The notion of the natural sublime became a way of accounting for the complex mixture of terror and delight that later travellers felt when confronted by the Alps and thereby transformed attitudes towards mountains.[45] John Baillie's *Essay on the Sublime* (1747) begins with the assertion that 'Nothing produces the [mind's] *Elevation* equal to large *Prospects*, vast extended Views, *Mountains*, the *Heavens*, and an immense *Ocean*' (p. 5).[46]

The importance of the eleven essays on 'the Pleasures of the Imagination' that Joseph Addison published in *The Spectator* from 21 June to 3 July 1712 (411–21) lies not only in their being 'the first sustained piece of writing on aesthetics in eighteenth-century England' (Monk, *The Sublime*, p. 57), but also in their wide circulation.[47] For Addison, the pleasures of the imagination may be distinguished into primary and secondary pleasures, stimulated by nature and works of art respectively. He begins paper 412 by suggesting that 'outward Objects' produce aesthetic pleasure if they are '*Great, Uncommon,* or *Beautiful*' (Addison and Steele, *The Spectator*, III, p. 540), and goes on to suggest that greatness is the major source of an aesthetic pleasure that later writers would call the sublime (Addison does not use the term). Features of the natural world that exhibit greatness include

> the Prospects of an open Champian Country, a vast uncultivated Desart, of huge Heaps of Mountains, high Rocks and Precipices, or a wide Expanse of Waters, where we are not struck with the Novelty or Beauty of the Sight, but with that rude kind of Magnificence which appears in many of these stupendous Works of Nature. (p. 540)

Addison's psychological account of the aesthetic effects of viewing 'stupendous Works of Nature' contains the germs of ideas that would later be elaborated in more extended and sophisticated discussions of the sublime (by Burke and Immanuel Kant):

> Our Imagination loves to be filled with an Object, or to graspe at any thing that is too big for its Capacity. We are flung into a pleasing Astonishment at such unbounded Views, and feel a delightful Stillness and Amazement in the Soul at the Apprehension of them. The Mind of Man naturally hates every thing that looks like a Restraint upon it, and is apt to fancy it self under a sort of Confinement, when the Sight is pent up in a narrow Compass, and shortned [*sic*] on every side by the Neighbourhood of Walls or Mountains. On the contrary, a spacious Horison is an Image of Liberty, where the Eye has Room to range abroad, to expiate at large on the Immensity of its Views, and to lose it self amidst the Variety of Objects that offer themselves to its Observation. (pp. 540–1)

There is some ambivalence here about mountains. Although 'huge Heaps of Mountains, high Rocks and Precipices' are examples of natural greatness, being encircled by mountains can also constrain the imagination. Addison's celebration of the pleasures that the imagination can derive from mountains, especially the 'unbounded Views' that may be seen from mountain peaks, nevertheless made a significant contribution to the growing enthusiasm in eighteenth-century Britain for travelling into mountainous regions in order to experience the 'pleasing Astonishment' of the sublime. (This enthusiasm was not shared by all writers, especially early on in the century, as we saw in the case of Defoe.)

Addison's account of the secondary pleasures of the imagination produced by written texts is also important for what follows. In essay 420, he implies that writers who 'describe visible Objects of a real Existence', such as historians, natural philosophers, travellers and geographers, can produce sublime pleasures of the imagination that match those of poets like Milton. Among such writers, however, 'there are none who more gratifie and enlarge the Imagination, than the Authors of the new Philosophy, whether we consider their Theories of the Earth or Heavens, the Discoveries they have made by Glasses, or any of their Contemplations on Nature' (pp. 574–5). It is notable that Addison includes 'Theories of the Earth' in this list. As I will argue in later chapters, the geotheory of the late seventeenth century and the geological travel writing of the late eighteenth century could generate sublime affect through requiring readers to envisage the powerful events and forces that had produced the earth's geomorphology in the deep past. In Peter de Bolla's terms, geological writing could thus operate as a discourse *of* the sublime, not merely describing sublime features and processes but also inducing sublime affect in readers.[48]

The most influential account of the sublime in eighteenth-century Britain was Burke's *A Philosophical Enquiry into the Origin of our Ideas of the Sublime and Beautiful*, which played a seminal role in promoting the cult of the sublime and encouraged writers and readers to see the dangers and pains associated with mountain travel in a positive light, thereby helping to make the Alps, the English Lake District, Snowdonia and the Scottish Highlands into prime destinations for tourists and artists. Burke locates terror, pain and danger at the heart of the sublime experience: 'Whatever is fitted in any sort to excite the ideas of pain, and danger, that is to say, whatever is in any sort terrible, or is conversant about terrible objects, or operates in a manner analogous to terror, is a source of the sublime' (*A Philosophical Enquiry*, I, vii, p. 39). The sublime is characterised by a complex feeling of terror and delight, the latter being defined as 'the sensation which accompanies the removal of pain or danger' (I, iv, pp. 36–7). The sublime, then, is associated with self-preservation: it is experienced when the self preserves itself from the threat of pain or danger by effort, or when the self contemplates pain or danger from a position of safety.

Like Addison, Burke distinguishes between the sublimity produced by nature and that produced by literature, though he sometimes confuses them. For the most part, as well, he treats the sublime as a psychological-cum-physiological experience rather than as a quality of natural objects or literary texts, though that distinction too is sometimes blurred. At the beginning of the second part of the *Enquiry*, Burke analyses the psychological experience caused by the natural sublime:

> The passion caused by the great and sublime in *nature*, when those causes operate most powerfully, is Astonishment; and astonishment is that state of the soul, in which all its motions are suspended, with some degree of horror. In this case the mind is so entirely filled with its object, that it cannot entertain any other, nor by consequence reason on that object which employs it. Hence arises the great power of the sublime, that far from being produced by them, it anticipates our reasonings, and hurries us on by an irresistible force. (II, i, p. 57)

The sublime in nature, then, paralyses the soul, completely occupies the mind, suspends reason, and carries us along with an irresistible force. Yet this potential annihilation of the self can prompt courageous or laborious effort and thereby stimulate a nervous system that has become over-relaxed in the debilitating world of civilised modernity, a condition which poses threats that are more dangerous than anything encountered in nature (IV, vi, pp. 134–5). Seeking out the pains, dangers and difficulties of arduous travel in remote and challenging landscapes can thus be seen as a kind of therapy for the educated middle classes of the period, whose safe and comfortable lifestyles are debilitating and potentially fatal. The Burkean sublime therefore gives theoretical legitimacy to the kind of courageous heroism claimed by the Romantic traveller, who represents himself (or occasionally herself) as exhibiting courage and fortitude in coping with terrifying natural places and conditions in order to achieve a valuable goal or reach a desired place.

Most of Burke's examples of natural objects that generate sublime experience, including mountains, do so through their extensive or three-dimensional magnitude, or what he calls 'Vastness' (II, vii, p. 72). But Burke also tentatively discusses objects and qualities that produce the sublime not through extension but through intensity or intensive magnitude (power, energy and so on) – a distinction that Kant would later reformulate as one between the mathematically sublime and the dynamically sublime.[49] In the second edition of the *Enquiry* of 1759, Burke added a section on 'Power' (II, v, pp. 64–70) in which he suggests that the most intensive of all intensive magnitudes is the power of God, the aesthetic impact of which strikes us the moment we open our eyes to view the immensity of the universe he created or contemplate ourselves as created beings. Sublime affect can be generated by our awareness of the immense force or labour needed to produce the great works of man, nature or God:

> Another source of greatness is *Difficulty*. When any work seems to have required immense force and labour to effect it, the idea is grand. Stonehenge, neither for disposition nor ornament, has any thing admirable; but those huge rude masses of stone, set on end, and piled each on other, turn the mind on the immense force necessary for such a work. Nay the rudeness of the work increases this cause of grandeur, as it excludes the idea of art, and contrivance; for dexterity produces another sort of effect which is different enough from this. (II, xii, p. 77)

Stonehenge is not sublime merely because of its extensive magnitude (its 'huge rude masses of stone, set on end, and piled each on other') but because it alerts us to the intensive magnitude of 'the immense force necessary for such a work'. As we will see, some of the most sublime geological formations that travellers encountered in Scotland in the eighteenth century, such as the basaltic columns of Fingal's Cave, were often compared to the most sublime products of human architecture in order to emphasise the extent to which they surpassed them. Indeed, the final geological traveller examined in this book, John MacCulloch, offered a suggestive account of the 'peculiar sentiment' produced by this impulse:

The sense of power is a fertile source of the sublime, and as the appearance of power exerted . . . is necessary to confer this character on architecture, so the mind, insensibly transferring the operations of nature to the efforts of art where they approximate in character, becomes impressed with a feeling rarely excited by her ordinary forms, where these are even stupendous. (*A Description of the Western Islands of Scotland*, I, p. 509)

As we will see, the travel writings of those geological travellers who read the Scottish terrain as the product of volcanic or plutonic processes in the distant past, such as Faujas and Hutton respectively, required the reader to imagine the 'immense force' that produced and shaped the 'huge rude masses of stone' that they encountered on their travels. Indeed, the characteristic geological assumption that the earth had been shaped, and was continually being shaped, by enormous dynamic forces made the earth itself into a sublime system powered by intensive magnitude. Geological travel writing about mountainous regions such as the Scottish Highlands therefore supplemented conventional responses to mountain grandeur with the dynamic sublimity generated by invoking the powerful forces and processes that had formed that grandeur.

But if Burke's *Enquiry* encouraged travellers to seek out the natural sublime in remote places, it also had complex implications for those who sought to write about their travels. Verbal description, Burke claims, is intrinsically incapable of conveying clear ideas and it is precisely this incapacity that allows it to convey or generate aesthetic affect:

It is one thing to make an idea clear, and another to make it *affecting* to the imagination. If I make a drawing of a palace, or a temple, or a landscape, I present a very clear idea of those objects; but then . . . my picture can at most affect only as the palace, temple, or landscape would have affected in the reality. On the other hand, the most lively and spirited verbal description I can give, raises a very obscure and imperfect *idea* of such objects; but then it is in my power to raise a stronger *emotion* by the description than I could do by the best painting. (II, iv, p. 60)

It is not surprising, therefore, that most of Burke's examples of sublimity come from texts rather than nature. His analysis of sublime passages – primarily from Homer, the Bible, Shakespeare and

Milton – insists that their sublime power derives not from raising clear ideas of the things represented but from the inherent power of language to raise strong emotions precisely through obscurity (II, iv, p. 61). Burke's claim, which anticipates Thomas De Quincey's distinction between the literature of knowledge and the literature of power, appears to make science and aesthetic affect incompatible with one another.[50] Yet, as Addison noted, geology was one of the sciences that was capable of generating the sublime. It does this partly because of its invocation of the powerful forces that had shaped the earth's terrain, but also because geology could only give obscure glimpses of those forces acting in the remote past.

Burke explores the sublime potential of language at greater length in the fifth part of the *Enquiry*. Drawing on Locke's account of the arbitrary nature of language in *An Essay Concerning Human Understanding*, Burke reiterates his earlier claim that words 'affect us in a manner very different from that in which we are affected by natural objects, or by painting or architecture' (V, i, p. 163).[51] The aim of poetry and rhetoric, for example, is the opposite of topographical or scientific description and drawing since it seeks 'to affect rather by sympathy than imitation; to display rather the effect of things on the mind of the speaker, or of others, than to present a clear idea of the things themselves' (V, v, p. 172). Despite their inability to present clear ideas of things, 'eloquence and poetry are as capable, nay indeed much more capable of making deep and lively impressions than any other arts, and even than nature itself in very many cases' (V, vii, p. 173). Poetry's supplementary power arises from three causes: our sympathy with the speaker's feelings; its capacity to represent things that have never occurred in nature or which no one has ever seen ('as God, angels, devils, heaven and hell'); and the facility it offers 'to make such *combinations* as we cannot possibly do otherwise' (V, vii, pp. 173–4). Milton's description in *Paradise Lost* of 'the travels of the fallen angels through their dismal habitation' is exemplary for Burke:

'— O'er many a dark and dreary vale
They pass'd, and many a region dolorous;
O'er many a frozen, many a fiery Alp;
Rock, caves, lakes, fens, bogs, dens and shades of death,
A universe of death. [*Paradise Lost*, II, 618–22]' (V, vii, p. 174)

These (slightly misquoted) lines describe the passage of the fallen angels across a geologically dramatic terrain. According to Burke, however, the accumulative effect of the monosyllabic list of geomorphic features that they pass over in line 621 is given its most powerful sublime charge by the final word, 'death':

> This idea or this affection caused by a word, which nothing but a word could annex to the others, raises a very great degree of the sublime; and this sublime is raised yet higher by what follows, a *'universe of Death.'* Here are again two ideas not presentable but by language; and an union of them great and amazing beyond conception; if they may properly be called ideas which present no distinct image to the mind. (V, vii, p. 175)

For Burke, even prose descriptions of landscapes or journeys do not convey or raise mental images in readers' minds. He presents a description of the course of the Danube through Europe and then claims that 'In this description many things are mentioned, as mountains, rivers, cities, the sea, &c. But let anybody examine himself, and see whether he has had impressed on his imagination any pictures of a river, mountain, watery soil, Germany, &c.' (V, iv, p. 167). From Burke's perspective, then, written accounts of travels necessarily struggle to convey clear ideas to readers and are more likely to convey the writer's sublime experience and perhaps induce sublime experience in the reader.

Although Burke's analysis of the sublime power of words draws on Locke's account of the arbitrary nature of language, it led to consequences that were the polar opposite of Locke's ambition – influenced by the Royal Society – to eliminate the abuses and imperfections of language so that philosophers, at least, might 'speak of things as they are' (*Essay*, III, ix, p. 452). Burke's claim that written descriptions tend to induce sublime affect rather than clear understanding therefore posed particular problems for scientific travel writing (which increasingly made use of pictorial illustrations to clarify verbal descriptions of natural features). Geological travel writing about mountainous regions was particularly prone to expressing and generating the sublime because it had the potential to add intimations of the intensive magnitude of immense geological forces to the general tendency in Romantic travel writing to record the aesthetic effects of extensive magnitude. The aesthetic resonance of geological travel writing, then, was always potentially in conflict with its attempt to present clear accounts of geological features and processes.

Perhaps even more challenging to readers' imaginative powers than the extensive magnitude of geological formations (such as mountains) and the intensive magnitude of the powers that had formed them (God and/or colossal geological processes) was the timescale over which such processes and forces appeared to have operated. The notion of the temporal sublime – the possibility that the mind's difficulty in conceiving the distant past might generate sublime affect – was first explored in David Hume's *A Treatise of Human Nature* (1739–40).[52] Geological writers of the period, such as the Comte de Buffon and John Playfair, coined and deployed sublime metaphors, such as the 'dark abyss' or the 'abyss of time', to describe the vast extensions to the age of the earth that geology was beginning to reveal.[53] The vertigo-inducing and potentially terrifying vision of 'deep time' opened up by geology in the second half of the eighteenth century thus added the fourth dimension of time to the three-dimensional sublimity of mountain grandeur and the dynamic sublimity of geological processes. Readers were invited to imagine the immense forces and processes that must have formed the earth's geomorphology over an immense time period in an unthinkably distant epoch in the past. Attending to the way geological knowledge informed the visual representation of the Highlands and Islands in the period, MacLeod concludes that 'time was the key to grandeur' (*From an Antique Land*, p. 165).

Klonk argues that 'Between 1790 and 1830 pictorial formulae like the sublime, the beautiful and the picturesque lost their privileged place in the perception of nature and were gradually displaced by a more phenomenalist mode of representation' and that 'this transformation corresponded to changes in the rhetoric and self-understanding of . . . geology' (*Science and the Perception of Nature*, p. 67). Heringman's attention to the way geology and literature were formed into separate professional disciplines in the early nineteenth century supports Klonk's claim, as does Rudwick's argument that geology was given a proper institutional and empirical basis with the formation of the Geological Society in 1807 (*Bursting the Limits of Time*, pp. 463–9). Yet the intimate interconnection between geology, aesthetics and literature continued well into the nineteenth century.

In 1822, in his capacity as President of the Royal Society, Humphry Davy presented William Buckland with the Royal Society's Copley Medal for his geological discoveries in Kirkdale Cave. In his speech, Davy enthused that 'the history of the past changes of the globe' produced by geology offered 'a sublime subject . . . for the exercise of the imagination!'. He went on to propose that

> If we look with wonder upon the remains of human works, such as the columns of Palmyra, broken in the midst of the desert, the temples of Pæstum, beautiful in the decay of twenty centuries, or the mutilated fragments of Greek sculpture, in the Acropolis of Athens, or in our own Museum, as proofs of the genius of artists, and power and riches of nations now past away; with how much deeper a feeling of admiration must we consider those grand monuments of nature, which mark the revolutions of the globe. (*Six Discourses Delivered before the Royal Society*, pp. 54–5)

O'Connor points out that this part of Davy's speech 'soon became one of the most quoted passages in the literature, doing public service in the epigraphs and chapter conclusions of geological books and museum guidebooks' (*The Earth on Show*, p. 90). Indeed, O'Connor demonstrates that the intimate interchange between geology and literature continued throughout the first half of the nineteenth century.

The Itinerary

This book focuses on the written tours of seven natural historians and geologists in roughly chronological order. The sequence of chapters attempts to reveal the mutually constitutive relationship between scientific and literary style – between the empiricist epistemology of early eighteenth-century natural history and the use of textual strategies that give the impression of neutral scientific observation, and between the dynamic visions of the earth developed by Romantic-period geology and the representation of self, journey and landscape in Romantic travel writing. Chapters 2 to 4 develop close analyses of the Scottish tours of three natural historians whose outlook, in the period between 1690 and 1770, was pre-geological and pre-Romantic, meaning that they tend not to represent Scotland's mountains as sublime, avoid speculation about the geological processes that formed them, and play down the difficulties and dangers of travel. Chapter 2 reveals that Martin Martin's *A Late Voyage to St. Kilda* (1698) and *A Description of the Western Islands of Scotland* (1703) were directly influenced by the Royal Society's guidelines on scientific travel. In Chapters 3 and 4 we will look at three natural history tours of Scotland that were influenced by Linnaeus: John Walker's 'Report on the Hebrides', completed in 1771, and Thomas Pennant's *A Tour in Scotland, MDCCLXIX* (1771) and *A Tour in Scotland and Voyage to the Hebrides, MDC-CLXXII* (1774, 1776). Chapters 5 to 8, by contrast, offer extended interpretations of geological tours of Scotland between 1784 and 1819 that emphasise the sublimity of Scotland's mountains, attempt to envisage the sublime geological processes that formed them, and play up the difficulties and dangers the travellers faced in exploring them (the Burkean sublime can thus be seen as having a decisive impact on the transformation in travel writing about Scotland in the long eighteenth century). Chapter 5 examines the first identifiably Romantic geological tour of Scotland – that of Faujas de Saint-Fond – in order to suggest that there is a mutually constitutive relationship between its representation of the author's arduous journey of geological discovery in the Highlands and Islands and his invocation of the colossal volcanic forces that had produced Scotland's terrain in the deep past. Chapter 6 seeks to dispel the belief that Hutton was an armchair geologist by developing a close analysis of the literary techniques of the extensive unpublished accounts of the geological tours of Scotland and England that he undertook from the 1760s to the 1780s. Chapter 7 examines Robert Jameson's accounts of his extensive tours of the Highlands and Islands in which he set out to refute Faujas's volcanic and Hutton's plutonic interpretation of Scotland's geomorphology. The final chapter generates an extended reading of John MacCulloch's *A Description of the Western Islands of Scotland* of 1819 partly because it was the most important geological survey of the region in the period, and partly because MacCulloch's close association with the Geological Society allows us to explore how geology and aesthetic travel writing began to go their separate ways.

Notes

1. See O'Gorman, *The Long Eighteenth Century*, and Baines, *The Long 18th Century*. For a pioneering collection of essays on geological travel writing, see Wyse Jackson (ed.), *Four Centuries of Geological Travel*; for an overview of 'geotourism' in Scotland from the late eighteenth century to the present, see Gordon and Baker, 'Appreciating Geology and the Physical Landscape in Scotland'.

2. For the extensive scholarship on the eighteenth-century 'discovery' of Scotland, see Moir, *The Discovery of Britain*; Lindsay, *The Discovery of Scotland* and *The Eye Is Delighted*; Holloway and Errington, *The Discovery of Scotland*; Cooper, *Road to the Isles*; Smout, 'Tours in the Scottish Highlands from the Eighteenth to the Twentieth Centuries'; Bray, *The Discovery of the Hebrides*; Andrews, 'The Highlands Tour and the Ossianic Sublime', in *The Search for the Picturesque*, pp. 197–240; Womack, *Improvement and Romance*; Gold and Gold, *Imagining Scotland*; Glendening, *The High Road*; Sawyers (ed.), *The Road North*; Rixon, *The Hebridean Traveller*; Grenier, *Tourism and Identity in Scotland*; McNeil, *Scotland, Britain, Empire*; Fielding, *Scotland and the Fictions of Geography*; Brown (ed.), *Literary Tourism, the Trossachs and Walter Scott*; MacLeod, *From an Antique Land*; and Rackwitz, *Travels to Terra Incognita*. On literary tourism in general, see Watson, *The Literary Tourist*.

3. See Durie, *Scotland for the Holidays*, p. 21; for lists of tours of Scotland, see Smout, 'Tours in the Scottish Highlands', and Rackwitz, *Travels to Terra Incognita*.

4. See Gilpin, *An Essay upon Prints*, *Observations on the River Wye* and *Observations, Relative Chiefly to Picturesque Beauty, Made in the Year 1776*.

5. For brief accounts of natural history's role in the history of mountain exploration and climbing in Scotland, see Mitchell, *Scotland's Mountains Before the Mountaineers*, pp. 36–43 and 87–94. On the transformation in attitudes towards mountains, see Nicolson, *Mountain Gloom and Mountain Glory*, Schama, *Landscape and Memory*, pp. 447–513, and Macfarlane, *Mountains of the Mind*.

6. See Macpherson, *The Poems of Ossian and Related Works*.

7. Also see Baines, 'Ossianic Geographies'.

8. On Waddell, and on imagined conformities between Ossian and geology more generally, see Gidal, *Ossianic Unconformities*.

9. For the key geological 'Places to Visit' in Scotland, including Siccar Point, the extinct volcanoes of Edinburgh, the Cuillin Hills of Skye, and Arran, see McKirdy et al., *Land of Mountain and Flood*, pp. 251–304.

10. See Hallam, *Great Geological Controversies*.
11. See Jameson, *An Outline of the Mineralogy of the Shetland Islands, and of the Island of Arran*, pp. 100–1, note.
12. See Rudwick, *Bursting the Limits of Time*, pp. 172–80; for Rudwick's summary of the various kinds of earth science in the period, see pp. 640–6.
13. For a similar idea, see Mitchell, '"The stratified record upon which we set our feet"'.
14. See Bacon, *The New Organon* (1620), especially the concluding 'Outline of a Natural and Experimental History' (pp. 222–38).
15. Shapin's *The Scientific Revolution* focuses on the Royal Society's Baconian aspects.
16. See Lovejoy, *The Great Chain of Being*, chapter 8, pp. 227–41.
17. See Bacon, 'Advice to the Earl of Rutland on his Travels'.
18. See Skouen and Stark (eds), *Rhetoric and the Early Royal Society*.
19. See Kuhn, *The Essential Tension*, pp. 147, 220.
20. See Foucault, *The Order of Things*, pp. 139–79, 245–52, 287–304 (pp. 158, 162).
21. See Holmes, *The Age of Wonder*.
22. On Romanticism and the sciences, see Piper, *The Active Universe*; Levere, *Poetry Realized in Nature*; Bewell, *Wordsworth and the Enlightenment*; Wyatt, *Wordsworth and the Geologists*; Shaffer (ed.), *The Third Culture*; Oerlemans, *Romanticism and the Materiality of Nature*; Heringman (ed.), *Romantic Science*; Knellwolf and Goodall (eds), *Frankenstein's Science*; Richards, *The Romantic Conception of Life*; Fulford (ed.), *Romanticism and Science*; and Ruston, *Shelley and Vitality* and *Creating Romanticism*.
23. For essays on geological travel, see Wyse Jackson (ed.), *Four Centuries of Geological Travel*.
24. See Laudan, *From Mineralogy to Geology*.
25. On the interrelationships between Romantic-period geology and Romanticism, see Levere, *Poetry Realized in Nature*, chapters 5 and 6; Bewell, *Wordsworth and the Enlightenment*; Wyatt, *Wordsworth and the Geologists*; and Dean, *Romantic Landscapes*.
26. See Kirwan, Preface to *Geological Essays*, pp. iii–xii (p. iii).
27. In Jardine, Secord and Spary (eds), *Cultures of Natural History*, p. 449. Heringman's edited collection on *Romantic Science* attends to the literary forms of Romantic natural history (see pp. 6–11).
28. See Walker, *Lectures on Geology*.
29. See Piper, *The Active Universe*; Levere, *Poetry Realized in Nature*; Kelley, *Wordsworth's Revisionary Aesthetics*; Bewell, *Wordsworth and the Enlightenment*; Wyatt, *Wordsworth and the Geologists*; and Dean, *Romantic Landscapes*.

30. See Heringman, *Romantic Rocks, Aesthetic Geology*, pp. 1–29, 138–60, 265.

31. On Romantic travel writing, see Thompson, 'Revealing the Self', in *Travel Writing*, pp. 96–129, and *The Suffering Traveller*; also see Parks, 'The Turn to the Romantic in the Travel Literature of the Eighteenth Century'; Batten, *Pleasurable Instruction*; Stafford, *Voyage into Substance*; Cardinal, 'Romantic Travel'; and Leask, *Curiosity and the Aesthetics of Travel Writing 1770–1840*.

32. See Humboldt, *Personal Narrative of a Journey to the Equinoctial Regions of the New Continent*.

33. See Fulford et al., *Literature, Science and Exploration in the Romantic Era*, pp. 2–4.

34. See O'Connor, *The Earth on Show*, p. 446; for O'Connor's reflections on reading scientific writing as literature, see pp. 1–27 and 445–53.

35. See Golinski, *Making Natural Knowledge*, especially chapter 4, pp. 103–32 and 186–206.

36. See Locke, *An Essay Concerning Human Understanding* (1689), book III, especially chapter 10, paragraph 34. Also see Walmsley, *Locke's Essay and the Rhetoric of Science*.

37. Rudwick derives the notion of the 'virtual witness' from Shapin, 'Pump and Circumstance'.

38. See Frye, 'The Mythos of Summer: Romance', in *Anatomy of Criticism*, pp. 186–206.

39. For the way scientific writing employs the conventions of Romance, Comedy, Tragedy and Satire, see Clark, 'Narratology and the History of Science', and Golinski, *Making Natural Knowledge*, pp. 192–4.

40. See Frye, *Anatomy of Criticism*, pp. 186–206.

41. See Rudwick, 'Geological Travel and Theoretical Innovation'.

42. See Nicolson, *Mountain Gloom and Mountain Glory*, and Heringman, *Romantic Rocks, Aesthetic Geology*.

43. See Longinus, 'On the Sublime', in Russell and Winterbottom (eds), *Classical Literary Criticism*, pp. 143–87. On the eighteenth-century sublime, see Monk, *The Sublime*; Hipple, *The Beautiful, the Sublime, and the Picturesque*; Weiskel, *The Romantic Sublime*; Brennan, *Wordsworth, Turner, and Romantic Landscape*; de Bolla, *The Discourse of the Sublime*; Ferguson, *Solitude and the Sublime*; Furniss, *Edmund Burke's Aesthetic Ideology*; Ashfield and de Bolla (eds), *The Sublime*; Shaw, *The Sublime*; Axelsson, *The Sublime*; Duffy and Howell (eds), *Cultures of the Sublime*; and Costelloe (ed.), *The Sublime*.

44. For Nicolson's discussion of Burnet's *Theory of the Earth* and the controversy it provoked, see *Mountain Gloom and Mountain Glory*, chapters 5 and 6, pp. 184–270.

45. John Dennis's early distinction between the sublime and the beautiful in *The Grounds of Criticism in Poetry* (1704) was influenced by his experience of the Alps, as was the Earl of Shaftesbury's celebration of mountains in *The Moralists* (1709). For the impact of the Alps on English travellers in the late seventeenth and early eighteenth centuries, see Nicolson, *Mountain Gloom and Mountain Glory*, pp. 271–323.

46. Scottish accounts of the sublime in the period included Gerard's *Essay on Taste* (1759), Home's *Elements of Criticism* (1762), Beattie's *Dissertations Moral and Critical* (1783), and Blair's *A Critical Dissertation on the Poems of Ossian* (1763) and *Lectures on Rhetoric and Belles Lettres* (1783).

47. See Addison and Steele, *The Spectator*, III, pp. 535–82. For relevant discussions of Addison's aesthetics, see Monk, *The Sublime*; Youngren, 'Addison and the Birth of Eighteenth-Century Aesthetics'; Fabricant, 'The Aesthetics and Politics of Landscape in the Eighteenth Century'; Widmayer, 'Mapping the Landscape in Addison's "Pleasures of the Imagination"'; Mastroianni, 'Joseph Addison's Pleasures of the Imagination'; and Furniss, 'Joseph Addison'.

48. See de Bolla, *The Discourse of the Sublime*, pp. 59–102.

49. See Kant, *Critique of the Power of Judgment* (1790); Kant's 'Third Critique' was not translated until 1892 and had limited impact in Britain during the period examined in the present book: see Wellek, *Immanuel Kant in England 1793–1838*, and Class, *Coleridge and Kantian Ideas in England, 1796–1817*.

50. See De Quincey, 'Letters to a Young Man Whose Education Had Been Neglected'.

51. See Locke, *An Essay Concerning Human Understanding*, book III, pp. 361–465.

52. See Hume, *A Treatise of Human Nature*, book II, part iii, sections 7–8, pp. 474–84. For a discussion of the temporal sublime, see Brady, *The Sublime in Modern Philosophy*, pp. 36–7.

53. See Playfair, 'Biographical Account of the Late Dr James Hutton', p. 73, and Buffon, *Les époques de la nature*. Also see Rudwick, *Bursting the Limits of Time*, pp. 139–49, and, for a general discussion of the development of ideas of geological time, see Rossi, *The Dark Abyss of Time*.

Chapter 2

Natural History, Travel and Early Explorations of Scotland's Natural History

Natural History and Travel Writing in the Scientific Revolution

Natural history has a long pedigree, stemming from classical writers such as Aristotle and Pliny the Elder. But modern natural history was shaped by the scientific revolution in seventeenth-century Britain. In *The Advancement of Learning* (1605), Sir Francis Bacon distinguished between natural history, natural philosophy and metaphysics on the basis that 'natural history describeth the variety of things; physic the causes, but variable or respective causes; and metaphysic the fixed and constant causes' (p. 97).[1] According to this, natural history is a descriptive discipline that is not intrinsically concerned with discovering causes. Bacon modified this, somewhat, in the introductory plan of his *Instauratio Magna* (1620), in which he outlines his programme for 'a renewal of the sciences' based on the inductive method. The beginnings of this renewal 'must come from a natural history, and a natural history of a new kind with a new organisation' (*The New Organon*, p. 20). This new kind of natural history would 'not so much amuse by the variety of its contents or give immediate profit from its experiments, as shed light on the discovery of causes and provide a first breast to feed philosophy' (p. 20). Natural history would not be limited to mere observation but would constrain nature to give up its secrets through devising experiments:

> we are making a history not only of nature free and unconstrained (when nature goes its own way and does its own work), such as a history of the bodies of heaven and the sky, of land and sea, or minerals, plants

and animals; but much more of nature confined and harassed, when it is forced from its own condition by art and agency, and pressured and moulded. (pp. 20–1)

The distinction here between a natural history based on observation and a natural history produced through the experimental harassment of nature anticipates later distinctions between natural history and natural philosophy (physics and chemistry). Even if experimental natural history works to 'shed light on the discovery of causes', it does so in order to 'provide a first breast to feed philosophy', a metaphor which suggests that natural history is different from and preparatory for natural philosophy. In what follows, I will use the term 'natural history' to refer to Bacon's call for the systematic description of 'the variety of things' – 'the bodies of heaven and the sky, of land and sea, or minerals, plants and animals' – rather than his proposal that nature should be experimentally harassed. The systematic observation of 'nature free and unconstrained' (on the moors and mountains), together with the gathering of samples for public and private collections, was, by and large, the kind of natural history that characterises natural history tours of Scotland between the 1690s and the 1770s. As we will see, such tours did not much concern themselves with questions of origins or causation.

The work of John Ray (1627–1705), Fellow of the Royal Society and 'father of English naturalists' (Mandelbrote, 'Ray, John', *ODNB*), can be taken as representative of natural history in Britain in the period. Ray's travels in Britain and Europe in the 1660s (with various collaborators, including Francis Willughby) provided the materials for his attempt to develop a system of plant classification based on morphology. Descriptions of the specimens observed and collected on Ray's British tours were included in his pioneering *Catalogus plantarum Angliae* (1670), which 'was notable not only for its thoroughness but also for the extensive medical and pharmacological notes which accompanied the descriptions of plants' (Mandelbrote, *ODNB*). In addition, Ray was convinced that 'the divine creation of plants implied a purpose to their existence, which might be discovered by putting them to use'. Ray's tour of Europe from 1663 to 1666, made with Willughby, Philip Skippon and Nathaniel Bacon, 'allowed him to expand his knowledge of plants, and build up a formidable collection of specimens' which 'occupied him for much of the rest of his life' and led to pioneering publications on natural history (Mandelbrote, *ODNB*).

The botanical collections that he and Willughby amassed were the basis of Ray's *Methodus plantarum nova* (1682), which developed his method of plant classification, and his *Historia generalis plantarum* (3 vols, 1686, 1688, 1704), a work which 'rejected classifications based on localities or properties in favour of ones based on the structure of plants, drawing on Ray's own studies of seeds and the specific differences of plants' (Mandelbrote, *ODNB*).

Seventeenth- and eighteenth-century natural history, then, was given over to empirical observation and description and sought to organise the animals, plants and minerals of a place or country into a general classificatory system based on intrinsic rather than accidental characteristics. It tended to avoid hypothetical speculation about the history or causation of the natural objects and life-forms it attended to and focused instead on discovering the uses for which nature, or God, had intended them. In the preface to his *Instauratio Magna*, Bacon stressed that the great renewal of the sciences that he was proposing would contribute to 'the uses and benefits of life' and to 'human progress and empowerment' (*The New Organon*, p. 13). As a branch of natural history, mineralogy shared its assumptions and aims, limiting itself to observation, description and classification, and seeking to contribute to national wealth through its practical application in mining and other industries.

By the end of the seventeenth century, as David Elliston Allen has shown, natural history had become a social activity in Britain through the formation of learned societies and journals. In addition to the creation of the Royal Society in 1660 and the publication of its *Philosophical Transactions* (from 1665 onwards), the formation of the Temple Coffee House Botanic Club 'in or about 1689' made it 'the earliest natural history society in Britain and probably in the world' (Allen, *The Naturalist in Britain*, p. 10). Crucial intellectual contexts, publications and institutions were also being formed in late seventeenth-century Scotland, especially in Edinburgh.

Natural history entailed a mode of writing and presentation as well as a mode of investigation. In his attempt to differentiate natural history and natural philosophy from the errors of the past, Bacon insists that the communication of the results of empirical and experimental method involves a new kind of stylistic discipline:

> in the choice of narratives and experiences we think that we have served men better than those who have dealt with natural history in

the past. For we use the evidence of our own eyes, or at least of our own perception, in everything, and apply the strictest criteria in accepting things; so that we exaggerate nothing in our reports for the sake of sensation, and our narrations are free and untouched by fable and foolishness. (*The New Organon*, p. 21)

As we will see, natural history travel writing was also required to conform to such stylistic constraints.

Travel writing is a very old genre whose origins go back to the ancient and medieval world.[2] But the expansion of travel in the early-modern period, along with the scientific revolution of the seventeenth century, transformed travel writing and natural history and forged new connections between them.[3] The exploration of the world was driven by scientific interest as well as colonial ambition and, in turn, offered new materials for science.[4] Natural history, indeed, depended on travel – domestic as well as foreign, local as well as distant – for the collection of specimens. The symbiotic relationship between travel writing and science was exemplified and strengthened by the Royal Society. Following Bacon's example, Fellows of the Royal Society produced guidelines on what travellers should observe and how they should report their observations.[5] John Woodward, who became a Fellow of the Royal Society in 1693, produced *Brief Instructions for Making Observations in all Parts of the World* (1696).[6] Robert Boyle issued 'General Heads for the Natural History of a Country' in the *Philosophical Transactions of the Royal Society* (1666), which was later posthumously published in an expanded version as *General Heads for the Natural History of a Country, Great or Small; Drawn out for the Use of Travellers and Navigators*. This short book begins by emphasising 'the great Improvements, that have of late been made of Natural History (the only sure Foundation of Natural Philosophy,) by the Travels of Gentlemen, seamen, and others' (p. 1). It seeks to make travel still more useful to natural history by offering guidelines that would allow travellers to be more scientific in their observations of unfamiliar places.

Boyle's four 'General Heads' are 'the Heavens, . . . the Air, the Water, [and] the Earth' (p. 2). The first head advises the traveller to note 'the Longitude and Latitude of the Place' and the effect they have on air, climate, length of longest and shortest days, and the 'fixt Stars' that can be seen or not seen there (pp. 2–3). The second head urges the traveller to observe and measure the air and its effects (pp. 3–5). The third head requires the traveller to observe and assess the various bodies of water that are found in a place and the plants, insects and fish they contain (pp. 5–6). The fourth head, concentrating on 'the Earth' of a place, is of most relevance to the mineralogical and geological travel writing studied in the present book. It explains that the earth of a place may be observed in two ways – in terms of 'It self' and in terms of 'Its Inhabitants, and its Productions, and those internal or external' (p. 7). Observing the earth of a place 'It self' involves taking particular account of physical geography:

> As to it self: What are its Dimensions, Situation, East, West, South or North, its Figure, its Plains, Hills or valleys, their Extent, the highest of the Hills, either in respect of the neighbouring Valleys, or the Level of the Sea; as also whether the Mountains lye scatter'd or in Ridges, and whether those run North or South, East or West, &c. What Promontories, Fiery or Smoaking Hills, &c. the Country has or hath not; whether subject to Earthquakes or not. . . . What kinds of Soyles are there, whether of Clay, Sand, Gravel, &c. What are its Products as to Minerals, Vegetables or Animals: And moreover how all these are or may be further improved for the Benefit of Man. (pp. 7–8)

Boyle's questions about the internal productions of the earth in particular places similarly focus on their use-value:

> By the Internal Production of the Earth are to be understood here, things procreated in the Bowels of the Earth, either for the Benefit or Hurt of Man; where Notice is to be taken, what way the one may be best found out, and the other most easily avoided or cured. Under these are comprehended Metals, Minerals, Stones Precious or Common, and how these Beds lye in reference to North or South, &c. What Clays and Earths it affords, e.g. Tobacco-pipe Clay, Marles, Boles, with their Physical or other Uses, Fullers Earth, Earth for Potters Ware, Soap, Earths, Axungiæ, &c. What Coals, Salts, or Salt-Mines, as Allom, Vitriols, Sulphurs, &c. it yields. As for Mines, you are to consider their Number, Situations, Depths, Signs, Waters, Damps, Quantities of Ore, goodness of Ore, and ways of reducing their Ores into Metals, &c. (pp. 10–11)

As we will see, these are precisely the kinds of questions that eighteenth-century natural historians and mineralogists would attend to during their travels in Scotland.

A few years after the publication of Boyle's *General Heads*, William Dampier wrote and published a series of travel books that combined adventurous sea travel with the natural history of exotic places in a way that exemplified the Royal Society's model of scientific travel writing. Thompson uses Dampier's *A New Voyage Round the World* (1697) to highlight the characteristic features of the scientific travel writing of the period, analysing the textual strategies of 'epistemological decorum' that were designed to convince the reader of the veracity of the author's observations about the unknown world (*Travel Writing*, p. 75).[7] Epistemological decorum governed both the mode of observing and the style of writing:

> Abstract or metaphysical speculations were to be kept to a minimum, as were subjective impressions, and personal thoughts and feelings. Instead, writers were advised to prioritise the observation of measurable, material phenomena in the external world. Hence Dampier's precise denotations of time, place, number and distance as he charts his movement around the Caribbean. The result is a narrative voice which makes much use of the first-person pronoun, in both its singular and plural forms, yet which nevertheless often seems very unemotive and impersonal. Rhetorically, this works to enhance the sense of Dampier as a dispassionate, rational and therefore reliable eyewitness to events and phenomena. (Thompson, *Travel Writing*, p. 76)

Dampier's account of his travels is written in a plain style, presented in a journal format, and employs dates, times, geographical locations, compass directions, distances, proper names and so on to convey a sense of scientific objectivity and veracity.[8] *A New Voyage Round the World* remained popular and influential throughout the eighteenth century, helping 'to establish procedural, formal and stylistic paradigms which were widely followed in eighteenth- and early nineteenth-century travel writing' (Thompson, *Travel Writing*, p. 78). Yet Thompson also charts the way that travel writing in the later eighteenth century underwent a Romantic revolution that gave new prominence to the traveller's subjective impressions and personal thoughts and feelings.[9] As we will see, this revolution had an impact on geological travel writing about Scotland in the second half of the eighteenth century, which began to foreground the traveller's subjective experience of exploring wild places alongside abstract or metaphysical speculations about the origins of geomorphology.

Geology in Seventeenth-Century Britain

Histories of science typically distinguish between mineralogy and geology on the basis that the latter is not merely concerned with describing and categorising rocks and minerals but seeks to understand the dynamic processes that produced, and perhaps continue to produce, the earth's materials and geomorphology.[10] Geology, then, broke with the static model of nature assumed by natural history. It is often claimed that this break characterised the emergence of geology proper at the end of the eighteenth century. But this story is complicated by the appearance in the second half of the seventeenth century of discourses and debates about the historical development of the earth's geomorphology and about the material processes that had created features such as mountains or had deposited what appeared to be the fossil remains of sea creatures on mountain tops throughout the known world.

In the seventeenth Observation of his *Micrographia: or, Some Physiological Descriptions of Minute Bodies made by Magnifying Glasses with Observations and Inquiries thereupon* (1665), Robert Hooke describes using his microscope to examine 'Petrify'd wood, and other Petrify'd bodies' (p. 111) and concludes that fossils really are the petrified remains of once-living creatures and plants.[11] Hooke's 'A Discourse of Earthquakes' (written in 1668) went further in attempting to explain 'the frequent finding of Shells and other Petrified Sea and Land Substances, scattered over the whole Terrestrial Superficies' (*Posthumous Works*, p. 277).[12] This discourse begins by reiterating the claim in *Micrographia* that the shells and fossils of sea creatures found on dry land are not sports of nature but genuine fossil remains of sea creatures. Hooke amasses a great deal of observational evidence for this, including his own first-hand discoveries and observations on the Isle of Wight (pp. 292, 297).[13] Accepting that fossils are the remains of sea creatures entails accepting that even the highest mountains were once covered by the sea. But Hooke rejects the claim that such remains can be explained by Noah's Flood and instead formulates the history of a dynamic earth which has been in a continuous process of re-formation – mainly due to earthquake activity – since the creation. For Hooke, earthquakes and volcanoes are evidence of subterranean fire; over the course of the earth's history they have repeatedly raised land masses from the depths of the earth or sea and swallowed them up again. Hooke's 'Discourse' culminates in a number of startling speculations:

> First, That there may have been in preceding Ages, whole Countries either swallowed up into the Earth, or sunk so low as to be drown'd by the coming in of the Sea, or divers other ways quite destroyed; As Plato's Atlantis, &c.
>
> Secondly, That there, many [sic] have been as many Countries new made and produced by being raised from under the Water, or from inward or hidden Parts of the Body of the Earth, as England.
>
> Thirdly, That there may have been divers Species of things wholly destroyed and annihilated, and divers others changed and varied . . .
>
> Fourthly, That there may have been divers new varieties generated of the same Species, and that by the change of the Soil on which it was produced; for since we find that the alteration of the Climate, Soil, and Nourishment doth often produce a very great alteration in those Bodies that suffer it; 'tis not to be doubted but that alterations also of this Nature may cause a very great change in the shape, and other accidents of an animated Body. And this I imagine to be the reason of that great variety of Creatures that do properly belong to one Species; as for instance, in Dogs, Sheep, Goats, Deer, Hawks, Pigeons, &c. . . .
>
> Fifthly, 'Tis not impossible but there may have been a preceding learned Age wherein possibly as many things may have been known as are now, and perhaps many more, all the Arts cultivated and brought to the greatest Perfection, Mathematics, Mechanicks, Literature, Musick, Opticks, &c. reduced to their highest pitch, and all those annihilated, destroyed and lost by succeeding Devastations. . . .
>
> Sixthly, 'Tis not impossible but that this may have been the cause of a total Deluge, which may have caused a destruction of all things then living in the Air . . .
>
> Seventhly, 'Tis not impossible but that some of these great alterations may have alter'd also the magnetical Direction of the Earth; so that what is now under the Pole or Æquator, or any other Degree of Latitude may have formerly been under another. (*Posthumous Works*, pp. 327–8)

The third, fourth and sixth of these hypotheses suggest that one of the consequences of the physical instability of the land masses of the earth is that species (perhaps including the human species) are subject to annihilation and transformation – a proto-evolutionary theory that challenged some of the basic assumptions of the Christian theology and natural history of the period.[14] The first, second and fifth hypotheses entail a revolutionary view of land masses and civilisations. Land masses that appear to be stable and permanent may actually have been raised from the seas or from the depths of the earth only relatively recently, and the countries and civilisations that have developed on them may at some point in the future be once again swallowed up by the sea or the earth.

Perhaps influenced by England's recent political instability, Hooke several times suggests that the fabric of England or Britain may have undergone such vicissitudes. He speculates that ''tis not improbable, but that many very Inland Parts of this Island, if not all, may have been heretofore all cover'd with the Sea, and have had Fishes swimming over it' (*Posthumous Works*, p. 291). If this was the case, as the discovery of fossils in upland areas of England implied, then 'all these Islands of Great Britain and Ireland' may have been raised 'out of the Sea' by an earthquake (p. 320). Hooke's supposition that earthquake activity may have shifted the earth's axis several times during its history also allows him to ask, in a later discourse, 'whether it may not have been possible, that this very land of England and Portland, did, at a certain time for some Ages past, lie within the Torrid Zone; and whilst it there resided, or during its Journeying or Passage through it, whether it might not be covered with the Sea to a certain height above the tops of the highest Mountains' (p. 343). Nothing, then, is stable or permanent – not even the position and fabric of England or Great Britain. In a lecture given to the Royal Society in February 1688, later published in his *Posthumous Works* (1705) as one of his 'Lectures and Discourses of Earthquakes, and Subterraneous Eruptions', Hooke anticipates that his critics may say that 'I have turned the World upside down for the sake of a Shell' (p. 411).[15] This phrase neatly summarises Hooke's geological theory and, by alluding to the English Revolution of forty years earlier, indicates his sense of its revolutionary implications.[16] Furthermore, as Humphry Davy and others have noticed, Hooke's geological theory anticipates, or may even have influenced, many of the revolutionary aspects of James Hutton's theory of the earth a century later.[17] Like Hutton's theory, too, Hooke's vision of a dynamic earth, in which land masses are raised from and swallowed by huge subterranean forces across vast periods of time, invokes what Immanuel Kant would later call the 'dynamically sublime in nature'.[18] Seventeenth-century geological theory, then, was already capable of producing what we may call the geological sublime.

John Ray's *Observations Topographical, Moral, & Physiological; Made in a Journey Through part of the Low-Countries, Germany, Italy, and France* (1673) also contributed to the geological debates of the period.[19] Ray met Nicolaus Steno on his tour and makes several references to his *Dissertationis Prodromus* (1669) in the *Observations*, especially regarding questions about the nature and origin of inland fossils of sea creatures. Ray accepts that the 'most probable' solution to the problem is Steno's and Hooke's view 'that they were originally the Shells or Bones of Living Fishes and other Animals bred in the Sea' (*Observations*, p. 120).[20] He goes on to identify some of the issues raised by this opinion. Firstly, if it is correct then the whole of Europe, including the Alps, must have once been covered by the sea (though the fossil evidence discounts the possibility that this can be equated with Noah's Flood) (pp. 125–6). Secondly, there is the problem of how the former sea-beds could have been transformed into dry land and raised up into mountains. If earthquakes had been responsible for this, as Hooke had suggested, then

> either the World is a great deal older than is imagined or believed, there being an incredible space of time required to work such changes as raising all the Mountains, according to the leisurely proceedings of Nature in mutations of that kind since the first Records of History: or that in the primitive times and soon after the Creation the earth suffered far more concussions and mutations in its superficial part then afterward. (pp. 126–7)

Thirdly, if all the fossils that have been found inland really are the remains of sea creatures, then the fact that some of them do not resemble known species means that some species have been lost to the world, a 'supposition which Philosophers hitherto have been unwilling to admit, esteeming the destruction of any one Species to be a dismembring the Universe and rendering it imperfect, whereas they think the Divine Providence is especially concerned to preserve and secure all the Works of the Creation' (p. 127). Ray goes on to rehearse other opinions about fossils – that they are not the remains of sea creatures but 'products of some Plastic [creative] power in the Earth' (p. 127) or that only some of them are genuine remains of sea creatures – but ends up reaffirming the views of Steno and Hooke (p. 131).

But the most controversial contribution to geological debates in the period was Thomas Burnet's *Telluris Theoria Sacra* (1681), first translated into English in 1684 as *The Theory of the Earth: Containing an Account of the Original of the Earth and of all the General Changes Which it hath already undergone, or is to undergo, Till the Consummation of all Things* (1684).[21] As Burnet's title indicates, his book is an example of what Martin Rudwick calls 'geotheory', which attempts to develop a general hypothesis about the earth that accounts for the formation of its geomorphology in the past and its future vicissitudes.[22] According to Burnet, his interest in such questions had been provoked by encountering the Alps and the Apennines on his Grand Tour of Europe of 1671:

> There is nothing doth more awaken our thoughts or excite our minds to enquire into the causes of such things, than the actual view of them; as I have had experience my self when it was my fortune to cross the *Alps* and *Appennine* Mountains; for the sight of those wild, vast and indigested heaps of Stones and Earth, did so deeply strike my fancy, that I was not easie til I could give my self a tolerable account of how that confusion came in Nature. (*The Theory of the Earth*, p. 140)

Burnet had been shocked by European mountains because they were neither beautiful nor useful and could not therefore be accommodated to the belief that God must necessarily have created a perfect world. In chapter XI, 'Concerning the Mountains of the Earth, their greatness and irregular Form, their Situation, Causes, and Origin', Burnet surveys the extensive portions of the earth that are covered by mountain ranges in order to prove to readers who live in temperate lowland regions that the earth as a whole is not so gentle and regular as they might imagine. He stresses that

> these mountains are plac'd in no order one with another, that can either respect use or beauty; And if you consider them singly, they do not consist of any proportion of parts that is referable to any design, or that hath the least footsteps of Art or Counsel. There is nothing in Nature more shapeless and ill-figured than an old Rock or a Mountain; and all that variety that is among them, is but the various modes of irregularity; so as you cannot make a better character of them, in short, than to say they are of all forms and figures, except regular. And . . . if you look upon an heap of them together, or a Mountainous Country, they are the greatest example of confusion that we know in Nature. (pp. 144–5)

In order to explain how the earth could be covered by such deformed objects and structures, Burnet deploys a potentially unstable combination of scripture and natural philosophy. He tries to prove that God had indeed originally created an earth that 'before the Deluge was smooth, regular and uniform; without Mountains, and without a Sea' (p. 51). He supports this hypothesis by suggesting that the original chaos out of which the earth was formed consisted of evenly blended materials and elements. The effects of gravity necessarily formed a perfect globe out of this chaos consisting of various layers, with the most dense in the centre and with a universal ocean, covered with an oily film, on the outside. Further precipitation of fine particles from the air combined with the oily film to form a perfectly smooth earthy shell or outer crust above the abyss of water and this became the inhabitable surface that was peopled by Adam and Eve and their descendants. Although this perfect earth had been produced by natural causes, it was also 'a piece of Divine Geometry or Architecture' (p. 65). For the reasons narrated in the Old Testament, God had subsequently destroyed his perfect world, again using natural means. The mundane shell had broken up and collapsed into the subterraneous waters, producing a new world – with rugged, irregular mountain chains, caverns and fathomless seas – out of the ruins of the original world.

Yet although Burnet is deeply troubled by the fact that mountains lack beauty, order and usefulness, he is also moved by their sublimity:

> The greatest objects of Nature are, methinks, the most pleasing to behold; and next to the great Concave of the Heavens, and those boundless Regions where the Stars inhabit, there is nothing that I look upon with more pleasure than the wide Sea, and the Mountains of the Earth. There is something august and stately in the Air of these things, that inspires the mind with great thoughts and passions; We do naturally, upon such occasions, think of God and his greatness: and whatsoever hath but the shadow and appearance of INFINITE, as all things have that are too big for our comprehension, they fill and over-bear the mind with their Excess, and cast it into a pleasing kind of stupor and admiration. (pp. 139–40)

As Marjorie Hope Nicolson suggests, 'Here, . . . for the first time in England we find a sharp distinction between the emotional effects of the *sublime* and the *beautiful* in external Nature' (*Mountain Gloom and Mountain Glory*, p. 222). She goes on to show that Burnet's *The Theory of the Earth* influenced the cult of the natural sublime in early eighteenth-century poetry (pp. 225–32). Burnet's book thus requires us to modify the standard account of the history of aesthetic taste, which tends to suggest that aesthetic enthusiasm for mountains did not emerge until the publication of Joseph Addison's essays on 'Taste and the Pleasures of the Imagination' in 1712 and Edmund Burke's *A Philosophical Enquiry into the Origin of our Ideas of the Sublime and Beautiful* in 1757 and 1759.[23] Yet the assumption that mountains might stimulate positive aesthetic experience was far from universal for much of the eighteenth century. Given that the protocols of natural history travel writing required the exclusion of personal experience and an emphasis on use-value, it is perhaps not surprising that natural history tours of Scotland in the period tend not to celebrate the sublimity of the Scottish Highlands. Yet as the natural sublime became more fashionable in the second half of the century, geological tours began to include positive aesthetic responses to Scotland's mountains.

Nicolson's account of the 'Burnet Controversy' that raged between 1685 and 1715 reveals that most of the key scientific figures of the period were drawn into supporting, developing or refuting Burnet.[24] In his *The Wisdom of God Manifested in the Works of the Creation* (1691) and *Three Physico-Theological Discourses* (1693), John Ray sought to oppose the rise of Lucretian atheism and mechanism, which he associated with Burnet as well as with Hobbes. John Woodward's *An Essay toward a Natural History of the Earth* (1695) was 'in part a sequel to Burnet's work, in part a reply to some of his arguments, in which Woodward believed that Burnet had not gone far enough' (Nicolson, *Mountain Gloom and Mountain Glory*, p. 246).[25] Edmund Halley 'was persuaded by the soundness of Burnet's conclusions about the effects of the Flood, though not satisfied with Burnet's hypothesis about its cause' (p. 243). He gave two papers at the Royal Society in December 1694 'in which he posited a natural rather than supernatural cause for the Deluge, which he found in "the casual Choc of a Comet"' (p. 243). Although Halley's theory greatly impressed his audience, he would not publish his papers for fear of incurring the censure of the Church (they were eventually published in the *Philosophical Transactions of the Royal Society* in 1726). William Whiston's *A New Theory of the Earth* (1696) also supported Burnet with 'a diluvian theory almost identical with Halley's' (Nicolson, *Mountain Gloom and Mountain Glory*, pp. 244–5).

The writings of Hooke, Ray, Burnet, Whiston, Woodward and others demonstrate that geological questions, approached in scientific as well as theological terms, had been raised in Britain well before the period focused on in the present book. Roy Porter argues that the outburst of geotheory in the late seventeenth century needs to be seen as a serious contribution to the history of geology: 'throughout eighteenth-century Britain, debate was conducted explicitly around the theories and outlooks of Burnet, Woodward and Whiston. Though dissociating themselves from them, Buffon, Raspe, Whitehurst and others nevertheless believed that *these* were the theories to be refuted in order to clear the decks' (*The Making of Geology*, p. 63). The almost ubiquitous assumption in the late seventeenth century that a universal flood had played a major role in forming and shaping the earth's rocks allows Rudwick to argue that the 'Neptunist' paradigm, usually associated with Abraham Gottlob Werner (1749–1817), had become 'the standard model' much earlier (*Bursting the Limits of Time*, p. 176). As we will see, however, late seventeenth-century geotheory appears to have had virtually no impact on the early phase of exploring Scotland's natural history – an omission that is in itself significant.

Discovering the Natural History of Scotland

The exploration of the old and new worlds in the sixteenth and seventeenth centuries was complemented by new interest in the 'discovery' and description of Britain itself.[26] Chorographic descriptions of, and travellers' reports about, Scotland can be traced back at least to the Middle Ages.[27] Among the great English Tudor topographies, William Camden's *Britannia* (first Latin edition in 1586) stands out for including an account of Scotland, though brief and based entirely on earlier writings rather than personal experience. The edition that is of most interest here is *Camden's Britannia, Newly Translated into English: With Large Additions and Improvements, published by Edmund Gibson* (1695). *Camden's Britannia* includes a much-augmented section on Scotland which begins with Camden saying 'Now I am bound for Scotland, with a willing mind' but then admitting that he 'shall with gentle touches lightly pass it over' because he does not know much about the country (p. 882). The text thus employs the language of a tour without narrating an actual tour, and although *Camden's Britannia* describes places of interest to the present book, especially the Highlands and Islands, it mentions minerals and fossils only in passing. Some of the additions that Gibson made to Camden's text are, however, notable in that they exemplify the new connections between chorographic description and natural history that had been forged in the seventeenth century. All but one of its English county lists of plants were made by John Ray. And included among the preliminary materials is a list of 'Treatises relating to Scotland, extracted out of Sir Robert Sibalds's *Materials for the Scotch-Atlas*'. These treatises include 'Metals and Minerals in Scotland, by D. Borthwick', 'Description of the High-lands of *Scotland*. MS', 'An account of the metals found in *Scotland*, by Mr. Atkinson MS.', and 'Scotia illustrata by Sir Rob. Sibalds' (no pagination).

The fact that Gibson's updated edition of *Camden's Britannia* included recent materials from Ray and Sir Robert Sibbald (1641–1722) indicates their prominence in the exploration and description of the natural history of England and Scotland respectively. Indeed, in the summer of 1661, Ray and Willughby made a tour of northern England and southern Scotland, making him 'the first naturalist to visit Scotland and record his findings' (Lindsay, *The Discovery of Scotland*, p. 70).[28] Although Ray did not publish an account of this tour, selections from his notes about his British journeys were posthumously published as 'Mr. Ray's Itineraries' in *Select Remains of the Learned John Ray* (1760). The Scottish section of 'Itinerary II' began on 17 August 1661 when Ray and Willughby rode north to Dunbar. Their ten-day tour included visits to Leith, Edinburgh, Linlithgow, Stirling and Glasgow. On the way back south they passed through Douglas and visited the lead mines at Leadhills, bidding farewell to Scotland on 26 August. Disappointingly, however, the only notes about natural history in Ray's account of Scotland in Itinerary II are his botanical observations on the Bass Rock, where he paid particular attention to the Soland Geese (pp. 191–3).

Sibbald was the most important pioneer in the seventeenth-century description of Scotland's geography, topography and natural history.[29] After studying at Edinburgh University and on the Continent, he 'briefly resided in London, where he met Sir Robert Moray and other virtuosi' and returned to Scotland at the end of October 1662.[30] In 1682, Sibbald was appointed as Scotland's Geographer Royal; in

1685, he spent another brief period in London, where 'he met Sir Robert Boyle . . . and other members of the Royal Society' (Withers, 'Sibbald, Sir Robert', *ODNB*).[31] Sibbald aspired to produce a comprehensive description of Scotland that would include its natural history. To that end, he 'published an Advertisement and a broadside circular requesting geographical information' from all corners of the land (Withers, *ODNB*). The questionnaire, as Porter points out, became 'a characteristic weapon in the armoury of the natural history project' and was often used in Scotland (*The Making of Geology*, p. 36). Sibbald's aims were further spelt out in *An Account of the Scottish Atlas; or, A Description of Scotland, Ancient and Modern* (1783). This text is both a report on progress and an attempt to recruit more respondents throughout Scotland to contribute descriptions of their districts. Sibbald announces that the 'Atlas of Scotland' 'Is to be in two Volumes; the one in Latin, the other in English' and that 'The Atlas of Scotland in English . . . is divided into two parts, the General and the special part'. The general part would focus on Scotland's history, while the special part would describe Scotland 'as it is now' (pp. 4, 5). Sibbald's account of the kinds of information which would be included in the description of contemporary Scotland recalls those in Boyle's 'Heads':

> Then *Scotland*, as it is now, is described, where is shewed the Extent and the Bounds of it, the Latitude of it, the Figure of it, under what Climate and Parallels; the length of the longest Day there; the Division of *Scotland* into three *Peninsulæ*, the South one, the Middle one and the North one. The Rivers upon each side running far into the Countrey are separated by a small Tract of Land from meeting, else they would make three Islands of the continent of *Scotland*. It is also divided by the Mountains, and by the Qualitie of the Soil, and Nature of the Inhabitants and their different manner of life, into the *High-Lands* and Low-lands, and the Highlanders and *Low-land men*. . . .
>
>   The *Islands* about *Scotland* are shewed, and there is an Account given of the Nature and Quality of the Soil, and the natural products of it: viz. the grains, Pot-herbs and Fruits, and other usefull Plants; The Animals; Four-footed Beasts domestick and wild, the Fouls, the Fishes, the Insects; the Metals and Minerals, the substances cast up by the Sea, the Mineral Waters; The Advantages by the Sea for Trade and Fishing; The great Rivers *Forth*, *Clyde* and *Tay*, with their Firths, of each of which there are particular Maps, with full Description of them; The Lochs and the rare properties of some of them. (*An Account of the Scottish Atlas*, p. 5)

For various reasons, however, the 'Scottish Atlas' was never published, although 'surviving manuscript material records about sixty-five local respondents' (Withers, *ODNB*). Many responses came from parish ministers, a source of local information that would be repeatedly drawn on in geographical and natural history writing about Scotland in the eighteenth century, including the Rev. Dr John Walker's 'Report on the Hebrides' (1771), Thomas Pennant's two-volume *A Tour in Scotland and Voyage to the Hebrides, MDCCLXXII* (1774, 1776), and Sir John Sinclair's multi-volume *Statistical Account of Scotland* in the 1790s.

Sibbald did, however, produce a major work on the natural history of Scotland. His *Scotia illustrate sive Prodromus historiæ naturalis* (1684) was published in Latin with a covering title page in English which summarises the project: Scotland Illustrated: or An Essay of Natural History, in *which Are Exquisitely displayed the Nature of the Country . . . And the Manifold Productions of Nature in its Threefold Kingdom, (viz.) Vegetable, Animal and Mineral . . . are now exactly Collected and Published Together; And their Various Uses; (Especially Medicinal and Mechanical, for the Necessity, as well as the Accommodation of Life.) Clearly laid open to all.*

Martin Martin's Pioneering Natural History Tours of Scotland

The first published tours of Scotland that came under the influence of the Royal Society and paid some attention to natural history and mineralogy were Martin Martin's *A Late Voyage to St. Kilda, the Remotest of all the Hebrides, or Western Isles of Scotland. With a History of the Island, Natural, Moral, and Topographical* (1698) and *A Description of the Western Islands of Scotland* (1703).[32] Martin's tours are often described as path-breaking topographical accounts of north-west Scotland. Yet, as Withers notes in his introduction, 'given the existence of earlier accounts of the Western Isles, albeit that many survived only in manuscript form, from Dean Munro's 1549 *Description of the Western Isles of Scotland* . . . and other geographical documents dating from the 1640s, 1670s and 1680s, the view that Martin's accounts mark the beginning of topographical description of the Hebrides cannot be allowed to stand' (p. 2).[33] It is possible to claim, however, that Martin was the first to write and publish scientifically motivated travel accounts of the north-western Scottish islands.[34] While his books are only occasionally concerned with the mineralogy of the places he visited (he is much more interested in flora and fauna), they can be used as an example of early travel writing about the natural history of the north-west of Scotland and as a template against which to measure some of the later mineralogical and geological tours examined in the present book.

Martin was a Gaelic speaker from Skye who graduated with an MA from Edinburgh in 1681 and with an MD from Leyden in 1710, after which he worked as a doctor in London until his death in 1719. While in Edinburgh in the 1680s Martin became involved in 'those networks of natural knowledge at that time centring upon Sir Robert Sibbald' (Withers, Introduction to Martin, p. 3). In these years, as we have seen, Sibbald was working on his 'Scottish Atlas', and Martin completed 'a short manuscript "Description of Sky" [Skye] for Sibbald's project' (p. 6). In London in the 1690s Martin came into the orbit of the Royal Society and this provided another impulse for his journeys to, and published works about, the Western Islands:

> he met, amongst others, the antiquarian, natural historian and collector, Hans Sloane, then Secretary of the Royal Society. It was under Sloane's patronage that Martin undertook both a tour of Lewis in 1696, and, more importantly, his trip to St Kilda in May 1697, which was to provide the crucial basis to his 1698 *Voyage*. It was with Sloane's guidance and support that Martin published his 'Several Observations in the North Islands of Scotland', in the Royal Society's *Philosophical Transactions* in October 1697. (p. 6)

As a native of Skye whose education had given him access to the centres of scientific enquiry in Edinburgh and London, Martin was able to bridge the gap between local and scientific knowledge of the places he visited. Although Martin is sometimes sceptical about the traditions and superstitions of the inhabitants of St Kilda and the other Western Islands of Scotland, wherever possible he also takes seriously local voices and experience. Martin's written accounts of the Hebridean islands can thus be read as staging a dialogue between different voices: 'Local information – the native voice, as it were – is often accompanied by our hearing Martin's "other voice", that of the scientist-cum-traveller who knows that his audience lies beyond the Hebrides' (Withers, Introduction to Martin, p. 8).

A Late Voyage to St. Kilda (1698) begins with a dedication to Charles Montague, President of the Royal Society. Its preface and opening paragraphs emphasise the role of the Royal Society in encouraging Martin to explore the natural history of the Western Islands of Scotland and exhibit various features which accord with the travel writing that came under the Royal Society's influence. Martin insists on the importance of exploring the natural history of the remote parts of the British Isles:

> It is a piece of weakness and folly merely to value things because of their distance from the place where we are Born: Thus Men have Travelled far enough in the search of Foreign Plants and Animals, and yet continue strangers to those produced in their own natural Climate. Therefore I presume that this following Relation will not prove unprofitable or displeasing, unless the great Advantages of Truth and unaffected plainness may do it a prejudice, in the Opinion of such as are more nice and childish than solid and judicious. (Martin, *A Late Voyage to St. Kilda*, no pagination)

Adhering to 'Truth and unaffected plainness', Martin emphasises his reliability by stressing that he undertook the dangerous journey to St Kilda solely in order accurately to observe and describe its natural history:

> The Ingenious Author of this Treatise is a Person whose Candour and Integrity guard him against all Affectation and Vanity; and his great desire to propagate the Natural History of the Isles of Scotland, makes him relate, without any disguise, the several particulars that fell under his accurate Observation. He was prompted by a generous Curiosity to undertake a Voyage through several Isles to St Kilda . . . and that in an open Boat, to the almost manifest hazard of his life, since the Seas and Tides in those Rocky Islands are more inconstant and ranging than in most other places. (no pagination)

Martin also stresses that the information he presents about St Kilda derives from his own observation or from the testimony and experience of the islanders, who can be believed precisely because of their remoteness from the modern world: 'they are a sort of People so Plain, and so little inclined to Impose upon Mankind, that perhaps no place in the World at this day, knows such Instances of true primitive Honour and Simplicity; a People who abhor lying Tricks and Artifices, as they do the most poisonous Plants, or devouring

Animals' (no pagination). Martin's emphasis on the 'true primitive Honour and Simplicity' of the people of St Kilda can be read as a response to 'the problem of many other travellers and reporters at this time, namely, how to get others to take seriously what is, essentially, the knowledge of "the vulgar sort"' (Withers, Introduction to Martin, p. 10). Martin, too, has necessarily avoided lying tricks and artifices, partly because he is incapable of them and partly because he is addressing a 'philosophic' readership that is well-read in the book of nature and trained in the disciplines of the Royal Society:

> The Author, perhaps, might have put these Papers into the Hands of some who were capable of giving them the politest turns of Phrase, and of making some pretty Excursions upon several passages in them; but he thought the Intelligent and Philosophic part of Mankind would value the Truth more in such Accounts, than any thing that can be borrowed from Art, or the advantages of more refined Language; and such do Contemplate the Books of Nature with so much diligence and application that they may admire the original spring of Power and Wisdom, that first set Nature it self in Motion, and preserves its regular course in all its wonderful and various Phenomena; and therefore it may be reasonably hoped, that the meanness of its dress will not be made use of as any considerable Objection against this preliminary Essay. (no pagination)

Martin's preliminary reflections, then, underline the epistemological decorum of his mode of observation and writing. He attempts to establish his reliability by employing textual strategies that are similar to Dampier's, including claims about his candour, integrity, disinterested observation, use of plain style, and emphasis on the difficulty and danger he underwent to gain the information he presents.

The archipelago of St Kilda, which was off the north-western edge of most maps of Scotland in the period, is the remotest part of the British Isles, lying forty-one miles (sixty-six kilometres) west of Benbecula in the Outer Hebrides.[35] It does appear, however, on the map of the Hebrides, drawn up by Herman Moll, that Martin included in A *Description of the Western Islands* (Figure 2.1). Martin had already presented a crude map of the St Kilda islands in *A Late Voyage to St. Kilda* (Figure 2.2) whose north-south orientation is virtually the reverse of the modern convention.

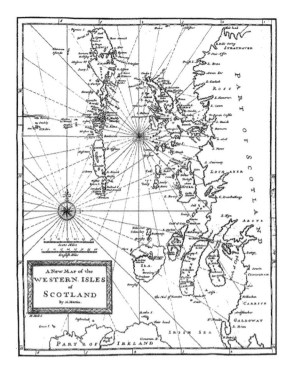

Figure 2.1 Herman Moll, 'A New Map of the Western Isles of Scotland', in Martin Martin, *A Description of the Western Islands of Scotland* (1703), between pp. 18 and 19. Reproduced by permission of the National Library of Scotland.

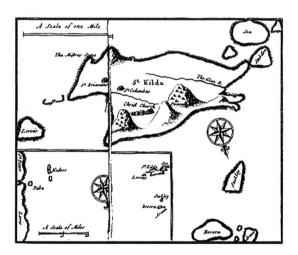

Figure 2.2 Martin Martin, 'Map of St Kilda', in *A Late Voyage to St. Kilda* (1698). Reproduced by permission of the National Library of Scotland.

The first chapter of *A Late Voyage to St. Kilda* begins by claiming priority – St Kilda 'being never hitherto described to any purpose, the Accounts which are given by [George] *Buchanan* and Sir *Robert Murray*, being but Relations from Second and Third Hands' (pp. 2–3).[36] The first chapter also offers a first-person account of the story behind Martin's journey and his efforts to visit the island. Driven by 'a Natural Impulse of Curiosity' stimulated by the description of the island by the present steward and by 'the Products of the Island, which were brought to me', Martin tells us that he attempted several times to visit St Kilda 'but in vain; until last Summer' when he had the opportunity to travel there with the islanders' new minister, Mr John Campbell: 'This Occasion I cheerfully embrac'd; and accordingly we embark'd at the Isle *Esay* [Ensay] in *Harris*, the 29th. of *May*, at Six in the Afternoon, 1697. the Wind at S.E.' (pp. 2–3). As in Dampier's *New Voyage*, details about place, date, time and wind direction work to convince the reader that the journey was really undertaken by the narrator and that he is reliable and possessed of the requisite scientific knowledge. Soon afterwards, however, geographical specificity is used to indicate the difficulties and danger of the voyage from Harris to St Kilda:

> We set Sail with a gentle Breeze of Wind, bearing to the *Westward*, and were not well got out of the Harbour, when Mr. *Campbell* observing the Whiteness of the Waves attended with an extraordinary Noise beating upon the Rocks, express'd his Dislike of it, as in those Parts a never-failing prognostick of an ensuing Storm; but the same appearing sometimes in Summer, before excessive Heat, this was slighted by the Crew. But as we advanced about two Leagues further, upon the Coast of the Isle *Pabbay*, the former Signs appearing more conspicuously, we were forc'd unanimously to conclude a Storm was approaching, which occasion'd a Motion for our Return; but the Wind and Ebb-Tide concurring, determin'd us to pursue our Voyage, in hopes to arrive at our desired Harbour, before the Wind or Storm should rise, which we judged should not be suddenly: But our fond Imagination was not seconded with a good Event, as appears by the Sequel; for we had scarce sail'd a League further, when the Wind inclined more *Southerly*, and alter'd our Measures; we endeavour'd by the help of our Oars to reach the *Haw-sker Rocks* [Haskeir Island and Haskeir Eagach], some Four Leagues to the *South*-Coast, which we were not able to effect, tho we consum'd the night in this vain expectation. (pp. 3–5)

Forced to continue, 'though labouring under the Disadvantages of Wind and Tide almost contrary to us', the travellers eventually espy 'the Isle *Borera* [Boreray], near Three Leagues *North* of St. *Kilda*, which was then about Four Leagues to the *South* of us' (pp. 6–7). Unable to land on Boreray, and constrained to remain there over-night by a storm which almost drove the ship out into the open ocean and caused 'our Men' to lay 'aside all hopes of life', the crew were eventually able to row to St Kilda (p. 9). It is important to note that this narrative account of the difficulty and danger Martin faced in crossing to St Kilda does not foreground his heroic subjective experience but authenticates and increases the value of the information he is about to present. By contrast, as we will see in later chapters, the geological travel writing about Scotland in the late eighteenth century, under the influence of Romanticism, typically foregrounds the heroic geological traveller's subjective experiences of difficulty, danger, discovery and delight.

A Late Voyage to St. Kilda is, as its title suggests, a 'voyage' – a contemporary genre term that seems to promise more of a travel nar-rative than the generic connotations of his later *A Description of the Western Islands of Scotland*.[37] Yet although Withers is right to say that 'neither the 1703 *Description* nor the 1698 *Voyage* can properly be termed a narrative' (Introduction to Martin, p. 10), *A Late Voyage to St. Kilda* does open with some of the conventions of travel nar-rative, beginning – as we have seen – with a first-person account of the journey to St Kilda, and employs them sporadically through the rest of the text. But after Martin describes how he and Campbell had to be carried to land by the local inhabitants, the rest of *A Late Voyage to St. Kilda* mostly consists of objective descriptions, in no particular order, of the physical environment, the island's flora and fauna and surrounding seas, and the people's mode of living, com-bining first-hand observation, scholarly references, and reports of the experiences and beliefs of the islanders. Attention to natural history is overwhelmingly concerned with botany and zoology, while com-ments on mineralogy are more or less limited to the following:

> There are several Veins of different Stone to be seen in the Rocks of the *South-East* Bay; upon the *North* side of this Rock is one as it were cut out by Nature, resembling a Tarras-Walk. The Chrystal grows under the Rock at the Landing-place; this Rock must be pierc'd a Foot or

two deep, before the Chrystal can be had from the Bed of Sand where it lies; the Water at the bottom is of a black Colour; the largest Piece is not above four Inches long, and about two in Diameter, each Piece Sexangular. (p. 21)

Here, mineralogical phenomena are located and described largely in terms of how they might be extracted for potential use.

Martin's preface to *A Description of the Western Islands of Scotland* echoes and develops the ideas in the preface to *A Late Voyage to St. Kilda*. It begins by claiming that the Western Islands 'have never been describ'd till now by any Man that was a Native of the Country, or had travelled them' (no pagination). Martin indicates that he is particularly qualified to write about them because he is both a native of the islands and has actually travelled around them. As in the earlier preface, he suggests that 'The Modern Itch after the Knowledge of Foreign Places' has contributed to a general ignorance of Britain, especially remote parts such as the Western Islands. As a consequence, the potential usefulness of the islands' natural history – much of which is known to the natives – has been neglected. At the same time, however, the scientific revolution of the previous century has generated a new kind of interest in nature and geography that was not available to earlier writers like George Buchanan: 'since his time, there's a great Change in the Humour of the World, and by consequence in the Way of Writing. Natural and Experimental Philosophy has been much improv'd since his days, and therefore Descriptions of Countries without the Natural History of 'em, are now justly reckon'd to be defective' (no pagination). Martin insists that the new concern with the empirical natural history of particular places distinguishes his *Description of the Western Islands* from all previous accounts: 'This I had a particular regard to in the following Description, and have every where taken notice of the Nature of the Climate and Soil, of the Produce of the Places by Sea and Land' (no pagination).

Yet Martin's stance as a savant of the recent scientific revolution does not lead him to assume that his mode of engaging with the natural world is superior to that of the inhabitants of the Western Islands. His identification with the islanders is bolstered by the claim that their interaction with their natural environment is virtually the same as that promoted by the Royal Society. He tells us that he has taken notice of 'the Remarkable Cures perform'd by the Natives merely by the use of Simples' and stresses that the use of such medicinal herbs is based on 'repeated Experiments' ('experiment' meant experience as well as a scientific test). He goes on to stress that his relation of such cures and usages is derived 'not only from the Authority of many of the Inhabitants, who are Persons of great integrity, but likewise from my own particular Observation; and thus with *Celsus* they first make Experiments, and afterwards proceed to reason upon the Effects' (no pagination).[38] The islanders, then, are sound natural historians whose inductive methodology resembles Martin's own: 'I hold it enough for me to furnish my Observations, without accounting for the Reason and Way that those Simples produce them; this I leave to the Learned in that Faculty' (no pagination). Despite the fact that the inhabitants of the Western Islands 'do for the most part labour under the want of knowledge of Letters, and other useful Arts and Sciences', then, 'they seem to be better vers'd in the Book of Nature, than many that have greater opportunities of improvement' (no pagination).

As well as more or less equating the islanders' mode of engaging with nature with that of the scientific revolution (thereby authenticating his own scientific style), Martin also implicitly suggests that the islanders' mode of speech is virtually the same as the style of science writing endorsed by the Royal Society (thereby authenticating his own writing style). He says that he hopes his empirical observation of the natural history of the Western Islands will 'make amends for what Defects may be found in my Stile and way of Writing'. But those 'defects' are characteristic of the islanders' use of language in general and precisely embody the philosophical and stylistic aspirations of the scientific revolution:

> for there's a Wantonness in Language as well as in other things, to which my Countrymen of the Isles are as much strangers, as to other Excesses which are too frequent in many parts of Europe. We study Things there more than Words, tho' those that understand our Native Language must own that we have enough of the latter to inform the Judgment, and work upon the Affections in as pathetick a manner as any other Languages whatever. (no pagination)

Here, Martin identifies with the linguistic propensities of his 'Countrymen' – who, we must recall, speak Hebridean Gaelic – by distinguishing their style, and his own, from the wanton excesses that are too frequent in many parts of Europe. It is notable that

Martin's claim that the islanders (including himself) 'study Things there more than Words' echoes John Locke's insistence, influenced by the Royal Society, on an absolute distinction between philosophical (or scientific) language, whose aim was to 'speak of things as they are', and the deceptive use of figurative language in other discourses.[39] Martin's extraordinary move, then, is to assert that the Gaelic speakers of the Western Islands of Scotland were intrinsically given to exercise such discipline and that he derived his own English style as much from them as from the Royal Society.

In contrast with *A Late Voyage to St. Kilda*, Martin's *Description of the Western Islands* almost wholly dispenses with first-person narrative in favour of impersonal observations of the Hebrides, island by island. Martin describes the following islands in the following order: Lewis and its surrounding islets; Harris; Benbecula; Skye; Bute, Arran, Ailsa and Gigha; Jura, Colonsay, Mull and Iona (but not Staffa); Tiree, Coll, Rum, Muck, Cannay and Eigg; St Kilda; Orkney and the Shetland Islands. This sequence distributes the islands into related groups but does not reproduce the order of a tour, as we can see from looking back at Martin's map of the Western Isles (Figure 2.1). Elizabeth Bray points out that

> [Martin] would have sailed across the dangerous seas by a variety of craft, ridden on horseback across the rough moors, or traversed them on foot. He had, however, pretensions as a man of science, and a contributor to learned journals. So he effaces himself. He withdraws the narrative thread – the story of his voyages and travels, his hosts and his personal experiences – leaving his observations strewn, like unthreaded beads, across his pages. With no coherent development, no line of argument or ordering of subject matter, his offering is whimsically disjointed. (*The Discovery of the Hebrides*, p. 14)

Martin's main focus is, once again, on the people's way of life and beliefs and on botany and zoology rather than mineralogy. Even more than in his earlier book, Martin's attention to natural history is concerned with the actual or potential use-value of the islands' natural resources. The lengthiest passage on mineralogy in *A Description of the Western Islands* appears in chapter VII, 'A Description of the Isle of Skye':

> THE Village *Borve*, and *Glenmore*, afford two very fine sorts of Earth, the one Red, the other White, and they both feel, and cut like melted Tallow. There are other Places that afford plenty of very fine white Marle

which cuts like Butter; it abounds most in *Corchattachan*, where an Experiment has been made of its Virtue; a quantity of it being spread on a sloping Hill, covered with Heath, soon after all the Heath fell to the Ground, as if it had been cut with a Knife, they afterwards sowed Barley on the Ground, which tho it grew but unequally, some places producing no Grain, because perhaps it was unequally laid on, yet the produce was thirty-five fold, and many stalks carried five Ears of Barley. This account was given me by the present possessor of the Ground, *Lachlin Mac-kinon.* . . .

. . . The village *Torrin* in *Strath*, affords a great deal of good White and Black Marble, I have seen Cups made of the White which is very fine. There are large Quarries of Freestone in several parts of this Isle, as at *Snisness* in *Strath*, in the *South* of *Borrie*, and Isle of *Rasay*. There is abundance of Lime-stone in *Strath* and *Trotterness*, some Banks of Clay on the *East* Coast are overflow'd by the Tide, and in these grow the *Lapis Ceranius*, or *Cerna Amonis* of different Shapes. Some of the breadth of a Crown-piece bearing an Impression resembling the Sun. Some are as big as a Man's Finger in form of a *Semicircle*, and furrowed on the Inner side, others are less, and have furrows of a Yellow Colour on both sides. These Stones are by the Natives called Cramp stones, because as they say they cure the Cramp in Cows, by washing the part affected with Water in which this Stone has been steep'd for some Hours. (pp. 132–4)

These paragraphs exemplify Martin's whole methodology. Blending, almost seamlessly, his own discoveries with what local people have told him (and perhaps what he gleaned from growing up on Skye), they attempt objectively to describe what is there rather than narrating his own adventure of discovery. These paragraphs also reveal a number of things about Martin's approach to mineralogy. Firstly, as Withers suggests, 'Martin's attention to the mineralogical wealth of Skye . . . is both a description of what is there and, in outline terms, a rough catalogue of its future potential' (Introduction to Martin, p. 8). Local traditional uses of mineral materials are treated as seriously and objectively as the use-values known to the world at large. The inhabitants of Skye and the scientific elite of the Royal Society share the assumption that nature is a store of objects and materials that have intrinsic uses for human beings that can be discovered empirically. Secondly, there is no apparent order to Martin's observations, despite the fact that John Ray had recently attempted to organise natural objects and life-forms into a classificatory system. Thirdly, Martin's account of the island's minerals is limited to description and observation. When he points out that *Lapis Ceranius* or *Cerna Amonis* (ammonites) 'grow' in banks of clay, for example, instead of engaging with contemporary debates about fossils and what they reveal about the history of the earth, Martin tells us why the natives call them 'Cramp stones'.[40]

Martin's apparent lack of interest in questions about the history and causal formation of geological phenomena cannot be explained by asserting that they could not have been formulated until the emergence of geology proper about a century later. As we have seen, the causal history of the earth's geomorphology had become particularly contested in late seventeenth-century Britain. The fact that this geological or geotheoretical controversy was at its height in the 1690s, precisely at the time when Martin was either in London or on his travels in the Western Islands of Scotland, shows that it was perfectly possible for him to engage in such speculations. Raising such questions would, however, have involved him in heated theological and scientific controversy. More pertinently, perhaps, the avoidance of such questions was also dictated by the scientific genre system of the period. The natural history of the late seventeenth and early eighteenth centuries confined itself to observation and description in accord with Bacon's demarcation of the different concerns of natural history, physic and metaphysic.

Another aspect of Martin's accounts of the Western Islands of Scotland that is markedly different from some of the travel writing we will look at in later chapters is that he does not respond aesthetically to the wild or mountainous landscapes he encountered. Burnet's ambivalent response to the Alps – combining or oscillating between horror and admiration – was a taste of things to come, but the dominant aesthetic values of the period precluded aesthetic delight in mountains. Moreover, the constraints of epistemological decorum that governed natural history also excluded expressions of such delight.

Although *A Late Voyage to St. Kilda* and *A Description of the Western Islands of Scotland* present pioneering accounts of the natural history of the Scottish islands, they cannot be called mineralogical or geological tours. Martin's natural history of the Scottish islands avoids geological questions and aesthetic responses to mountainous landscapes not because they were not yet culturally possible, but because of the disciplinary conventions and constraints that natural history travel writing set for itself. Such writing confined itself to objective observation and description, avoiding speculations about history or causality and reports of the traveller's subjective or aesthetic experience. In these and other ways, the disciplines of natural history shaped a quite different kind of travel writing about the Highlands and Islands of Scotland to that which would emerge in the second half of the eighteenth century under the interrelated influences of Romanticism and geology. In the following two chapters we will examine two of the pre-eminent travelling natural historians who toured Scotland – John Walker and Thomas Pennant – whose writing about Scotland's natural history generally adheres to the generic conventions of natural history, maintaining epistemological decorum and passing over the rigours of travel and subjective experience in order to present objective observations and descriptions of the natural history itself.

Notes

1. For Bacon's vision of an all-encompassing scientific project, see *The New Organon*, especially 'Outline of a Natural and Experimental History' (pp. 222–38).
2. See Thompson, *Travel Writing*, pp. 34–44.
3. See Raven, *English Naturalists from Neckham to Ray*; Allen, *The Naturalist in Britain*, especially chapters 1 to 3; Findlen, 'Natural History'; Iliffe, 'Science and Voyages of Discovery'; Bowen, *Empiricism and Geographical Thought*; Jardine et al. (eds), *Cultures of Natural History*; and Withers, 'Reporting, Mapping, Trusting' and *Geography, Science and National Identity*, pp. 1–29. On the scientific revolution in seventeenth-century England, see Shapin, *The Scientific Revolution*.
4. See Hulme and Jordanova (eds), *The Enlightenment and its Shadows*, especially pp. 1–15 and 18–34.
5. See Bacon, 'Advice to the Earl of Rutland on his Travels' and 'Of Travaile'.
6. For a discussion of Woodward's *Brief Instructions* and an illuminating analysis of the notion of place in eighteenth-century geography and natural history, see Withers, 'Geography, Natural History and the Eighteenth-Century Enlightenment'.
7. Also see chapter 4, 'Reporting the World' (pp. 62–95), especially the section on 'Gaining the Reader's Trust' (pp. 72–86).

8. See Dampier, *A New Voyage Round the World*, I, p. 1.

9. See Thompson, *Travel Writing*, pp. 96–129, and *The Suffering Traveller*.

10. See Laudan, *From Mineralogy to Geology*, and Rudwick, *Bursting the Limits of Time*.

11. See Hooke, *Micrographia*, pp. 107–12.

12. See Hooke, *Posthumous Works*, pp. 277–328.

13. See Drake, 'The Geological Observations of Robert Hooke (1635–1703) on the Isle of Wight'.

14. For an account of the period's assumptions about nature and their compatibility with Christian theology, see Willey, *The Eighteenth-Century Background*, pp. 1–26. On the possibility of Hooke's theory of evolution, see Drake, 'Hooke's Ideas of the Terraqueous Globe and a Theory of Evolution'.

15. See Hooke, *Posthumous Works*, pp. 277–450. For discussions of Hooke's geology, see Drake, *Restless Genius* and 'Hooke's Concepts of the Earth in Space'; Drake and Komar, 'A Comparison of the Geological Contributions of Nicolaus Steno and Robert Hooke'; Rappaport, 'Hooke on Earthquakes'; and Rossiter, 'The First English Geologist'. Also see Purrington, *The First Professional Scientist*, and Rossi, *The Dark Abyss of Time*.

16. The phrase 'the world turned upside down' was used by Henry Denne in *Grace, Mercy and Peace* (1645); see Christopher Hill, *The World Turned Upside Down*.

17. For Davy's suggestion that Hooke anticipated Hutton, see Siegfried and Dott (eds), *Humphry Davy on Geology*, pp. 40, 54. Also see Drake, 'The Geological Observations of Robert Hooke (1635–1703) on the Isle of Wight', pp. 26–8, and 'The Hooke Imprint on the Huttonian Theory'; Davies, 'Robert Hooke and his Conception of Earth-History'; and Oldroyd, 'Robert Hooke's Methodology of Science as Exemplified in his "Discourse of Earthquakes"'.

18. See Kant, *Critique of the Power of Judgment*, pp. 143–58.

19. For Ray's contributions to geology, see Raven, *John Ray, Naturalist*, chapter 16. Also see Ray, *Miscellaneous Discourses Concerning the Dissolution and Changes of the World*.

20. Steno's pioneering geological work was published in *De Solido Intra Solidum Naturalita Contento Dissertationis Prodomus*; see Cutler, *The Seashell on the Mountaintop*.

21. I have used the second English edition, published in 1691.

22. For Rudwick's account of 'geotheory' as a scientific genre, see *Bursting the Limits of Time*, pp. 133–80. On the geological theories of the period, see Rappaport, *When Geologists Were Historians*.

23. On the eighteenth-century sublime, see Monk, *The Sublime.*

24. See *Mountain Gloom and Mountain Glory*, pp. 225–70. For Nicolson's account of Burnet and the Burnet controversy, see chapters 5 and 6 (pp. 184–270). A discussion of Burnet and Ray can be found in Willey, *The Eighteenth-Century Background*, pp. 27–42. Also see Porter, *The Making of Geology*, chapter 3, 'The Re-creation of the Earth' (pp. 62–90).

25. Nicolson overstates the scientific nature of Woodward's arguments. For Porter's discussion of Woodward as one of 'the age's foremost students of the earth', see *The Making of Geology*, pp. 62–90.

26. See Moir, *The Discovery of Britain.*

27. See Lindsay, *The Discovery of Scotland*, and Rackwitz, *Travels to Terra Incognita.*

28. For Ray's life and work, see Raven, *John Ray, Naturalist.* On Ray's contribution to the development of natural history, see McMahon, 'Constructing Natural History in England, 1650–1700'.

29. For an account of Sibbald's geography of and in Scotland, see Withers, *Geography, Science and National Identity*, pp. 70–87.

30. On Sir Robert Moray, or Murray, see Allan, 'Moray, Sir Robert (1608/9?–1673)', *ODNB.*

31. See Emerson, 'Sir Robert Sibbald, Kt, the Royal Society of Scotland and the Origins of the Scottish Enlightenment', and Withers, 'Geography, Science and National Identity in Early Modern Britain: The Case of Scotland and the Work of Sir Robert Sibbald, 1641–1722'.

32. Although Daniel Defoe's *A Tour through the Whole Island of Great Britain* (1724–6) covered much more of Scotland than Martin's tours, it only rarely touches on Scotland's natural history and avoids geological and geotheoretical questions altogether.

33. Bray describes Martin's *Description of the Western Islands* as 'the earliest first-hand record of the Hebrides' (*The Discovery of the Hebrides*, p. 13). Rixon's *Hebridean Traveller* locates the 'discovery' of the Hebrides much earlier than Martin.

34. On Martin Martin, see Withers, *Geography, Science and National Identity*, pp. 87–96.

35. See Fleet et al., *Scotland: Mapping the Nation*, pp. 167–9. For an extensive survey of the early maps of Scotland, see Moir (ed.), *The Early Maps of Scotland to 1850.*

36. See Buchanan, *The History of Scotland* (1790).

37. On the genre of the 'voyage' in the period, see Thompson, *Travel Writing*, pp. 19–20.

38. Martin is presumably referring to Aulus Cornelius Celsus (c. 25 BC – c. 50 AD), author of *De Medicina.*

39. See Locke, *An Essay Concerning Human Understanding* (1689), book III, especially chapter 10, paragraph 34. Also see Walmsley, *Locke's Essay and the Rhetoric of Science*.

40. The resemblance between ammonites and coiled rams' horns led Pliny the Elder to call them *ammonis cornua* ('horns of Ammon') because the Egyptian god Ammon was typically depicted wearing rams' horns. For the identification of crampstones as ammonites, see Marren and Maybey, *Bugs Britannica*, p. 462.

Chapter 3

John Walker's 'Report on the Hebrides' (1764–1771)

John Walker (1731–1803), Regius Professor of Natural History at the University of Edinburgh from 1779 until his death in 1803, was a protégé of Henry Home (Lord Kames) and William Cullen and a colleague of Dugald Stewart, Joseph Black and other Edinburgh professors who helped to shape the Scottish Enlightenment. Walker 'was the first professor of Natural History who gave lectures, held class meetings, prepared syllabuses for his students and organised work in the laboratory' (McKay, 'Introduction', p. 4). Among his students were some of the most prominent Scottish natural historians, geologists and university teachers of the following generation, including Robert Jameson, his protégé and successor to the chair of natural history, John Playfair, Professor of Natural Philosophy, Sir James Hall, President of the Royal Society of Edinburgh, and Thomas Charles Hope, Professor of Medicine and Chemistry.[1] Walker thus played a significant role in disseminating knowledge of natural history in Scotland and was a major influence on the tenor of Scottish natural history, mineralogy and geology in the period. In this chapter I develop a close reading of his 'Report on the Hebrides' (1771) which was based on an extensive tour of the Hebrides and parts of the Highlands that he made in 1764. Although this report remained unpublished until Margaret McKay's edition in 1980, it was the first important tour of the region by an expert in natural history and mineralogy.

Walker's passion for natural history led him to begin exploring Scotland at an early age. While studying divinity at the University of Edinburgh (1746–9), Walker went on collecting trips in the Edinburgh area, alone, with William Cullen or with other friends, in search of minerals. After graduating in 1749 he was ordained into the Church of Scotland, beginning as a preacher in Kirkudbright in 1754 and spending the rest of his life as a parish minister in Glencorse (1758–62), Moffat (1762–82) and Colinton (1782–1803).[2] At Glencorse, he went 'on botanical and mineralogical expeditions to the nearby Pentlands, adding to current knowledge of species of plants and rocks' (McKay, 'Introduction', p. 1).[3] At Moffat, Walker searched 'the fields and mountains, breaking rocks, gathering minerals, visiting mines, collecting flowers and "even weeds".... Continuing the habits he formed as a boy, Walker travelled far in pursuit of mineral specimens for his collection, which was becoming extensive' (Scott, 'Biographical Introduction', p. xix).[4] Between the early 1750s and the early 1780s, Walker's passion for natural history led him to 'traverse almost the entire mainland of Scotland' (Eddy, *The Language of Mineralogy*, p. 103).

After taking up the chair of natural history in 1779, Walker played a central role in creating and developing natural history institutions in Edinburgh. As Keeper of Edinburgh's Natural History Museum he greatly enhanced its collection, making it a crucial place to visit for geological tourists. He was a founding member of the Royal Society of Edinburgh in 1783 and joint secretary of the physical section until 1796. He was also 'active in the organisation of the Natural History Society of Edinburgh in 1782' (McKay, 'Introduction', p. 2). Walker's status as a natural historian was recognised when he was made a Fellow of the Royal Society of London in 1794. He published articles and papers in the *Philosophical Transactions of the Royal Society*, the *Transactions of the Royal Society of Edinburgh* and the *Transactions of the Highland Society of Scotland*. But much of Walker's work remained unfinished or unpublished at his death, a situation partly remedied when his friend Charles Stewart gathered together and published Walker's *Essays on Natural History and Rural Economy* and the two-volume *An Economical History of the Hebrides and Highlands of Scotland* in 1808. Walker spent many years working on a 'Flora Scotica' but abandoned it after the publication of John Lightfoot's *Flora Scotica* in 1777.[5] His other major work, a 'Natural History of the Hebrides', remained uncompleted.

Eighteenth-Century Natural History: Mineralogy and Geotheory

In eighteenth-century Britain, natural history and mineralogy kept their distance from geotheory. Most theories of the earth in the period assumed that most types of rock had been formed early in the earth's history by sedimentation or crystallisation in the 'mineral soup' of a universal ocean whose level had subsequently fallen to reveal the present land masses. As Martin Rudwick points out, the 'Neptunist' system developed in John Woodward's *Natural History of the Earth* (1695 and 1726) 'was adopted by a wide range of savants throughout Europe', though 'a growing awareness of the sheer thickness of the ['secondary'] formations, many of them composed of finely layered sediments, made [a] short timescale increasingly implausible', meaning that 'by midcentury the equation with the biblical Flood had been generally abandoned' (*Bursting the Limits of Time*, p. 175).[6] Alternatives to the diluvial model became more prominent from the 1760s onwards. 'Vulcanists' interpreted some of the earth's materials and geomorphology as evidence for considerable volcanic activity over long periods of the earth's history.[7] Despite their differences, both geotheories attempted to identify the causal origins of rocks and geomorphology and saw the earth as a dynamic system that had changed through an immensely long history.

By contrast, the defining concerns of eighteenth-century natural history – empirical description, the attempt to create general classificatory systems and promote the commercial exploitation of the natural world – were inherited from the Baconian natural history of seventeenth-century pioneers such as John Ray and Francis Willughby.[8] Natural history focused on the 'observation of Matter of Fact' and the exploration of 'the most desert Rocks and Mountains, as [well as] the more frequented Valleys and Plains' in search of evidence and specimens (Porter, *The Making of Geology*, pp. 34–5).[9] Ezio Vaccari has shown that the eighteenth-century natural history explorer was an 'organized traveller' influenced by the guidelines on fieldwork that had begun to appear in published instruction manuals in the late seventeenth century, such as John Woodward's *Brief Instructions for Making Observations in all Parts of the World: as also for Collecting, Preserving and Sending over Natural Things* (1696).[10] Discoveries made in the field were supplemented by the reports of other travellers and through the use of circulated questionnaires. The goal was to produce natural histories of particular regions and to construct a general system of classification. Conceived as a branch of natural history, mineralogy did not concern itself with theories about the formation of minerals and rocks but was an ahistorical, empirical enterprise that thought of the earth and its natural objects as static. Minerals were treated as natural kinds that had existed in their present state since the creation.

Eighteenth-century natural history came to be dominated, of course, by the work of the Swedish botanist and zoologist Carl Linnaeus. The various editions of Linnaeus's *Systema Naturae* (first published in 1735) elaborated his enormously influential classificatory system, which introduced a binomial nomenclature and located organisms in five principal groups according to class, order, genus, species and variety. Linnaeus's *Oeconomia Naturae* (1749), which was 'heavily indebted to British natural theology, particularly the writings of John Ray and William Derham',

> described a world of eternal order and static harmony governed by stable proportions, fixed species, regular flows, and cyclical patterns. Each of the three kingdoms of nature – minerals, plants, and animals – underwent the same eternal cycle of 'propagation, preservation, and destruction.' All species had an 'allotted place,' and all places had a species to fill it. (Jonsson, *Enlightenment's Frontier*, p. 59)

In *Flora Lapponica* (1737), Linnaeus offered an account of his 1732 natural history tour to Lapland that became an inspiring model of arduous but rewarding natural history travel to the supposedly resource-rich but as yet unimproved northern mountainous regions of Europe. The first English translation of Linnaeus's and his followers' work – Benjamin Stillingfleet's *Miscellaneous Tracts Relating to Natural History, Husbandry and Physick* (1741) – included Linnaeus's 'Oration Concerning the Necessity of Travelling in One's Own Country' (1741), in which he recalled the rigours and joys of his exploration of Lapland and sought

> to shew by instances, that the natural philosopher, the mineralogist, the botanist, the zoologist, the physician, the œconomist, and all others, initiated in any part of natural knowledge, may find in travelling thro' our own countrey . . . such things, as may not only gratify, and satiate their curiosity; but may be of service to themselves, their country and all the world. (p. 12)[11]

Linnaeus's taxonomic system and his emphasis on the interest and utility of exploring the natural history of one's own country, and especially northern countries, had a defining impact on some of the natural historians examined in the present book. According to Jonsson,

> early adherents and popularizers of Linnaeus's method of classification and economic botany in Britain [included] John Walker, John Hope, James Robertson, John Lightfoot, John Stuart of Killin, Sir Joseph Banks, Daniel Solander, and James Anderson. They shared a common faith in the analytic power of Linnaeus's system and its utility as the basis for new ways of mastering the natural world. (*Enlightenment's Frontier*, p. 57)

But it was Walker who first took up Linnaeus's project in Scotland:

> As an aspiring young naturalist in search of patronage, Walker wrote to Linnaeus in early 1762 to announce his intention of promoting botany in Scotland and to profess his allegiance to the 'sex system.' Linnaeus responded warmly and showed particular interest in the prospect of discovering new alpine plants in Scotland. . . . A few months later, Walker wrote back to report that he had begun a survey of the Scottish mountains. He stressed his attention to altitude, probably in deference to Linnaeus's theory of alpine transplantation. Walker told Linnaeus that he had used the barometer and 'geometric mensuration' to relate his plant identifications to the height over the sea. (Jonsson, *Enlightenment's Frontier*, p. 63)

Walker's reading of Linnaeus deeply informed his explorations of Scotland, especially his tour of the Highlands in 1764. These tours, and the specimens he gathered on them, formed the basis of his teaching of natural history, geology and mineralogy at the University of Edinburgh. In his lectures Walker echoed Linnaeus in emphasising the fundamental importance of fieldwork for the natural historian: 'neither here [in the lecture theatre], nor in the closet, nor in the best furnished Museum, can any one ever expect to become a thorough naturalist. The objects of nature themselves must be sedulously examined in their native state. The Fields of the Mountains must be harvested, the woods and waters must be explored.'[12] Walker also produced printed materials for his students, including a sequence of classificatory systems – *Schediasma fossilium* (1781), *Delineatio fossilium* (1782) and *Classes fossilium* (1787) – that were based on but also modified Linnaeus.

Cultural and Political Contexts

Walker's tour of the Hebrides in 1764 and his 1771 report need to be understood in terms of the close connection between natural history, economic improvement and the British state's complex political responses to the Highlands and Islands of Scotland in the post-Culloden period.[13] Military occupation involved repressing clan culture, building roads and a Military Survey that eventually produced the exquisite Roy Map of Scotland (along with Paul Sandby's pioneering Highland landscapes). The Hanoverian state also attempted to pacify the Highlands and Islands by annexing the estates of some of the leading Jacobites and using the revenues to improve agriculture, industry, trade and education in the region:

> Following the 1745 rebellion, the Scottish Court of the Exchequer had been authorised to take charge of the estates which were forfeit to the Crown owing to the owners' attainder for treason. Forty-one estates were taken over. The majority of these were sold to repay debts, but thirteen were annexed to the Crown by act of Parliament in 1752. The rents and profits were to be used 'for the Purposes of civilising the Inhabitants upon the said Estates, and other Parts of the Highlands and Islands of Scotland, and promoting amongst them the Protestant religion, good Government, Industry and Manufactures, and the Principles of Duty and Loyalty to his Majesty, his Heirs and Successors, and to no other use or Purpose whatsoever'. (McKay, 'Introduction', p. 6)

Before the 'civilising' process could begin it was necessary to survey the Highlands and Islands 'to ascertain what conditions were like and what resources lay beyond the Highland line' (McKay, 'Introduction', p. 6). As a consequence,

> An upsurge of scientific interest in the Highlands began in the 1760s as the Board for the Annexed Estates sponsored a series of tours of the region by natural historians and agricultural writers. While the Reverend Walker explored the Western Isles, the Welsh mining engineer John Williams charted the resources of the Annexed Estates on the mainland between 1763 and 1775. The chemist William Cullen advised the board on the properties of alkali and conducted experiments on weed ashes near Loch Lomond. The engineer James Watt, inventor of the separate condenser for steam engines, made a survey on behalf of the Annexed Estates for the Crinan Canal project. (Jonsson, *Enlightenment's Frontier*, p. 47)

These tours and surveys resulted in reports and publications which 'were organized around the interconnected tasks of inventory and exploitation. Sections on local climate, diseases, soil, mineral resources, and the character of indigenous people were followed by advice on the best crops or industries to introduce and the optimal means of managing them' (Jonsson, p. 48). The project managed by the Board of Annexed Estates can thus be seen as attempting to impose order on the natural world and on the people of the Highlands at one and the same time with the aim of making both into useful resources.

The Scottish Enlightenment's assumptions about the need to 'improve' the Highlands and Islands after 1745 were shaped by the stadial theory of historical progress which claimed, in the words of Adam Smith, that 'There are four distinct states which mankind pass thro: – Ist, the Age of Hunters; 2dly, the Age of Shepherds; 3dly, the Age of Agriculture; and 4thly, the Age of Commerce' (*Lectures on Jurisprudence*, p. 14). Smith's lectures on jurisprudence were not published at the time, but 'unequivocal expressions' of the four-stage theory in Scotland included Lord Kames's *Sketches of the History of Man* (1774, 1779), John Millar's *Origin of the Distinction of Ranks* (1779) and Hugh Blair's *A Critical Dissertation on the Poems of Ossian* (1763).[14] Stadial theory provided an intellectual rationale for the attempt to lift the Highlands out of the hunter-gatherer and pastoral stages of human development into the more advanced agricultural and commercial stages. But it was also used to authenticate the Ossian poems as a genuine product of the Highland past and encouraged the view that the Highlands, past and present, were a locus of primitive martial virtue that provided a source of warriors, more able and willing than southerners debilitated by commercial life, to fight Britain's imperial wars.[15] After the publication of Macpherson's *Fragments of Ancient Poetry Collected in the Highlands of Scotland* (1760),

> a group of Edinburgh lawyers and literati [established] funds to enable Macpherson to explore [the Highlands] more deeply. He made two trips, the first in August and September 1760 and the second between late October 1760 and early January 1761, visiting Perthshire, Argyll, Inverness-shire, and the islands of Skye, North and South Uist, Benbecula, and Mull. He collected manuscripts and oral versions of songs and ballads on these trips. (Thomson, 'Macpherson, James', *ODNB*)

Macpherson therefore toured the Highlands and Islands in search of Ossianic songs and ballads only three or four years before Walker made his own tour for the Board of Annexed Estates to assess the region's natural resources. Although these tours were undertaken for quite different ends, they were motivated by similar concerns about the fate of the Highlands after 1745.

Walker's patron, Lord Kames, played an active role both as an agricultural improver and as an advocate of Ossian's poetry. He became a commissioner for the Board of Annexed Estates in 1761 and a member of other engines of improvement such as The Highland Society of Scotland. He carried out a large-scale improvement project on his Blair Drummond estate near Stirling, where he cleared and drained a huge area of moss with the help of Highland labourers.[16] He was also one of the sponsors of Macpherson's tour of the Highlands in search of Ossianic manuscripts and remnants and he 'used a good part of the *Sketches of the History of Man* (1774) to launch a broadside on behalf of the Gaelic "Homer." This literary campaign in turn clearly colored his views of Highland improvement, tingeing the civilising mission with fashionable melancholy' (Jonsson, *Enlightenment's Frontier*, p. 30).[17]

Walker's Preparation and Method

Walker initially became acquainted with Lord Kames in 1750 when he was minister of Glencorse. In March 1764, probably encouraged by Kames, Walker proposed to the Board of Annexed Estates 'that he should "take a tour thro' the Highlands", and make a "faithful and distinct report". The proposal was accepted, expenses of £60 were allowed, and Lord Kames drew up Walker's instructions, "to examine the natural histories of these countries, their population, and state of their agriculture, manufactures and fisheries"' (McKay, 'Introduction', p. 6). As minister of Moffat, Walker could not set out on a lengthy tour without permission from the Church of Scotland. He therefore 'suggested to the General Assembly that he should take the opportunity given by his commission from the Board of Annexed Estates to report on the religious and educational state of the Highlands for the Church' (McKay, 'Introduction', p. 6). He also suggested to the Society for Promoting Christian Knowledge that he could complete an earlier report on the state of their schools in the Scottish Islands. Both organisations accepted Walker's proposals and he was therefore 'freed from his parochial responsibilities but faced with the onerous tasks of making reports to each of his three sponsors' (McKay, 'Introduction', p. 6). Walker's 1764 tour of the Highlands and Islands, then, was not that of a Romantic traveller in search of wilderness and adventure, but was commissioned by organs of state and church in order to survey the people's material and spiritual conditions and assess the commercial potential of natural resources in the name of 'improvement'.

In addition to the instructions of the Board of Annexed Estates, drawn up for him by Kames, Walker developed his own guidelines about what he should do, observe and collect on his Scottish tours that 'bear a strong resemblance to the instructions to travelling collectors given by Boyle, Woodward and Cullen' (Eddy, *The Language of Mineralogy*, pp. 104, 106). When he heard about Walker's forthcoming tour of the Hebrides, Thomas Pennant, who was then working on his *British Zoology* and would make his own groundbreaking tours of the Highlands and Islands a few years later, wrote to Cullen in order to recommend 'to Mr Walker a thorough Attention to the Zoology of the western Isles' and went into great detail about what he should observe, collect, stuff and bottle (Pennant to Cullen, 21 April 1764, quoted by McKay, 'Introduction', p. 7). Pennant's letter highlights the characteristic assumption that natural history was not an individualistic pursuit but a collaborative enterprise that involved bringing specimens back to centres of Enlightenment as well as *in situ* description. It also indicates that the Western Isles were still regarded in the 1760s as a remote and exotic region where strange species might flourish.

A letter from Walker to Lord Bute on 8 February 1765 indicates that he followed the example of earlier natural history projects, such as that of Sir Robert Sibbald examined in the previous chapter, in deriving information from local ministers: 'Though the Commission I had from the General Assembly cost me a great deal of Time and Travel, yet it was very usefull to me upon many accounts, especially in procuring me the Assistance and Information of the Clergy, in everything I wanted' (quoted by McKay, 'Introduction', p. 10). The composition of the 'Report on the Hebrides' over a six-year period (from 1765 to 1771) also allowed Walker to incorporate information received after completing his journey:

> Walker was sent data after his return which appear in the text of the report. His correspondence with Macnicol, minister of Lismore, too late to be of use in 1771, perhaps gives an indication of what demands he made on his fellow ministers; he asked for information on fish, their Gaelic and English names, snakes, deer bones, seals, tides, numbers of people over eighty, what 'Selma' means and any other Ossianic names Macnicol could suggest, the rents of farms and the kind of flax sown. (McKay, 'Introduction', p. 10)

The fact that Walker included information from parish ministers in his report indicates that he regarded his personal observation of the Hebrides during his extensive data-collecting voyage as just one source of information to be supplemented by facts derived from local sources. Walker also did a great deal of background research while writing up his report:

> His manuscript papers in the library of the University of Edinburgh show detailed work on the Sibbald manuscripts in the Advocates' Library (he owned a 1742 catalogue of the library), including notes on the animal and bird life of the Hebrides, natural products and numbers of fighting men. He transcribed information on natural manures and minerals from Sir Alexander Murray's 'True Interest of Britain and Ireland' . . . Besides his large collection of botanical and geological treatises, Walker's own library contained works of Sibbald, Pennant's 'British Zoology', [and] Martin Martin's 'Voyage to St Kilda' . . . Walker also drew on Martin Martin's 'Description of the Western Isles' and George Buchanan's 'History of Scotland'. (McKay, 'Introduction', p. 11)

In the report itself, it is often not clear whether the information Walker presents is derived from his own on-the-spot observation or from his other sources. The report is not a narrative of Walker's journey and experience, but an empirical account of the places he visited. Natural history travellers in the eighteenth century embarked on journeys into new regions in the spirit of discovery rather than self-discovery. The lack of focus on Walker himself is also a matter of genre: his text is a report, not a tour. Walker needed to meet the requirements of the Board of Annexed Estates, which sought information about the Hebrides which would help direct its attempt to stimulate economic and agricultural improvement. Walker's approach also echoes the assumptions and methods of the new science of 'statistics' that had recently been developed in Germany by figures such as Gottfried Achenwall as a way of collecting systematic information 'on the geography, topography, political circumstances, religion, culture and the special way of life of inhabitants from a particular region' (Klemun, 'Writing, "Inscription" and Fact', p. 56).

Walker's request that Macnicol should inform him about Selma and other Ossianic names indicates the curious combination of Linnaeus's natural history and Ossianic enthusiasm that characterised the Scottish Enlightenment's view of the Highlands in the period. Walker was intrigued by the notion that particular places in the Highlands and Islands were imbued with the romance of Ossianic associations. Indeed, 'Walker was among the first literati to defend the authenticity of Macpherson's poetry by collecting information about his alleged sources in the Highlands. Like many other travellers, he also sought to discover in situ the Highland locales that best corresponded to the landscapes described in the poems' (Jonsson, *Enlightenment's Frontier*, p. 97). As McKay notes,

> Walker delighted in identifying places he visited with sites in the stories. He described to Lady Kames 'the spot of Fingal's residence . . . a green promontory skirted with wood' at Selma. In Appin he encountered 'a circle of Druidical stones which alone would almost authenticate his (Ossian's) poems were there nothing else'. ('Introduction', p. 4)

Walker's 1764 Tour of the Hebrides

Walker set out on his tour of the Hebrides in June 1764. He sailed 'from Greenock to Campbeltown in the "custom House wherry" provided for the expedition and then over to Ireland for provisions, where he visited the Giant's causeway and took "a fine pillar of it" for the foundation stone of the Edinburgh Museum' (McKay, 'Introduction', p. 7). The Giant's Causeway had been made famous throughout Europe when 'a pair of engravings based on prizewinning paintings by the Irish artist Susanna Drury . . . [were] published in 1744' (Rudwick, *Bursting the Limits of Time*, p. 44). After leaving Ireland, Walker sailed to Islay. On 27 June, he crossed the Sound of Islay to make experiments on one of Jura's mountains and then worked his way northwards, exploring most of the major islands and parts of the mainland in a thorough fashion:

> [He] was in Colonsay on the 29th of June and then spent nearly the whole of July travelling from Iona, where he camped, collected lichens used for dyeing and toured the Abbey ruins, to Mull, Coll, Tiree, Rum, Eigg and Canna. On the 30th of July he was in Barra and in South Uist on the 31st. It took him a fortnight to see Benbecula, North Uist, Berneray, Vallay, Pabbay, Ensay and Harris, and on the 16th of August he was at Stornoway. . . . Walker [then] crossed the Minch, visited Assynt, and then went to Skye. He left the cutter and crossed to Glenelg, saw Kintail, Glenshiel and Lochaber, and then on to Morvern. He went south by Glenspean, Fort Augustus, Badenoch and Taymouth. On December 9th, the minister of Moffat returned at last to his manse – seven months and two days after setting out. (McKay, 'Introduction', p. 8)

Walker's tour can be followed on a map of 'The Hebrides in Relation to Mainland Scotland' included in McKay's edition of Walker's *Report on the Hebrides* (Figure 3.1).

On 10 December, Walker wrote to Lord Kames, giving him a summary of the tour:

> Upon looking into my Journal, I find the Miles I have travelled are as follows:
>
>> sailed 1,263
>> rowed in a boat 280
>> rode 1,087
>> walked 528
>
> The hardships I met with were greater indeed than I would have chosen, but they were what I expected, and were in most cases, unavoidable. The Entertainment I had from the Business I was engaged in, and the surveying a sort of new World, made me even bear them with Pleasure, and I expect still more in reflecting upon them. (Quoted by McKay, 'Introduction', p. 8)

Walker thus travelled about 3,000 miles in seven months, on seas and across terrains that were remote and potentially dangerous.

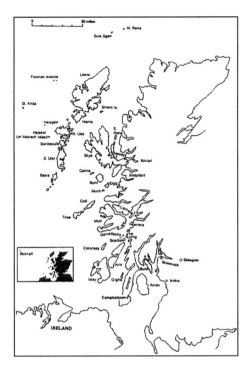

Figure 3.1 Margaret M. McKay, 'The Hebrides in Relation to Mainland Scotland', in McKay (ed.), *The Rev. Dr. John Walker's Report on the Hebrides of 1764 and 1771*, p. 34.

Although he refers to the hardships and rewards of exploring this 'sort of new World' in his letter to Kames, the fact that they are hardly ever mentioned in the report itself indicates that Walker systematically excluded personal experience from the text that he handed in to the Board of Annexed Estates in 1771.

'Report on the Hebrides': Textual Analysis

Walker's 'Report on the Hebrides' exhibits a number of the conventions associated with natural history travel writing of the period, as explored in the previous chapter. Walker's report begins with a short introduction 'To His Majesties Commissioners at the Board of Annexed Estates' in which he stresses that the data he presents 'were collected with the utmost Care, during the Course of above Seven Months, in a Journey by Land and Water of upwards of 3,000 miles, through the Islands North of Cantire and the adjacent parts of the Highlands' (p. 33). Walker highlights the interrelation between the style of his report and its role in promoting the state's political control and economic improvement of its remote regions:

> [The report] consists for the most part of a Narration of Facts designed to serve as so many Data, from which, every intelligent Person, though he has never seen these Countries, may form a proper Idea of their Oeconomy and Improvement. And, in this View, it is hoped, they may be of Use to those who have the Police of these distant parts of Scotland, under their immediate Inspection. (p. 33)

Walker's report purports to present an objective, empirical account of the places, people and physical environment of the Hebrides rather than narrating a particular individual's experience of them on a single journey. Focus on the observed rather than the observer is marked by the report's sparse use of first-person pronouns, in singular or plural forms. Yet the author figure nonetheless performs a key function in the report. Walker stresses that the report's trustworthiness is based on the trustworthiness of his own direct observations and his judgement of what he gathered from other informants:

> Being conscious of no Intention to Mislead, I persuade myself no Person will here be misinformed through Design though I cannot be equally certain, that amidst such a Multiplicity of Facts, I have been no where Missled [sic]. What I saw I can affirm; but many things related, must rest on the authority of others; though no Informations were admitted, whose Evidence was not in a high Degree unexceptionable. (p. 33)

Although the report consists of a collection of empirical facts originating from the collective effort of many contributors, the author retains an important function both as the traveller who had first-hand experience of the places described and as a guarantor of the report's objectivity and reliability.

Like many travellers in the period, Walker raises the value of his report, though not his own intrepidity, by emphasising the remoteness and primitiveness of the places he visited, along with the fact that they are almost unknown to the outside world:

> There is no Corner of Europe, so little known even to the Inhabitants of Britain, as the Islands which are here described. We have long had more

Information concerning the Islands of Asia; and it is likely will soon be better acquainted with those in the far distant parts of the Southern Hemisphere; than we are with the Islands adjacent to our own Coasts, and which make part of the Kingdom. (pp. 33–5)

Walker thus compares his tour of the Hebrides with James Cook's exploration of the southern Pacific Ocean from 1768 to 1771 on the *Endeavour* – a voyage into a new world that, through the work of Joseph Banks, made a major contribution to natural history.[18] As with Cook and Banks, Walker's encounter with 'primitive' people is imbued with ambiguity and ambivalence:

Their Soil remains, as it was left at the Creation: The Inhabitants, when compared to their Fellow Subjects, with Respect to Arts; are in almost the same Situation as in the Days of Oscian [*sic*], yet they are Countries capable of being greatly advanced by Agriculture; capable of many of the most important Species of manufacture: possessed of the most valuable Fisheries in Europe. (p. 35)

The natural resources of the Highlands and Islands might be profitably exploited if the people were trained in the arts of agriculture, fishing and manufacturing. But such improvement can only come about through the intervention of the enlightened state: 'Unassisted Exertions of Industry are not to be expected from a People still in the Pastoral Stage of Society; nor from unenlightened Minds are we any where to expect the sudden Discontinuance of bad Customs' (p. 35). Walker's suggestion that the inhabitants of the Highlands and Islands 'are in almost the same Situation as in the Days of Oscian' is an example of what Jonsson calls 'northern time travel' in that 'Highland tours offered a time machine for the adherents of stadial theory. Travellers felt themselves moving backward in time the farther into the region they penetrated' (*Enlightenment's Frontier*, p. 50). Walker's observation may thus reveal a trace of the eighteenth-century celebration of 'primitive' people influentially articulated in Jean-Jacques Rousseau's *Discours sur l'origine de l'inégalité* (1755) even as it provides a warrant for their 'improvement'. But if it is difficult to gauge the tone of the statement that the people of the Hebrides are 'still in the Pastoral Stage of Society', Walker also says that they are 'a sensible, hardy, and laborious Race of People' (p. 35). Although the Hebrideans need the state's assistance to lift them into the agricultural and commercial stages of advanced civilisation, they have a 'Disposition to Industry' that will help them make the most of such assistance (p. 35).

Walker had been required by the Board of Annexed Estates to report on a wide range of features of the places and peoples of the Hebrides, and included natural history only when it could contribute to the general purpose of improvement:

> Many curious Discoveries in natural History ocurred [*sic*] in the Course of this Journey. But here I judged it more proper to confine myself to a general Description of the Countries; of their Soil and Climate, and of the Customs and Manners of the People. To mark everywhere the Prices of Labour and of Commodities: the Nature and Extent of the Exports and Imports; and the Causes of Population and Depopulation. To describe the present state of Agriculture; Manufacture and Fishery, and to point out the most obvious Methods for the Advancement of these Usefull [*sic*] Arts. Natural History however could not be wholly omitted as it affords such frequent and favourable Opportunities, of turning the Truths of Science to the Purposes of Life. (p. 33)

While the final sentence of this passage indicates the perceived connection between natural history and economic usefulness, the suggestion that 'Many curious Discoveries in natural History ocurred in the Course of this Journey' which were not directly relevant to the report indicates that natural history sometimes exceeds the bounds of usefulness and that Walker excluded observations that were not immediately relevant to his brief. As we will see, however, he was not always able to prevent 'curious Discoveries in natural History' from intruding into his official report, even though they appeared to have no utilitarian value.

The 'Report on the Hebrides' contains sections on twenty-one Hebridean islands in an apparently random sequence that is quite different from that of Walker's actual journey: Lewis, Harris, St Kilda, North Uist, Benbecula, South Uist, Barra, Rockall, Islay, Jura, Colonsay, Oronsay, Gigha, Iona, Mull, Coll, Tiree, Rum, Skye, Eigg and Canna. The account of each island is divided into subsections with titles such as 'Situation', 'Extent and Rental', 'Number of people', 'Soil', 'Exports', 'State of Agriculture', 'Manufacture' and 'Fishery'. The following discussion is confined to Walker's accounts of those islands – Islay, Jura, Mull and Skye – which include particularly interesting mineralogical or geological features.

The 'Report on the Hebrides' sometimes attends to large-scale physical geography as well as to local details of natural history. In his description of the 'Soil and Climate' of Islay, Walker notes that 'The Island of Ila differs remarkably in its Structure and the Nature of its Fossils, from the Coast of Ireland on the one Hand, and that of Cantire on the other' (p. 98). Whereas coal 'abounds on the Cantire Coast immediately opposite to it', there 'is not the smallest Appearance of Coal in Ila' (p. 98). And while 'two remarkable Fossils' – the 'Rock of which the Giants Causeway is composed, and the white sort of Limestone which is so prevalent in Ireland' – 'extend along the whole Irish Coast, that looks to Ila . . . there is not a Vestige of either of these Stones in Ila' (p. 98). But Walker's observation of these geological discontinuities does not lead to speculation about large-scale geological structures or causal processes but merely serves as a framework for delineating natural resources.

A section on Islay's 'Mines' reveals that although the island has no coal or white limestone, it does contain Whinrock (basalt) dykes and metallic veins 'lodged in Limestone' in a disposition that 'is very singular' and that poses problems for 'the most experienced Miner':

> the Limestone in which [the veins] are Lodged consists of extensive Strata, of great Breadth, . . . which run for several miles in Length. The streek of this Limestone is nearly South to North, and it dips to the East, not as Limestone generally does, at a small Angle, but precisely like Whinrock, in Edge Seams at an Angle of between 70 and 80 Degrees to the Horison. This great Body of Limestone is intersected by Whinstone Dykes, from 6 inches to 50 Feet thick, which run across that part of the Island, East and West, at Right Angles to the Limestone; and the Course of each is regularly continued even after the Intersection. (p. 106)

This passage exhibits several features that are characteristic of the mineralogy of the period. It confines itself to objective description and measurement – identifying materials, length, thickness, angles of dip and intersection, compass directions and so on – and highlights the problems of mining the metallic veins in the limestone. And while the passage does, necessarily, describe and measure these geological features *in situ*, it avoids any speculation about their history or causes. Walker carefully observes the way the limestone is fissured by Whinstone dykes and veins of metallic ore, but makes no attempt to discuss how such intrusions might have been formed.

Yet Walker does occasionally make gestures towards explanatory causes. In the first of a sequence of trips to Jura by eighteenth-century natural historians, mineralogists or geologists (including Banks and Pennant), Walker crossed the Sound of Islay on 27 June 1764 in order to make scientific experiments on one of Jura's mountains (or 'Paps'). Walker begins his account with a confused description of the orientation of Jura and Islay, claiming that they 'extend lengthways, only two or three points from East and West' and that this orientation is contrary to that of the rest of the Western Isles and of Britain itself (Jura's actual orientation is roughly south-west to north-east). Walker accounts for what he takes to be the odd orientation of these islands by suggesting that they conform to that of the nearest parts of the mainland – Knapdale and the Mull of Kintyre. While this is not quite true (the Mull of Kintyre is nearer to a north-south orientation than Jura or Islay), it leads Walker into unusual, though undeveloped, speculations about the formation of the earth's crust:

> The Direction therefore of Ila and Jura, though contrary to that of the other Hebrides, appears to be the Effect of the same Cause. Of that Cause, which made Britain itself run parallel with the Coast of Scandinavia; and stretched out Macagascar [*sic*] in a Line with Africa. Of that great Law, which seems to have subsisted at the Formation of the Earth by which all the Islands upon the Globe in general, are extended in length in the same Direction with the Coast of the next adjacent Continent. (p. 111)

It is notable, however, that Walker does not explain or speculate about the cause and great law he refers to, perhaps because such speculation was outside the remit of his report and of natural history in general. But the passage does anticipate Walker's speculation about the cause of mountains and mountain chains in his geology lectures at the University of Edinburgh in the 1780s and 1790s:

> A great number of late and present philosophers have attributed [mountains] to Volcanoes.
>
> But their regular form, their regular chains, their general direction, their continued ridges, the salient and receding angles, their strata and the matter of which they consist, evidently shew that they never have arisen from such partial or contiguous Causes as Earthquakes or Volcanoes, but that they owe their origin to a Cause more universal and much more

uniform. It is upon the whole much more probable that they have been formed in water than either by earthquakes or volcanoes. (*Lectures on Geology*, p. 170)

Both passages appear to echo the Comte de Buffon's *Théorie de la terre* (1749), which invokes Newton's laws of universal gravity and momentum in order to argue that the earth's landforms and mountain chains were formed in a north-south orientation by the long-term east-west motion of tides in a universal ocean that originally covered the earth. Yet Walker was wary of geotheory and particularly critical of Buffon and other French theorists. In a letter to Lord Kames, written on 29 February 1776, he says that 'Those very qualities which make [the French] shine in other parts of literature, make them bad theorists. From Des Cartes down to Buffon, France has certainly produced the worst system mongers that ever put pen to paper' (quoted by Eddy, *The Language of Mineralogy*, p. 164).[19] The problem with such system-mongers, in Walker's view, is that they conjure theoretical systems out of thin air and then proceed to look for evidence to support them. In his lectures on natural history Walker warned his students to avoid theories of the earth in favour of empirical observation, description and classification. However, as Eddy points out, one of the few instances where Buffon is not criticised 'is in the "Mountains" section of his geology lectures where Walker discusses the mountaintop angles in parallel mountain ranges. There he avers that Buffon's "System", in accordance to reliable observations concerning mountaintop angles, correctly assumes that the tops of the Alps had been formed by water' (*The Language of Mineralogy*, p. 166).[20]

Walker went to Jura in order to carry out two experiments on the summit of the island's highest mountain, though he may have climbed Beinn a' Chaolas (734m, 2,408ft) rather than Beinn an Oir (785m, 2,575ft).[21] On what is the first recorded ascent of one of the Paps of Jura, Walker attempted to ascertain the relationship between height, atmospheric pressure and the boiling point of water, thus building on the work of Daniel Gabriel Fahrenheit and Jean-Jacques d'Ortous de Mairan. In the first experiment, Walker used a barometer to measure the mountain's height:

In Order to ascertain the Height of the Paps of Jura, I filled a Barometer on the 27th June, on the Shore of the Sound of Ila, at 7 O'clock in the morning, when the Mercury stood at 29 Inches and 7 tenths. We set off at 10 O'clock; and it cost us Seven Hours of excessive Fatigue, to get to the Summit of the highest Mountain. Here, at 5 in the afternoon, I again filled the same Barometer, when the Mercury stood at 27 Inches and 1 Tenth: a Column of Air therefore, of the height of this Mountain, is equal to two Inches and six tenths of Mercury. And assuming Dr. Halley's calculation of 90 feet to each Tenth, the Perpendicular Height of the Mountain turns out to be 2,340 English Feet above the Level of the Sea. (p. 114)

In addition to measuring the height of Beinn a' Chaolas (only 68 feet short of the 734 metres marked on the current OS map), Walker recorded the difference in the boiling point of water at sea level (213 degrees Fahrenheit) and on the summit (207 degrees). Given that the atmospheric pressure remained the same throughout the day, Walker concludes that the boiling point of water falls by one degree for every 390 feet of ascent. Walker's account in 'Report on the Hebrides' gives the impression that his ascent of this mountain was undertaken solely in order to carry out these scientific experiments (which were not obviously relevant to the aims of his tour). As we will see later, however, Walker subsequently produced an expanded and quite different description of his experience of climbing the mountain.

In his account of the 'Natural Productions' of Mull (pp. 162–4), Walker notes that 'There are some very strong Appearances of Coal, at three different places in the parish of Ross in Mull' (p. 162). The unusual feature of these coal seams is that they are 'lodged in Whinstone. This would render the working of them extremely precarious. Since no Person has any Experience of Coal situated in such a Manner. Yet the Discovery of Coal in any of the Western Islands, is a matter of such Importance to the Fisheries, as would justify a considerable Trial, at the last mentioned Place' (p. 162). Another potential source of income generation in the south-west extremity of Mull is the red granite that Iona Abbey was built out of and that might be quarried and shipped to Glasgow to be 'wrought into tables Chimney pieces and other Ornaments' and 'exported into England and other European Countries to great Advantage' (pp. 163–4).

The south-west corner of Mull also features a basaltic columnar formation that resembles the Giant's Causeway:

the most exact Representation of the Giants Causeway in Ireland, is to be seen at the Red Cave of Seba [Shiaba] at the South Western Extremity of the Isle of Mull.

Here, the Whin rock is disposed in regular prismatick Columns nearly perpendicular, from four to Seven Sides, though they are most usually hexagonal. The Columns are from one to three Feet in Diameter, but are not anywhere so far uncovered, that their whole Length can be seen. They appear hereabouts in several of the Sea Cliffs, but in one place, they form the Beach for above 200 Feet, and being uncovered at Top afford a Causeway to walk upon like that in the County of Antrim, which like that likewise slopes gradually into the Sea beyond the lowest Ebb.

. . .

The Stone of which they are composed, is thought to be the Basaltes of Pliny. Though a compound Stone it is of a very fine Grain, has a good black Colour, admits of a tolerable Polish, and by its extreme Hardness, is admirably fitted for Duration, as appears from the Sepulchral Monuments in Icolumbkil [Iona], where it has for Ages stood exposed to the Weather without being the least impaired. (pp. 164–5)

Here, Walker confines himself to description and comparison, with virtually no trace of speculation about how the basalt columns might have been formed. His suggestion that basalt's durability is demonstrated by the fact that the 'Sepulchral Monuments' of Iona have 'for Ages stood exposed to the Weather without being the least impaired' indicates natural history's concern for usefulness and its limited sense of geological time. Yet the large pyramidal columns of basalt that made up the Giant's Causeway had been the subject of debate by British naturalists since the late seventeenth century, and Walker was writing at a time when the European-wide controversy about the nature and origin of basalt was well under way.[22] Various features of basalt encouraged mineralogists to believe that it had been formed in the universal primeval ocean postulated by the standard geotheoretical model. Basaltic prismatic columns were interpreted by many mineralogists as 'enormous crystals . . . consistent with basalt's consolidation by water' (Laudan, *From Mineralogy to Geology*, p. 182). In 1763 and 1766, however, while exploring the Auvergne region of central France, Nicolas Demarest linked prismatic columnar basalts and 'what appeared to be flows of basalt back to the volcanic cones. On that basis, he claimed that basalts had a volcanic origin' (Laudan, p. 183). Demarest's 'Mémoire sur l'origin et la nature du basalte' was not published until 1774, but in 1763 Rudolf Erich Raspe's *An Introduction to the Natural History of the Terrestrial Sphere* drew on Robert Hooke's theory of subterranean heat in order to argue for the igneous origin of basalt and for the significance of volcanoes as major geological agents (Laudan, p. 184).[23] Yet the classification of basalt as an igneous rock was a minority view in the 1760s; indeed, Laudan claims that 'The conviction that basalt's mineralogy indicated consolidation from water . . . [still] seemed . . . self-evident in the 1770s and 1780s' (p. 182).[24] Walker appears to have adopted his own version of the Neptunist model and 'held that basalts and other minerals that contained or resembled crystals were most probably formed in water and not by heat. Indeed, his mineralogy lectures [of 1797] state that basalts were not igneous, and were a form of primary strata' (Eddy, *The Language of Mineralogy*, pp. 172–4).[25]

In describing the 'face of the Country' of Skye, Walker is so clearly impressed with its mountains that he describes them at length, despite the fact that this does not meet the requirements of his sponsors:

> The Quillin [Cuillin] Mountains, which are amongst the highest in the British Isles, are situated upon the West Coast, about the middle of the Island. These Mountains, or rather Sceletons of Mountains, appear at a Distance, like a huge Congeries of Buildings and Spires in Ruins; and upon approaching their Summits, all is sharp, ragged and naked, without either Earth or Herbage. Further North, the West Coast rises in a Train of Mountains called by the Sailors, Macleods Tables, from their singular Shape, being each of them pyramidal and flat at the Top, like a truncated Cone.
>
> Upon the East side of the Island, there are also considerable Mountains, but very differently shaped from any of the former, and composed of very different Materials. They consist chiefly of Columnar Whinstone, and are generally flat at Top and abrupt and perpendicular on one Side. This is the Appearance of the Hills at the Giants Causeway in Ireland, of Salisbury Hill at Edinburgh, of the Hill which lies to the North of Stirling, and of many others in the Islands of Mull and Canna. All the Hills of this Figure, are composed of that sort of Whinstone, which generally in some degree or other, affect a Columnar Shape, and is disposed in huge Strata nearly inclined to the Horizon. (p. 204)

Walker clearly assumes that these mountains are worth describing in their own right and makes no attempt to identify their potential use-value. But his description confines itself to locations, shapes, heights, appearances, composition and local names, thus avoiding questions about the formation of mountains or basaltic columns. Although he clearly feels compelled to describe Skye's remarkable mountains, he avoids what would become the main point of mountains for Romantic travellers – their aesthetic qualities and psychological impact.

Walker returns to his brief at the end of his section on Skye with an account of the island's commercially useful 'Natural Productions' – which include coal, limestone, 'Smectis' (a kind of fuller's earth), black lead and 'Amiantus' (a kind of asbestos). Echoing Martin Martin's observation sixty years earlier, Walker reports that 'There is a pure white Marble of a fine Grain' found in two places 'in the Country of Strath in this Island. The one near the Church of Kil-christ, and the other about 2 Miles distant at the Village of Torrin upon Loch Slapan' (p. 215).[26] He informs his sponsors that 'There are extensive Strata of it at both places . . . [which] are from one to three feet thick, very solid and entire, without Cracks or Fissures, so that it might be raised in very large Blocks, sufficient for any Purpose of Architecture' (p. 215). Walker's observation of Skye's limestone, whose use-value was well understood, concentrates on potentially interesting geological features:

> There is Limestone in several parts of the Country of Trotternish, and at Braccis in Strath, along the Sea Shore, there are extensive Tracts of coarse Limestone filled with petrified Shells, and with Cornua Ammonis, a Figured Fossil, which has not yet been discovered anywhere else in Scotland. These Rocks ly [*sic*] all horizontal and stretch East and West, but are intersected by Whinstone Dykes, from one to four Feet broad, which run South to North, inclined to the Horizon at an Angle of above 80 degrees. (p. 215)

Walker is recording here what he takes to be the first discovery of fossilised ammonites in Scotland, but while he and most contemporary natural historians no longer doubted that fossils were the remains of organic creatures, he does not discuss the implications of finding the fossils of an extinct group of marine animals on a sea-shore in Skye.[27] This is particularly notable because, as Rudwick points out, ammonites were the 'most striking . . . and certainly the most frequently cited' examples of shellfish fossils that had no counterpart in the present world and were therefore seen by many naturalists as 'strong evidence – perhaps the best evidence of all – for extinction on a large scale' (*Bursting the Limits of Time*, pp. 247–8).[28] In his lectures on natural history twenty years later, Walker noted that '*Cornu ammonis* so plentiful in England to the number of thirty-nine species has never been in recent or living state' (Scott, 'Biographical Introduction', p. xliii). Yet Walker did not countenance the possibility of extinction, which would have violated the paradigm of the Great Chain of Being that was fundamental to the natural history project.[29]

On his return from the Hebrides at the end of 1764, Walker faced the task of writing three separate reports on his findings. His report for the General Assembly was handed over in 1765 and published in *The Scots Magazine* in December 1766.[30] He eventually delivered the 'Report on the Hebrides' to the Commissioners of Annexed Estates in March 1771 and 'there were suggestions that it should be published, but these Walker resisted, maintaining that "it was intended for their private Use, and not at all for Publication at least in its present form". Walker was intending to use the material in the report for a "Natural History of the Hebrides"' (McKay, 'Introduction', pp. 9–10). Shortly after presenting his report, Walker persuaded the Commissioners to support another trip to survey the islands which he had not been able to visit in 1764. The expedition of 1771 'produced [a] second report for the Church but nothing for the Commissioners. They had promised him a further payment when he completed the proposed "Natural History of the Hebrides", but it was never finished' (McKay, 'Introduction', p. 10).[31] The Board of Annexed Estates was wound up in 1784 and thereafter the Highland improvement project 'shifted into the domain of voluntary associations like the Highland Society of London, founded in 1778, the Highland Society of Edinburgh, created in 1784, and the joint stock company of the British Fisheries Society, launched the following year. The two latter associations in particular offered a new locus for Highland travel and natural history' (Jonsson, *Enlightenment's Frontier*, p. 54).

'History of the Island of Jura'

Towards the end of his *Tour in Scotland, MDCCLXIX*, Pennant reports that he visited Moffat on his way south to Carlisle and says that Walker, who was then 'minister of the place, showed me in manuscript his natural history of the Western Isles, which will do him much credit whenever he favours the world with it' (p. 216).

Pennant's statement suggests that Walker showed him his unfinished 'Natural History of the Hebrides' rather than the 'Report on the Hebrides' that would be completed two years later. In the introduction to *An Economical History of the Hebrides and Highlands of Scotland*, published five years after his death, Walker notes that the text of his 'Report on the Hebrides' had gone missing some time after it was delivered to the Board of Annexed Estates (p. 2). The manuscript was discovered in the King's Library in the British Museum at the end of the nineteenth century and first published in McKay's edition in 1980.[32] Scott is therefore mistaken when he claims that 'The Hebrides report was first published' in *An Economical History of the Hebrides* ('Biographical Introduction', p. xx). Whereas the 'Report on the Hebrides' was based on his 1764 tour, Walker tells us that the *Economical History* was 'the result of six journies made into the Highlands and Hebrides, from the year 1760, to the year 1786, during which, a greater extent of these distant parts of the kingdom was surveyed, than what had probably ever been traversed by a former traveller' (p. 1). And while the 'Report on the Hebrides' consists of surveys of individual islands, the *Economical History* is a much more extensive general survey of the whole region, containing systematic observations on topics such as 'Extent and Population', 'Tenure of Lands', 'Buildings and Inclosures', agricultural instruments and methods, livestock and crops, and a subsection on fossils.

Walker's posthumous *Essays on Natural History and Rural Economy* is also closely related to the 'Report on the Hebrides'. It includes a number of essays about the natural history and mineralogy of particular places in Scotland, but the most interesting essay for my purpose is the 'History of the Island of Jura'.[33] McKay claims that parts of the 'Report on the Hebrides' 'are nearly identical to a MS "History of the Island of Jura"' (*The Rev. Dr. John Walker's Report on the Hebrides*, p. 237, n. 1). Yet there are significant differences between the account of Walker's visit to Jura in the unpublished 'Report on the Hebrides' and that in the 'History of the Island of Jura' that appeared in *Essays on Natural History*.

For the most part, 'History of the Island of Jura' is straightforward natural history writing, presenting non-narrative empirical information about 'Dimensions', 'Mountains', 'Rocks', 'Waters', 'Harbours', 'Eddies', 'Climate', 'Inhabitants', 'Diseases', 'Plants', 'Fossils' and so on. But the essay also offers a much more extended narrative of Walker's ascent of Beinn a' Chaolas than that in 'Report on the Hebrides'. After noting that the aim of climbing the mountain was to conduct the two experiments we looked at earlier, Walker's account involves a remarkable fusion of scientific observation with physical and aesthetic experience:

> Some Highland gentlemen were so good as to go along to conduct us. And a box with barometrical tubes, a telescope, a large kettle, water, fewel, provisions, and a couple of fowling-pieces, loaded seven or eight servants.
>
> The first part of our progress lay through deep bogs, from which we sometimes found it very difficult to extricate ourselves. We then came to a chain of small but steep hills, where the heather struck us to the breast, and which were cut every where with deep glens and gullies, which we could not have ascended on the opposite side, without the assistance of the junipers and strong heather, with which they were covered. We next travelled along the rocky skirts, of three or four extensive hills, and came to a small gloomy lake, at the foot of the highest mountain. Upon this side, which was to the south, we found the ascent impracticable, being so abrupt and full of precipices, which obliged us to make a circuit to the east. Here we had before us, a very steep and continued ascent of about one thousand five hundred feet of perpendicular height, and composed entirely of loose rocks and stones. They lay upon the side of the mountain, like a great stream, and upon the least motion, gave way all about us, which made our progress both tedious and dangerous. With great difficulty, we made our way against these hurling ruins of the mountain; and at last, after an ascent of seven hours, with excessive fatigue, we gained the summit.
>
> It was now five o'clock in the afternoon, the day was serene, not a cloud in the firmament, and the atmosphere uncommonly clear; so that the view we now enjoyed, of the earth and seas below, made us forget the toil of our ascent. Every way we turned, we had a prospect of sea and land, as far as the eye could reach. The sea in many places running out to the sky, and in others, terminated by lands and islands of various shapes, forming a very singular and grand horizon. ('History of the Island of Jura', in *Essays on Natural History*, pp. 229–30)

Rather than an empirical report about the natural history of the mountain, this passage is a narrative of actions and experience. Although the many first-person pronouns are all plural, other features of the text indicate that Walker is reporting his own subjective experience.

While Walker does mention in the 'Report on the Hebrides' that it took him 'Seven Hours of excessive Fatigue, to get to the Summit of the highest Mountain', that is the only deviation from the objective reporting of the conduct and results of the experiments. By contrast, the account in the 'History of the Island of Jura' makes much more of the difficulty, danger and fatigue of the ascent. It also records what we might call the aesthetic pay-off when Walker and his companions are rewarded with a sublime panoramic view of mountains, islands and seas that 'made us forget the toil of our ascent'. Perhaps half a dozen years earlier, Burke's *Philosophical Enquiry into the Origin of our Ideas of the Sublime and Beautiful* (1757/1759) had stressed the effects of labour and overcoming difficulty and danger in producing the soul-expanding delight of the sublime.[34] By the end of the eighteenth century, this aesthetic economy had become conventional in narratives of climbing mountains, though was still capable of subtle developments of the kind that Wordsworth produced in various passages of the 1805 *Prelude*.[35] Other markers of the sublime in Walker's narrative include emphasis on the experiencing subject's elevation (literal and metaphorical) and a consciousness that expands to the limits of the horizon and beyond. The spectator views 'the earth and seas below' and is at the centre of a massive 360 degree panorama. The eye is active rather than passive, reaching towards and beyond its limits. As its etymology suggests, the natural sublime is produced by geographical or geomorphic features that appear to push back or go beyond normal limitations: 'The sea in many places running out to the sky, and in others, terminated by lands and islands of various shapes, forming a very singular and grand horizon.'

Walker goes on to describe in more detail the 'prospect' seen from the summit of Beinn a' Chaolas:

> *Prospect.* – On one hand we had a thousand hills; the whole alpine country of Argylshire, the ancient Albion. Here only, our view was intercepted, and that only by mountains at the distance of above fifty miles. In another quarter, we saw distinctly the whole of the Hebrides, and Deucaledonian ocean. Southwards, the vast promontory of Cantire lay under our eye; and beyond it, in one view, all the west of Scotland rising to the great mass of mountains in the head of Clydesdale and Nithsdale: in another view, the spiry summits of Arran, and the whole Irish sea, with its shores, to the Isle of Man. From the south to the west, the north of Ireland lay as a plain before us, further than the eye could reach. The

impetuous strait between the Mull of Cantire and the Fair Head, with its lofty cliffs, was at hand; through which the Irish sea is filled every tide, by the pouring in of the Atlantic. The promontory of the Giants Causeway appeared near and distinct; and beyond it, the high land of Inis-huna, the north extremity of Ireland; beyond this, to the Hebrides, nothing but air and ocean. (pp. 230–1)

Although the term 'prospect' would later be associated with the aesthetics of picturesque tourism introduced by pioneers such as William Gilpin in the 1780s,[36] it was used in early eighteenth-century loco-descriptive or topographic poetry to refer to the landscape seen from the summit of hills and mountains.[37] Such views were often loaded with moral or political significance, as in James Thomson's description in *Spring* (1728) of a view from a hill on George Lyttelton's Hagley Park estate in Worcestershire:

> Meantime you gain the height, from whose fair brow
> The bursting prospect spreads immense around;
> And, snatched o'er hill and dale, and wood and lawn,
> And verdant field, and darkening heath between,
> And villages embosomed soft in trees,
> And spiry towns by surging columns marked
> Of household smoke, your eye excursive roams –
> Wide-stretching from the Hall in whose kind haunt
> The hospitable Genius lingers still,
> To where the broken landscape, by degrees
> Ascending, roughens into rigid hills
> O'er which the Cambrian mountains, like far clouds
> That skirt the blue horizon, dusky rise. (ll. 950–62)

From this 'height', the prospect seems to 'burst' the limits of everyday vision and experience, and 'spreads immense around'. The eye, too, 'excursive roams – / Wide-stretching' to the limits of the expanded horizon. From this vantage point, the landscape exhibits the aesthetic, moral and political values of 'order in variety' that shaped much of the poetry and politics of the period. Hill is varied with dale, wood with lawn, field with heath, villages with trees, towns with villages, nature with culture, and the beautiful landscape of the hospitable estate gradually roughens into sublime Welsh mountains that 'skirt the blue horizon'. Also characteristic of the early eighteenth-century celebration of British landscape was the attempt to imbue it with classical associations – as in Thomson's use of 'Cambrian', from the Latin name for Wales which derived, according to Geoffrey of Monmouth, from the name of one of Brutus's sons.[38]

Walker's account of his experiences on Beinn a' Chaolas contains echoes of such passages of prospect poetry, along with the dynamics of the Burkean sublime. From Walker's high vantage point, the eye/I dominates huge landforms: 'the vast promontory of Cantire lay under our eye', and 'the north of Ireland lay as a plain before us'. The sublime experience generates an undecidable interplay between limits and limitlessness. Walker's own 'bursting prospect spreads immense around', and as the eye (and the I) surveys the panorama it is virtually without impediment, intercepted only in one direction by the alpine mountains of Argyll more than fifty miles away. The plain of the north of Ireland extends 'further than the eye could reach', though Walker's eye extends with it: 'The promontory of the Giants Causeway appeared near and distinct; and beyond it, the high land of Inis-huna, the north extremity of Ireland; beyond this, to the Hebrides, nothing but air and ocean'. Walker's prospect also exhibits unity in variety – mountains and plains, seas and shores, air and oceans are bound together in the 360 degree panorama and in the experience of the viewing subject at its centre. The passage also endows the landscape with classical resonances: the Sea of the Hebrides becomes the 'Deucaledonian ocean', and the alpine country of Argyll is called 'the ancient Albion', a provocative suggestion, perhaps drawn from the story in Geoffrey of Monmouth, which makes this region of western Scotland, rather than England, into the core of an imagined ancient Britain. These classical associations are deployed alongside a Gaelic place name –'Inis-huna' – from the poems of Ossian.[39]

Walker also employs the trope of indescribability that features so often in the eighteenth-century and Romantic sublime, but it is the internal experience of the beholder rather than the landscape that is beyond the powers of description:

> The emotions of the mind of the beholder, arising from the grandeur of this scene, are not to be excited by any description. The extent of prospect from this mountain is indeed surprising, not much under three hundred miles, south and north. But the curvature of the earth is here greatly overcome by the elevation of the spectator, and the great height

of the distant lands. Nothing else could render the Isle of Skye and the Isle of Man at the same time visible. At three such views, the naked eye might extend from the one extremity of Britain to the other. To stretch the eye over so many different seas, over such a multitude of islands, and such various countries, in different kingdoms, is perhaps a scene, that can nowhere be beheld in Europe, but from the summit of Jura. (pp. 231–2)

The prospect Walker describes is a fascinating blend of the Burkean sublime and the geographical precision of a natural historian. The extent of prospect from the top of the mountain is now measurable at 'not much under three hundred miles'. This extent is surprising, even to the natural historian who understands that the limits created by the curvature of the earth are 'greatly overcome by the elevation of the spectator', a phrase which refers, of course, to the spectator's height above sea level but perhaps also suggests the spectator's psychological elevation in relation to the physical objects that are laid out beneath him. In an intriguing move, Walker computes and imaginatively multiplies his panoramic view in order to envision a God-like vantage point from where three such views could be combined to enable his 'naked eye' to 'extend', without the assistance of the telescope carried by one of the servants, 'from the one extremity of Britain to the other'. Such a composite view would allow the beholder to oversee the unity in variety of Britain's complex political make-up. As a Scot who had contributed to the British government's attempt to shore up the parliamentary union of England and Scotland in the aftermath of Culloden, Walker makes the summit of a mountain in the remote island of Jura (and himself) the centre not only of a panoramic vision of the landscape of Scotland, Ireland and Wales (a Celtic fringe made central) but also of the whole British Isles. The unity within variety that Walker envisions is perhaps not just that of the physical land mass, but also a political vision of Britain that both celebrates the Union of Parliaments and recognises internal national and cultural differences.

Walker's extended account of his experience of climbing Beinn a' Chaolas in his 'History of the Island of Jura' itself exhibits unity in variety in terms of register and genre, modulating effortlessly between aesthetic rapture and scientific precision, travel writing inspired by prospect poetry and natural history. This fusion of, or dialogue between, the registers of the natural sublime and natural history is, to my knowledge, unique in Walker's writings, the vast majority of which adhere to the methods and outlook of natural history that Walker practised throughout his life and taught at the University of Edinburgh. As such, this passage has more in common with the writings of some of the Romantic-period geologists examined in later chapters than with the general tenor of Walker's natural history writing.

Although Walker's various accounts of the natural history of the Highlands and Islands of Scotland were not published in the period, the discoveries and observations he made on his field trips and tours, along with the methodology that he developed on and for them, formed the basis of his lecture course in natural history at the University of Edinburgh. In turn, Walker's lectures deeply influenced those of his students who went on to make their own mineralogical and geological journeys in Scotland and produced key publications in the story I am tracing. It is also possible that one of Walker's manuscript accounts of the Hebrides influenced Pennant to undertake his second tour of Scotland in 1772 in order to explore the islands that Walker had recently surveyed. In Pennant, however, and still more in the writings of later geological travellers in Scotland, the fusion of scientific analysis and aesthetic response that appears briefly and unexpectedly in Walker's 'History of the Island of Jura' would become much more prevalent, especially in the 'Romantic geology' that emerged towards the end of the century.

Notes

1. See Harold Scott's 'Biographical Introduction' to Walker, *Lectures on Geology*, pp. xxiv, xxx. For Walker's class lists, see Eddy, 'The University of Edinburgh Natural History Class Lists' and *The Language of Mineralogy*, pp. 229–50. Also see Withers, 'Walker, John (1731–1803)', *ODNB*.
2. Walker wrote the parish reports on Glencorse (1795) and Colinton (1797) for Sir John Sinclair's *Statistical Account of Scotland*. In the eighteenth century, Colinton was known as 'Collington'.
3. For the correspondence between Walker and Linnaeus, see Walker, *Lectures on Geology*, pp. 253–62; for a chronological list of Walker's correspondence from the mid-1750s to 1803, see Eddy, *The Language of Mineralogy*, pp. 219–28.
4. See Walker, 'Notice of Mineralogical Journeys, and of a Mineralogical System'.

5. Much of Lightfoot's first-hand information about Scotland's plants was gathered as a member of the expedition group, along with John Stuart, on Pennant's tour of Scotland in 1772. On Lightfoot's and Stuart's extended collaboration as natural historians and climbers of Scottish mountains, see Mitchell, *Scotland's Mountains Before the Mountaineers*, pp. 41–3. For bibliographies of Walker's manuscripts and publications, see his *Lectures on Geology*, pp. 272–4, and Eddy, *The Language of Mineralogy*, pp. 254–6, 271–3.

6. See Woodward, *An Essay toward a Natural History of the Earth*.

7. See Hallam, *Great Geological Controversies*, pp. 1–28.

8. See Bacon, *The New Organon*, especially the concluding 'Outline of a Natural and Experimental History' (pp. 222–38).

9. Porter quotes Hans Sloane and Edward Lhwyd.

10. See Vaccari, 'The Organized Traveller'.

11. The first account in English of Linnaeus's life and work was Richard Pulteney's *General View of the Writings of Linnaeus* (1781), which included a summary of Linnaeus's account of 'The Fossil Kingdom' (pp. 131–66).

12. Walker, 'A General View of its Literary History', *Notes and Lectures on Natural History* (1789), pp. 40–1, quoted by Eddy, *The Language of Mineralogy*, p. 21.

13. See Youngson, *After the Forty-Five*, and Jonsson, *Enlightenment's Frontier*. Also see Phillipson and Mitchison (eds), *Scotland in the Age of Improvement*, and Withers, 'Improvement and Enlightenment'.

14. See Berry, *The Idea of Commercial Society in the Scottish Enlightenment*, p. 39.

15. See Stafford, *The Sublime Savage*, pp. 163–80; Andrews, *The Search for the Picturesque*, pp. 197–240; Withers, 'The Historical Creation of the Scottish Highlands'; and Baines, 'Ossianic Geographies' and *The House of Forgery in Eighteenth-Century Britain*, pp. 103–24.

16. See Jonsson, *Enlightenment's Frontier*, pp. 11–12.

17. See Home (Lord Kames), *Sketches of the History of Man*, I, pp. 42, 307–8.

18. See Holmes, *The Age of Wonder*, pp. 1–59.

19. For Scottish criticism of Buffon in the period, see Wood, 'Buffon's Reception in Scotland'.

20. See Walker, *Lectures on Geology*, p. 172.

21. Mitchell, however, taking Walker at his word, believes that he made the first recorded ascent of Beinn an Oir (*Scotland's Mountains Before the Mountaineers*, pp. 150–1).

22. See Porter, *The Making of Geology*, pp. 40, 113; Rappaport, 'The Earth Sciences'; Klonk, 'Science, Art, and the Representation of the

Natural World'; and Rudwick, *Bursting the Limits of Time*, pp. 62–3, 94, 105–8, 204–7.

23. Also see Carozzi, 'Rudolf Erich Raspe and the Basalt Controversy'.

24. Although Hallam describes the two competing interpretations of basalt as 'Neptunist' and 'Vulcanist' (*Great Geological Controversies*, p. 6), this is an over-simplification.

25. See Walker, *An Epitome of Natural History*.

26. See Martin, 'A Description of the Western Islands of Scotland Circa 1695' and 'A Late Voyage to St Kilda', p. 89.

27. On the debates about fossils in the seventeenth and eighteenth centuries, see Porter, *The Making of Geology*, pp. 46–53, 165–70.

28. For later developments in the discussion of fossils in the period, see Rudwick, *Bursting the Limits of Time*, pp. 194–203, 239–87.

29. See Lovejoy, *The Great Chain of Being*.

30. See 'Dr. John Walker's Report to the Assembly 1765, Concerning the State of the Highlands and Islands'.

31. See 'Dr. John Walker's Report Concerning the State of the Highlands and Islands, to the General Assembly 1772'.

32. See Walker, 'Report on the Hebrides', King's MS 105, The British Library.

33. Walker, 'History of the Island of Jura', in *Essays on Natural History and Rural Economy*, pp. 219–82.

34. Scott dates the MS 'History of the Island of Jura' to '*ca.*1765' (Walker, *Lectures on Geology*, p. 273); McKay notes that 'The MS "History of the Island of Jura" is in the Laing collection in the Library of the University of Edinburgh' (p. 237, n. 1). Kames's discussion of 'Grandeur and Sublimity' in *Elements of Criticism*, I, pp. 150–78, is less interesting and relevant than Addison's or Burke's.

35. On the history of the representation of mountains, see Nicolson, *Mountain Gloom and Mountain Glory*, and Macfarlane, *Mountains of the Mind*. Emphasis on overcoming difficulty and danger also featured in the shift in the representation of travel experience in the late eighteenth century, as traced in Thompson's *The Suffering Traveller*.

36. See Gilpin, *Observations on the River Wye* (1782), *Observations, Relative Chiefly to Picturesque Beauty, Made in the Year 1776* (1789), and *Three Essays: - On Picturesque Beauty; - on Picturesque Travel; and, on Sketching Landscape* (1792).

37. For a discussion of early eighteenth-century 'prospect poetry' in these terms, see Andrews, *The Search for the Picturesque*, pp. 3–23.

38. According to Geoffrey of Monmouth, Brutus conquered Britain after the fall of Troy and when he died it was divided between his three sons: 'Locrinus, who was first-born, inherited the part of the island

which was afterwards called *Loegria* [a Latinisation of the Welsh name *Lloegr*, 'England'] after him. Kamber received the region which is on the further bank of the River Severn, the part which is now known as Wales but which was for a long time after his death called Kambria from his name. . . . Albanactus, the youngest, took the region which is nowadays called Scotland in our language. He called it Albany, after his own name' (*The History of the Kings of Britain*, part II, p. 75).

39. 'Inis-huna' is 'presumably Wales; "that part of South-Britain which is next to the Irish coast"; "the western coast of South Britain"; "*green island*"' (in Macpherson, *The Poems of Ossian and Related Works*, p. 564).

A Country Torn and Convulsed: Pioneering Geological Observations in Thomas Pennant's Tours of Scotland (1769, 1772)

Thomas Pennant (1726–98) was one of the foremost natural historians in eighteenth-century Britain. According to G. R. de Beer, he was 'the leading British zoologist after Ray and before Darwin' (*Tour on the Continent*, p. vi).[1] Pennant's most important scientific work, *The British Zoology*, first published in 1766, 'was organized according to the classificatory systems of John Ray' and 'established him in the eyes of contemporaries as a leading European natural historian' (Withers, 'Pennant, Thomas', *ODNB*).[2] In his early twenties, Pennant began publishing articles on various aspects of natural history in the Royal Society's *Philosophical Transactions* and undertook natural history tours of Cornwall, Wales and Ireland. In 1755 he began a correspondence with Carl Linnaeus that 'continued . . . till age and infirmities obliged [Linnaeus] to desist' (*The Literary Life of the Late Thomas Pennant*, p. 3).[3] Yet although Pennant adopted Linnaeus's binomial system, he thought him a poor ornithologist and zoologist and saw himself as 'loyally protecting the heritage [and system] of John Ray as improved by himself' (Gascoigne, *Joseph Banks and the English Enlightenment*, p. 104). In 1765, he went on a six-month tour of Europe, travelling through France, Switzerland, Germany and the Netherlands and meeting fellow naturalists, including the Comte de Buffon, whose highly influential multi-volume *Histoire naturelle, générale et particulière* had begun to be published sixteen years earlier. Pennant was elected fellow of the Royal Society in 1767, 'began that correspondence with Gilbert White, . . . which, together with White's correspondence with Daines Barrington, formed the basis of White's *Natural History of Selborne* (1789)' (Withers, *ODNB*), and first met Joseph Banks in 1768. Despite Pennant's stature as a natural historian, however, little attention has been paid to his contribution to mineralogy and the history of geology.[4] In this chapter, however, I suggest that Pennant played a significant part in the revolutionary discovery that Scotland's terrain had been partly shaped by volcanic activity in the distant past.

Pennant undertook two groundbreaking tours of Scotland and published accounts of them in *A Tour in Scotland, MDCCLXIX* (1771) and *A Tour in Scotland and Voyage to the Hebrides, MDCCLXXII* (1774, 1776). These tours played a key role, along with James Macpherson's Ossian poems of the 1760s, in representing the Highlands and Islands of Scotland as attractive places for a growing number of travellers and tourists. For Brian D. Osborne, Pennant's appreciation of 'the grandeur and natural beauty of Scotland' made him 'one of the first generation of travellers who saw in wild mountain scenes anything more than an awful wilderness' ('Introduction', *A Tour in Scotland, 1769*, p. xviii).[5] For Withers, by contrast, although 'Pennant was certainly aware of Scotland's visual grandeur', the central theme of his tours is Scotland's natural history ('Introduction', *A Tour in Scotland and Voyage to the Hebrides, 1772*, p. xx).[6] This aspect of Pennant's Scottish tours helped to make the Highlands and Islands into primary destinations for travellers in search of the natural history of the northern wilds of Britain. There is some validity in both these readings of Pennant's tours. In what follows, I try to show that there are significant interconnections between Pennant's natural history of the geological features of the Highlands and Islands, his aesthetic response to landscape, his self-representation as a traveller, and his prose style.[7] A close reading of Pennant's texts will enable us to continue mapping the pre-geological, pre-Romantic interface between the natural history of the mineral kingdom and the stylistic and generic features of the eighteenth-century natural history tour. This reading will allow us in later chapters to contrast Pennant's natural history tours of Scotland with the Scottish travel writings of the 'Romantic geologists' of the following decades.

Natural History, Mineralogy, Geology

As we have seen in previous chapters, the defining concerns of eighteenth-century natural history – empirical observation, description and classification – were inherited from the Baconian natural

history of seventeenth-century pioneers such as Ray and Francis
Willughby. As Roy Porter points out, natural history defined itself
against the cosmogonies or speculative theories of the earth that
flourished at the end of the seventeenth century, focusing instead
on the 'observation of Matter of Fact' and on exploring 'the most
desert Rocks and Mountains, as [well as] the more frequented
Valleys and Plains' in search of evidence and specimens (*The Making
of Geology*, pp. 32–41).[8] Discoveries made in the field were supplemented by the reports of other travellers and through the use of circulated questionnaires. The goal was to produce natural histories of
particular regions and to construct a general system of classification.
Mineralogy attempted to imitate the methodology that had been
so successful in investigating plants and animals, treating minerals,
rocks and 'fossils' as natural kinds that had existed in a relatively
static state since the creation. Mineralogy did not concern itself with
theories about the origins or historical development of its materials
and forms and was therefore quite different from the geology that
emerged in the late eighteenth century, which assumed that the earth
was a dynamic system and studied its geomorphology in terms of its
history and/or causation.

Yet although Porter distinguishes between mineralogy and geology
in these ways, he also stresses the contribution that mineralogy made
to the formation of geology. Furthermore, the static view of the earth
that characterised mineralogy began to be challenged in the second
half of the eighteenth century by interpretations of strata, earthquakes
and volcanoes that suggested that the earth had had an extremely
long dynamic history (*The Making of Geology*, pp. 38–41, 112–14,
120–7). The problematic goal of producing a Linnaean classification
of rocks and minerals gave way to the attempt, by mineralogists such
as Abraham Gottlob Werner, to classify them according to their supposed causes and temporal sequence of formation.[9] Mineralogy thus
got caught up in contemporary controversies about the history and
formative causes of the earth's crust. While the Neptunist mineralogy
developed by Werner and others held that the earth's materials and
topography had mostly resulted from the effects of one or more inundations by a universal ocean, Vulcanist mineralogy interpreted some of
the same materials and features as evidence for considerable volcanic
activity over long periods of the earth's history.[10] Both sides in the dispute assumed that the goal of mineralogy was no longer static classification but the discovery of causation and historical sequence. Both Porter

and Rachel Laudan therefore see mineralogy as anticipating, making possible, or even morphing into the geology that emerged at the turn of the century, a seismic paradigm shift in which 'The static had given way to the dynamic' (Porter, *The Making of Geology*, p. 218).

Given that these developments in the earth sciences were well under way at the time Pennant toured Scotland, his approach to mineralogy, indebted to Ray's natural history, might initially appear outmoded. Pennant is primarily concerned with making empirical observations that contribute to the natural history of animals, plants and minerals in Scotland, together with what we might call a natural history of the people. His tours exemplify natural history as a mode of doing science, a mode of travel, and a mode of writing. His prose style reinforces the impression that his observations and descriptions are strictly factual, thus forging an implicit correspondence between natural history and literary style. One of the rhetorical strategies of Pennant's tours of Scotland, for example, is a tendency to omit first-person pronouns where they would normally be expected, thus creating the impression that Pennant's observations do not pass through his individual subjectivity but are neutral facts about the world. Pennant downplays his personal experience and achievements on his tours and makes light of the hazards of travelling through what was at the time one of the most challenging terrains in Britain. In contrast to Romantic-period geological travellers of the following generation, who fashion themselves as quest-heroes who overcome difficulty and danger in order to arrive at remote places and radical theories of the earth, Pennant's attention to geological features prioritises observation and description over causal theory, precludes imaginative voyaging into deep time, and does not attempt to understand their place within a history of the earth's evolving system of forces and materials.[11] Pennant's admission in the first volume of *A Tour in Scotland, MDCCLXXII* that the intricate folding of the strata of coal and stone at Whitehaven that he saw en route to Scotland was due to 'Operations of nature past my skill to unfold' (p. 56) suggests, through a quiet pun, that theoretical speculation about the causal origins of geological features was beyond his capacity or outside his remit. Whether or not Pennant was being overly modest, the reluctance to engage in geotheory or geohistory was characteristic of the natural history of the period.

Yet although Pennant's writing style, aesthetic values, self-image as a traveller, and scientific outlook appear to derive from the natural history of an earlier age, I will suggest that his tours helped to make the landscapes of Scotland into key resources for 'Romantic geologists' by identifying and tentatively exploring, against the grain of his outlook as a natural historian, the interrelations between sublime mountain features and their geological formation in deep time. In particular, I concentrate on Pennant's discovery of what he took to be the remains of extinct volcanoes in various parts of Scotland and the remnants of a massive basaltic formation in the Inner Hebrides – discoveries for which Pennant has not received any credit.

Collective Collecting

Samuel Johnson famously said of Pennant in 1778 that 'he's the best traveller I ever read; he observes more things than anyone else does' (Boswell, *The Life of Samuel Johnson*, p. 671).[12] Johnson correctly identifies the keynote of Pennant's travel writing, but James Boswell, for once, disagrees with his hero's judgement, revealing a fundamental misunderstanding of what Pennant was trying to do in his tours:

> I could not help thinking that this was too high praise of a writer who had traversed a wide extent of country in such haste, that he could put together only curt frittered fragments of his own, and afterwards procured supplemental intelligence from parochial ministers, and others not the best qualified or most impartial narrators, whose ungenerous prejudice against the house of Stuart glares in misrepresentation. (*The Life of Samuel Johnson*, p. 671)

Yet neither of Pennant's tours could be said to have involved traversing Scotland in haste, and neither text consists of 'curt frittered fragments'. Boswell misrepresents Pennant's project, partly because of political antipathies, partly because he appears not to understand Pennant's scientific project or method, and partly because he was looking back from the perspective of 1791 at a time when the generic conventions of the tour had changed significantly from the 1760s and 1770s, shifting from objective reportage to a Romantic focus on the individual traveller's inner and outer experience.[13] For Pennant, empirical observation is more important than personal experience, and this allows him to incorporate information from other sources in precisely the way that Boswell objected to.

On his first tour of Scotland, Pennant made use of the specialist knowledge of some of Scotland's leading natural historians, including Robert Ramsay, John Hope, John Walker and David Skene. Perhaps already planning a second tour, he included two sets of 'Queries' among the appendices at the end of the first edition of *A Tour in Scotland, MDCCLXIX*. These queries were 'Addressed to the Gentlemen and Clergy of North-Britain, respecting the Antiquities and Natural History of their Parishes, with a View of exciting them to favor the World with a fuller and more satisfactory Account of their Country, than it is in the Power of a Stranger and transient Visitant to give' (p. 287). The first set of twenty-seven questions is concerned with the history, sociology and antiquities of parishes. The second set relates 'to the Natural History of the parish' and includes several queries about mineralogical or geological features:

I. What is the appearance of the country in the parish; is it flat or hilly, rocky or mountainous?

IV. Is there sand, clay, chalk, stone, gravel, loam, or what is the nature of the soil?

X. Are there any and what mines; what are they; to whom do they belong; what do they produce?

XI. Have you got any marble, moorstone, or other stone of any sort, how is it got out, and how worked?

XV. Are there any remarkable caves, or grottos, natural or artificial? Give the best description and account thereof you can.

XVIII. Are there any chalk-pits, sand or gravel-pits, or other openings in the parish, and what?

XIX. On digging wells or other openings, what strata's of soil do they meet with, and how thick is each?

XXI. Is there any marl, Fuller's earth, potters earth, or loam, or any other remarkable soils, as ochre, etc.

XXII. Are there any bitumen, naptha, or other substances of that nature found in the earth?

XXVIII. Are there any petrifying springs or waters that incrust bodies, what are they?

XXX. Are there any figured stones, such as echinitæ, belemnitæ, &c. Any having impression of plants or fishes on them, or any fossil marine bodies, such as shells, corals, &c. or any petrified parts of animals: where are they found, and what are they?

Pennant also published a letter in *The Scots Magazine* of April 1772, one month before setting out on his second tour, addressed 'To every Gentleman desirous to promote the Publication of an Accurate Account of the Antiquities, Present State, and Natural History of SCOTLAND'. Accompanying the letter was a set of twenty-two queries, adapted from those published at the end of his first tour, designed to elicit information about the people, topography, commerce, agriculture and local antiquities of Scotland's parishes. Curiously, Pennant reduced his queries related to the mineral kingdom to just two:

2. What remarkable natural caves, rocks, or mountains: what picturesque scenes worth drawing?
19. Please to observe and collect against my coming, specimens of all sorts of earths, clays, stones, marbles, pebbles, sands, asbestus, minerals, and ores; also bituminous fossils, petrified shells, wood, fossil-wood, in short, fossils of all denominations.

Pennant reassured his addressees that he would deposit all such items with Dr Robert Ramsay, then keeper of the Natural History Museum in Edinburgh and Professor of Natural History at the University.[14]

In publishing and circulating questionnaires to parish ministers and other provincial gentlemen, Pennant was following a long-standing practice in natural history and making thorough preparations for his second tour of Scotland. The 'Advertisement' at the beginning of *A Tour in Scotland, MDCCLXXII* reveals that these preparations included recruiting two expert travelling companions: 'the Rev. Mr. *John Lightfoot*, lecturer of *Uxbridge*, [to whom] I am obliged for all the botanical remarks featured over the following pages. . . . [And] Rev. Mr. *John Stuart* of *Killin*, for a variety of hints, relating to customs of the natives of the highlands, and of the islands' (I, p. iii).[15] Withers notes, as Pennant fails to, that the expeditionary team also included Moses Griffith, Pennant's 'servant and an "able artist" who produced the many sketches later published as engravings' ('Introduction', p. xvi).[16] Pennant also used his 'Advertisement' to acknowledge his debts 'to the several gentlemen who favoured me at different times with accounts and little histories of the places of their residence, or their environs' (I, p. iii). At the beginning of the second volume, he announces that he is peculiarly indebted to nineteen named individuals for information about various localities that he visited on the second half of his 1772 tour. The fact that Pennant travelled with these companions and sought the aid of the clergymen of the parishes that he visited throughout Scotland meant that his 1772 tour, even more than his 1769 tour, would not be limited to the observations of an individual traveller but was intended to make a substantial, objective contribution to the natural history of Scotland. Pennant thereby followed in the footsteps of the seventeenth-century naturalists who first inspired him, making it a non-personal, collective enterprise which draws on and coordinates the knowledge and findings of local experts.

Itineraries

Pennant includes an itinerary of his tour at the end of *A Tour in Scotland, MDCCLXIX* which can be followed on J. Bayly's 'Map of Scotland, the Hebrides and Part of England adapted to Mr Pennant's Tours', which was included in the 1777 and subsequent editions of Pennant's *A Tour in Scotland, MDCCLXIX* and *A Tour in Scotland and Voyage to the Hebrides, MDCCLXXII* (Figure 4.1). Pennant entered Scotland on 17 July 1769, riding north from Berwick along the North Sea coast. During a week's stay in Edinburgh he visited the college and its museum, and the new Royal Botanic Garden near Calton Hill. Pennant then headed north into the Grampian Mountains, making use of the military road built by General George Wade in 1728–30.[17] At Blair Atholl, he cut across country towards Braemar via Glen Tilt (twenty years before Hutton) and then made his way east through Ballater to Aberdeen. From there, he headed along the coast to Inverness and rode north to Duncansby Head and John o' Groats, from whence 'is a full view of several of the Orkney islands' across the Pentland Firth (p. 153). He then headed south-west to Loch Ness, where he rode along the more recent of Wade's two military roads towards Fort Augustus and took Wade's 1726 road to Fort William,

Figure 4.1 J. Bayly, 'A Map of Scotland, the Hebrides and Part of England adapted to Mr Pennant's Tours' (London: B. White, 1777) (detail). Reproduced by permission of the National Library of Scotland.

where the weather prevented him from seeing the summit of Ben Nevis and from visiting the Parallel Roads of Glen Roy.[18] From Fort William Pennant took the military road across the mountains to Kinlochleven and thence over the Devil's Staircase to the King's House at the head of Glen Coe. He crossed Rannoch Moor to Tyndrum, rode west to Loch Awe and then turned south to Inverary. From there he rode round the heads of Loch Fyne and Loch Long, crossing over the 'Rest and Be Thankful' pass before reaching Tarbet on the western bank of Loch Lomond, 'the most beautifull of the Caledonian lakes' (p. 194). He then took the military road south to Glasgow and completed a 'most agreeable and prosperous Tour' back in Edinburgh (p. 215). On 18 September, Pennant headed south, visiting John Walker in Moffat, who 'shewed me in manuscript his natural history of the western isles' (p. 216), and crossed the border into Cumberland on the following day. Osborne calculates that Pennant 'covered over 1200 miles in nine weeks' 'On horseback, over poor roads and mountainous country' ('Introduction', p. xvii).

Whereas Pennant's first tour had largely been restricted, where possible, to the half-dozen or so military roads built by Wade and William Caulfield earlier in the eighteenth century, a large part of his second tour involved sailing, walking and riding around 2,000 miles along the north-west coast of Scotland – 'one of the most treacherous coasts in Europe' – to visit Hebridean islands and parts of the Highlands that were 'far beyond the reach of the military roads' (Crane, *Great British Journeys*, pp. 164, 167). The 'off-road' part of the tour began at Greenock on 17 June 1772 when Pennant and his companions embarked on 'the Lady Frederic Campbell, a cutter of ninety tuns, Mr. Archibald Thompson master' (I, p. 179). Using the Admiralty charts produced by Murdoch Mackenzie, Pennant visited an impressive number of the Western Islands and peninsulas over the following two months, including Bute, Arran, Ailsa Craig, Kintyre, Gigha, Jura, Isla, Oronsay and Colonsay, Iona, Rum, Skye, Loch Broom, Ardnamurchan, Mull and Lismore.[19] He then spent about six weeks, beginning in the middle of August 1772, on an extended exploration of mainland Scotland that occupies about half of the second volume.

Natural History and Aesthetic Experience

Natural history and aesthetic appreciation were potentially interconnected responses to landscape in the eighteenth century, especially in topographic poems such as James Thomson's *The Seasons* (1726–30). The dominant aesthetic category of British tourism – the picturesque – involved a detached description of the natural world which easily correlated with the observational mode of natural history.[20] But the picturesque was fundamentally challenged by mountainous landscapes of the kind encountered in northern Scotland. In his *Observations, Relative Chiefly to Picturesque Beauty, Made in the*

Year 1776, On several Parts of Great Britain; Particularly the High-Lands of Scotland (1789), partly based on a tour of Scotland made only a couple of years after Pennant's tours, William Gilpin is often driven to abandon his own aesthetic category – the picturesque – in favour of notions of grandeur and sublimity derived from Joseph Addison's *Spectator* essays on the pleasures of the imagination of 1712 and Edmund Burke's *A Philosophical Enquiry into the Origin of our Ideas of the Sublime and Beautiful* (1757/1759). Addison's and Burke's aesthetic terms allowed poets and tourists to describe both the imposing physical nature of mountains and their powerful emotional and psychological impact. But although Pennant made his tours of Scotland only a couple of years after Macpherson's Ossian poems had made the Scottish Highlands and Islands into Britain's pre-eminent sublime landscape, his scientific style involved trying to maintain a low-key response to these landscapes. As a result, there is often a tension in Pennant's texts between the contradictory impulses of the picturesque and the sublime which correlates, I suggest, with a parallel tension between mineralogy and geology.

When Pennant visited Edinburgh during his first tour of Scotland, his observations of Arthur's Seat and Salisbury Crags – features that would soon become significant in the history of geology – oscillate between these different modes of scientific analysis and aesthetic response:

> Near [Holyrood] palace are the *Parks* first inclosed by *James* V. within are the vast rocks known by the names of *Arthur*'s Seat and *Salisbury*'s Craigs; their fronts exhibit a romantic and wild scene of broken rocks and vast precipices, which from some points seem to over-hang the lower parts of the city. Great columns of stone, from forty to fifty feet in length, and about two feet in diameter, regularly pentagonal, or hexagonal, hang down the face of some of these rocks almost perpendicularly, or with a very slight dip, and form a strange appearance. Considerable quantities of stone from the quarries have been cut and sent to *London* for paving the streets, its great hardness rendering it excellent for that purpose. Beneath these hills are some of the most beautiful walks about *Edinburgh*, commanding a fine prospect over several parts of the country. (*A Tour in Scotland, MDCCLXIX*, p. 52)

Pennant's description of the basaltic columns of Salisbury Crags employs the characteristic mode and terminology of mineralogical description and avoids speculation about their composition or origins.

Similarly, there is no suggestion that Arthur's Seat is part of an extinct volcano (its volcanic provenance was not readily accepted by Edinburgh's geologists, even after it was pointed out by Faujas de Saint-Fond in 1784). Pennant's attention to the way the stone has been used for commercial purposes exemplifies the link between mineralogy and economic exploitation, while his use of the term 'fine prospect' invokes the contemporary cult of the picturesque. But when he writes that the fronts of Arthur's Seat and Salisbury Crags 'exhibit a romantic and wild scene of broken rocks and vast precipices', he ventures into impressionistic hyperbole derived from the cult of the sublime. Yet, Pennant characteristically omits the sublime's defining characteristic – its impact on the perceiving subject.

But the static view of nature assumed by both natural history and the picturesque was tested to the limit by the mountains of the Scottish Highlands. There are moments in Pennant's tours when the sublime features of mountain topography almost inevitably stimulate speculation about the dynamic geological processes that formed them in the distant past. On his second tour, for example, an astonishing mountain landscape in Ross-shire prompts geological reflections:

> Ascend a very high mountain . . . Pass under some great precipices of limestone, mixed with marble: from hence a most tremendous view of mountains of stupendous height and generally of conoid forms. I never saw a country that seemed to have been so torn and convulsed: the shock, whenever it happened, shook off all that vegetates: among these aspiring heaps of barrenness, the sugar-loaf hill of *Suil-bhein* [Suilven] made a conspicuous figure: at their feet, the blackness of the moors by no means assisted to cheer our ideas. (*A Tour in Scotland, MDCCLXXII*, I, pp. 364–5)

Yet Pennant does not go beyond registering the impression that these stupendous mountains appear to have been 'torn and convulsed' by powerful forces at some point in the past and might be of volcanic origin (as the term 'conoid' implies). As we will see, however, there are other passages in Pennant's second tour in particular where the sublime grandeur of Scotland's mountainous terrain coaxes him still further into wondering about the dynamic volcanic processes that forged that landscape in the ancient past.

The Discovery of Extinct Volcanoes in Scotland

Pennant made his tours of Scotland at a time when geological debate in Britain and Europe had begun to pay increasing attention to the nature and effect of volcanoes.[21] Neptunist geotheory, the 'standard model' of the earth's formation and development in the eighteenth century, assigned only a minor role to volcanoes.[22] Yet the second half of the eighteenth century witnessed an increasing attention to active and extinct volcanoes and the extent to which they had shaped, and continued to shape, the earth's geomorphology. Sir William Hamilton, Patrick Brydone and Sir James Hall were just some of 'the Britons who pioneered investigation of Continental volcanoes' in the period (Porter, *The Making of Geology*, p. 163). Hamilton published a number of papers on Vesuvius and Etna in the Royal Society's *Philosophical Transactions* between 1767 and 1772 which were republished in his *Observations on Mount Vesuvius* (1772), thereby making Vesuvius and Etna into necessary viewing on the Grand Tour and helping to make volcanoes into classic manifestations of the sublime.[23] While Hamilton brought active volcanoes to the attention of British naturalists, the writings of geological travellers such as Jean-Étienne Guettard and Nicolas Demarest about the Auvergne region of the French Massif Central, which began to appear in the early 1750s, presented early glimpses of the extent to which volcanic activity in the ancient past had moulded vast landscapes.[24] As K. L. Taylor points out, 'Within a quarter century of Guettard's famous report on the extinct volcanoes of France, similar phenomena were being reported in neighbouring Velay, and in Vivarais, notably by Barthélemy Faujas de Saint-Fond' ('Geological Travellers in Auvergne', p. 76). Shortly after Pennant's second tour of Scotland, John Strange asserted 'that a few days tour in such countries as Auvergne, Velay, and the Venetian state are worth a seven years apprenticeship at the foot of mount Vesuvius or Ætna' ('An Account of Two Giants Causeways', pp. 32–3).

The mid-century debate about volcanoes overlapped with a developing controversy about the nature and origin of basalt.[25] As Laudan notes, 'We now assume that [basalt] flowed from volcanic vents in the earth's crust, in a type of vulcanism known as submarine or Hawaiian. Matters were not so clear in the late eighteenth century; neither its place in the succession, nor its mineralogy, nor its stratigraphic relations, nor evidence from contemporary volcanoes decisively indicated its origin' (*From Mineralogy to Geology*, p. 181). Various features of basalt appeared to support the Neptunist theory that it had been formed by crystallisation in a primeval ocean. Prismatic basaltic columns were interpreted by many mineralogists as 'enormous crystals . . . consistent with basalt's consolidation by water' (*From Mineralogy to Geology*, p. 182). In the Auvergne in 1763 and 1766, however, Demarest linked prismatic columnar basalts and 'what appeared to be flows of basalt back to the volcanic cones. On that basis, he claimed that basalts had a volcanic origin' (*From Mineralogy to Geology*, p. 183).[26] Demarest's 'Mémoire sur l'origin et la nature du basalte' was not published until 1774, but in 1763 Rudolf Erich Raspe's *An Introduction to the Natural History of the Terrestrial Sphere* drew on Robert Hooke's theory of subterraneous heat in order to argue for the igneous origin of basalt and for the significance of volcanoes as major geological agents (*From Mineralogy to Geology*, p. 184). One of Hamilton's papers supported Raspe's theory, arguing 'for the igneous origin of crystalline rocks such as basalt, which in turn suggested widespread volcanic activity over geological time' (Morson, 'Hamilton, Sir William', *ODNB*). Yet the classification of basalt as an igneous rock was a minority view in the 1760s; indeed, Laudan claims that 'The conviction that basalt's mineralogy indicated consolidation from water . . . [continued to seem] self-evident in the 1770s and 1780s' (*From Mineralogy to Geology*, p. 182).

Porter points out that the investigation of European volcanoes in the late eighteenth century had an important impact on the interpretation of Britain's geomorphology, resulting in 'the revolutionary conception that the British Isles harboured ancient volcanoes, identifiable through landscape features and/or formations of lava, pumice, tufa and basalt' (*The Making of Geology*, p. 162). In *A Tour in Scotland, MDCCLXIX*, Pennant's attention to possible volcanic features in Scotland is limited and tentative. In *A Tour in Scotland, MDCCLXXII*, however, his observations gradually convinced him that Scotland's landscape contained the remains of extinct volcanoes. On the northern side of the harbour of East Tarbert on the Kintyre peninsula, he tells us, 'the rocks are of a most grotesque form: vast fragments piled on each other; the faces contorted and undulated in such figures as if created by fusion of matter after some intense heat; yet did not appear to me a lava, or under any suspicion of having been the recrement of a vulcano' (I, p. 188). Pennant becomes more confident, however, about the volcanic origins of other features he observes on the 1772 tour. His description of Arran, which includes the suggestion that a feature near the summit of 'the great hill *Dunfuin*' a couple of miles south-east of Brodick is likely to 'have been the effect of a *vulcano*' (I, p. 211), constitutes one of the first published suggestions that the island had been partly shaped by volcanic processes. Towards the end of the first volume, Pennant reports having explored a hill at 'Beregonium', the supposed site of an ancient city on the southern shore of Loch Etive, from which

> are dug up great quantities of different sorts of pumices, or *scoria*, of different kinds: of them, one is the *pumex cinerarius*; the other the *P. molaris* of *Linnæus*; the last very much resembling some that Mr. *Banks* favored me with from the island of *Iceland*. The hill is doubtless the work of a *vulcano*, of which this is not the only vestige in *North-Britain*. (I, p. 412)

Here, Pennant is more interested in the potentially volcanic remains around Beregonium than in the belief that it was the site of an ancient 'city', and he does not associate it with Ossian's Selma, as later enthusiasts did.[27] In his *Observations on a Tour through the Highlands and Parts of the Western Isles of Scotland* (1800), Thomas Garnett, educated at Edinburgh University and recently Professor of Natural Philosophy at Anderson's Institution in Glasgow, presents a Vulcanist interpretation of Scotland's geomorphology and repeats, almost word-for-word, Pennant's analysis of the hill at 'Beregonium'.[28] But although Garnett frequently refers to Pennant, he fails to acknowledge his priority in identifying the apparently volcanic nature of this hill. Indeed, Garnett conforms to a general pattern of overlooking Pennant's path-breaking contributions to the gradual realisation of the extent to which Scotland's landscape had been formed by volcanic activity in the distant past.

In the second volume of *A Tour in Scotland, MDCCLXXII*, Pennant suggests that the castle hill of Finehaven is an extinct volcano as well as a British antiquity:

> Above the castle, is the hill called the castle hill of *Finehaven*, a great eminence or ridge, with a vast and long hollow in the top. Along the edges are vast masses of stone, strongly cemented by a semi-vitrified substance, or *lava*. . . .

This hill is certainly the effect of a *volcano*; at the one end of the hollow are two great holes of a funnel shape, the craters of the place through which the matter had been ejected. One is sixty feet in diameter, and above thirty deep . . .

On both sides of the hill are found in digging great quantities of burnt earth, that serve all the purposes of *Tarras* or the famous *pulvis puteolanus* or *Puzzolana* [a type of porous volcanic ash], so frequent in countries that abound with volcanoes, and so useful for all works that are to lie under water. (II, p. 166)[29]

Pennant also reports his discovery of 'a considerable quantity of *lava*' on the Hill of Kinnoull near Perth, which is 'a proof of its having been an antient *volcano*' (II, p. 119). Several later travellers would visit this hill because of its supposed volcanic nature. As we will see in the following chapter, Faujas de Saint-Fond's exploration of Scotland in 1784, published in his *Travels in England, Scotland, and the Hebrides* in 1799, deployed his expertise on volcanic geomorphology to interpret the landscape of the Highlands and Islands as almost entirely made up of the products of ancient volcanoes and volcanic activity. Towards the end of his tour, Faujas passed through Perth in order to examine 'the hill of Kinnoul' and found considerable evidence of its volcanic origins. But although he makes several references to Pennant, Faujas does not acknowledge his role in alerting the world to this volcano or to any of Scotland's other volcanic remains.[30]

Following Pennant's tours, reports of volcanic remnants in Scotland started to appear in the *Philosophical Transactions of the Royal Society*, including Thomas West's 'An Account of a Volcanic Hill near Inverness' (1777), which makes no mention of Pennant, and Abraham Mills's 'Some Account of the Strata and Volcanic Appearances in the North of Ireland and Western Islands of Scotland' (1790), which describes volcanic features in several of the Inner Hebridean islands and makes three references to Pennant's 1772 tour without mentioning its identification of volcanic remains in Scotland. Similarly, John MacCulloch's comprehensive survey of the 'trap islands' in *A Description of the Western Islands of Scotland* (1819), which we will examine in Chapter 8, barely mentions the names of any forerunners.[31]

The gathering evidence of Scotland's volcanic past was not uncontested. Volcanic interpretations of Scotland's geomorphology were anathema to Edinburgh's Neptunist natural historians. John Walker

and Robert Jameson steadfastly denied the existence of ancient volcanoes in Scotland and would not have accepted Mills's pronouncement
in the 1790 *Philosophical Transactions* that 'columnar basalts . . . are
now, by almost universal consent, acknowledged to be of volcanic origin' (p. 88). In his lectures on geology at the University of Edinburgh,
Walker insisted that 'In Scotland there are few if any Earthquakes, and
those that have been observed are of no importance. Therefore we
cannot expect Volcanoes here, any more than we can expect a Volcanic Earthquake; and for this reason, that we have no volcanic or . . .
inflammable materials for breeding or feeding Volcanoes' (*Lectures on
Geology*, pp. 211–12).[32] Walker, then, rejected the theory of subterranean heat and treated volcanoes as relatively minor shapers of geomorphology, limited to known volcanic areas and caused by superficial
chemical or mineral deposits. As we will see in Chapter 7, Jameson's
Mineralogy of the Scottish Isles (1800) offers a sustained critique of
the Vulcanist interpretation of Scotland's topography and belittles and
dismisses the volcanic features identified by Pennant, Faujas de Saint-
Fond and Garnet.

The Discovery of Staffa

Pennant's most spectacular discovery of volcanism in Scotland began
with his recognition of the basaltic nature of the island of Staffa
off the western coast of Mull, which he describes as 'a new giant's
causeway, rising amidst the waves; but with columns of double the
height of that in *Ireland*; glossy and resplendent, from the beams of
the Eastern sun' (I, p. 298).[33] It is generally assumed that Staffa was
'discovered' by Sir Joseph Banks on his way to explore Iceland's volcanic landscape and that Pennant was merely a conduit for relaying
Banks's journal account to the outside world by inserting into his tour
an 'Account of Staffa, by Joseph Banks, Esq.' (I, pp. 299–309). My
revision of this story demonstrates that Pennant saw Staffa's basaltic
pillars before Banks and shows that he went on to view Staffa as part
of an astonishingly massive and mostly submerged geological formation that stretched from Ireland to Skye.

Neither Banks nor Pennant can be said to have discovered Staffa in
the strict sense. The island had probably been named by the Vikings,
had long been known to local people and was probably known to the

monks of Iona.[34] Banks's 'Account of Staffa' in Pennant's second tour begins by noting that he first heard about Staffa from 'an *English* gentleman, Mr. *Leach*', whom he met at Sir Allan Maclean's house at Drimnen on the Morvern peninsula opposite Tobermory, who 'no sooner saw us than he told us, that about nine leagues from us was an island where he believed no one even in the highlands had been, on which were pillars like those of the *Giant's-Causeway*' (in Pennant, I, p. 299). The circumstantial details of his own account thus indicate that at least one 'gentleman' had visited Staffa before Banks. Furthermore, Banks's Iceland journal reveals that Staffa was, indeed, inhabited by a small family when he visited the island with Daniel Solander, Uno von Troil, John Cleveley the Younger, Mr Leach, Mr Maclean's son, and others.[35]

But the geological wonders of Staffa were unknown, at least to the outside world, when Pennant and Banks made their separate sea voyages northward along the western coast of Scotland in the summer of 1772. Staffa was first mentioned in print in George Buchanan's *The History of Scotland* (1582). Buchanan drew his information from the manuscript 'Description of the Occidental i.e. Western Islands of Scotland by Mr Donald Monro who travelled through many of them in Anno 1549', which describes Staffa in one sentence and makes no mention of its geology or Fingal's Cave.[36] Although Martin Martin visited and described Mull and Iona, there is no reference to Staffa in *A Description of the Western Islands of Scotland* (1703). In 1760, Richard Pococke's ambitious tour of Scotland, which was not published until 1887 but which Pennant seems to have read in manuscript, includes observations of basaltic columns on the crossing to Iona but does not refer to Staffa.[37] Walker spent nearly a month of his 1764 tour of the Hebrides on and around Iona, and was excited to discover geological features 'at the South Western Extremity of the Isle of Mull' that resembled the Giant's Causeway (McKay (ed.), *The Rev. Dr. John Walker's Report on the Hebrides*, p. 164), but he makes no mention of Staffa.

Banks explored Staffa on 12 and 13 August 1772, but Pennant had sailed past Staffa and noted its basaltic pillars a month earlier on 11 July (*A Tour in Scotland, MDCCLXXII*, I, p. 298). Pennant had not been able to land on the island because of 'rocky seas', but he got Griffith to produce 'an accurate view . . . of its Eastern side' (I, p. 300) which shows the basaltic pillars to the south of the island, but not Fingal's Cave, which Pennant does not mention (Figure 4.2). But although Pennant was the first naturalist to have sighted Staffa,

STAFFA

Figure 4.2 Moses Griffith, 'an accurate view' of Staffa's 'Eastern side' (detail), in Thomas Pennant, *A Tour in Scotland, MDCCLXXII*, I, between pp. 300 and 301. By permission of University of Glasgow Library, Special Collections.

it is notable that he does not contest Banks's claim to priority. That Pennant found it a 'great consolation' to be able to insert Banks's 'Account of Staffa' into his tour, along with copies of some iconic engravings by John F. Millar, James Miller and John Cleveley, 'the professional draughtsmen who accompanied Banks in 1772' (Klonk, *Science and the Perception of Nature*, pp. 74–5), again suggests that the observation of the natural history of Scotland was more important for him than elevating his own status as a path-breaking observer or intrepid traveller. As a consequence, his role in making Staffa into one of Scotland's talismanic places for Romantic travellers and geologists has generally been underplayed.

Banks's 'Account of Staffa' does not fit seamlessly into Pennant's text, however. Stylistic differences between the two writers indicate that my characterisation of Pennant's style cannot be extended without qualification to natural history in general in the period. Far more than Pennant, for example, Banks foregrounds his own subjectivity, personal experience and claims to priority. Banks writes that, after staying overnight on Staffa, he and his party were impatient 'to see the wonders we had heard so largely described'; at first light they 'arrived at the S.W. part of the island, the seat of the most remarkable pillars; where we no sooner arrived than were struck with a scene of magnificence which exceeded our expectations, though formed, as we thought, upon the most sanguine foundations' (in Pennant, *A Tour in Scotland, MDCCLXXII*, I, p. 300). Banks began a long-standing trend by comparing the basaltic formations on Staffa to architectural features and insisting that this natural architecture exceeds even the achievements of ancient Greece. The most sublime feature of all is a magnificent cave:

> With our minds full of such reflections we proceeded along the shore, treading upon another *Giant's Causeway*, every stone being regularly formed into a certain number of sides and angles, 'till in a short time we arrived at the mouth of a cave, the most magnificent, I suppose, that has ever been described by travellers.
>
> The mind can hardly form an idea more magnificent than such a space . . . (in Pennant, I, p. 301)

As well as making the cave the epitome of the sublime and indicating its impact on the perceiving subject, Banks forged a link between its spectacular geology and the Ossian poems by reporting that the island's most striking basaltic feature was called 'Fingal's Cave':

> We asked the name of [the cave]. Said our guide, the cave of *Fhinn*; what is *Fhinn*? said we. *Fhinn Mac Coul*, whom the translator of *Ossian*'s works has called *Fingal*. How fortunate that in this cave we should meet with the remembrance of that chief, whose existence, as well as that of the whole *Epic* poem is almost doubted in *England*. (in Pennant, I, p. 302)[38]

Banks's description of Fingal's Cave was complemented by an influential visual image produced by one of his artists and published in Pennant's tour (Fig. 4.3).[39] MacLeod offers an insightful analysis of the way this illustration refashions this natural feature to look like the product of art:

FINGAL'S CAVE IN STAFFA.

Figure 4.3 Plate based on James Miller's drawing of Fingal's Cave, in Thomas Pennant, *A Tour in Scotland, MDCCLXXII*, I, between pp. 302 and 303. By permission of University of Glasgow Library, Special Collections.

By manipulating the vertical columns which line the cave into smooth pillars, heightening the roof, and shifting the island mass to extend behind rather than alongside the cave, Cleveley [or Miller] created a visual echo of Banks' eulogy to its cathedral-like structure. This image formed the prototype for subsequent versions, such as the frontispiece to Faujas de St Fond's *Voyage en Angleterre* (1797), which distorted the height and regularity of the basalt columns still further in order to enhance the cave's resemblance to the nave of a cathedral. (*From an Antique Land*, p. 139)

After expressing his enthusiasm for Staffa's aesthetic qualities and Ossianic associations, Banks shifts gear to natural history, emphasising that they are quite different registers and modes of experience: 'Enough for the beauties of Staffa, I shall now proceed to describe it and its productions more philosophically' (in Pennant, I, p. 302). Banks's philosophical account includes sets of tabulated measurements of the cave and its pillars and descriptions of the rock materials that make up the cave and island (in Pennant, I, pp. 303–9), thus remaining squarely within the remit of natural history that he would later reimpose on the Royal Society.[40] Although Banks notes that the stratum below the basaltic pillars of the cave has 'very much the appearance of a *Lava*' (in Pennant, I, p. 306), which would imply that volcanic action had played some part in the formation of Fingal's Cave, he does not develop that suggestion, despite the fact that his account of Iceland in his journal reveals his expertise in the analysis of volcanic phenomena.[41] Banks and Pennant both note that Staffa's pillars are formed of basalt (in Pennant, I, pp. 308–9), but neither of them considers questions of causation or history, perhaps because the origin and nature of basalt remained in dispute in the early 1770s.

The Ruins of Creation

When Pennant pointed out the resemblance between one of the pumices from 'Beregonium' on the west coast of mainland Scotland and Banks's Icelandic specimens, he was of course unaware of the possibility that both sets of volcanic rocks might have been produced by the same phase of intense volcanic activity that took place between sixty-five and twenty-three million years ago during the Palaeogene period when the Atlantic Ocean began to open up, dividing Scotland from America, and which encompassed Greenland and Iceland as well as northern Ireland, the west coast of Scotland and the Inner Hebrides.[42] Yet, by this point in his second tour, Pennant had begun to piece together parts of this formation, envisaging that a vast basaltic structure, mostly hidden under the sea, extended from the north coast of Ireland all the way to Skye. As with his discovery of volcanoes on the mainland, however, Pennant's pioneering role in the reconstruction of this massive volcanic formation has gone unrecognised.

On his way to Skye, Pennant sighted 'the rock *Humbla*, formed of *Basaltic* columns', which he informs us 'was discovered by Mr *Murdock Mackenzie*' (I, p. 310).[43] On Skye, Pennant visited

> a high hill, called *Briis-mhawl*, about a mile South of *Talyskir*, having in the front a fine series of genuine basaltic columns, resembling the *Giant*'s causeway: the pillars were above twenty feet high, consisting of four, five and six angles, but mostly of five: the columns less frequently jointed than those of the *Irish*; the joints being at great and unequal distances, but the majority are entire . . . The stratum that rested on this colonnade was very irregular and shattery, yet seemed to make some effort at form. The ruins of the columns at the base made a grand appearance: these were the ruins of creation: those of *Rome*, the work of human art, seem to them but as the ruins of yesterday.
>
> At a small distance from these, on the slope of a hill, is a tract of some roods entirely formed of the tops of several series of columns, even and close set, forming a reticulated surface of amazing beauty and curiosity. This is the most northern *Basaltes* I am acquainted with; the last four in the *British* dominions, all running from South to North, nearly in a meridian: the *Giant's Causeway* appears first; *Staffa* succeeds; the rock *Humbla* about twenty leagues further, and finally the column of *Briis-mhawl*: the depth of ocean in all probability conceals the lost links of this chain. (I, pp. 334–5)

By suggesting that the ruins of the columns at the base of the geological formation he discovered at 'Briis-mhawl' 'were the ruins of creation', in comparison with which 'those of *Rome* . . . seem . . . but as the ruins of yesterday', Pennant indicates both their grandeur and the long timescale involved in the creation and destruction of this feature. Pennant is also implicitly suggesting that his discovery is comparable to Banks's discovery of Fingal's Cave, whose natural architecture, he had claimed, exceeds even the achievements of ancient Greece (in Pennant, I, p. 301). Indeed, Pennant's apparently modest account of his discovery of what he takes to be a massive geological formation stretching from northern Ireland to Skye would appear to outdo Banks. Yet Pennant plays down the potential sublimity of these physical and temporal dimensions and does not speculate about the dynamic forces that might have produced such an enormous geological structure.

Pennant had indeed identified parts of a geological formation which was even more extensive than he imagined and would gradually be reconstructed by geological travellers over the following hundred years or so. D. R. Oldroyd and B. M. Hamilton point out that Sir Archibald Geikie's work on Eigg, which he visited in 1864 and described in *The Scenery of Scotland* (1865), 'suggested that the basaltic lavas of the Hebrides, parts of the mainland, and also across in Northern Ireland, might be mere fragments of what was formerly one vast tract of basaltic lavas' ('Themes in the Early History of Scottish Geology', p. 40).[44] The bulk of the second volume of Geikie's *The Ancient Volcanoes of Great Britain* (1897) is given over to 'The Volcanoes of Tertiary Time', whose eruptions 'assumed . . . colossal proportions' in the north-west

and took the form of fissure-eruptions by which many thousands of square miles of country were deluged with lava. From the South of Antrim all along the West of Scotland to the north of the Inner Hebrides remains of these basalt-floods form striking features in the existing scenery. The same kind of rocks reappear in the Faroe Islands and in Iceland, so that an enormous tract of North-western Europe, much of it now submerged under the sea, was the scene of activity of the Tertiary volcanoes. In entering, therefore, upon a consideration of the British Tertiary volcanic rocks, we are brought face to face with the records of the most stupendous succession of volcanic phenomena in the whole geological history of Europe. Fortunately these records have been fully preserved in the British Isles, so that ample materials remain there for the elucidation of this last and most marvellous of all the volcanic epochs in the evolution of the continent. (p. 108)[45]

But Geikie's account of the gradual discovery and reconstruction of the stupendous volcanic formations in the north-west of Scotland limits Pennant's contribution to relaying Banks's account of Fingal's

Cave to the outside world (*Ancient Volcanoes*, II, p. 109). The earliest important contribution, in Geikie's view, was made by John White-hurst in the second edition of *An Inquiry into the Original State and Formation of the Earth* of 1786, 'who gave a good account of the basalt cliffs of Antrim, and regarded the basaltic rocks as the result of successive outflows of lava from some centre now submerged beneath the Atlantic' (II, p. 109). More developed observations appeared in Mills's 'Some Account of the Strata and Volcanic Appearances in the North of Ireland and Western Islands of Scotland' (*PTRS*, 1790). A decisive contribution was made by Faujas de Saint-Fond, who 'at once recognized the volcanic origin of the basalts of Mull, Staffa and the adjoining islands. His account of the journey, published in Paris in 1797, may be taken as the beginning of the voluminous geological literature which has since gathered round the subject' (II, p. 109).[46] Geikie also commends MacCulloch's survey of the 'trap islands' in *A Description of the Western Islands of Scotland*, the most comprehensive discussion of the basaltic islands of the north-west coast of Scotland in the period covered by the present book (see Chapter 8). MacCulloch refers, for example, to the 'beautiful and conspicuous collection of [basaltic columns] at Great Brish Meal' and says that 'ranges of tolerably defined pillars are also to be seen in many places of this neighbourhood' (*A Description of the Western Islands*, I, p. 374), but he does not mention that Pennant (and Jameson) had visited and described 'Great Brish Meal' before him.

Pennant's pioneering contribution to the reconstruction of the volcanic formation that extends from the north of Ireland to Skye and beyond was therefore largely ignored by subsequent geological travellers and historians.[47] Yet the implications of Pennant's finds were not overlooked by the leaders of the Neptunist school in late eighteenth-century Edinburgh. By 1798, as we have seen, the volcanic interpretation of basalt had become a serious challenge to Neptunist geotheory, which is perhaps why Jameson's account of his own exploration of Skye in 1798 refers rather dismissively to Pennant's basaltic formation on 'Briis-mhawl': 'at little Breeze hill, which is near to the vale of Talysker, there is a pretty colonade of basalt pillars, which, Mr Pennant, in his voyage to the Hebrides, erroneously mentions as the most northern groupe of columns in Scotland' (*Mineralogy of the Scottish Isles*, II, pp. 73–4). Yet when

Jameson later 'discovered' his own impressive columnar formation (of volcanic pitchstone rather than basalt) on Eigg, he ironically extended the colossal formation that Pennant had envisaged
(though he did not associate it with volcanic action).

Pioneering Fieldwork

Pennant's outlook on his journeys through the Highlands and
Islands mostly eschews speculations about past and future, cause
and effect, in favour of observations and measurements of static
features that are severed from causality and history. His mode of
scientific observation, self-representation and writing style may be
illuminatingly compared with the writings of later 'Romantic' geologists, such as Faujas de Saint-Fond's celebration of Staffa's sublime
geology, Hutton's account of Arran, or John Playfair's responses to
Hutton's on-the-spot analysis of Siccar Point. In Romantic geology, speculating about geological origins and processes typically
generates the aesthetic/psychological experience of wonder. For
these later writers, arduous journeys of geological discovery into
the sublime terrain of the Scottish mountains led to encounters with
geological formations that give glimpses into the sublime reaches
of deep time. For Faujas, the journey into the Scottish Highlands
and Islands is a journey into the imaginary past of Ossian and the
ancient past of stupendous geological processes. When Faujas travels to Staffa, the journey itself seems to take place in Ossianic time,
and Fingal's Cave becomes a portal to an even earlier geological
era of volcanic upheaval. Hutton's geological discoveries on Arran
enable him imaginatively to recreate the sequence of events that
formed the island in the deep past and to anticipate its eventual
destruction through the action of uniform processes of erosion over
an enormous time span.

Yet although Pennant was one of Britain's foremost natural historians, who set out to write pioneering natural history tours of
Scotland's Highlands and Islands, what he encountered and discovered there forced him to begin to envision the dynamic shaping
forces that had fashioned the surface of the earth over enormous
time periods. Pennant's careful observations of geomorphic features

can be regarded as pioneering fieldwork for the geological exploration of Scotland in later decades, and his identification of a range of topographical features that he believed were the remnants of ancient volcanoes can be seen to have contributed to the revolutionary concept that the British Isles harboured ancient volcanoes – a concept that was central to Romantic geology's view of the earth as a dynamic system that had been active for an enormously long time. If the history of earth science in the eighteenth century can be plotted in terms of the shift from Enlightenment mineralogy to Romantic-period geology, as both Porter and Laudan suggest, then Pennant's tours of Scotland can be located on the fault-line of that shift.

Notes

This chapter is an extended and revised version of an essay in Constantine and Leask (eds), *Enlightenment Travel and British Identities*, pp. 163–81.

1. Also see Anderson, *Deep Things out of Darkness*, pp. 81–2.
2. Pennant's *British Zoology*, 3 vols (1768–9), was supplemented by a fourth volume in 1770.
3. See The Linnaean Correspondence, <http://linnaeus.c18.net/Letters/display_bio.php?id_person=1193> (last accessed 15 May 2017).
4. Pennant is not mentioned at all in Laudan's *From Mineralogy to Geology* or in Oldroyd's *Thinking about the Earth*; Davies, *The Earth in Decay*, mentions Pennant only once (p. 279), while Rudwick's *Bursting the Limits of Time* sees Pennant merely as the conduit for Joseph Banks's account of Staffa (p. 77); although Dean's *James Hutton and the History of Geology* suggests that Hutton read Pennant's *A Tour in Scotland, MDCCLXXII*, it otherwise ignores him (p. 13). Porter's *The Making of Geology*, however, recognises at least part of Pennant's contribution to British geology (pp. 102, 114, 120, 162).
5. On Pennant's responses to landscape in Scotland, see Smethurst, 'Peripheral Vision, Landscape, and Nation-Building in Thomas Pennant's Tours of Scotland, 1769–72'.
6. Withers discusses Pennant's tours of Scotland in 'Geography, Natural History and the Eighteenth-Century Enlightenment'.
7. For a literary analysis of natural history writing, see Heringman (ed.), *Romantic Science*, and Smethurst, *Travel Writing and the Natural World*.
8. Porter quotes Hans Sloane and Edward Lhwyd.

9. See Laudan, *From Mineralogy to Geology*, pp. 70–102. On eighteenth-century natural history and mineralogy, see Rudwick, *Bursting the Limits of Time*, pp. 37–48, 59–71.
10. See Hallam, *Great Geological Controversies*, pp. 1–28.
11. On travel writing in the Romantic period, see Thompson, *The Suffering Traveller*.
12. On the relationship between Pennant's and Johnson's tours of Scotland, see Jemiely, 'Thomas Pennant's Scottish Tours and *A Journey to the Western Islands of Scotland*'; Jenkins, '"And I travelled after him": Johnson and Pennant in Scotland'; and Chalmers, 'Scottish Prospects: Thomas Pennant, Samuel Johnson, and the Possibilities of Travel Narrative'.
13. See Thompson, *The Suffering Traveller*; Parks, 'The Turn to the Romantic in the Travel Literature of the Eighteenth Century'; Batten, *Pleasurable Instruction*; Stafford, *Voyage into Substance*; and Cardinal, 'Romantic Travel'.
14. Robert Ramsay was appointed to the newly created Professorship of Natural History in 1767 and held the chair, without teaching, until his death in 1779, when he was succeeded by John Walker. The collaborative natural history project set up by Pennant's tours and questionnaires was continued in Scotland by Charles Cordiner in his *Antiquities and Scenery of the North of Scotland in a Series of Letters to Thomas Pennant* (1780) and *Remarkable Ruins and Romantic Prospects of North Britain*, 2 vols (1788–95).
15. Lightfoot's fieldwork in Scotland resulted in his *Flora Scotica* (1777). Stuart was an important local natural historian as well as a Gaelic scholar whose 'knowledge of the Scottish mountain flora was almost without equal' (Mitchell, 'Loch Lomondside Depicted and Described: 5. Early Natural Historians'). Stuart was minister of Luss from 1777 to his death in 1821 and wrote the report on 'The Parish of Luss' in Sir John Sinclair's *Statistical Account of Scotland*. For an account of Stuart's and Lightfoot's collaboration as natural historians and climbers of Scottish mountains, see Mitchell, *Scotland's Mountains Before the Mountaineers*, pp. 41–3.
16. On Griffith's contribution to the visual representation of the Highlands and Islands in the period, see MacLeod, *From an Antique Land*, p. 38. For a more extended account, see Moore, *Moses Griffith*.
17. On the military roads built in the Highlands by General George Wade and William Caulfield, see Ang and Pollard, *Walking the Scottish Highlands*.
18. Unable to visit the Parallel Roads of Glen Roy himself, Pennant gathered information about them in Appendix III (pp. 253–7).

19. On Murdoch Mackenzie's charting of the western coast of Scotland, see Bray, *The Discovery of the Hebrides*, pp. 58–69; for her discussion of Pennant's exploration of the Hebrides, see pp. 70–87.

20. The best account of the picturesque is Andrews, *The Search for the Picturesque*.

21. See Porter, *The Making of Geology*, pp. 160–5, and Laudan, *From Mineralogy to Geology*, pp. 181–93.

22. For Rudwick's account of the standard model, see *Bursting the Limits of Time*, pp. 172–80.

23. For the way Hamilton's publications helped to make volcanoes 'a popular subject in art and poetry and to cause a visit to Vesuvius to be a necessary stage on the grand tour', see Morson, 'Hamilton, Sir William (1731–1803)', *ODNB*. On the sublimity of volcanoes, see Duffy, *The Landscapes of the Sublime*, chapter 2, pp. 68–101.

24. See Taylor, 'Geological Travellers in Auvergne, 1751–1800'. Also see Hallam, *Great Geological Controversies*, pp. 6–9, and Rudwick, *Bursting the Limits of Time*, pp. 203–12. The extinct volcanoes of the Auvergne region of the French Massif Central were first reported in Guettard, 'Mémoire sur la minéralogie de l'Auvergne'.

25. On the basalt controversy, see Rappaport, 'The Earth Sciences', and Klonk, 'Science, Art, and the Representation of the Natural World'; also see Rudwick, *Bursting the Limits of Time*, pp. 62–3, 94, 105–8, 204–7. For a catalogue of historical publications and illustrations, see Ashworth, *Vulcan's Forge and Fingal's Cave*.

26. See Demarest, 'Mémoire sur l'origin et la nature du basalte'.

27. See Gidal, *Ossianic Unconformities*, pp. 76–8, 143.

28. See Garnett, *Observations on a Tour through the Highlands and Parts of the Western Isles of Scotland*, I, pp. 279–80.

29. Shortly after the publication of Pennant's second tour, John Williams, in his *Account of Some Remarkable Ancient Ruins, Lately Discovered in the Highlands, and Northern Parts of Scotland* (1777), identified a vitrified fort on the summit of 'Finaven' (pp. 39–40), a claim which offered an alternative interpretation of some of Pennant's volcanoes.

30. See Faujas Saint-Fond, *Travels in England, Scotland, and the Hebrides*, II, p. 185.

31. See MacCulloch, *A Description of the Western Islands of Scotland*, I, pp. 235–587; II, pp. 1–79.

32. Walker's assertion that volcanoes were not to be found in Scotland was wrong, of course; see Upton, *Volcanoes and the Making of Scotland*.

33. The large pyramidal columns of basalt that made up the Giant's Causeway had long been the subject of debate by British naturalists (see Porter, *The Making of Geology*, pp. 40, 113).

34. For surmises about the local islanders' and Iona's monks' knowledge of Staffa, see MacCulloch, *The Wondrous Isle of Staffa*, pp. 5–7. For a useful account of early travellers' responses to Staffa, see Bunting, *Love of Country*, pp. 103–30.

35. Banks's journals of his Iceland trip were first published in Rauschenberg, 'The Journals of Joseph Banks's Voyage up Great Britain's West Coast to Iceland'. Banks published brief notices of his 'discovery' of Staffa in *The Scots Magazine*, 34 (1772) and *The Gentleman's Magazine*, 42 (1772). Uno von Troil, *Letters on Iceland*, presents an account of Staffa by one of Banks's party. For accounts of Pennant's and Banks's visits to Staffa, see Bray, *The Discovery of the Hebrides*, pp. 70–87, 88–97. On 'The Creation of Fingal's Cave', see Shortland, 'Darkness Visible', pp. 5–10.

36. See MacCulloch, *The Wondrous Isle of Staffa*, p. 3, and Martin, 'A Description of the Western Islands of Scotland Circa 1695' and 'A Late Voyage to St Kilda', with 'A Description of the Occidental i.e. Western Islands of Scotland, by Mr Donald Monro who travelled through many of them in Anno 1549', p. 317, n. 29.

37. See Pococke, *Tours in Scotland*, p. 77. For Pennant's knowledge of Pococke's manuscript, see Kemp's introduction, pp. lxix–lxx.

38. See Faujas Saint-Fond, *Travels in England, Scotland, and the Hebrides*, I, pp. 50–1, note. For a discussion of the origin of the name of Fingal's Cave, see MacCulloch, *The Wondrous Isle of Staffa*, pp. 105–13.

39. This iconic image of Fingal's Cave seems to have been made by James Miller, not John Cleveley, as is often claimed. See Ksiazkiewicz, 'Geological Landscape as Antiquarian Ruin'.

40. Heringman notes that 'In his first decade as president of the Royal Society, Banks had successfully asserted the priority of natural history' over natural philosophy (*Romantic Science*, p. 2).

41. For Banks's description of the volcanic nature of Iceland, see Rauschenberg, 'The Journals of Joseph Banks's Voyage up Great Britain's West Coast to Iceland', pp. 214–25.

42. See McKirdy et al., *Land of Mountain and Flood*, pp. 150–6.

43. Mackenzie's charting of the Hebrides between 1748 and 1769 is discussed by Bray in *The Discovery of the Hebrides*, pp. 58–69; his *Nautical Descriptions of the West Coast of Great Britain, from Bristol Channel to Cape-Wrath* was published in London in 1776.

44. See Geikie, *The Scenery of Scotland*, pp. 141–4, 167–73.

45. For modern geological interpretations of the volcanism of the Inner Hebrides, see Whittow, *Geology and Scenery in Scotland*, chapters 11 to 13; Gillen, *Geology and the Landscapes of Scotland*, chapter 7; and McKirdy et al., *Land of Mountain and Flood*, pp. 151–4.

46. For a contemporary map of Ireland and Scotland which suggested that the basalt features on Mull, Staffa, Eigg, Rum and Skye were once part of a larger formation, see Conybeare, 'On the Geological Features of the North-Eastern Counties of Ireland'.

47. Porter briefly mentions Pennant's contribution to 'the revolutionary conception that the British Isles harboured ancient volcanoes', noting that 'the prismatic basalt formations on Staffa and other Scottish Isles now began to be connected with volcanic action, or at least with flows of molten rocks, whether on the land surface or the sea-bed (Pennant, 1771)' (*The Making of Geology*, p. 162).

Chapter 5

Astonishing Productions of Volcanic Combustion: Barthélemy Faujas de Saint-Fond's *Travels in England, Scotland, and the Hebrides* (1784, 1799)

Barthélemy Faujas de Saint-Fond (1741–1819), who became the first professor of geology at the Museum of Natural History in Paris in 1793, developed an expertise in volcanic geomorphology through extensive explorations of the French Massif Central in the 1770s and early 1780s. As noted in the previous chapter, following Jean-Étienne Guettard's report on the extinct volcanoes of the Auvergne region of central France, Faujas discovered 'similar phenomena . . . in neighbouring Velay, and in Vivarais' (Taylor, 'Geological Travellers in Auvergne', p. 76). Martin Rudwick points out that

> The fine engravings in [Faujas's] handsome volume *Researches on Extinct Volcanoes* (1778) made accessible to others what he claimed was clear field evidence for the Vulcanist interpretation of basalt: his proxy pictures demonstrated that there was a clear connection between prismatic basalts and what were unmistakably volcanoes, albeit ones apparently long extinct. (*Bursting the Limits of Time*, p. 108)[1]

In 1784, Faujas toured England and Scotland, and his account of this tour was eventually published in Paris in 1797, having been delayed by the turmoil of the French Revolution.[2] An English translation was published in London two years later as *Travels in England, Scotland, and the Hebrides; Undertaken for the Purpose of Examining the State of the Arts, the Sciences, Natural History and Manners, in Great Britain*. As we saw in the previous chapter, Sir Archibald Geikie claimed in 1897 that this book made the most important contribution in the eighteenth century to the emerging recognition of the existence of ancient volcanoes in Scotland.[3] Faujas's extended title announces that his two volumes contain 'Mineralogical Descriptions of the Country round Newcastle; of the Mountains of Derbyshire; of the Environs of Edinburgh, Glasgow, Perth, and St. Andrews; of Inverary, and other Parts of Argyleshire; and of THE CAVE OF FINGAL'. Indeed, Faujas repeatedly indicates that his 'principal object' in crossing the channel was 'a journey to the island of Staffa' (I, p. 161), the geological wonders of which had been revealed to the world a decade earlier by Joseph Banks and Thomas Pennant.

Faujas's tour of Scotland can be traced on a section of J. Bayly's 'Map of Scotland, the Hebrides and Part of England adapted to Mr Pennant's Tours', which was included in the 1777 and subsequent editions of Pennant's *A Tour in Scotland, MDCCLXIX* and *A Tour in Scotland and Voyage to the Hebrides, MDCCLXXII* (Figure 5.1). Faujas took the eastern route into Scotland, passed through Edinburgh and crossed the country to Glasgow. From Glasgow his journey to Staffa took him through Dumbarton, Luss, Tarbet, Inverary, Dalmally, Oban and Mull. After visiting Staffa he retraced his steps to Dalmally, travelled to Tyndrum via Glen Lochy, and then passed through Killin, Kenmore, Perth and St Andrews, and returned to Edinburgh along the coastal road through Kirkcaldy.

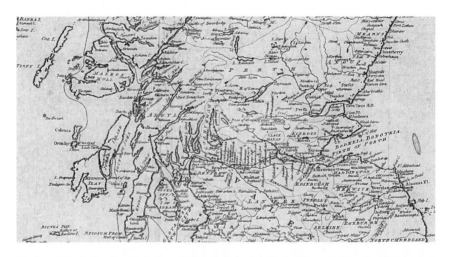

Figure 5.1 J. Bayly, 'A Map of Scotland, the Hebrides and Part of England adapted to Mr Pennant's Tours' (London: B. White, 1777) (detail). Reproduced by permission of the National Library of Scotland.

My interest in Faujas's *Travels in England, Scotland, and the Hebrides* is partly in the way it considerably extends earlier observations of the remains of extinct volcanoes in Scotland. Faujas toured Scotland with a fully formed theory of the origins and formation of mountain scenery and was the first writer to interpret Scotland's mountain terrain as largely made up of the remnants of violent volcanic activity in the distant past. According to Faujas, much of the apparently solid and stable geomorphology of the Highlands and Islands is composed of petrified currents and spurts of burning lava produced by terrible shocks and convulsions at a distant period when subterraneous conflagrations devoured the materials of the earth and reconfigured them into peaks and colonnades. The landscape of Scotland's ancient past is represented as a dynamic system as violent and sublime as any of the classic volcanic landscapes (such as Etna and Vesuvius) that fascinated Enlightenment savants and travellers. By repeatedly comparing Scotland's volcanic geomorphology to that of Velay and Vivarais, and other important sites in Europe, Faujas ranked the Scottish Highlands and Islands alongside landscapes whose exploration had revolutionised geology in the second half of the eighteenth century. As we will see, however, Faujas's Vulcanist interpretation of Scotland's landscape was rejected by two of the most prominent Scottish geologists of the period – James Hutton and Robert Jameson – who were otherwise at odds as proponents of Plutonist and Neptunist geotheories respectively.

But my larger argument in the present chapter concerns the way Faujas's *Travels in England, Scotland, and the Hebrides* constitutes the first 'Romantic' geological tour of Scotland. It does this in several ways. It interprets Scotland's geomorphology as compelling evidence that the earth was a dynamic system that had undergone a number of major 'revolutions' in its long history, most of which had been obscured in what Paolo Rossi calls 'the dark abyss of time' by succeeding revolutions.[4] The notion of a dynamic earth correlates with the emerging 'Romantic' science of the second half of the eighteenth century which saw nature not as an inert mechanism but as a dynamic system of subtle powers and forces – or, in Wordsworth's phrase, an 'active universe'.[5] By viewing Scotland's mountains as the products of powerful geological processes that took place in the unthinkably distant past, Faujas adds the geological sublimity of deep time to emerging Romantic responses to the spatial grandeur of Scotland's mountains. Faujas, indeed, is the first writer examined in the present book who responded to Scotland's mountainous landscape in a fully Romantic way. While natural history aspired to objective empirical description of static objects of nature, Faujas's response to the geomorphology of Scotland involves subjective emotion (usually astonishment) and imaginative reconstruction in ways that correlate with the increasing emphasis on the emotions and the imagination in Romantic theories of mind and poetry in the period.[6] Astonishment, which Edmund Burke identified as the highest effect of the sublime in nature, becomes a leitmotif of *Travels in England, Scotland, and the Hebrides*.[7] By staging the interaction between dynamic geology and the dynamic mind, Faujas reveals that subject and object mutually influence or affect each other in ways that are akin to Romantic theories of the imagination's creative interaction with the natural world. If Faujas made volcanic activity the major shaping force of Scotland's landscape, Wordsworth claimed in the 'Preface to *Lyrical Ballads*' (1800) that good poetry is the 'spontaneous overflow of powerful feelings' and Lord Byron described it as 'the lava of the imagination whose eruption prevents an earth-quake'.[8] Faujas's *Travels in England, Scotland, and the Hebrides* also exemplifies the paradigm shift, traced by Carl Thompson, in which emphasis on the suffering and subjective experience of the traveller marks the onset of Romantic travel writing.[9] Faujas's text pays as much attention to the subjective experience of his travelling self as it does to the geology of Scotland, foregrounding his heroic fortitude as he and his companions endure the difficulties and dangers of journeying through the Highlands and Islands in the late eighteenth century. The endurance of difficulty and danger as a necessary prelude to aesthetic delight was a central strand of Burke's account of the sublime and of Wordsworthian epiphany.[10]

In addition, *Travels in England, Scotland, and the Hebrides* deploys elements of the genre of Romantic quest as Faujas strives to reach his ultimate goal – the island of Staffa, which Banks had made into an irresistible fusion of sublime geology and Ossianic Romanticism. James Macpherson's publication of *Fragments of Ancient Poetry* (1760), *Fingal* (1761/1762) and *The Works of Ossian* (1765), aided by Hugh Blair's 'A Critical Dissertation on the Poems of Ossian' (1763), had played a major role in kick-starting Romanticism in France.[11] Blair summarised the Ossianic image of Highland Scotland's landscape as follows:

The events recorded, are all serious and grave; the scenery throughout, wild and romantic. The extended heath by the sea shore; the mountain shaded with mist; the torrent rushing through a solitary valley; the scattered oaks, and the tombs of warriors overgrown with moss; all produce a solemn attention in the mind and prepare it for great and extraordinary events. ('A Critical Dissertation', p. 356)

As we will see, Faujas's accounts of the landscapes he passed through on his travels in Scotland were thoroughly imbued with Ossian. Faujas's ultimate goal – Fingal's Cave – represented the most powerful fusion of Ossianic sublimity and volcanic geology. As Eric Gidal puts it, Banks's and Pennant's reports on Staffa

helped publicize the island to an even wider audience keen to experience through travel the emotional sublimity of Ossianic verse side by side with the wondrous remains of volcanic eruption and oceanic erosion. Fingal's Cave . . . perfectly combined folkloric romance, sublime aesthetics, and scientific curiosity in a remote and difficult-to-access location at the margins of the British archipelago. (*Ossianic Unconformities*, p. 9)

Heading North

The first volume of *Travels in England, Scotland, and the Hebrides* contains a fascinating account of Faujas's experience of Enlightenment London, including visits to the Royal Society, Greenwich Observatory, Kew Gardens, the British Museum, and meetings with scientific luminaries such as Joseph Banks, Nevil Maskelyne, and William and Caroline Herschel. Through a letter of recommendation from Benjamin Franklin, Faujas also met John Whitehurst, whose *Inquiry into the Original State and Formation of the Earth* had recently been published in London in 1778. Roy Porter describes Whitehurst's geotheory as the 'leading theory of the age'; it combined the idea of a universal primeval ocean with the effects of subterraneous heat, held that a massive 'earthquake-cum-volcano' had precipitated the Noachian Deluge, and claimed that the earth remained both dynamically active and subject to the regular, gradual and continuous processes of nature.[12] Whitehurst made the Peak District into a landscape of geological wonders, and Noah Heringman's analysis of eighteenth-century travel writers' responses to it includes Faujas's account of the Devil's Cave, which 'presents conflicting responses of scientific precision and rationalized wonder' (*Romantic Rocks*, p. 246). But although Faujas makes geological observations in England on his journey to and from Scotland, it is clear that his main interest is in Scotland. He and his party (Count Paul Andreani of Milan, William Thornton, M. de Mecies, and several unnamed servants) set out for Scotland in chapter 5 and cross the border halfway through the first volume; the rest of volume I and the bulk of volume II are devoted to observations and experiences north of the border.

After a brief stay in Edinburgh, Faujas and his companions set out on the road to Glasgow, noting abundant evidence of ancient volcanic activity en route. Three days exploring the geology in the 'environs of Glasgow' led Faujas to announce that there must once have been volcanoes in the Glasgow area comparable to Vesuvius (I, pp. 205–26). Faujas and his party – now including an unnamed 'draughtsman . . . from Edinburgh' (I, p. 226) – headed north on 14 September 1784, passing through Dumbarton and intending to stay overnight in Luss on the west bank of Loch Lomond in order 'to have an opportunity next morning of examining at our ease that beautiful lake . . . [which] is regarded as one of the wonders of the country' (I, p. 232). But having been refused a place to stay in the only hut at Luss, the travellers had to continue on through the night and after a 'tedious and painful journey' arrived 'at half past three in the morning at a place called Tarbet, which was also a single house' (I, p. 234). From Tarbet, Faujas headed west towards Inverary on William Caulfield's military road that took travellers round the head of Loch Long, over the 'Rest and Be Thankful' pass, and round the head of Loch Fyne – a route now followed by the A83 through a remote mountainous landscape that remains imposing.[13] Faujas reports that 'We were nearly six hours in this dismal passage, the road through which is almost impassable; at last it suddenly opened on Loch-Fyne, in Argyllshire' (I, p. 240). After experiencing several days of the civilised, almost Parisian hospitality of the Duke of Argyll at Inverary Castle, the party headed north on the military road to Dalmally, immediately experiencing the 'striking contrast' of entering 'the midst of a chain of mountains of the wildest aspect' where the 'gloomy appearance' of banks of black schistus in the looming mountains 'seems to announce to passengers the mourning of nature in this frightful solitude' (I, pp. 264–5).

Faujas's *Travels* gives the impression that to journey into the Scottish Highlands is to travel back into the remote past of human culture as well as the deep time of geological processes. He presents a detailed description of the dress of a group of Highlanders he encountered at Dalmally and remarks that it has been worn 'from a very remote antiquity' (I, p. 269). He also describes in detail the 'remains of some very ancient monuments' in the vicinity of the local church (I, p. 282). Faujas was also interested in 'monuments of a different kind' at Dalmally (I, p. 290). He acquired the services of Patrick Fraser, the local schoolmaster, to act as guide and interpreter on the route to Oban. Fraser had studied at Edinburgh and spoke English, 'Celtic', Greek and Latin. Faujas found Fraser particularly interesting because he was 'passionately fond of the verses of Ossian; and often made excursions among the inhabitants of the mountains in quest of further fragments of those ancient poems' (I, p. 271). These excursions are implicitly analogous to Faujas's excursions into the same mountains in search of fragments of the ancient volcanic history of the earth.

Among those Mountains which the Exploits of Fingal Have for Ever Signalised

Faujas presents an extended and compelling narrative of the travellers' daunting journey of twenty-four miles through the mountains from Dalmally to Oban along a road which was 'so bad, that it is scarcely passable in carriages' and often required them to walk (I, p. 303). This route, led by Fraser, followed a partially constructed military road round the head of Loch Awe and through the Pass of Brander. Admiring the prospects, attending to the mineralogy of the mountains and examining ancient monuments, the travellers made slow progress, passed up the opportunity to spend the night at Bun Awe halfway to Oban, lost the half-formed road, and got benighted on a mountain in a terrifying thunderstorm. Fraser, who was himself completely lost, did his utmost to extricate the travellers from this dangerous situation. After scouting ahead, he advised that they should 'turn to the left, to avoid falling into the sea; that he believed he heard a stream about two hundred toises distant, and that by gaining its bed we might find some outlet from the rugged track in which we were involved' (I, pp. 314–15).[14] These expedients led the travellers into further danger:

> We turned and arrived with great difficulty, at the brink of a small torrent; but the declivity of the bank was rapid, and the noise of the water announced a deep hollow. It was, however, necessary to attempt this difficult passage through briars and stones. The first carriage and chaise got down without any accident. The second overturned, but was got up before the horses were hurt, and there was nothing damaged but some of our baggage. The third succeeded better.
>
> Having entered the bed of the rivulet we coasted along its banks, walking up to the knees in water. In about a quarter of an hour the noise of a cascade, not far from us, suddenly stopped our progress. A ray of the moon penetrated through the dark clouds, and by its light we observed a few tufted trees, a small meadow, and some cultivated fields. 'We are not far from a house', exclaimed Patrick Fraser, 'we must call for help to enable us to get out of this abyss'. (I, p. 315)

Although the travellers were greatly fatigued and alarmed by their adventure, it also heightened their imaginative and aesthetic responsiveness:

> William Thornton, who possessed a lively imagination, and was passionately fond of the ancient poetry of this country, observed that the place where we were, was not without charms; that it was calculated to inspire grand and romantic ideas; and if he had a glass of rum to drive away the cold, he should be able to write an ode immediately. – 'We are', said he, 'among those mountains which the exploits of Fingal have for ever signalized. The immortal Ossian has trod upon this ground. – His name is dear to the Muses. – My imagination warms.'
>
> He had scarcely repeated these words, which he pronounced with a tone of enthusiasm, when an old man, with his head uncovered, his hair white, and dressed in a floating drapery of the same colour, started up before us. 'It is Ossian!' cried Thornton, 'It is the divine poet himself! Let us prostrate ourselves before him.' The figure, however, which said not a word in reply to this address, and even did not deign to cast a look towards us, stalked gravely across the stream, and suddenly disappeared.
>
> Is it an illusion? Is it a dream? We all exclaimed; for we had all seen the same object, seen it distinctly by the light of the moon. We were astonished, and remained for some time in a state of uneasy expectation; at last we heard the voices of men coming to our assistance. From them we learned that the water-fall was only the sluice of two mills, which had

been opened, and the white phantom an old miller, who, awakened by our cries, ran in his shirt bareheaded to our assistance; but who, seeing horses and carriages, and hearing a language which he did not under-stand, went off, without saying a word, to call his neighbours. These obliging highlanders came eagerly to help us out of our difficulties. They could not conceive how our carriages had descended the steep bank of the stream without being dashed to pieces. It required all the address and strength of these athletic men to draw the chaises out of this abyss. They formed a kind of road with pick-axes, and carried the chaises, as it were, on their shoulders. (I, pp. 316–18)

This episode is interesting for a number of reasons. Firstly, it presents travel in Highland Scotland as fraught with difficulty and danger, thus raising the price of the observations and discoveries that Faujas makes later on. Faujas and his party figure as suffering travellers who exhibit heroic fortitude in ways that correspond with some of the characteristic features of the emerging mode of Romantic travel writing. Secondly, it represents the travellers as imaginative enthusiasts for the Romantic landscape of Scotland and the poetry of Ossian. Thirdly, the Highland-ers are represented as hospitable, heroic and physically robust, fully at home in, and almost a part of, the Highland landscape. Fourthly, the narrative technique and reported speech could easily form part of a Romantic novel rather than a travelogue. The narrative heightens the reader's imaginative engagement and suspense, invites the reader to share the traveller's vision of a ghostly Ossianic figure, and then explains the apparition with matter-of-fact details. The text thus shares features with the 'supernatural explained' technique deployed by contemporary Gothic novelists such as Anne Radcliffe.[15] A further aspect of the episode is the way it foregrounds the role of the imagination, in protagonists and readers, in a way that becomes implicitly analogous to the role of the imagination, in geologist and reader, in reconstructing the dynamic pro-cesses that formed the terrain in which such adventures can occur.

Astonishing Volcanic Geology on the Rugged Coast of Morven

Following the pattern set by earlier natural history travel writers, Faujas tends to separate his summaries of the natural history of particular places from his general narrative. Yet this distinction is often undermined or blurred in that the more formal natural history sections tend to be as equally given to narrative, subjective experience and conjecture as the narrative chapters. Faujas's practice of natural history writing is therefore quite different from what we have seen in earlier chapters. This transformation of natural history can be seen in Faujas's account of Oban, which is formally divided into a description of his general experience and observations (I, pp. 319–29) followed by a separate chapter which presents a 'sketch' of the 'Natural History of the Environs of Oban' (I, pp. 330–60).

In his introductory narrative, Faujas tells us that he remained at Oban for a few days with Fraser and a servant because, unlike his companions, he was unwilling to risk the crossing to Mull in a small boat and opted to wait for a larger fishing vessel. At Oban, he imagined himself 'on the rugged coast of Morven' (I, p. 321), the name of Fingal's kingdom in book III of *Fingal* and located by Macpherson as 'All the North-west coast of Scotland' (*The Poems of Ossian*, p. 428).[16] Here, Faujas spent a few blissful days exploring the local geology, spoilt only by a piper who insisted on playing every evening under his bedroom window. For Faujas, the sea cliffs and mountains of Oban combine Ossianic romance with sublime geological features produced by 'some great revolution in nature, [which] deserves the attention of those who love studies connected with the theory of the earth' (I, p. 328). Relentless Atlantic storms over an enormous time period have exposed the geological structures of Oban's sea cliffs and mountains, revealing features which bear witness to the processes which created them in the deep past:

> A boisterous sea, which beats furiously against the steep rocks, that serve it for a barrier, has disclosed the structure of these hills, which appear to have been heaped one above another by terrible convulsions, and by the action of the two elements of fire and water, in constant opposition to one another.
>
> The bases of these mountains are so worn away, that their flanks are, in a manner, laid open, which gives the observer an opportunity of studying the materials which compose them. He is at first astonished to find so much variety and so much confusion. However great his knowledge, he would soon find himself puzzled, if the vestiges of subterraneous fires, which are easily recognized, did not enable him to explain this discordant collection, so contrary to the usual course of nature.
>
> I examined and re-examined these different materials, with great perseverance; and, far from being discouraged by this chaos, I felt an

increasing interest in exploring it. I was animated also by the desire of being useful to those who should visit the same place after me, by fixing their attention on the most remarkable objects, and presenting them with the sketch of a labour which may put it in their power to make more discoveries than I have done, without having the same difficulties to encounter. (I, pp. 328–9)

This passage foregrounds the subjective experience of the geologist in the face of astonishing geological features which initially appear to be a confused 'discordant collection' of materials that is 'so contrary to the usual course of nature'. The geologist, however great his knowledge, is at first astonished and puzzled by this confusion and chaos, but his desire to understand it and enable others to make more discoveries leads him to examine and re-examine the formations 'with great perseverance'. The key to the puzzle, for Faujas, is that the geologist with relevant experience can easily recognise the 'vestiges of subterraneous fires' that identify these formations as the products of ancient volcanic activity.

But although the following chapter on the 'Natural History of the Environs of Oban' attempts to bring some order to an 'astonishing assemblage of various substances so heterogeneous in appearance' (I, p. 335), it similarly foregrounds the role of subjective experience and hermeneutical processes. Faujas tells us that he was astonished to see that the sea cliffs 'in the environs of Oban' consist of 'vast walls of pudding-stone, some of which are more than two hundred feet high, and sixty feet thick' which 'extend uninterruptedly along the coast, from the right side of the harbour, fronting the sea, to a distance of more than three miles' (I, p. 350). He goes on to note that

> this remarkable pudding-stone, formed by a natural cement of the greatest hardness, is sometimes shaped into insulated peaks, which rise in the form of pyramids, or needles, and present the idea of grand monuments, erected by human hands. I declare, that from the time I have made natural history my principal occupation and pleasure, and during my numerous travels, I have never met with an object of this kind which so much astonished me. (I, p. 351)

The geology of the Oban area, then, is even more astonishing than that of volcanic regions such as Vivarais which Faujas had helped to make into classic sites in the history of geology. While Burke had insisted that astonishment is the highest effect of the sublime in nature, he also claimed that custom and familiarity could nullify the sublime. But Faujas suggests here that knowledge and experience of natural history increase the savant's astonishment at the natural products of the earth's ancient past that confront us in their grandeur. Extensive knowledge and experience allow the savant to notice and explore such features in the first place, and the difficulty of working out the astonishing causal processes that created them increases their impact on the expert observer. The ability to compare and contrast geological features from various locations brings to light singularity as well as similarity. Familiarity with natural history and natural philosophy thus works to defamiliarise particular natural features and adds extra dimensions to the observer's aesthetic response.

The examination of samples of the pudding stone with 'powerful microscopes' allows Faujas to conclude that the geomorphology of the environs of Oban was created by submarine volcanic eruptions:

> The more one examines this immense assemblage of stony substances rounded by attrition, the more one studies the form of these enormous masses, their position in the vicinity of lavas, and their physiognomy (if I may use the expression) – the more also are they found to differ from the ordinary beds of pebbles, which the waters have accumulated in such abundance in various places. One is, therefore, induced to compare them to certain volcanic eruptions, in which water, heated to the highest degree of ebullition, enters into concourse with fire, and the different elastic emanations generated by subterraneous combustion. This may have been the cause of these sudden and tumultuous petrifactions, of which the remains of ancient extinct volcanos every where afford us examples.
>
> I am thence pretty much inclined to ascribe the origin of these astonishing ramparts and huge pyramids of pudding-stone, to volcanic eruptions of a similar nature. For it must be supposed that the sea experiences furious convulsions, when its bottom is rent asunder by violent explosions and earthquakes, produced by water converted into the state of vapour by these terrible convulsions. Vast quantities of matter must then necessarily be displaced; pebbles and stony fragments are united and blended with slime, sand, and volcanic rubbish of every sort, which act as a cement; and there thence result solid masses, which are able to adhere together afterwards, by the effect of a gluten so much the more tenacious, as it is produced by the two most active solvents known, namely, fire and water. (I, pp. 355–7)

Robert Jameson would later claim that he was unable 'to compre-hend this explanation' of the formation of Oban's geology (*Min-eralogy of the Scottish Isles*, I, p. 199). But here I want to attend to the way this passage, once again, foregrounds the processes of analysis and imaginative reconstruction that enable Faujas to envis-age the astonishing geological processes in the deep past that must have produced this 'immense assemblage of stony substances'. The geologist examines objects, compares them with other phenomena, makes suppositions about causes, feels an inclination to ascribe ori-gins, imagines what the sea 'experiences' when its bed is rent asunder by submarine volcanoes and earthquakes and what must then hap-pen. The complex geology of contorted topography sets the mind in motion to work out the dynamic processes that must have pro-duced it. Dynamic geology triggers dynamic aesthetic experience and dynamic interpretive activity.

These passages from Faujas's 'Natural History of the Environs of Oban' exemplify the way that his natural history of particular places is often as equally given to narrative, subjective experience and conjecture as the travel narrative chapters. Natural history here involves the imaginative reconstruction of sublime geological events and processes of the distant past and requires the active participation of an imaginative, geologically informed reader.

Superb Monuments of a Grand Subterraneous Combustion

Faujas's account of the geomorphology of the Oban area forms the climax of volume I of *Travels in England, Scotland, and the Hebri-des*. Volume II centres on Faujas's visit to Staffa, the ultimate goal of his quest narrative. It begins with an account of Faujas's voyage to the island of Mull in the company of 'a young British Officer of the name of McDonald, who had come to wait at Oban for a favour-able opportunity of going to the isle of Sky, which was the place of his nativity' (II, pp. 1–2). McDonald, who 'understood the Earse or Celtic language' and wished to visit Staffa, replaced Fraser as the expedition's interpreter (II, p. 2). After being rowed to Mull, Faujas and McDonald rode from Aros to Lachlan McLean's house at Torloisk on the west coast, undergoing another experience of getting lost and benighted on a lengthy and arduous journey on a 'detestable' road (II, p. 15). When he eventually arrived at his host's house, Faujas learned that the rest of his party had gone to Staffa that morning in two small boats, that the weather had become tempestuous, and that they had not returned as expected. When they did return after two further days of anxious expectation, their narrative of the 'many struggles and dangers' they faced in getting to and getting off Staffa in rough seas serves to increase Faujas's concerns about his desire to visit the island (II, p. 20):

> The details of the adventures of my poor friends, did not much encourage me to attempt the same voyage. Mr. McLean also did not cease to impress me with the inconstancy of the weather, the dangers of disembarking on the island, the advanced period of the season, and his apprehensions lest, could we even seize a favourable moment to waft us thither, we should not find it equally easy to return, and lest we should be obliged to remain there, not only several days like our friends, but perhaps for several months. (II, p. 25)

McLean added his own account of several danger-filled trips that he had made to Staffa, and Faujas inserts a quotation from Pennant to the same effect (II, p. 26, note). The accumulated effect of these travellers' tales is to heighten anxiety, suspense and desire at the prospect of the impending voyage to Staffa. Faujas presents his dilemma in the form of the internal soliloquy of a questing hero working himself up to face the final, most dangerous stage of his quest, addressing himself in a series of questions that are not merely rhetorical:

> All these accounts were not very encouraging, especially to one, who, like me, is almost always sick on the water; but curiosity overcame the suggestions of fear and prudence. What, said I, incessantly to myself, shall I have come in a manner to the very entrance of this renowned cave, and from such a distance too, without enjoying a view of it? Shall I thus easily forego the opportunity of obtaining new information and instructive facts, on a subject of natural history in which I feel so much interest as that of ancient volcanos? and shall I not be able to accomplish what my fellow-travellers have performed? Or, shall I hesitate to encounter the same danger? All these reflexions irrevocably fixed my determination; and I resolved to set out at sunrise next morning, if the sea should be anywise passable. (II, p. 26)

In fact, the weather was unusually fine the following morning, and Faujas was joined on his voyage by Mr McDonald 'and my intrepid friend William Thornton', who had only just returned from Staffa with the other party (II, p. 26).

The epic tone of Faujas's account of his voyage to Staffa is heightened, and the interplay between literary and scientific genres intensified, when he tells us that the three travellers embarked 'under the auspices of the genius who presides over the science of Nature, and to whom we addressed a short invocation' (II, p. 29). They are then rowed to Staffa by 'four young and bold Hebridians, who appeared to undertake this short voyage with pleasure; for they are fond of every thing which reminds them of Ossian, and they seemed to regard it an honour to conduct strangers to the cave of Fingal' (II, p. 28). Indeed, the boatmen are represented as characters who might have emerged from the pages of Ossian: 'To testify to the chearfulness with which [the fine day] inspired them, they began to chaunt in chorus the songs of Ossian. There is not a native of these islands, from the oldest to the youngest, that is not able to repeat, from memory, long passages or hymns of that ancient and celebrated bard' (II, pp. 29–30). Once safely landed on Staffa, Faujas tells us that the two families who then lived on the island in abject poverty welcomed them in a ritual that involved passing a bowl of milk around in a circle, again adding to the sense that these travellers had stepped back into the Ossianic past (II, p. 32). The journey to Staffa and Fingal's Cave thus becomes an Ossianic adventure and even the three travellers accrue an Ossianic aura.

At the conclusion of the welcoming ceremony, Faujas and his friends 'went to work . . . without losing a moment of time' in order to investigate Fingal's Cave and the rest of the island. The results of Faujas's investigation are presented in his 'Description and Natural History of the Isle of Staffa' (II, pp. 38–62), a separate chapter which 'is principally intended for such as employ themselves in the natural history of stones and minerals. If it be considered as rather tedious by those who are not attached to that study, it will be easy for them to pass on to other subjects' (II, p. 37). Faujas warns us that, in contrast with the accounts of Staffa given by Banks and his fellow traveller Uno von Troil, who 'principally attended to the picturesque scenes', he will enter 'into those details which are more particularly interesting to naturalists' (II, p. 41).[17] The chapter includes 'Dimensions of the Cave of Fingal' and a detailed account of the 'Mineralogy of the

Isle of Staffa' (II, pp. 52–3, 57–62). His overall conclusion is that the geological features of Staffa and Fingal's Cave indicate that the island is an extinct volcano which 'has been exposed for so many ages to the fury of a sea full of currents, and agitated with tempests, that it may well be said to have left only the skeleton of a volcanic isle, much more considerable in former times' (II, p. 58). Despite Faujas's warnings, however, this chapter is far from tedious and is not limited to natural history. Indeed, natural history is interlaced with subjective and aesthetic responses from the outset:

> This superb monument of a grand subterraneous combustion, the date of which has been lost in the lapse of ages, presents an appearance of order and regularity so wonderful, that it is difficult for the coldest observer, and one the least sensible to the phænomena which relate to the convulsions of the globe, not to be singularly astonished by this prodigy, which may be considered as a kind of natural palace. (II, pp. 41–2)

Having attempted to distinguish his response from those of Banks and von Troil, Faujas quotes at length from their accounts in order to 'shelter myself from all critical observation on the emotions which I experienced while contemplating the most extraordinary of any cavern known' (II, p. 42). He quotes the passage from Banks's journal, published in Pennant's 1772 tour and examined in the previous chapter, in which Banks says that Fingal's Cave is 'the most magnificent . . . that has ever been described by travellers' and that 'The mind can hardly form an idea more magnificent than such a space' (II, p. 43). Faujas then quotes the following passage from von Troil's *Letters on Iceland* (1780):

> 'when we behold the cave of Fingal, formed by nature, in the isle of Staffa, it is no longer possible to make a comparison, and we are forced to acknowledge that this piece of architecture, executed by nature, far surpasses that of the Louvre, that of St. Peter at Rome, and even what remains of Palmira and Pestum, and all that the genius, the taste, and the luxury of the Greeks, were ever capable of inventing.' (II, p. 44)[18]

These quotations serve to authenticate Faujas's own emotional response:

> Such was the impression made by the cave of Fingal on Sir Joseph Banks, and on the bishop of Linkœping. I have seen many ancient volcanos,

and I have given descriptions of several superb basaltic causeways and delightful caverns in the midst of lavas. But I have never found any thing which comes near this, or can bear any comparison with it, either for the admirable regularity of the columns, the height of the arch, the situation, the forms, the elegance of this production of nature, or its resemblance to the master-pieces of art: though this has no share in its construction. It is therefore not at all surprising that tradition should have made it the abode of a hero. (II, pp. 44–5)

Faujas refers to his extensive experience of ancient volcanoes and basaltic causeways in order to insist on the singularity of Fingal's Cave, and he authenticates his emotional response by showing that Banks and von Troil responded in a similar way. Yet it is striking that such a response should appear in a chapter devoted to a 'Description and Natural History of the Isle of Staffa', given that the disciplinary assumptions of natural history necessarily exclude such emotions and exclamations. Natural history here is being displaced by Romantic geology.

Extraordinary Products of Subterraneous Combustion on Mull

After his extended description of Staffa, Faujas presents a general account of Mull, including the hospitality he experienced at Mr McLean's house at Torloisk and his experience of climbing Ben More, which he identified as volcanic in origin. Following his 'ordinary mode of proceeding', Faujas then switches from travel narrative to natural history, collecting his geological findings on Mull in a separate chapter entitled 'Natural History of the Island of Mull' (II, pp. 105–43) so 'that such of my readers as are interested in that science may find the objects which refer to it, united under one head, and that those to whom the subject may be indifferent or tiresome, may easily pass it over' (II, p. 104). As in the other instances we have looked at, however, Faujas's chapter on the natural history of Mull is as enthralling as the main narrative.

In his 'Natural History' of Mull, Faujas recaps his experience of the various stages of his journey round the island, revealing that he found evidence of extinct volcanoes everywhere he went.[19] But the bulk of this chapter is given over to an extended analysis of what he earlier refers to as 'one of the most astonishing productions of volcanic combustion that I ever had an opportunity of observing' (II, p. 102). His description of this feature, which he discovered near 'Achnacregs' (presumably Auchnacraig, on the east coast of Mull directly opposite the island of Kerrera), suggests that it might be a trap vein associated with a 'ring dyke' or a 'cone sheet', both of which are quite common on Mull:[20]

> To the north of Achnacregs, on the right side of the road from the house, and about six hundred toises distant from it, we observed, close by the sea, a natural platform of a semi-circular shape, situated on an eminence which is about a hundred and fifty feet above the level of the water, and which is entirely composed of black lavas of a basaltic nature. This small plain, which has a gentle slope, is bounded on the south by a perpendicular volcanic cliff.
>
> A vast detached wall lines a portion of the circle, formed by a basaltic rock which rises in the opposite quarter, and there thence results a kind of antique circus that fills one with astonishment at the first glance, and gives this singular place the appearance of a ruin as extraordinary as picturesque.
>
> The objects assume a new character of grandeur in proportion as they are approached; and the picture becomes more striking when the height of the wall and its astonishing regularity are viewed from a near situation.
>
> At first, one is lost in considering how, or from what motive, human beings should have raised, in a place so remote and desert, a monument presenting the image of a Roman circus. The further the observer advances, the more surprising does this kind of arena become. A large angular breach in the midst of the wall permits the eye to discover the interior of this antique ruin. On approaching the opening he feels a lively curiosity intermixed with uncertainty, respecting the nature of the object presented to his view. Such at least were the sensations that my companions and myself experienced the first time that we went to see this remarkable place, which we conceived, even when quite close to it, to be a monument of art.
>
> There is nothing here, however, but the work of nature, and one of the most extraordinary productions of subterraneous combustion; no less astonishing, perhaps, in its kind, than that which gave existence to the cave of Fingal. (II, pp. 125–6)

By emphasising the scale of this feature, the powerful forces that had formed this extraordinary production of subterraneous combustion, and its immense antiquity, Faujas invokes all the resources of the geological sublime. But what also interests me in this passage is that rather than objectively describing and analysing the geological feature itself, Faujas offers a narration of the perceiving subject's gradual coming to terms with it. At first glance, the observer is filled with astonishment because 'this singular place' has 'the appearance of a ruin as extraordinary as picturesque'. As the observer approaches the formation, 'The objects assume a new character of grandeur . . . and the picture becomes more striking when the height of the wall and its astonishing regularity are viewed from a near situation'. But the illusion that this is a ruined antique building is not immediately dispelled by a nearer approach, and the observer is thrown into perplexity: 'At first, one is lost in considering how, or from what motive, human beings should have raised, in a place so remote and desert, a monument presenting the image of a Roman circus. The further the observer advances, the more surprising does this kind of arena become.' Although 'this antique ruin' enables the 'eye' to 'discover [its] interior', the observer's perplexity is not dispelled: 'On approaching the opening he feels a lively curiosity intermixed with uncertainty, respecting the nature of the object presented to his view.' The hermeneutic suspense is partly resolved in the following paragraph – this is a geological rather than an architectural ruin – but the sense of sublimity and astonishment are, if anything, heightened by this revelation.

As well as narrating the observer's subjective experience of engaging with this geological feature, Faujas also emphasises its singularity. Although comparisons are made with Fingal's Cave, the Mull ring dyke affects Faujas, a seasoned observer of the products of ancient volcanoes, because he has never seen anything like it before. In his imaginative reconstruction of the geological processes which must have formed this feature, Faujas invokes the actions of known or plausible geological processes, but stresses that they have combined here to produce a unique feature. While he insists that the earth's geomorphology has been shaped by natural processes that are consistent across time and in all places, they can nonetheless work to produce singular and astonishing features in particular places and circumstances. Just as Romantic poetry gave a new importance to local places, in contrast to the generalising tendency of Enlightenment poetry, so too does the Romantic geologist value individual geological formations in particular locations.[21]

Faujas also foregrounds the problem of writing about singularity. He compares the appearance of the basaltic wall with 'the manner in which the wood for firing is arranged in the wood-yards of Paris' (II, p. 128) and emphasises the necessity of using comparisons with ordinary objects in describing singular and extraordinary geological phenomena:

> I am obliged to use this trivial comparison, in order to make myself better understood. It is not easy to be perspicuous, and at the same time to avoid fatiguing the reader with details too minute or imperfectly expressed, when it is necessary to describe objects which Nature seems to have produced in her capricious moments, to embarrass us with aberrations of which she exhibits a few examples only. (II, p. 129)

In addition to using commonplace similitudes, however, Faujas also deploys the trope of inexpressibility that had become conventional in accounts of sublime phenomena and experience: 'I am fully conscious of my inability to express all that I saw, or felt, on seeing the volcanic circus in the vicinity of Achnacregs' (II, p. 129). The emphasis here is at least as much on the inner experience of the observer and on the observer's effort to communicate that experience as it is on the nature of the geological phenomenon itself. These passages stage the encounter between geologist and geological formation, highlighting the effect the object has on the subject and the subject's efforts at understanding that object and communicating its effects. As such, Faujas's writing here is closely akin to the way Romantic poetry stages the complex mutually constitutive encounter between poet and natural world.

After presenting the measurements of this geological monument, Faujas highlights the difficulty of conceiving 'how the lava, when flowing, could have formed a wall so high, of such regular construction, unconnected with any other mass, and composed entirely of differently sided prisms, placed horizontally by the side of each other, with such order and symmetry, that the art of the most able stone-cutter could never have arranged them with equal dexterity' (II, p. 131). He nonetheless attempts imaginatively to reconstruct the natural processes that built this imposing 'circus' and simultaneously narrates the means by which he came to a 'remarkable theory' (II, p. 132). Understanding this theory requires an effort of imagination on the part of the reader as well as the observer:

Let the reader imagine to himself, for a moment, two streams of lava of a considerable thickness, which at the time of some great eruption, have flowed parallel to each other, with an interval of several toises between them. The case is not without a precedent, at Ætna, the volcano of the isle of Bourbon, and elsewhere. From these two streams result a long and deep gallery, or a kind of covert-way, more or less straight, more or less circular or winding, according to local circumstances, and the obstacles which might have occurred in their progress. (II, pp. 132–3)

With the two parallel lava walls in place, Faujas imagines – and requires us to imagine – that another stream of basaltic lava flowed into this 'mould' and 'thus created a wall something similar to the cased walls of the Romans' (II, p. 136). The outer walls, which Faujas supposes were less solid than the basaltic core, were then eroded by the sea to leave a wall which 'would appear to have been erected in a miraculous manner, and to have arisen out of the earth as an amphitheatrical decoration' (II, p. 137). He then claims that his imaginative reconstruction 'is precisely what happened in the present case' (II, p. 137). Volcanoes, then, although they are 'frequently the agents of destruction, are able to create, or rather to imitate, by a succession of accidental circumstances, productions which cannot be effected by mankind without much labour and a train of tedious and difficult means and combinations' (II, p. 141). The only remaining aspect of this basaltic wall twenty-five feet and ten inches high that needs to be explained is that it is now forty feet above the level of the sea. Given the supposed role of the sea in forming it, Faujas concludes that 'it must follow that the sea has fallen sixty-five feet ten inches in that quarter, unless we suppose that the coast has been elevated by the incalculable efforts of some vast subterraneous explosion' (II, p. 142).

Faujas, then, makes much of this volcanic feature on Mull's east coast and his effort to interpret it. It is thus notable that both Jameson and John MacCulloch would later go out of their way to trivialise this feature and Faujas's enthusiasm for it. In *Mineralogy of the Scottish Isles*, Jameson summarily dismisses Faujas's interpretation of this formation:

The occurence [*sic*] of veins of basalt crossing a similar rock, seems to be very rare; as I am well informed, that foreign mineralogists, have never observed such appearances. Mr Faujas St. Fond, in describing this part of the island, seems to have been much struck with one of these veins, which he compares to a circus; and has given a long detail, of the way in which it may have been formed. This was all very unnecessary, as this vein does not differ from many others to be observed in the island; and the idea which Mr St. Fond raises of its magnificence, is far stretched – it is trifling when compared with the grand appearances upon the coasts of Isla and Jura. (I, pp. 203–4)

Jameson insists that Faujas was mistaken in his Vulcanist interpretation of the basaltic vein near Auchnacraig and implies that his inexperience led him into overblowing and mystifying what is actually a common-place feature in the Western Islands. In *A Description of the Western Islands of Scotland* (1819), MacCulloch writes that

> I must not terminate this account [of Mull] without mentioning the frequency of trap veins throughout the island. These are indeed so invariably present in all parts of Scotland where trap predominates, that I have rarely thought it necessary to give a particular description of them, unless where they were attended with unusual or instructive appearances. I know of few such in Mull. They are frequently conspicuous for their permanence after the surrounding strata have been removed, a character which they also possess in Isla, in Jura and elsewhere. One of them has been described in high colouring by Faujas de St. Fond, but there are innumerable others far more conspicuous in the northern division of the island. (I, p. 578)

Shortly after exploring this geological feature on Mull, Faujas returned to Oban. He travelled to Dalmally on 7 October without further misadventure, and then took the military road through Glen Lochy to Tyndrum. From Tyndrum he proceeded to Kenmore on Loch Tay, and then passed through Perth in order to examine 'the hill of Kinnoul' (II, p. 185), a desire which must have been stimulated by Pennant's suggestion in part II of his *Tour in Scotland, 1772* that it was an extinct volcano.[22] From Perth, Faujas headed east to St Andrews and then took the coastal road through Kirkcaldy towards Edinburgh, seeing evidence of ancient volcanic activity, together with erratic boulders and standing stones, all along the way.

Edinburgh's Geology and Geologists

Chapter 14 of volume II of *Travels in England, Scotland, and the Hebrides* is given over to an extended description of Faujas's second stay in Edinburgh (II, pp. 222–54). He begins with an account of Edinburgh's institutions related to 'The sciences, literature, natural history, and the arts', including the Antiquarian Society, the College of Physicians, the College of Surgeons, the Medical Society and the High School of the City (II, p. 222). Edinburgh University is characterised by a list of 'the names of those who were at this time its professors' – a list that includes many of the principal figures of the Scottish Enlightenment (II, p. 223). The Royal Society of Edinburgh, formed the previous year out of the Edinburgh Philosophical Society, is characterised by a similar list, including Adam Smith, James Hutton and John Playfair (II, p. 224). Faujas 'visited, as often as possible, the celebrated chymist, Dr. Black' (II, p. 231), 'had the pleasure of dining with Doctor Cullen, . . . one of the most celebrated physicians of Europe' (II, p. 237), and 'saw several other men distinguished in various branches of literature, among whom were Doctor Anderson, Sir John Dalrymple, and the celebrated historian Doctor William Robertson' (II, p. 240). In addition, 'That venerable philosopher, Adam Smith, was one of those whom I visited most frequently' (II, p. 240).

The presence of these men and institutions in Edinburgh, along with the chair of natural history occupied by John Walker and 'The cabinet of natural history, in the university',[23] leads Faujas to proclaim that the city is on the verge of becoming an important centre for the study of Scotland's rich natural history (II, p. 229). Yet, despite the fact that Walker's lectures made use of the collection of minerals he had gathered during his extensive travels in the Highlands and Islands, Faujas asserts that mineralogy is the least developed of the sciences in Edinburgh:

> Lithology, and the study of minerals, have as yet made little progress in Scotland. There are therefore few collections of these objects. Doctor James Hutton is, perhaps, the only individual in Edinburgh who has placed in his cabinet some minerals and a number of agates, chiefly found in Scotland; but I observed, that he had not been sufficiently careful in collecting the different matrices which contained them. I therefore experienced more pleasure in conversing with this modest philosopher than in examining his collection, which presented me with nothing new, since I had seen and studied upon a large scale and in the places where nature had deposited them, almost all the specimens of his collection.
>
> Doctor Hutton was at this time busily employed in writing a work on the theory of the earth. (II, pp. 229–30)

These comments indicate that Faujas visited Hutton at his home on St John's Hill in Edinburgh, that the two geologists probably discussed their related but different geotheories, and that Faujas may have read Hutton's theory of the earth in draft. Dennis Dean surmises that Hutton and his guest probably walked together 'to Arthur's Seat, which Saint-Fond . . . immediately (and for Hutton unacceptably) identified as an extinct volcano' (*James Hutton and the History of Geology*, p. 15).

Indeed, Faujas 'found the greatest part of the learned men of this city obstinately prejudiced' against his claim that Arthur's Seat, Salisbury Crags, the castle rock and Calton Hill are all volcanic and that 'the operation of subterranean fire is manifest every where around Edinburgh' (II, pp. 250, 253). Unfortunately, the 'large collection of volcanic substances, and other interesting mineralogical specimens' that Faujas gathered in and around Edinburgh and throughout Scotland were lost when the ship carrying them back to France sank off the coast of Dunkirk (II, p. 249). 'If my valuable collection had not been lost', Faujas suggests, 'I should have described a series of volcanic productions which would have removed every doubt on this subject, and demonstrated that the vicinity of Edinburgh has been the prey of ancient volcanos, since it still exhibits lavas similar to those of Etna and Vesuvius' (II, pp. 253–4).

Dean suggests that Hutton was one of 'the learned men of this city' who was 'obstinately prejudiced' against Faujas's volcanic interpretation of Edinburgh's hills. Hutton's resistance was influenced by his desire to maintain a distinction between lava and basalt:

> While Hutton clearly favoured observations supporting the igneous origin of basalt, he demurred from identifying basalt with lava. Though both flowed from volcanoes, lava, he believed, had been erupted from the volcano's mouth or some other surface aperture. Basalt, on the other hand, was wholly subterranean, though it could be exposed subsequently through the erosion of overlying sediments. (*James Hutton and the History of Geology*, p. 14)

Hutton's reluctance to accept the volcanic origins of Edinburgh's hills highlights a fundamental difference between Plutonist and Vulcanist geology. While both theories stress the role of subterranean heat and pressure in shaping the earth's geomorphology, they envisage different mechanisms and look for different evidence. Hutton wanted to distinguish between basalt and lava because he assumed that basaltic intrusions were empirical evidence for his theory that many rocks and elevated formations were 'indurated' and raised by subterraneous heat and pressure.[24] Hutton was, of course, very familiar with Arthur's Seat and Salisbury Crags, whose basaltic features were interpreted in support of his own theory:

> 'On the south side of Edinburgh,' he observed, 'I have seen, in little more than the space of a mile from east to west, nine or ten masses of whinstone [basalt] interjected among the strata' [*Theory*, I, pp. 153–4]. This was primarily at Salisbury Crags, adjacent to Arthur's Seat, where part of the relevant exposure is now termed 'Hutton's Section'. (Dean, *James Hutton and the History of Geology*, p. 11)[25]

Modern geologists would say that Faujas and Hutton were both partly right: while Arthur's Seat is the remnant of an ancient volcano, Salisbury Crags is the glaciated remains of a Carboniferous sill.[26]

The British reception of Faujas's *Travels in England, Scotland, and the Hebrides* was varied and revealing. Hutton does not mention Faujas in his *Theory of the Earth* (1795), but the reviews in London journals were generally favourable.[27] In his *Observations on a Tour through the Highlands and Part of the Western Isles of Scotland, Particularly Staffa and Icolmkill* (1800), Thomas Garnett quotes Faujas favourably several times.[28] But the mainstream of Edinburgh's geology, committed to the Neptunist model of the earth's formation and development, either ignored or dismissed Faujas's interpretation of Scotland's geomorphology. Walker does not mention Faujas in his lectures on natural history, and firmly rejects the possibility that Scotland contains volcanoes or vestiges of volcanoes. In his *Mineralogy of the Scottish Isles* (1800), Jameson – Walker's protégé and successor to the chair of natural history – emphatically rejects Faujas's theory, methodology and conclusions:

> Professor Faujas de St. Fond has given us a short account of the mineralogy of the environs of Glasgow; but his descriptions are unluckily obscured by a rigid adherence to a theory which has no foundation in nature. He considers all the rocks we have now mentioned, as lavas; and those he denominates balsatic, porphyritic, and granitic lavas. I do

not hesitate a moment in saying, that, in my opinion, there is not in all Scotland the vestige of a volcano. I do not rest this assertion upon my own authority, (for that would be presumptuous;) but upon that of Dr. Walker, who has examined more of the mineralogy of Scotland than any man now living, and whose collection of Scotch fossils is the largest that has ever been made. Besides, it wars with every principle of systematic classification, to arrange and denominate fossils from any *theory* we may adopt as to their formation. (I, p. 5)

It would be facile to point out that Faujas was right and that Walker and Jameson were wrong regarding the presence of ancient volcanoes in Scotland. It is more interesting and revealing to try to reconstruct the assumptions that fuelled this geological disagreement. Jameson criticises Faujas for allowing his false Vulcanist theory to distort his observations of the mineralogy of the environs of Glasgow and for intermixing 'his theoretical speculations with the description of the strata' of the Oban area (I, p. 198). Jameson, then, like his teacher, assumes that it is possible to put aside theory and that doing so will allow the mineralogist to present fully objective observations. Faujas's *Travels in England, Scotland, and the Hebrides*, however, suggests that geotheory and imaginative reconstruction play a central creative role in interpreting geological processes and formations. For Faujas, the earth's crust has been shaped by a series of dynamic revolutions in deep time and the observer is compelled to enter into a dynamic, imaginative relationship with the vestiges of those revolutions in order to understand their nature and origins. For Walker and Jameson, however, while the landscape of Scotland had been formed in the distant past by dynamic aqueous forces, it was now more or less static and required the natural historian to observe it in a neutral manner: subject and object remain separate and have no effect on one another. But although Walker and Jameson supposedly rejected geotheory in favour of empirical observation, their travel writings and lectures were deeply informed by their commitment to the standard Neptunist theory of the earth. While Faujas can be called the pioneer of a Romantic Vulcanist interpretation of Scotland's landscape, the mainstream of Edinburgh geology, as represented in Walker's lectures on natural history and Jameson's tours of Scotland, was committed to empirical natural history underwritten by a Neptunist theory that was taken as a given. Nonetheless, as we will see in Chapter 7, Jameson's 'objective' readings of Scotland's geomorphology were intrinsically shaped by his desire to refute Faujas and Hutton and did so, moreover, by deploying and reworking his own imaginative and aesthetic responses to astonishing geological features.

Notes

1. See Faujas de Saint-Fond, *Recherches sur les volcans éteints du Vivarais et du Velay* and *Minéralogie des volcans ou description de toutes les substances produites ou rejetées par les feux souterrains*.
2. Faujas de Saint-Fond, *Voyage en Angleterre, en Ecosse et aux Iles Hebrides*.
3. See Geikie, *The Ancient Volcanoes of Great Britain*, II, p. 109.
4. See Rossi, *The Dark Abyss of Time*.
5. On the Romantic vitalist view of nature, see Piper, *The Active Universe*; Levere, *Poetry Realized in Nature*; Bewell, *Wordsworth and the Enlightenment*; Heringman (ed.), *Romantic Science*; and Holmes, *The Age of Wonder*.
6. The centrality of the imagination to Romanticism has long been a given, but see Engell, *The Creative Imagination*.
7. See Burke, *A Philosophical Enquiry into the Origin of our Ideas of the Sublime and Beautiful*, p. 57.
8. See Byron's letter to Annabella Milbanke, 29 November 1813, in Marchand (ed.), *Byron's Letters and Journals, Vol. 3: 1813–1814*, pp. 178–80 (p. 179).
9. See Thompson, *The Suffering Traveller and the Romantic Imagination*.
10. The interrelationship between epiphany and the endurance of danger and difficulty in Wordsworth's poetry is best seen in the 1805 *Prelude*, especially in the climbing Snowdon episode in book 13.
11. For the impact of Ossian on French Romanticism, see Carboni, 'Ossian and Belles Lettres', and Hook, 'The French Taste for Scottish Literary Romanticism'.
12. See Porter, *The Making of Geology*, pp. 124–7.
13. On the military roads built in the Highlands by General George Wade and William Caulfield, see Ang and Pollard, *Walking the Scottish Highlands*.
14. In France before 1812, one *toise* was the equivalent of six *pieds* (just under two metres).
15. On the 'supernatural explained' in Gothic novels of the period, see Clery, *The Rise of Supernatural Fiction*, pp. 106–14.
16. 'Morvern' is actually the name of the land mass NNW of Oban across Loch Linnhe.

17. For Banks's account of his two days on Staffa, see Rauschenberg, 'The Journals of Joseph Banks's Voyage up Great Britain's West Coast to Iceland', pp. 206–9.

18. See von Troil, *Letters on Iceland*, pp. 266–88.

19. On Mull's volcanic terrain, see Stephenson, *Mull and Iona: A Landscape Fashioned by Geology*, and Gillen, *Geology and Landscapes of Scotland*, pp. 157–9.

20. See Friend, *Scotland: Looking at the Natural Landscapes*, pp. 180–96; Gillen says that 'ring dykes were intruded in abundance' on Mull (*Geology and Landscapes of Scotland*, p. 158); also see Emeleus and Bell, *The Palaeogene Volcanic Districts of Scotland*, pp. 126–34.

21. On the importance of 'locality' in geological history, especially at the end of the eighteenth century, see Oldroyd, 'Non-written Sources in the Study of the History of Geology'. On the importance of local places in Romantic poetry, see Bate, *The Song of the Earth*, pp. 205–42; Lamont and Rossington (eds), *Romanticism's Debatable Lands*; Stafford, *Local Attachments*; and Fielding, *Scotland and the Fictions of Geography*, pp. 4–11.

22. See Pennant, *A Tour in Scotland, MDCCLXXII, Part II*, p. 476.

23. See Withers, '"Both Useful and Ornamental": The Rev. Dr. John Walker's Keepership of Edinburgh University's Natural History Museum'.

24. In his 'Observations on Granite' (1794), Hutton says that his *TRSE* 'Theory of the Earth' paper maintained 'that all the solid strata of the earth had been consolidated by means of subterraneous heat, softening the hard materials of those bodies; and that in many places, those consolidated strata had been broken and invaded by huge masses of fluid matter similar to lava, but, for the most part, perfectly distinguishable from it' (p. 77). This is a summary of his argument in 'Theory of the Earth' (*TRSE*, 1788), which was expanded to form the second section of chapter 1 of his *Theory of the Earth*.

25. For Hutton's interpretation of Arthur's Seat and Salisbury Crags, see *Theory of the Earth*, I, pp. 153–8, and II, pp. 417–18; on Calton Hill, see *Theory of the Earth*, I, pp. 96–7, 158. Also see Hutton's 'Of Certain Natural Appearances of the Ground on the Hill of Arthur's Seat'.

26. See Friend, *Scotland: Looking at the Natural Landscapes*, pp. 161–79.

27. See Anon, 'Travels of Citizen B. Faujas Saint-Fond', a favourable review with extensive quotations. There are substantial extracts, especially from Faujas's account of the adventurous journey from Dalmally to Oban, in *The Monthly Epitome and Catalogue of New Publications* (1797–1802), vol. 3, pp. 60–7.

28. See I, pp. 227–9, and II, pp. 126–8.

Chapter 6

James Hutton's Geological Tours of Scotland (1764–1788)

James Hutton (1726–97), Scotland's most famous geologist, is often described in biographies and popular histories as the 'founder' of modern geology and as the first savant who challenged the Christian Church's view, based on Bishop Ussher's reading of the Bible, that the earth was about six thousand years old.[1] But most scholarly histories of geology which take a European-wide perspective tend to downplay Hutton's contribution to the history of geology and point out that he was far from being the first natural historian to push back the limits of time beyond the biblical span.[2] Such histories also tend to view Hutton's work not as geology but as 'geotheory' – a genre which Martin Rudwick defines as aiming to develop an a priori theoretical model that would explain the system and causal development of the earth's geomorphology (*Bursting the Limits of Time*, pp. 133–9).[3] Stephen Jay Gould seeks to dispel the 'myth' that Hutton developed his theory after extensive empirical investigation, suggesting that it was pre-shaped by a model of cyclical time which virtually eliminates any possibility of imagining a sequential history of the earth and by 'an unswerving conviction' that the earth 'was constructed as a stable abode for life, in particular for human domination' (*Time's Arrow*, pp. 61–91, 74). In what follows, however, I want to examine the role that empirical fieldwork played in the formulation and reformulation of Hutton's theory of the earth, paying particular attention to the contribution of his geological tours of various parts of Scotland in the 1780s, the manuscript accounts of which remained unpublished for a hundred years after Hutton's death and which Rudwick and Gould overlook. Without wishing to reinstate claims that Hutton was the founder of geology, I will highlight the way Hutton's discoveries in Scotland challenged the standard geotheoretical paradigm of the period and revolutionised the interpretation and representation of Scotland's landscape.

Most geotheories in the late eighteenth century, as we have seen, were variants of 'Neptunism', whose characteristic assumption was that most rocks, apart from those produced by the odd volcano, were chemical precipitates or sedimentary deposits from a primeval universal ocean whose sequence revealed the order of their formation. Hutton's geotheory broke with the Neptunist model in several fundamental ways. For Hutton, the primary agency in the production of rock materials was not oceanic precipitation but subterraneous heat and pressure, and the land masses had not emerged from the primeval ocean's subsidence but had been raised (and were continually being raised) by the same subterraneous forces (a theory which led to him being labelled a 'Plutonist'[4]). And while most Neptunist theories held that the formation of the earth's rocks and geomorphology had been completed in the recent or distant past and they were not subject to any further significant change, Hutton argued that rocks and landforms are continually being eroded by weathering agents, carried by streams and rivers to the bottom of the oceans, consolidated or transformed by subterraneous heat and pressure and then uplifted by those forces to become new land masses. Such processes, he argued, have acted uniformly over a vast timescale and will continue to do so without prospect of an end, a vision he articulated in the most famous and controversial sentence he ever wrote: 'The result, therefore, of our present enquiry is, that we find no vestige of a beginning, – no prospect of an end' ('Theory of the Earth', p. 304). According to G. Y. Craig, Hutton's description of this 'geostrophic cycle' constitutes 'possibly the single most important concept in modern geology' and this is the main reason why Hutton has been celebrated as the founder of geology (*James Hutton's Theory of the Earth*, p. 5).[5]

An early version of Hutton's geological theory was first aired in the spring of 1785 in a paper read at two successive meetings of the Royal Society of Edinburgh (by Joseph Black on 7 March, and Hutton himself on 4 April). Shortly afterwards, a twenty-eight-page *Abstract of a Dissertation Read in the Royal Society of Edinburgh . . . Concerning the System of the Earth, its Duration, and Stability* was published to enable discussion in the Royal Society. In early 1786, Hutton's 'Theory of the Earth; or an Investigation of the Laws Observable in the Composition, Dissolution, and Restoration of Land upon the Globe' was published as an author's separate before appearing two years later in the first volume of the *Transactions of the Royal Society of Edinburgh*. The centrality of this article for Hutton is indicated by the fact that a slightly revised version was used as the opening chapter of his *Theory of the Earth, with Proofs and Illustrations* (1795).[6]

I have argued elsewhere that the account of the earth's geological system in Hutton's 'Theory of the Earth' exhibits a number of features that allow us to call it a Romantic geology.[7] Firstly, although Hutton's geology is grounded in a Newtonian view of the material world, his representation of nature and the earth appears more and more Wordsworthian as his argument develops. If the system of the earth is initially figured as a complex machine designed by a wise creator, it ends up as a self-sustaining organism whose design bears witness to the wisdom and goodness of nature itself. Secondly, Hutton, along with many other 'Romantic' scientists in the second half of the eighteenth century, breaks from Newtonianism by seeing nature not as a mechanism made up of inert material bodies but as a system of active 'powers' and 'forces'.[8] Thirdly, Hutton's vision of the dynamic forces that had shaped and reshaped the earth over a colossal period of time ramped up the power of the 'geological sublime' and thereby contributed to the Romantic culture of the period. In what follows, I demonstrate that Hutton's geotheory emerged out of evidence gathered on numerous wide-ranging tours and field trips in Scotland and England during more than thirty years.

Hutton's Geological Excursions prior to 1785

In the first volume of his *Theory of the Earth*, Hutton replied to Richard Kirwan's criticism of his claim in 'Theory of the Earth' that granite is a relatively recent igneous rock that is not found universally in the rock sequence. Hutton's account of granite directly contradicted Kirwan's Neptunist belief that granite was the first rock to be precipitated from the primeval ocean and was therefore the underlying basic rock throughout the world.[9] In his response, Hutton emphasised how little granite he had found on his geological travels prior to publishing his 'Theory of the Earth':

> I had examined Scotland from one end to the other before I saw one stone of granite in its native place. I had, moreover, examined almost all England and Wales (excepting Devon and Cornwall) without seeing

more of granite than one spot, not many hundred yards of extent . . . I had travelled every road from the borders of Northumberland and Westmoreland to Edinburgh. From Edinburgh, I had travelled to Port-Patrick, and from that along the coast of Galloway and Airshire to Inverary in Argyleshire, and I had examined every spot between the Grampians and the Tweedale mountains from sea to sea, without seeing granite in its place. I had also travelled from Edinburgh by Crieff, Rannock, Dalwiny, Fort Augustus, Inverness, through East Ross and Caithness to the Pentland-Frith or Orkney Islands, without seeing one block of granite in its place. It is true, I met with it on my return by the east coast, when I just saw it, and no more, at Peterhead and Aberdeen (*Theory of the Earth*, I, pp. 213–14)

Hutton admits that he was not looking for granite during this phase of his geological investigations and notes that 'I have, since that time, seen it in different places; because I went on purpose to examine it' (I, p. 214). Much of the present chapter will be devoted to analysing Hutton's accounts of his search for granite-schistus junctions in the late 1780s, but what is striking about the above passage is its revelation of the wide extent of his geological exploration of England, Scotland and Wales prior to 1785. Jean Jones points out that 'Hutton's interest in geology had developed in the 1750s in parallel with his interest in agriculture. During the next three decades he made extensive journeys through much of England and Wales and most regions of Scotland except the north-west and the Hebrides' ('Hutton, James', *ODNB*). As she suggests, 'Only the journeys he made in the 1780s are well documented and some historians of science have branded him as a theorist, unaware that his theories were preceded by thirty years of investigation at home and effort in the field.'

An early indication of the extent of Hutton's geological exploration of Britain over more than three decades appeared in John Playfair's 'Biographical Account of the Late Dr James Hutton', which Playfair read to the Royal Society of Edinburgh on 10 January 1803 and which was published two years later in the Society's *Transactions*. In this biography of his late friend, Playfair sets out to demonstrate that Hutton had arrived at his theory of the earth through geological travel and Baconian methodology. We need to bear in mind, though, that Playfair was attempting to defend Hutton's geotheory against attacks by Neptunists such as Kirwan and Robert Jameson, who condemned it as atheistic and based entirely on theoretical conjecture.[10]

After graduating with an MD from Leiden in 1749, with a thesis entitled *De sanguine et circulatione microcosmi*, Hutton returned to Edinburgh and 'resolved to apply himself to agriculture', having 'inherited from his father a small property in Berwickshire' (Playfair, 'Biographical Account', p. 43). In the following two years he made frequent visits to his farm at Slighhouses, west of Berwick-upon-Tweed, and became acquainted with Sir John Hall of Dunglass, whose son, Sir James Hall, would become a Huttonian geochemist who accompanied Hutton on some of his later field trips in Scotland.[11] In order 'to study rural economy in the school which was then reckoned the best, . . . [Hutton] went into Norfolk, . . . living in the house of a farmer, who served both for his landlord and his instructor' (p. 43). During this period, Hutton investigated England's mineralogy and geology as well as its agricultural methods (p. 44). Dennis Dean suggests that it was at Yarmouth that Hutton 'first observed a river in flood carrying away "part of our land, to be sunk at the bottom of the sea" and a storm making its hostile attack on the coast; both helped to convince him that "in the natural operations of the world, the land is continually perishing"' (*James Hutton and the History of Geology*, p. 5).[12] Dean stresses the importance of Hutton's fieldwork in Norfolk and elsewhere in England in shaping his early geological speculations:

> Using a methodology he would repeat throughout his life, Hutton had formulated some far-reaching geological suppositions from his concentrated attention to a small geographical area. Because he believed all natural processes to be constant, ubiquitous, and virtually eternal, Hutton set out to discover corroborative evidence in other locales. Among his several foot journeys toward that end, he seems to have undertaken a major one that led him south along the coast of Suffolk (. . . Crag deposits), probably to London, south again to the Sussex coast (prominent chalk cliffs), then west to the Isle of Wight (spectacular erosion and contortions) and along the Dorset coast for some distance. He stopped short of Cornwall, which was almost the only part of English geology Hutton would never see. (*James Hutton and the History of Geology*, pp. 6–7)

Playfair suggests that the first general conclusion that Hutton drew from these early explorations in the field was 'that a vast proportion of the present rocks is composed of materials afforded by the destruction of bodies, animal, vegetable, and mineral, of more ancient formation' ('Biographical Account', p. 56). The second conclusion was 'that all the present rocks are without exception going to decay, and their materials descending into the ocean' (p. 56). Although these conclusions were not in themselves original, Hutton linked them together to form the original insight that 'they are two steps of the same progression; and that, as the present continents are composed from the waste of more ancient land, so, from the destruction of them, future continents may be destined to arise' (p. 56). Hutton's next step was to consider

> this succession of continents as not confined to one or two examples, but as indefinitely extended, and the consequence of laws perpetually acting. Thus he arrived at the new and sublime conclusion, which represents nature as having provided for a constant succession of land on the surface of the earth, according to a plan having no natural termination, but calculated to endure as long as those beneficent purposes, for which the whole is destined, shall continue to exist. (pp. 56–7)

In order to complete this early version of the geological or 'geostrophic' cycle, Hutton needed a mechanism that could transform eroded detritus into new rocks and form continents out of the waste of more ancient land. Playfair claims that Hutton approached this problem and arrived at his core proposition – that subterraneous heat is the agent which consolidates eroded materials into rocks and raises them above the surface – not through a ready-made hypothesis but through a long period of empirical analysis and logical deduction (p. 57).

From 1754 to 1767, or thereabouts, Hutton resided on his farm in Berwickshire, from where he continued to develop his knowledge of geology by making field trips and tours in Scotland:

> Though the years Hutton spent at Slighhouses . . . have often been represented as a fallow period in his life, they actually included intensive fieldwork throughout much of Scotland. As in Norfolk, Hutton walked or rode out whenever he could, seeking further evidence to support his theory. 'I have been examining the south alpine country of Scotland, occasionally, for more than forty years,' he would write no later than 1795 (*Theory*, I, 335). This deliberate research culminated in 1764, when he toured extensively throughout northeastern Scotland with his friend George Clerk-Maxwell. From Edinburgh they proceeded through Crieff, Dalwhinnie, Fort Augustus, Inverness, and East Ross into Caithness (at the very north of Scotland), then returned along the coast through Aberdeen. (Dean, *James Hutton and the History of Geology*, pp. 8–9)

Hutton, then, undertook his first major geological tour of northern Scotland in the same year that John Walker made his tour of the Hebrides and parts of the Highlands for the Board of Annexed Estates.

In late 1767 or early 1768 Hutton left his farm to live in Edinburgh, where he became part of a network of Enlightenment intellectuals and was a founding member of the Royal Society of Edinburgh (Dean, p. 3). Living in Edinburgh enabled Hutton to explore the impressive geology of the city and its environs, especially Arthur's Seat and Salisbury Crags.[13] His observations on Arthur's Seat and Salisbury Crags (and in Derbyshire in 1774) raised questions about the nature and origin of basalt, especially in the form of intrusive veins and sills, that were currently being debated in the basalt controversy. If basalt could be identified as an igneous rock, rather than an aqueous precipitate, it would greatly strengthen Hutton's supposition about the existence and effects of subterraneous heat:

> According to his primary source, Alex Frederic Cronstedt's *Essay Towards a System of Mineralogy* (1758; English translations 1770, 1772), . . . basalt was usually found as veins in rocks of another kind, 'running commonly in a serpentine manner, contrary or across to the direction of the rock itself' (*Theory*, I: 151). Hutton himself found and described 'a fine example of this kind' (152) in 1764, while on the road to Crieff. By this time he had also thoroughly investigated the basaltic phenomena closer to home. 'On the south side of Edinburgh,' he observed, 'I have seen, in little more than the space of a mile from east to west, nine or ten masses of whinstone interjected among the strata' (153–154). This was primarily at Salisbury Crags, adjacent to Arthur's Seat, where part of the relevant exposure is now termed 'Hutton's Section'. (Dean, *James Hutton and the History of Geology*, p. 11)

As we saw in the previous chapter, however, in 1784 Hutton refused to accept Faujas de Saint-Fond's volcanic interpretation of Salisbury Crags and Arthur's Seat because he wanted to maintain a distinction between basalt and lava. For Hutton, whereas lava was emitted from the mouths of volcanoes, basalt was a more general product of subterraneous heat and pressure not limited to volcanic activity.[14] Thus it is misleading, but not uncommon, to describe Hutton's geotheory as 'Vulcanist'. Whereas Vulcanists argued that far more of the earth's rocks and geomorphic features had been produced by volcanic activity than the Neptunist model recognised, Hutton introduced a third, more revolutionary paradigm into the debate by giving a much more significant and general role to subterraneous heat (making him a 'Plutonist').

In addition to highlighting Hutton's geological fieldwork and tours, Playfair also seeks to represent Hutton as an unprecedented intuitive genius who transformed mineralogy into a branch of physical science which focused on the temporal and causal vicissitudes of 'fossils' (natural objects found in the ground) and of the earth itself:

> with an accurate eye for perceiving the characters of natural objects, he had in equal perfection the power of interpreting their signification, and of decyphering those ancient hieroglyphics which record the revolutions of the globe. There may have been other mineralogists, who could describe as well the fracture, the figure, the smell, or the colour of a specimen; but there have been few who equalled him in reading the characters, which tell not only what a fossil *is*, but what it *has been*, and declare the series of changes through which it has passed. ('Biographical Account', p. 89)[15]

Playfair's metaphors here suggest that Hutton's unique genius resided in his ability to read, decipher and interpret the hieroglyphic characters of natural objects and fossils in order to reveal not only what they are (the domain of mineralogy) but also the revolutionary changes they, and thus the globe itself, have undergone in the deep past (the domain of geology). As we will see, the most spectacular representation of Hutton's interpretive power appears in Playfair's account of Hutton's unfolding of the sequence of geological revolutions that must have occurred to produce the famous unconformity at Siccar Point.

Although Hutton's theory of the earth was partly based on empirical evidence that he had been gathering on geological tours of England and Scotland over almost thirty years, the 1785 'Abstract of a Dissertation Read in the Royal Society of Edinburgh' relies entirely on a rational deduction about the formation of rock materials derived from the principles of physics and chemistry and on a 'moral' argument grounded in assumptions about the 'wisdom of nature' in constantly producing 'a soil, adapted to the growth of plants . . . in order to support the system of this living world' ([Hutton], *Abstract of a Dissertation Read in the Royal Society of Edinburgh*, pp. 28–9).

Although the Royal Society of Edinburgh became a hospitable arena in which Hutton and his followers presented their geological theory and discoveries (Porter, *The Making of Geology*, p. 145), the general tenor of natural history in Edinburgh in the 1780s was not receptive to abstract theorising, and criticisms of Hutton in these terms began to appear in print from 1788 onwards.[16] But whether or not the reception of Hutton's paper to the Royal Society of Edinburgh was hostile in the way Dean suggests (pp. 17–19), it is the case that shortly after its presentation in the spring of 1785 Hutton embarked on a series of geological tours and field trips in Scotland in quest of more evidence to support his theory.

Hutton's Geological Tours of Scotland between 1785 and 1788

Between 1785 and 1788, Hutton explored Glen Tilt in the Highlands just south of the Cairngorms, the Southern Uplands of Galloway in south-west Scotland, the island of Arran in the Firth of Clyde, the Jed Water south of Jedburgh in the Borders, and Siccar Point on the coast of Scotland to the east of Edinburgh.[17] These locations are marked on the map in Figure 6.1. Accompanying Hutton on these tours was a variety of friends and colleagues, including Hall, Playfair and John Clerk of Eldin, with Clark making a series of drawings of the landscapes and geological structures that they saw. Although his 'Theory of the Earth' barely mentions these tours of Scotland or the evidence he was beginning to gather on them, Hutton summarised some of his findings in his 'Observations on Granite' (*TRSE*, August 1794). He also offered brief descriptions of his discoveries in Arran and the Southern Uplands in chapter 6 of the first volume of *Theory of the Earth*, including an account of his exploration, with Playfair, of south-east Scotland, beginning with Dunglass Burn, late in the spring of 1788, and moving on to the unconformities at Jedburgh, Siccar Point and elsewhere.[18] But Hutton reserved the full accounts of his Scottish tours of the 1780s for a projected third volume of *Theory of the Earth*. His death in 1797 prevented that, thus allowing critics ever since to attack him not only for his theory but also for failing to support it with adequate empirical evidence.

Figure 6.1 Map of places visited on Hutton's geological tours of Scotland, from G. Y. Craig (ed.), *James Hutton's Theory of the Earth: The Lost Drawings*, p. 25.

Hutton's manuscript material for the third volume of *Theory of the Earth*, including three chapters devoted to his tours of Glen Tilt, Galloway and Arran, remained unpublished until 1899, when Archibald Geikie edited and published it for the Geological Society of London.[19] Hutton had intended to use Clerk's drawings and watercolour sketches as illustrations for the third volume, but most of them went missing after Hutton's death and were not available to Geikie. Fortunately, these 'lost drawings' were rediscovered in 1968 by John Clerk of Penicuik, one of Clerk's descendants, and published in 1978 in *James Hutton's Theory of the Earth: The Lost Drawings*, edited by G. Y. Craig. (The black and white reproductions given below of some of Clerk's images do scant justice to the exquisite colouring of the originals, facsimiles of which can be seen in the folder that accompanies *The Lost Drawings*.) Geikie's edition of the material intended for the third volume of *Theory of the Earth*, together with Craig's edition of the 'lost drawings', helps us to reconstruct Hutton's Scottish travel writings of the 1780s as originally envisaged.

In what follows, I want to read Hutton's unpublished tours of Scotland in the late 1780s as examples of Romantic geology that transformed the geological interpretation of Scotland's landscape. A close textual analysis will allow me to contest the long-standing and often unexamined assumption that his writing was so bad that his geological contributions remained unintelligible or inert until they were transformed into lucid prose by Playfair's *Illustrations of the Huttonian Theory of the Earth* (1802). As well as being important episodes in the history of geology, Hutton's unpublished tours exhibit a number of literary qualities. Hutton's narratives can be read, for example, in terms of the way they draw on the conventions of the quest myth, as summarised by Northrop Frye (*Anatomy of Criticism*, pp. 186–206). They are structured as a sequence of minor adventures that lead up to the main adventure, and Hutton figures as a heroic pioneer in pursuit of the secrets of nature (in the form of buried treasure), battles against negative antagonists (Edinburgh's Neptunists), overcomes difficulties to arrive at truth through a series of natural epiphanies, and brings back precious objects (rock samples and drawings of geological features) found on the quest. Metaphors of desire, hunting and the uncovering of nature's inner secrets shape the narratives and give particular resonance to common geological terms such as 'exposures'. In one of the tours, as we will see, Hutton employs linguistic strategies more reminiscent of the Romantic novel than scientific reports. Such language and strategies generate a vivid representation of the experience of scientific discovery, enabling readers to become virtual witnesses of, or virtual participants in, Hutton's geological quests in relatively remote parts of Scotland.[20]

In Quest of Intrusions and Unconformities

Hutton initially undertook his tours of Scotland in the 1780s in order to find and examine places where granite was juxtaposed with other rock materials, especially the metamorphic rocks that he called 'schistus'.[21] Hutton anticipated that exposed granite-schistus junctions would reveal granite veins running through the overlying or adjacent rocks. Such features would confirm, he believed, that granite is an igneous rock and that it had been forced into the surrounding rocks in a molten state by subterranean heat and pressure.[22] This would in turn support his theory that those forces were the main agents in the formation of rock materials and the uplift of land masses. It would also, incidentally, undermine the Neptunist claim that granite was a primary sedimentary rock or aqueous precipitate. Playfair explains that Hutton's discovery or failure to discover a granite intrusion on his Scottish tours would be 'an *instantia crucis* [that would] subject his theory to the severest test' ('Biographical Account', p. 67). Playfair's use of this Baconian term insists again on Hutton's empirical methodology and indicates the importance of granite veins to his theory. Bacon explains in aphorism 36 of *The New Organon* (1620) that 'we take the term from the *signposts* which are erected at forks in the road to indicate and mark where the different roads go' (p. 159). The presence or absence of granite veins in adjacent sedimentary or metamorphic rocks would thus decisively indicate whether Hutton or the Neptunists were on the right road. Hutton, then, was in search of evidence to support a theory, which is one of the reasons his written tours are structured as quests. As we will see, however, Hutton also found evidence that he seems not to have expected (junctions between stratified rock formations that exhibited 'unconformity') that allowed him to elaborate his theory in spectacular ways.

A Journey to the North Alpine Part of Scotland in the Year 1785

In the summer of 1785 Hutton and Clerk explored Glen Tilt and the surrounding area of north-east Perthshire in the Scottish Highlands. The Tilt begins at Loch Tilt on the confines of Aberdeenshire and flows south-west and then south to Blair Atholl, where it enters the River Garry after a course of fourteen miles. It can be located and traced on Bayly's 'Map of Scotland, the Hebrides and Part of England adapted to Mr Pennant's Tours' (Figure 6.2).

Playfair spells out the reasons why Hutton chose to explore this glen:

> One of the places where he knew that a junction of the kind he wished to examine must be found, was the line where the great body of gran- ite which runs from Aberdeen westward, forming the central chain of the Grampians, comes in contact with the schistus which composes the

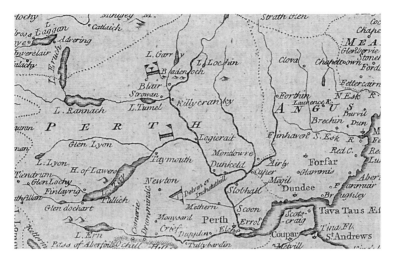

Figure 6.2 J. Bayly, 'A Map of Scotland, the Hebrides and Part of England adapted to Mr Pennant's Tours' (London: B. White, 1777) (detail). Reproduced by permission of the National Library of Scotland.

inferior ridges of the same mountains toward the south. The nearest and most accessible point of this line seemed likely to be situated not far to the eastward of Blair in Athol, and could hardly fail to be visible in the beds of some of the most northern streams which run into the Tay. Dr Hutton having mentioned these circumstances to the Duke of Athol, was invited by that nobleman to accompany him in the shooting season into Glentilt, which he did accordingly, together with his friend Mr Clerk of Elden, in summer 1785. ('Biographical Account', p. 68)

Hutton begins his written account of the tour, which was intended to form chapter 4 of the projected third volume of *Theory of the Earth*, by claiming that the Scottish Highlands contain 'everything requisite for establishing a natural history, not only of this, but of every other alpine country' (*Theory of the Earth*, III, p. 4). Hutton spells out why the Highlands might be regarded as typical of the geological make-up of mountain regions in general and how the evidence he found there reversed prevailing assumptions about the creation of mountains and the order in which different rock materials were formed:

the Highlands of Scotland, as well as the Alps of Switzerland, Savoy and other alpine countries, may be considered as composed of two things, mountains of schistus and mountains of granite. Some naturalists consider these mountains as being the primitive parts of the globe, or as having no origin from whence we may derive them in the operations of the globe; while others, here acknowledging a species of stratification, suppose them only to be primary in relation to other strata of which we certainly know the origin. In this case of primary and posterior, naturalists have thought to distinguish granite as being the primary in relation to the schistus mountains which they thus suppose as having been formed posterior to it; but as I have just now found evidence of the contrary in a journey which I have made to the Highlands, it will not be unacceptable to the public to know the state in which those things are found and to be informed of the place where any naturalist, who is willing to be satisfied from his own examination, may have an opportunity of gratifying his curiosity, and perhaps discovering something interesting to science and useful to those philosophers who enquire into the origin of things. (III, pp. 8–9)

The place where any natural philosopher might find decisive evidence about the origin of things, and thus confirm and perhaps develop Hutton's claims, is the 'long narrow valley' of the River Tilt (III, p. 11).[23] Hutton and Clerk travelled with the Duke of Atholl and a hunting party to Forest Lodge, about ten miles up the glen, where they soon found abundant evidence that supported Hutton's theory:

> We have both these points now perfectly decided; the granite is here found breaking and displacing the strata in every conceivable manner, including the fragments of the broken strata, and interjected in every possible direction among the strata which appear. This is to be seen, not in one place only of the valley, but in many places, where the rocks appear, or where the river has laid bare the strata. (III, p. 13)

Although Hutton is reporting his discovery of crucial evidence in support of his theory, his prose is notably restrained, especially when compared with Playfair's account:

> When they had reached the Forest Lodge, about seven miles up the valley, Dr Hutton already found himself in the midst of the objects which he wished to examine. In the bed of the river, many veins of red granite, (no less, indeed, than six large veins in the course of a mile), were seen traversing the black micaceous schistus, and producing, by the contrast of colour, an effect that might be striking even to an unskilful observer. The sight of objects which verified at once so many important conclusions in

his system, filled him with delight; and as his feelings, on such occasions, were always strongly expressed, the guides who accompanied him were convinced that it must be nothing less than the discovery of a vein of silver or gold, that could call forth such strong marks of joy and exultation. ('Biographical Account', pp. 68–9)

Hutton's restraint in reporting his discoveries in Glen Tilt can also be contrasted with his suggestion that curiosity and desire play a central role in scientific exploration and are not satisfied but whetted by the discovery of apparently decisive evidence:[24]

In matters of science, curiosity gratified begets not indolence, but new desires. We now wished to see the extent of that granite which we had found; and whether it were one continued mass of granite to the River Dee, where perhaps nothing but granite mountains are to be found, at least where chiefly these abound. We had hitherto made the Duke's hunting-lodge in Glen Tilt our head-quarters. His Grace now proposed to move us farther into the wilderness, and also to entertain us with the deer-hunting in his forest. We travelled up the Tilt, crossed the Tarf which runs into the Tilt, and came to the other hunting seat of Fealar, the most removed, I believe, of any in Britain from the habitations of men. Here we were near the summit of the country, where the water runs into the three great rivers Tay, Spey, and Dee. The Duke was successful in killing three harts and one hind, all in excellent condition; and our curiosity was gratified in finding both the granite and alpine schistus in this summit of the Highlands, between Glen More and Glen Beg. (III, pp. 16–17)

Hutton implicitly compares the hunt for the geological secrets of the earth with the hunting of deer, and suggests that the chase led them still 'farther into the wilderness' to the most remote hunting lodge in Britain. As we saw in the introductory chapter, Rudwick's essay on 'Geological Travel and Theoretical Innovation' suggests that groundbreaking geological field trips are analogous to pilgrimages in that they typically involve an often arduous and transformative journey into an unfamiliar 'liminal' place in which the geologist experiences a kind of revelation triggered by the encounter with geological features that challenge conventional paradigms and interpretations. Hutton's excursion into Glen Tilt and Glen Tarff fits Rudwick's model. In these liminal spaces, far removed from the physical and intellectual environment of

Edinburgh, Hutton discovered and interpreted geological features that challenged the fundamental assumptions of Neptunist geotheory.

Hutton's observations in Glen Tarff revealed that granite is not the only rock that may be forced into schistus in a molten state under pressure. He notes, for example, 'that besides the granite which has been made to flow in breaking and displacing the strata of the alpine stone, there have been also masses of fluid porphyry interjected among those elevated strata' (III, p. 21). Hutton found a boulder in Glen Tarff, weighing about four hundred pounds (about 180 kg), which contained 'a vein which traversed both the mass of granite and broken schistus' (Craig (ed.), *The Lost Drawings*, p. 19) and had it transported to his house in Edinburgh; Clerk's drawing (Figure 6.3) presented readers with a proxy image.[25] Such finds enable Hutton to conclude that 'our alpine country consists of indurated or erected strata of slate, gneiss, and limestone, broken and injected with granite and porphyry' (III, p. 24). He thus repeats with new confidence the conclusions he had arrived at in his 1785 paper. In the Highlands of Scotland, as in the rest of the world, 'Nature acts upon the same principle in her operations, in consolidating bodies by means of heat and fusion, and by moving great masses of fluid matter in the bowels of the Earth' (III, pp. 25–6).

Hutton then turns his attention to another aspect of his theory – the claim that uplifted land masses are gradually and continuously eroded by weathering agents over enormous periods of time and that much of the detritus is carried away by rivers and deposited on the sea-bed (where it is eventually consolidated into new rocks).

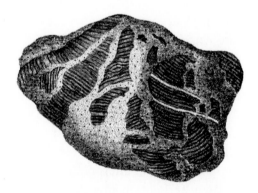

Figure 6.3 John Clerk of Eldin, Boulder from Glen Tarff (1785), in G. Y. Craig (ed.), *James Hutton's Theory of the Earth: The Lost Drawings*, p. 30.

Hutton's observation in and around the River Tay at Dunkeld of elevated river plains and rounded stones that could only have come from Glen Tarff is interpreted as

> evidence of the long succession of time upon this elevated country, and great operation of water, in wasting and wearing the materials of this high land, in forming the valleys between the mountains, and carrying an immense mass of matter from the summits of those mountains into the sea. It must not be alleged that this is too great an effect for the operation of this river, which from the longest records of our history makes but trifling alterations upon its bed; neither must it be supposed that this had been the effect of some great catastrophe which may have happened to the globe. (III, pp. 28–9)

Hutton's tour of the Glen Tilt area in the summer of 1785 thus yielded what he took to be decisive evidence in support of two of the main aspects of his theory of the earth – the agency of subterraneous heat and pressure in forming igneous rocks and raising land masses, and gradual erosion by flowing water over a vast time period. Although such exciting evidence is not mentioned in Hutton's 'Theory of the Earth' separate that was published a few months later in early 1786, it may well have influenced the confident manner in which he articulates that theory.

A Journey to the South Alpine Parts of Scotland in the Year 1786

Hutton's account of his exploration of the Southern Uplands of south-west Scotland in 1786, intended as chapter 5 of the third volume of *Theory of the Earth*, begins by explaining that the evidence that he had found in and around Glen Tilt had stimulated rather than satisfied his desire to find further proof in other parts of Scotland (III, pp. 31–3). Hutton's and Clerk's tour of the coast of south-west Scotland can be traced on J. Bayly's 'Map of Scotland, the Hebrides and Part of England adapted to Mr Pennant's Tours' (Figure 6.4).

Hutton and Clerk were told at Newton Stewart ('N. Town Stewart' on the map, just north of Wigtown) that local people, even the overseers of mines, had not found granite in the region and could therefore offer them no help in their quest. Left to their own devices, Hutton and

Figure 6.4 J. Bayly, 'A Map of Scotland, the Hebrides and Part of England adapted to Mr Pennant's Tours' (London: B. White, 1777) (detail). Reproduced by permission of the National Library of Scotland.

Clerk soon notice indications that they might find granite-schistus junctions on 'Cairns Muir, a great round mountain, exposed immediately to view from that part of the road upon the coast. Therefore being now determined, we put up our chaise at the village of Ferrytown, and procured horses and a guide to conduct us through the muir in pursuit of the object which we had in view' (III, p. 44). In describing their exploration of this 700 metre mountain, Hutton emphasises that the geologist's desire to see and know is at once impeded and excited by the way nature sometimes resists and sometimes fulfils that desire:

> To a naturalist nothing is indifferent; the humble moss that creeps upon the stone is equally interesting as the lofty pine which so beautifully adorns the valley or the mountain: but to a naturalist who is reading in the face of rocks the annals of a former world, the mossy covering which obstructs his view, and renders indistinguishable the different species of stone, is no less than a serious object of regret. Such was our case, in viewing a mountain which seemed as if cut asunder in order to gratify our particular desire. . . . [H]ere we had the most desirable section exposed to our view, and had nothing to do but remove the thin veil with which the mineral face of nature was disguised. It was not without much pains and labour that we thus proceeded to investigate what could not appear at first sight; and it was not without some regret that we left so noble a section unfinished, or

without a full delineation of an object so decisive in its nature and of such extent. We saw, however, enough to describe upon principle what we here had learned. (III, pp. 46–7)

The natural historian is interested in all aspects of nature, including the moss that covers rocks and stones and trees. But to the geologist, anything that conceals rock sections and frustrates the attempt to read the annals of a former world is to be regretted and, if possible, removed. Although the mountain initially looks as if it has been 'cut asunder in order to gratify our particular desire', exposing 'the most desirable section . . . to our view', Hutton and Clerk are forced, with pains and labour, to 'remove the thin veil with which the mineral face of nature was disguised'. Even then, they are not able fully to satisfy their desire. One of 'The drawings which Mr. Clerk took upon this occasion' (III, p. 47) is particularly interesting in the way it represents the relationship between these savants and this natural feature (Figure 6.5). As well as providing a vivid proxy image of the geological feature, this drawing includes images of Hutton and Clerk working at and interpreting the exposure, whose size both overwhelms them and connotes their heroic labour on the mountainside. The figure at the centre of the image appears to stand at the threshold of deep time, reading the annals of a former world on what almost

Figure 6.5 John Clerk of Eldin, Granite veins exposed on Cairnsmore of Fleet, in G. Y. Craig (ed.), *James Hutton's Theory of the Earth: The Lost Drawings*, p. 50.

seems like a semi-transparent screen whose luminous glow hints at the subterranean fire at the core of Hutton's theory. Hutton appears, indeed, to be about to penetrate the mountain, setting out on a journey to the centre of the earth.

Hutton's representation of geological exploration as driven by the desire to discover or uncover exposures that will reveal the secrets of the earth is part of a larger discursive formation in the period. The gendering of the scientific quest was ubiquitous from the seventeenth to the early nineteenth century, from Francis Bacon's *The New Organon* (1620) to Humphry Davy's 'Discourse Introductory to a Course of Lectures on Chemistry' (1802). Davy, for example, rhetorically asked his audience at the Royal Institution 'who would not be ambitious of becoming acquainted with the most profound secrets of nature, of ascertaining her hidden operations, and of exhibiting to men that system of knowledge which relates so intimately to their own physical and moral constitution?' (p. 320). Such attitudes are dramatised and criticised in Mary Shelley's *Frankenstein* (1818/1831), whose eponymous protagonist reports that 'with unrelaxed and breathless eagerness, I pursued nature to her hiding places' and eventually 'succeeded in discovering the cause of generation and life' after 'days and nights of incredible labour' (pp. 55, 53). As Jan Golinski puts it, 'Images of nature as a female, unveiled by male researchers, had a pervasive ideological role' in Enlightenment science (*Making Natural Knowledge*, p. 66).[26] Hutton's writings, and some of Clerk's drawings, then, fashion Hutton as a masculine explorer engaged in the heroic and laborious endeavour of exposing and penetrating the inner secrets of a nature figured as female.

As they make their way along the south-west coast between Kirkcudbright and the Solway Firth, Hutton represents himself and Clerk as intrepid travellers on 'a road which perhaps was never passed in a chaise before' (III, p. 54). Expectations are raised, apparently fulfilled, and then disappointed: granite and schistus outcrops are easily seen but the vital junction, which might reveal intrusions, remains hidden (III, pp. 54–5). The explorers press on eagerly, anticipating that the sea at the Solway Firth might have created the exposures they seek:

> The road from Coend Kirk, if it may be called a road, leads to a little sandy bay of the sea, just within the limits or entry of the Solway Firth. Here it is common to ride along the sands when the sea has ebbed, in

leaving the shore and making to Saturness [Southerness] Point near Arbigland, whither we were bound. The road was this way nearer, easier, and far more expeditious; but this was not our object; for now the rocky shore appeared, and we had every reason to expect to find something interesting in this critical spot. We therefore left the chaise, which we had for a long way attended on foot, to find its way up the hill, while we ran with some impatience along the bottom of the sandy bay to the rocky shore which is washed by the sea, it being then low water. We saw the schistus pretty erect, but variously inflected, as is usual, upon our right, where the land terminated in the sea. Upon the left again, we had the granite appearing through the sandy shore; and above, the granite hill seemed to impend upon the erected strata, if these reached so far into the land. We saw the place nearly where the granite and the schistus upon the shore must be united; but this place was bushy; and thus our fears and expectations remained for a moment in suspense. But breaking through the bushes and briars, and climbing up the rocky bank, if we did not see the apposition of the granite to the side of the erected strata so much as we would have wished, we saw something that was much more satisfactory, and to the purpose of our expedition. This was the granite superinduced upon the ends of those broken strata or erected schisti. We now understood the meaning of the impending granite which appeared in the hill above this place; and now we were satisfied that the schistus was not only contiguous with the mass of the granite laterally, but was also in the most perfect conjunction with this solid rock which had been superinduced upon the broken and irregular ends of the strata.

But even this view of things, decisive as it was, did not fill up the measure of our satisfaction, which was to be still farther gratified with the only possible appearance which could now remain, in order to complete the proof with every species of evidence which the nature of things could admit of. For here we found the granite, not only involving the terminations of the broken and elevated strata, but also interjected among the strata, in descending among them like a mineral vein, and terminating in a thread where it could penetrate no farther. Mr. Clerk's drawing, and a specimen which I took of the schistus thus penetrated, will convince the most sceptical with regard to this doctrine of the transfusion of granite. (III, pp. 55–9)

This remarkable passage is written with a breathless eagerness more reminiscent of the climax of a Romantic novel of the period than of a scientific report or even a travel narrative. Hutton's first-person account represents himself and Clerk as characters traversing a landscape suffused with desire, in quest of an exposure which the landforms repeatedly promise, satisfy in part, and only yield up at the climax. These characters run 'with some impatience along the bottom of the sandy bay to the rocky shore'; their 'fears and expectations remained for a moment in suspense' because the anticipated exposure is concealed by vegetation; breaking through 'the bushes and briars' they gratify their desire to know the meaning of the surrounding rock formations, only to gain further satisfaction when they view an exposure that 'complete[s] the proof with every species of evidence which the nature of things could admit of'.

The impression that this passage could easily appear in a Romantic novel is created not only by the way the characters pursue their quest through a landscape that both lures them onward and defers their satisfaction until the last moment, but also by Hutton's use of paradoxical deictic markers ('was-now') that override the normal distinction between 'is-now' and 'was-then':

> but this *was* not our object; for *now* the rocky shore appeared, and we had every reason to expect to find something interesting in this critical spot . . . We *now* understood the meaning of the impending granite which appeared in the hill above this place; and *now we were* satisfied . . . our satisfaction . . . *was to be* still farther gratified with the only possible appearance which could *now* remain . . .

At the time Hutton was writing this passage, the use of 'was-now' formulations was being developed in third-person novels, though this technique would not become a dominant style until Jane Austen's sustained use of empathetic narrative allowed readers both to participate in and to criticise the inner experiential lives of third-person characters.[27] Literary critics and theorists have paid a great deal of attention to third-person empathetic narration in the nineteenth- and early twentieth-century novel, but they have largely ignored the use of the 'was-now' paradox in first-person narrative.[28] Yet, as Sylvia Adamson has shown, the 'she-was-now' formula introduced by the Romantic novel was made possible by an 'I-was-now' form developed in seventeenth-century Puritan conversion autobiographies, most prominently in John Bunyan's *Grace Abounding* (1666).[29] In carrying out the intense self-scrutiny of their sinful past lives that Puritanism demanded, writers like Bunyan employ the 'I-was-now' form most prominently in critical conversion moments in ways that collapse past and present into an illusion of experiential immediacy.[30] Bunyan uses the form throughout *Grace Abounding* in the retrospective narration of key moments in which he realised his state of sin or received intimations of God's grace. Both kinds of insight are juxtaposed in the final, most intense epiphany:

> At the apprehension of these things, my sickness was doubled upon me, for now was I sick in my inward man, my Soul was clog'ed with guilt, now also was all my former experience of Gods goodness to me quite taken out of my mind, and hid as if it had never been, nor seen: Now was my Soul greatly pinched between these two considerations. *Live I must not, Die I dare not*: now I sunk and fell in my Spirit, and was giving up all for lost; but as I was walking up and down in the house, as a man in a most woful state, that word of God took hold of my heart, *Ye are justified freely by his grace, through the redemption that is in Christ Jesus*, Rom. 3.24.
>
> Now was I as one awakened out of some troublesome sleep and dream, and listening to this heavenly sentence, I was as if I heard it thus expounded to me . . .
>
> Now was I got on high; I saw myself within the arms of Grace and Mercy; and though I was before afraid to think of a dying hour, yet now I cried, Let me die; now death was lovely and beautiful in my sight. (Bunyan, *Grace Abounding*, p. 73)

In contrast to the concentrated uses of 'I-was-now' forms in *Grace Abounding*, other first-person early-modern narratives, such as the sea voyages collected in Richard Hakluyt's *Principal Navigations* (1598–1600), reveal a comparatively low percentage of was-now tokens. The key difference, perhaps, between Hakluyt's *Navigations* and *Grace Abounding* is that the former concentrates on external places and events, while the latter is concerned almost exclusively with intense internal experience.[31]

It is striking that Hutton should employ first-person 'was-now' deictic markers, along with the other markers of subjective experience that we have noted, in a text intended to be included in his major work of natural history. We might expect, indeed, that Hutton's text would be more like Hakluyt's than Bunyan's in this respect. Adamson claims that scientific writing of the eighteenth century, partly in reaction to Puritan enthusiasm, sought to eliminate deictic markers of subjectivity in order to suggest that science was entirely a matter of objective experimental evidence.[32] Although Isaac Newton's *Opticks* (1704), one of the paradigmatic texts of eighteenth-century natural philosophy, does make use of 'was-now' deictics, it does so in a way that is crucially different from Hutton's usage. Out of about one hundred uses of 'now' as an adverb and conjunction in the fourth edition of 1730, eleven occur in adverbial form in relation to the past tense of the verb 'to be', always in reporting the results of experiments. The use of 'was-now' forms is most concentrated in book II, part iv, Obs. 11, where Newton reports his 'very strange and surprizing' 'Observations concerning the Reflexions and Colours of thick transparent polish'd Plates'. Notably, however, even in this flurry of 'was-now' phrases, the subject of the verb is almost invariably the natural phenomenon rather than Newton himself, as in the following: 'the first of those luminous Rings was now grown equal to the second of those dark ones' (*Opticks*, pp. 289, 309). Although Newton does use the first-person pronoun in *Opticks*, in the one instance where 'I' appears in a sentence with a 'was-now' form, the subject is still the phenomenon rather than the experimenter: 'Wherefore I covered that Part of the Glass with black Paper, and letting the Light pass through another Part of it which was free from such Bubbles, the Spectrum of Colours became free from those irregular Streams of Light, and was now such as I desired' (*Opticks*, p. 88). While it is clearly not possible to generalise these findings without more extensive research, Newton's *Opticks* indicates that although the 'was-now' form does feature in reporting experimental findings in the natural philosophy of the period, Hutton's usage may be relatively novel in combining 'was-now' with first-person pronouns.

It is particularly revealing that a scientific travel narrative of the late eighteenth century should present its intense moments of geological discovery in ways that echo the moments of spiritual self-discovery in seventeenth-century Puritan conversion narratives. Such Puritan texts represent a high point in the focus on subjective experience in the seventeenth century (anticipating the Romantic focus on internal experience at the end of the eighteenth century). Yet although Hutton is primarily concerned with the external events of his travels and the geomorphology of his findings, he also reveals the internal experience of the naturalist-traveller and it is when he records the most climactic moments of discovery that he reaches for the paradoxical deictics of 'was-now'. If 'was-now' markers occur most intensively at the critical conversion moments in seventeenth-century Puritan autobiographies, in Hutton they occur at critical moments of epiphany when the long-expected revelation of decisive exposures seems about to occur and when crucial evidence about the natural history of the earth is about to be revealed.

One explanation of Hutton's stylistic usage is that he is writing scientific travel literature rather than a treatise. As we have seen in earlier chapters, a number of critics have argued that travel writing at the end of the eighteenth century underwent a shift from objective reportage to a more Romantic focus on the individual traveller's inner and outer experience. Nigel Leask questions this standard account by relocating the 'disjuncture between scientific and literary travel writing in the decades *after* 1790–1820' (*Curiosity and the Aesthetics of Travel Writing*, p. 7). 'In the earlier decades', he suggests, 'travel writing struggled to integrate . . . anecdotal personal narrative with "curious" or "precise" observation.' Yet Hutton, it might be said, succeeds in integrating scientific and Romantic travel writing precisely in those moments of epiphany when the discovery of geological evidence is fused with the discoverer's excited experience of that discovery.

It is also important to recall Heringman's argument that geological writing had not yet fully distinguished itself from the network of other discourses and practices – travel writing, landscape aesthetics, topographic poetry and so on – in which it developed.[33] In addition, Rudwick's suggestion that there are similarities between groundbreaking geological field trips and religious pilgrimages might lead us to wonder whether the parallels between Hutton's and Bunyan's climactic moments might be typical of scientific journeys of discovery in general. We also need to bear in mind, as Rudwick emphasises in *Bursting the Limits of Time* and as Ralph O'Connor demonstrates in *The Earth on Show*, that geological writers of the period attempted to persuade their readers to accept their theoretical claims by making them feel that they were 'virtual travellers' who shared in the journey of discovery and 'virtual witnesses' to the evidence in the field. One effect of Hutton's use of 'we-were-now' forms in the above passage is to conflate the 'now' of the experience, the 'now' of the writing, and the 'now' of the reading, thus involving the reader in the plural pronoun and in the present-tense experience of expectation, delay and eventual discovery. A climactic moment in Hutton's discovery of the secrets of the earth's geological system is vividly shared by the reader, as if the difference between time present and time past had been collapsed. Such a manipulation of the reader's experience of time is wholly germane to Hutton's geological project, which is to decipher the formative events of the earth's distant past in the now of the geological evidence – simultaneously opening up and bridging the unthinkable gulf between the awesome processes that must have taken place in deep time and their traces in the rock formations he discovers and interprets for the reader.

An Examination of the Mineral History of the Island of Arran

Hutton concludes chapter 5 by announcing that the geological features found 'in the south alpine region of Scotland' had finally confirmed his theory of the earth (III, pp. 60–1). As before, however, confirmation served to whet rather than satisfy his desire to seek further evidence in other enticing locations in Scotland. Hutton defers the account of his trip to Arran by inserting three chapters, taking up a hundred pages in Geikie's edition, in which he correlates his findings in Scotland with those of geologists in other parts of the world, especially those in the volumes of Horace-Bénédict de Saussure's *Voyages dans les Alpes* (1779–96) that had then been published. When he finally turns to his findings on Arran in chapter 9 Hutton reveals that his desire to visit the island had originally been stimulated by seeing it from more than fifty miles away:

> The extremely alpine appearance of Arran from the continent of Scotland, even at the distance of the middle of the country, *i.e.*, from the Shott Hills, had long been a subject of admiration to me; and it was there that I had always expected to have the nature of mountains, that is to say, the steps of nature in their origin and decay, better investigated than any other-where. (III, p. 193)

Arran, then, is an island of promise whose exploration will potentially reveal the geological history of mountains. When Hutton finally made the crossing to Arran in August 1787, he went with Clerk's son, 'Mr John Clerk junior' (III, pp. 191–2). As Playfair notes in his

'Biographical Account', John Clerk junior took over his father's role by making 'several drawings, which, together with a description of the island drawn up afterwards by Dr Hutton, still remain in manuscript' (p. 70).[34]

Geikie included a simplified sketch-map of Arran's geology in his edition of the third volume of Hutton's *Theory of the Earth* (Figure 6.6). He points out that this map 'is generalised and reduced from the latest work of the Geological Survey. For the sake of adapting it to Hutton's narrative only those groups of rock are represented which he describes' (III, pp. 202–3, note).

Hutton announces that 'In setting out upon that expedition, I had but one object in view; this was the nature of the granite, and the connection of it with the contiguous strata' (III, p. 193). Although the sixty-one-year-old Hutton had already gathered enough evidence in support of his theory about granite, he searched with boyish eagerness for exposed granite-schistus junctions all over the northern

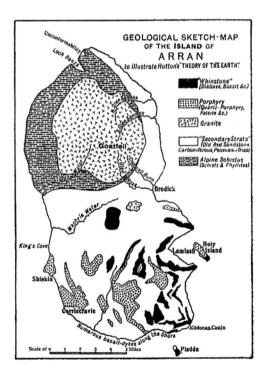

Figure 6.6 Geological sketch map of the island of Arran, from James Hutton, *Theory of the Earth, with Proofs and Illustrations*, III, p. 203.

part of the island, spurred on by repeated frustration. Hutton eventually found satisfactory exposures of intrusive granite veins in adjacent schistus on a solo foray into North Glen Sannox, and only after that did he and Clerk make similar finds on Glenshant Hill and in the Cnocan Burn. Playfair reports these finds in his biography and notes that Hutton 'brought a specimen of some hundred weight' from North Glen Sannox back to Edinburgh, 'consisting of a block of schistus, which includes a large vein of granite' (p. 70).

But Hutton found more on Arran than he had anticipated. Rather than remaining fixated on granite-schistus conjunctions, he turned to a consideration of the geomorphology and geohistory of Arran as a whole, beginning with a general overview in which he notes the island's division into a granite mountain range to the north and a lowland area to the south made up primarily of sedimentary rocks arranged in horizontal strata (III, pp. 201–16). The fact that the Highland Boundary divides Arran in this way means that the island is often described as a Scotland in miniature, and this is one reason why it remains of special interest to geologists today.[35] Playfair represents Arran as 'one of those spots in which nature has collected, within a very small compass, all the phenomena most interesting to a geologist. A range of granite mountains, placed in the northern part of the island, have their sides covered with primitive schistus of various kinds, to which, on the sea-shore, succeed secondary strata of grit, limestone, and even coal' ('Biographical Account', pp. 69–70). Hutton, indeed, views Arran as a geological microcosm of the whole planet that promises to reveal the secrets of the system of the earth itself, as well as of mountains (III, p. 199).

One of the discoveries on Arran that allowed Hutton to begin to think of the island not only as a microcosm of the earth but also as a key to unfolding the earth's geohistory was an interface not between granite and schistus but between schistus and stratified sedimentary rocks. As Playfair notes, the 'primitive schistus of various kinds' that covers the sides of the granite mountains in the north of Arran is succeeded on the sea-shore by various kinds of secondary strata. Hutton claims that he had been searching for this kind of junction for a long time (though it is not mentioned in earlier chapters):

> The immediate connection of the alpine schistus with the strata of the low country is an object which I have long looked for, I may almost say in vain. I expected to have seen it in entering the Grampian mountains, . . . but I

was disappointed in my expectations. . . . I have in like manner looked for it in both sides of the southern mountains of Scotland, and that in several places, without receiving any satisfaction upon that subject. In the island of Arran I have sought it carefully without finding it, in a place where I thought it was certainly to be found; and I found it, in a place where I had not thought almost of looking for it. (III, pp. 230–2)

This passage works to stimulate our anticipation of Hutton's account of his discovery of the now famous unconformity just north-east of Newton Point at the northern tip of Arran – the first unconformity to be discovered in Britain and now a place of pilgrimage and study for geologists and geology students:[36]

Loch Ranza at the north end of the island, is properly within the alpine schistus; but, in tracing the shore, upon the east side of the loch or bay, we come to the extremity of this schistus district. Here the first thing that occurs is the immediate junction of the inclined strata of schistus and the other strata which here appear to be a composition of sandstone and limestone; these strata are equally inclined with the schistus, but in the opposite direction. Those two different kinds of stratified bodies rise to meet each other; they are somewhat confused at the immediate junction; but some of the sandstone or calcareous strata overlap the ends of the alpine schistus. (III, p. 235)

Hutton presents a more precise description of the Lochranza uncon-formity in the first volume of *Theory of the Earth*:

It was but a very small part that I could see; but what appeared was most distinct. Here the schistus and the sandstone strata both rise inclined at an angle of about 45°; but these primary and secondary strata were inclined at almost opposite directions; and thus they met together like the two sides of a *lambda*, or the rigging of a house, being a little in disorder at the angle of their junction. From this situation of those two masses of strata, it is evidently impossible that either of them could have been formed originally in that position; therefore, I could not here learn in what state the schistus strata had been in when those of the sand-stone, &c. had been superinduced. (I, pp. 429–30)

Hutton does not immediately explain the significance of the Lochranza unconformity in either account. But within twenty pages or so of his unpublished 'Mineral History of the Island of Arran', some of its implications begin to emerge in his speculations about the origins of Arran as a whole:

> It must appear that the island of Arran was originally composed of strati-fied bodies, in which two species may be distinguished; on the one hand, the alpine schistus, much changed by fusion from its original state, and containing no visible mark of organized bodies; and on the other, strata probably of later formation, less changed by fusion, and containing marks of organized bodies. (III, pp. 262–3)

Although it is true that Hutton exhibited little interest in the historical sequence of the fossil record,[37] he is clearly interested here in the possibility that the presence or absence of fossils might reveal temporal and causal differences in rock formation that correlate with the temporal succession indicated by the Lochranza unconformity. That the island consists of at least two kinds of stratified rock that have undergone different degrees of metamorphosis indicates that its basic building materials must have been formed under the sea in at least two separate phases over a very long time. The fact that these stratified materials have been intruded and broken up not only by the massive granite upwelling that formed the mountains of the northern part of the island but also by multiple intrusions of all kinds of rock material into the various stratified rocks over the whole island supports Hutton's assumption that Arran must have been created a very long time ago when the complex strata that had been formed under the sea were raised above sea level by subterraneous heat and pressure.[38] The original size and shape of the Arran land mass cannot even be guessed at because the island's geomorphology indicates that it has been exposed to erosive forces over an enormous time period since it 'first [proceeded] from the bowels of the earth or bottom of the sea' (III, p. 264).

Having conjured up these startling visions of Arran's complex formation under the sea, its uplift above the sea by subterraneous heat and pressure, and its subsequent erosion over an enormous period of time, Hutton goes on to speculate about the island's past connections with the surrounding land masses in ways that heighten the aesthetic power of his Arran story still further:

> The great number of whinstone dykes upon the west coast in the shire of Ayr, opposite Arran, *i.e.*, from Scalmorly [Skelmorlie] almost to Irwin [Irvine] similar to those which we find in that island, give reason

to conclude that these are continued under ground, or that they had proceeded originally from one mass. We thus are led to believe that the island of Arran and the shire of Ayr had been raised from the bottom of the sea at the same time, or in the operation of the same causes; and that therefore those two coasts were once continuous land, which was afterwards preyed upon by the water, and disjoined by the sea. (III, pp. 265–6)

By observing the erosive forces of the sea on Arran and suggesting that the islands of Pladda and the Holy Island (and perhaps even Ailsa Rock) were once part of Arran, Hutton begins to open up his speculations to include the likely future of the planet:

> By thus ascertaining the first step in our cosmological speculation, we advance with some degree of certainty into the annals of a continent which does not now appear; and in tracing these operations which are past, we foresee distant events in the course of things. We see the destruction of a high island in the formation of a low one; and from those portions of the high land or continent which remain as yet upon the coast and in the sea, we may perceive the future destruction, not of the little island only, which has been saved from the wreck of so much land, but also of the continent itself, which is in time to disappear. Thus Pladda is to the Island of Arran what Arran is to the island of Britain, and what the island of Britain is to the continent of Europe. (III, pp. 261–2)

On the eve of the French Revolution, in a period when writers were concerned about the potential decline and fall of the British Empire, and even of Britain itself, and speculating about the ruins of empires in general, Hutton's long geological perspective indicates that the very fabric of the British Isles is a relatively temporary product of the geostrophic cycle, destined to destruction not by sin, or loss of virtue or valour, or political corruption, but by the slow but relentless continuation of the geological processes that formed it in the first place. Hutton's interpretation of Arran's geology and the story it tells about the past and future of the planet offers sublime glimpses of colossal processes taking place infinitesimally slowly over unthinkable time periods, and promises the eventual slow-motion destruction of everything we take to be solid and permanent. His vision is nonetheless an optimistic one in that he sees the destruction of cherished landscapes and landforms as a necessary process in that it provides the eroded materials needed for the geostrophic cycle to continue to produce new land masses that will sustain life long after Scotland, Britain and Europe will have disappeared from the face of the earth. Such a long-term perspective enables Hutton to claim that his theory of the earth 'is confirmed from the natural history of Arran' (III, p. 267).

Jedburgh and Siccar Point (1787 and 1788)

We might expect that the sublime epiphanies that Hutton experienced on Arran would constitute the completion of his geological quest. Yet, as Playfair observes,

> The least complete of the observations at Arran was that of the junction of the primitive with the secondary strata, which is but indistinctly seen in that island, and only at one place. Indeed, the contact of these two kinds of rock, though it forms a line circumscribing the bases of all primitive countries, is so covered by the soil, as to be visible in very few places. ('Biographical Account', pp. 70–1)

As a consequence Hutton undertook two further expeditions in Scotland whose object was no longer granite-schistus junctions but those elusive junctions between 'primitive' and 'secondary' strata that exhibited unconformities of the kind glimpsed on Arran. Having proven to his own satisfaction that granite is an igneous rock that has been forced in a molten state into older overlying schists, Hutton put all his attention on discovering unconformities between inclined schists and overlying sedimentary rocks because these formations appeared to confirm his theory that the earth's geomorphology has been formed by repeated revolutions of the geostrophic cycle.

Because the manuscript intended to form the third volume of *Theory of the Earth* comes to an end with the chapter on Arran, to complete the story of Hutton's geological tours of Scotland we need to turn to chapter 6 of the first volume of *Theory of the Earth* and to Playfair's biography of Hutton. It is notable that Hutton's *Theory of the Earth* makes no mention of his search for granite intrusions in Glen Tilt, Galloway and Arran and concentrates instead on his later quest for unconformities. In chapter 6 of the first volume, Hutton briefly refers to the unconformity on Arran (I, pp. 429–30), but it is the unconformity near Jedburgh that he describes and analyses at length:

one day, walking in the beautiful valley above the town of Jedburgh, I was surprised with the appearance of vertical strata in the bed of the river, where I was certain that the banks were composed of horizontal strata. I was soon satisfied with regard to this phenomenon, and rejoiced at my good fortune in stumbling upon an object so interesting to the natural history of the earth, and which I had been long looking for in vain. (I, p. 432)

What most interests Hutton, however, is that 'above those vertical strata, are placed the horizontal beds, which extend along the whole country' (I, p. 432), and he spends the bulk of the first part of the chapter in thinking through how such a juxtaposition could have come about and what it means for his geotheory. The elder John Clerk made a drawing of the Jed unconformity (Figure 6.7) which was later used for one of the six engravings in *Theory of the Earth*.

Hutton assumes that everyone will agree that the vertical strata of schistus must have been formed in a horizontal orientation out of sediments gathered at the bottom of the sea. More controversially,

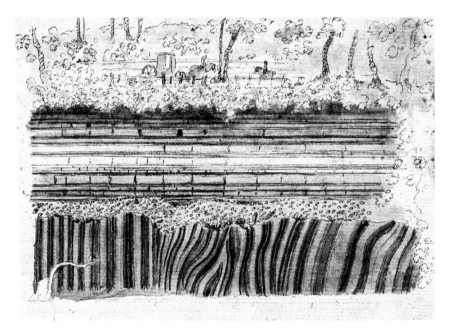

Figure 6.7 John Clerk of Eldin, Unconformity at Jedburgh: original drawing of the engraving for plate III of Hutton's *Theory of the Earth*, I (1787), from G. Y. Craig (ed.), *James Hutton's Theory of the Earth: The Lost Drawings*, p. 57.

he then proposes that subterraneous heat and pressure had hardened these strata, folded them into an upright orientation, and then raised them well above the surface of the ocean to produce an extensive mountainous area. A long period of erosion followed in which 'the effects of either rivers, winds, or tides' had washed bare 'the surface of the vertical strata'. At a still later period, 'this surface had been . . . sunk below the influence of those destructive operations, and thus placed in a situation proper for the opposite effect, the accumulation of matter prepared and put in motion by the destructive causes' (I, pp. 434–5). The unconformity is complicated by the fact that 'a certain pudding-stone' is to be found 'interposed' between the vertical and horizontal strata (I, p. 436). The fact that the pudding stone is in a hardened state is taken by Hutton as evidence that the remnants of the eroded schistus mountains had once more been subjected to the 'indurating' effects of subterraneous heat and pressure (I, p. 438). The overlying horizontal beds of Old Red Sandstone must have been laid down upon the hardened pudding stone at the bottom of the sea and then consolidated by plutonic forces, after which the whole structure had once more been raised above the sea by those same forces and subsequently laid bare by the erosive effects of the river (I, pp. 439–42). The Jed unconformity, then, must have been produced by several revolutions of the geostrophic cycle involving erosion, sedimentation, induration, uplift, erosion, sinking, further sedimentation and so on, over enormous periods of time.

But Hutton's most important and famous unconformity was the one he found at Siccar Point in 1788 on a boat trip he made with Playfair and Hall. Siccar Point is a rocky promontory in Berwickshire located on the coast about thirty-five miles east of Edinburgh between Dunglass and Fast Castle. The Siccar Point unconformity, which is now a Site of Special Scientific Interest and a Geological Conservation Review site, consists of almost vertical beds of marine Lower Silurian greywackes that are approximately 435 million years old and are overlain by gently sloping beds of non-marine Upper Devonian conglomerates that are approximately 375 million years old (Figure 6.8). Although Hutton did not know how old these rocks were, he did realise that the unconformity must have been formed over an enormous time period. Hutton's *Theory of the Earth* offers only a brief description of this now world-famous unconformity and does not analyse it. Hutton notes that late in the spring of 1788 he

Figure 6.8 'Siccar Point', by Dave Souza (2008), Wikimedia Commons ©
Dave Souza.

and Playfair visited Sir James Hall on his estate at Dunglass in order
to explore the Lammermuir Hills and the coast where they run into
the North Sea. He describes how the party embarked in a boat at
Dunglass Burn and 'set out to explore the coast' between Dunglass
and Fast Castle and perhaps on to St Abb's Head (I, p. 458). It was
on this boat trip that 'at Siccar Point, we found a beautiful picture
of this junction [between schistus and sandstone] washed bare by the
sea' (I, p. 458).

The fact that *Theory of the Earth* says relatively little about Siccar
Point perhaps prompted Playfair to offer his own extended account
of the expedition in his biography of Hutton. Playfair's narrative is
perhaps the most famous and often-quoted passage in the history of
geology and it helped to make Siccar Point into an internationally
famous place of geological pilgrimage. Playfair's account is worth
quoting at length:

> The ridge of the Lammer-muir Hills, in the south of Scotland, consists
> of primary micaceous schistus, and extends from St Abb's-head west-
> wards, till it join the metalliferous mountains about the sources of the
> Clyde. The sea-coast affords a transverse section of this alpine tract at
> its eastern extremity, and exhibits the change from the primary to the
> secondary strata, both on the south and on the north. Dr Hutton wished
> particularly to examine the latter of these, and on this occasion Sir James

Hall and I had the pleasure to accompany him. We sailed in a boat from Dunglass, on a day when the fineness of the weather permitted us to keep close to the foot of the rocks which line the shore in that quarter, directing our course southwards, in search of the termination of the secondary strata. We made for a high rocky point or head-land, the Siccar, near which, from our observations on shore, we knew that the object we were in search of was likely to be discovered. On landing at this point, we found that we actually trode on the primeval rock, which forms alternately the base and the summit of the present land. It is here a micaceous schistus, in beds nearly vertical, highly indurated, and stretching from S.E. to N.W. The surface of this rock runs with a moderate ascent from the level of low-water, at which we landed, nearly to that of high-water, where the schistus has a thin covering of red horizontal sandstone laid over it; and this sandstone, at the distance of a few yards farther back, rises into a very high perpendicular cliff. Here, therefore, the immediate contact of the two rocks is not only visible, but is curiously dissected and laid open by the action of the waves. The rugged tops of the schistus are seen penetrating into the horizontal beds of sandstone, and the lowest of these form a breccia containing fragments of schistus, some round and others angular, united by an arenaceous cement.

Dr HUTTON was highly pleased with appearances that set in so clear a light the different formations of the parts which compose the exterior crust of the earth, and where all the circumstances were combined that could render the observation satisfactory and precise. On us who saw these phenomena for the first time, the impression made will not easily be forgotten. The palpable evidence presented to us, of one of the most extraordinary and important facts in the natural history of the earth, gave a reality and substance to those theoretical speculations, which, however probable, had never till now been directly authenticated by the testimony of the senses. We often said to ourselves, What clearer evidence could we have had of the different formation of these rocks, and of the long interval which separated their formation, had we actually seen them emerging from the bosom of the deep? We felt ourselves necessarily carried back to the time when the schistus on which we stood was yet at the bottom of the sea, and when the sandstone before us was only beginning to be deposited, in the shape of sand or mud, from the waters of a superincumbent ocean. An epocha still more remote presented itself, when even the most ancient of these rocks, instead of standing upright in vertical beds, lay in horizontal planes at the bottom of the sea, and was not yet disturbed by that immeasurable force which has burst asunder the solid pavement of the globe. Revolutions still more remote appeared in the distance of this extraordinary perspective. The mind seemed to grow giddy by looking so far into the abyss of time; and while we listened with earnestness and admiration to the philosopher who was now unfolding to us the order and series of these wonderful events, we became sensible how much farther reason may sometimes go than imagination can venture to follow. ('Biographical Account', pp. 71–3)

In Playfair's reconstruction, Hutton's on-the-spot analysis of the Siccar Point unconformity had an astonishing impact, carrying his giddy listeners across the abyss of time to glimpse a series of events that overwhelmed their imagination. It is thus notable that Playfair, in recalling the climax of Hutton's endeavour, twice reaches for the paradoxical deictics of 'was-now' constructions – the second of which is in the third person ('the philosopher . . . was now'). It may be, as I suggested earlier, that the 'was-now' paradox, with its disruptions of grammatical and temporal logic, best conveys (or produces) the experience of Hutton's listeners and readers as they 'grow giddy by looking so far into the abyss of time'. We might say that 'was-now' is a grammatical unconformity that is highly appropriate in attempting to describe or generate the disorienting effects of attempting to conceive the full implications of geological unconformity. The grammatical technique also helps to persuade readers of the explanatory power of Hutton's theory by inducing them to feel that they are sharing in the intense experience of those who listened to Hutton in front of the Siccar Point exposure, allowing them to becoming virtual witnesses not only of the evidence in the field but also of the ancient processes that it points to. As Playfair puts it, 'We felt ourselves necessarily carried back to the time when the schistus on which we stood was yet at the bottom of the sea.'

Informed Wonder

The publication of the two versions of Hutton's theory of the earth in 1786/1788 and 1795 precipitated a heated controversy in which Hutton's Plutonism, apparent suggestion of an eternal earth, and seeming reliance on deductive theoretical hypothesis were all attacked. We can only speculate about the possible impact on this controversy if the projected third volume of *Theory of the Earth* had been published in 1795. Contemporary readers would have had a very different picture of Hutton's theory and the evidence for it. Yet prevailing paradigms and theories tend to shape the observation and interpretation of evidence even in those naturalists who claim to be inductive empiricists. The manuscripts of Hutton's Scottish tours were held by Playfair after Hutton's death, and C. J. Nicholas and P. N. Pearson have suggested that Playfair may have discussed them with John Walker, his former teacher at the University of Edinburgh.[39] As we will see in the following chapter, when Robert Jameson, also a former student of Walker, explored Arran in the late 1790s he seems to have known more about Hutton's findings on the island than are revealed in *Theory of the Earth*, though he claimed not to be able to see the features that Hutton saw or reinterpreted them to support his own Neptunist theory. Even today, more than a century after their rediscovery and publication, Hutton's manuscript tours of Scotland have not been fully taken into account by historians of Romantic-period geology, many of whom perpetuate the assumption that Hutton was an armchair geologist whose theory of the earth had more in common with the tradition of speculative theories stemming from Thomas Burnet than with the empirical fieldwork that came to characterise geology in the nineteenth century.[40]

A literary reading of Hutton's geological tours of Scotland helps us to speculate about their potential impact upon readers if not on the history of geology. Along with the 1786/88 paper and chapter 6 of the first volume of *Theory of the Earth*, the Scottish tours undermine the often-repeated assertion that Hutton was an inept writer. While some of the writing and organisation of the first two volumes of *Theory of the Earth* are confusing and opaque, the geological travel writing in the projected third volume is often lucid and powerful and potentially generates the informed wonder that was the hallmark of Romantic science.[41] Attention to Hutton's use of literary techniques and conventions – narrative strategies associated with quest romance, figurative language, authorial self-fashioning, the manipulation of the sublime, the use of paradoxical deictics and so on – highlights the ways these texts dramatise the journey of scientific discovery and induce the reader to participate in the dynamic experience of desire, frustration, fulfilment and awe. These written tours would have allowed Hutton's readers to imagine that they were virtual participants in the geological quest conducted by a savant whose self-fashioning made him a reliable guide through Scotland's geomorphology and the landscapes of deep time. Indeed, it is possible to suggest that had they been published in 1795, Hutton's geological tours would have made a significant contribution to the tradition of scientific travel writing and the Romantic 'discovery' of Scotland.

Notes

This chapter is a revised and extended version of Furniss, 'James Hutton's Geological Tours of Scotland'.

1. For claims that Hutton was the founder of modern geology, see Geikie, *Geological Sketches at Home and Abroad*, pp. 286–311, and *The Founders of Geology*, pp. 150–200; Bailey, *James Hutton – The Founder of Modern Geology*; Dean, *James Hutton and the History of Geology*; McIntyre and McKirdy, *James Hutton: The Founder of Modern Geology*; Oldroyd and Hamilton, 'Themes in the Early History of Scottish Geology'; Baxter, *Revolutions in the Earth*; and Repcheck, *The Man Who Found Time*. The misconception that Hutton was the first geologist to challenge Ussher's calculation of the age of the earth is recycled by Baxter and Repcheck.

2. See Porter, *The Making of Geology*; Gould, *Time's Arrow, Time's Cycle*; Laudan, *From Mineralogy to Geology*; and Rudwick, *Bursting the Limits of Time*, pp. 158–72.

3. For Rudwick's informed, but sometimes problematic, account of Hutton's geotheory, see *Bursting the Limits of Time*, pp. 158–72. On the complex relationship between theory and empirical evidence in Hutton's work, see Laudan, *From Mineralogy to Geology*, pp. 128–31; also see Leveson, 'What Was James Hutton's Methodology?'.

4. On the controversies between 'Neptunists, Vulcanists and Plutonists' and between 'Catastrophists and Uniformitarians', see Hallam, *Great Geological Controversies*.

5. The term 'geostrophic cycle' was coined by Tomkeieff in 'James Hutton and the Philosophy of Geology'. Playfair's 'geological cycle' (*Illustrations of the Huttonian Theory of the Earth*, p. 128) seems preferable.

6. For the way this chapter revises the 1788 paper, see Dean, *James Hutton and the History of Geology*, pp. 66–7.

7. See Furniss, 'A Romantic Geology'. Also see Heringman, *Romantic Rocks*, pp. 109–18. Hutton's impact on Romantic poetry has been explored by a number of scholars, including Leask, 'Mont Blanc's Mysterious Voice', and McKusick, '"Kubla Khan" and the Theory of the Earth'.

8. On the Romantic vision of nature's active powers, see Piper, *The Active Universe*, and Levere, *Poetry Realized in Nature*. For an important correction to the view that Newton's universe was inert, see Gabbey, 'Newton, Active Powers, and the Mechanical Philosophy'.

9. See Kirwan, 'Examination of the Supposed Igneous Origin of Stony Substances'. For a general discussion of the dispute about granite in the period, see Read, *The Granite Controversy*.

10. See, for example, Jameson, 'Is the Huttonian Theory of the Earth Consistent with Fact?', read to the Royal Medical Society of Edinburgh in 1796. On the controversy between Jameson and Hutton, see Flinn, 'James Hutton and Robert Jameson'.

11. See Jones, 'Hall, Sir James, of Dunglass, fourth baronet (1761–1832)', *ODNB*.

12. Quoting Hutton, *Theory of the Earth*, I, pp. 185–6.

13. See Hutton, 'Of Certain Natural Appearances of the Ground on the Hill of Arthur's Seat'. On the importance of Salisbury Crags to Hutton, see *Theory of the Earth*, I, pp. 153–4; Craig (ed.), *James Hutton's Theory of the Earth: The Lost Drawings*, p. 27; and Dean, *James Hutton and the History of Geology*, pp. 11–15.

14. See Dean, *James Hutton and the History of Geology*, pp. 14–15.

15. As was common in the period, Playfair uses the term 'fossil' to mean a natural object found in the ground. As Hutton admitted in a letter in 1770, 'I never considered the different kinds of figured bodies found in strata further than to distinguish betwixt animal and vegetable, sea and land objects, the mineralization of those objects being more the subject of my pursuits than the arrangement of them into their classes' (Hutton to John Strange, quoted by Dean, *James Hutton and the History of Geology*, p. 9). The fact that organic fossils would soon become the central concern of European geology was one of the factors that made Hutton's geotheory appear outdated in the early nineteenth century.

16. For early criticism of Hutton's deductive theorising, see Walker, *Essays on Natural History and Rural Economy*, pp. 336–7. Also see Williams, *The Natural History of the Mineral Kingdom*, I, pp. xxiii–lxii. The most extended early criticism of Hutton is de Luc, 'To Dr. James Hutton, F.R.S. Edinburgh, on his Theory of the Earth'. Also see Jameson, *An Outline of the Mineralogy of the Shetland Islands*, and Kirwan, 'On the Huttonian Theory of the Earth' and 'Examination of the Supposed Igneous Origin of Stony Substances'. For an overview, see Dean, *James Hutton and the History of Geology*, pp. 46–57, 79–101, 126–62, and Hallam, *Great Geological Controversies*, pp. 1–63. For the Edinburgh controversy between Wernerian Neptunism and Huttonian Plutonism

in the early nineteenth century, see Davies, *The Earth in Decay*, and Hallam, *Great Geological Controversies*, pp. 18–23.

17. For accounts of Hutton's tours of Scotland in the 1780s, see Baxter, *Revolutions in the Earth*, pp. 146–61, and Dean, *James Hutton and the History of Geology*, pp. 15–46.

18. See Hutton, 'Observations on Granite' and *Theory of the Earth*, I, chapter 6, section I (pp. 421–53) and section II (pp. 453–72).

19. The text of Hutton's manuscript for the projected third volume of *Theory of the Earth* can also be found in Dean (ed.), *James Hutton in the Field and in the Study*.

20. On the notion of the 'virtual witness' in the geological writing of the period, see Rudwick, *Bursting the Limits of Time*, pp. 74–5.

21. As Geikie points out, 'Under the term "schistus," Hutton included not only what are now discriminated as "schists," but also all rocks associated with the schists and possessing a bedded character, such as quartzites and limestones. He also applied the same term to the highly inclined and contorted greywackes, grits and shales (Silurian) of the Southern Uplands of Scotland' (Hutton, *Theory of the Earth*, III, p. 6, note).

22. See Nicholas and Pearson, 'Robert Jameson on the Isle of Arran', p. 31. Also see Hutton, 'Observations on Granite' (read at the Royal Society of Edinburgh in January 1790 and August 1791).

23. The importance of Glen Tilt in the history of geology is recognised in the fact that it has been made a Joint Nature Conservation Committee Geological Conservation Review site (GCR Number 2695, NN960720).

24. For an account of the role of curiosity in travel writing of the period, see Leask, *Curiosity and the Aesthetics of Travel Writing*.

25. Hutton's geological collection went missing after his death, partly through Robert Jameson's neglect. See Jones, 'The Geological Collection of James Hutton'.

26. See Jordanova, *Sexual Visions: Images of Gender in Science and Medicine*.

27. On the emergence of empathetic narrative and deictics, see Adamson, 'Literary Language', pp. 671–3.

28. See Adamson, 'Subjectivity in Narration'.

29. See Adamson, 'From Empathetic Deixis to Empathetic Narrative'.

30. See Adamson, 'From Empathetic Deixis to Empathetic Narrative', p. 216.

31. See Adamson, 'From Empathetic Deixis to Empathetic Narrative', p. 209.

32. See 'Literary Language', p. 662.

33. See Heringman, *Romantic Rocks*, p. 1.

34. Craig suggests that 'there are reasons to believe that the drawings [of Arran] reproduced [in *The Lost Drawings*] are not by John Clerk, jnr., but by his father' (*The Lost Drawings*, p. 53).

35. For Arran's significance for geologists, see Whittow, *Geology and Scenery in Scotland*, pp. 67–79; Gillen, *Geology and Landscapes of Scotland*, pp. 161–3; and McKirdy et al., *Land of Mountain and Flood*, pp. 297–301.

36. The itinerary of Lochranza Field Study and Activity Centre includes a day's investigation of Hutton's Unconformity; see <https://www.lochranzacentre.co.uk/> (last accessed 5 June 2017).

37. See Porter, *The Making of Geology*, p. 166, and Gould, *Time's Arrow, Time's Cycle*, pp. 86–8.

38. See Tyrrell, 'Hutton on Arran'.

39. See Nicholas and Pearson, 'Robert Jameson on the Isle of Arran, 1797–1799', p. 33.

40. See Gould, *Time's Arrow, Time's Cycle*, pp. 61–97, and Porter, *The Making of Geology*, pp. 184–96.

41. See Holmes, *The Age of Wonder*.

Chapter 7

Natural History among the Mountains of a Wild Country: Robert Jameson on Arran, 1797 and 1799

As well as studying natural history with John Walker at the University of Edinburgh (1792–3), Robert Jameson (1774–1854) also studied mineralogy and geology with Abraham Gottlob Werner at the Bergakademie in Freiberg in 1800.[1] When Walker died in December 1803, Jameson replaced him as Regius Professor of Natural History, a post he held for the next fifty years. As a teacher, writer and editor, and through various institutional positions, Jameson championed Werner's Neptunist mineralogy and geotheory for much of the rest of his life.[2] In 1808, he published *Elements of Geognosy*, the first full exposition of Werner's mineralogy, and founded the Wernerian Natural History Society, acting as its president for nearly half a century.[3] He also promoted Werner's ideas by founding and editing *Memoirs of the Wernerian Society* (from 1811) and the *Edinburgh Philosophical Journal* (from 1819).[4]

Jameson and Hutton

In 1796, primed by Walker's teachings and Werner's writings, Jameson contributed to the Neptunist critique of Vulcanism and Plutonism by reading two papers to the Royal Medical Society of Edinburgh entitled 'Is the Volcanic Opinion of the Formation of Basaltes Founded on Truth?' and 'Is the Huttonian Theory of the Earth Consistent with Fact?'.[5] In the first of these papers, as Dennis R. Dean points out, Jameson 'noted that the volcanic theory was first proposed in 1763 by Demarest, who affirmed that basalt had the same external character as lava. On this gross error, Jameson observed, "succeeding geologists

have founded a most extraordinary chimera, attributing the formation of basalts to fire!'" (*James Hutton and the History of Geology*,
pp. 97–8).[6] Reiterating an assertion that Walker made in his lectures,
Jameson insists that 'though basalt occurs frequently in volcanic
countries, it also appears in Scotland, where no such volcanoes have
ever been detected' (Dean, *James Hutton and the History of Geology*,
p. 98). Jameson concludes by saying that

> Upon such a basis is the famous Volcanic theory founded, which for
> many years consigned three fourths of our Globe into the hands of
> Pluto, until the immortal *Werner*, from a careful examination of nature,
> declared the absurdity of such a hypothesis (if it can be so called). He
> did not endeavour to confute it by subtlety of argument, but with facts,
> sunk it into utter oblivion. Mr Kirwan, in his admirable book of Fossils,
> has also given us a very able defence of the Neptunian hypothesis; which
> he has farther confirmed by new and important facts. (In Nicholas and
> Pearson, 'Robert Jameson on the Isle of Arran', p. 33)[7]

Facts also demonstrated, Jameson argued, that Hutton's theory of
the earth was not consistent with fact. These two papers indicate that
Jameson was already familiar with some of the key texts in the con-
troversy between Neptunism, Vulcanism and Plutonism, including
Werner's article about his observations in Scheibenberg,[8] Kirwan's
Elements of Mineralogy (1794), and Hutton's 'Theory of the Earth'
(*TRSE*, 1788) and *Theory of the Earth* (1795).

In the 1790s, Jameson undertook various tours of Scotland's
Highlands and Islands in order to gather evidence that would support Neptunism and refute Vulcanist and Huttonian interpretations
of Scotland's geomorphology. In 1794, accompanied by his younger
brother Andrew, Jameson spent three months exploring the geology,
mineralogy, zoology and botany of the Shetland Islands. He made
a second tour in Scotland two years later with the London chemist
Charles Hatchett. Thereafter, he toured Arran in 1797 and 1799,
the Western Islands and the Highlands in 1798, and Orkney and the
north-east coast of Scotland in 1799.[9] Jameson kept journals on these
tours and wrote up his findings in *An Outline of the Mineralogy of
the Shetland Islands, and of the Island of Arran* (1798) and *Mineralogy of the Scottish Isles; with Mineralogical Observations Made in a
Tour through Different Parts of the Mainland of Scotland* (1800).[10]
In this chapter I concentrate on Jameson's tours of Arran in 1797

and 1799, comparing and contrasting the accounts of the island in his handwritten journals with the published versions in these books.

One of the intriguing questions with regard to Jameson's tours of Arran concerns the extent of his knowledge of Hutton's findings on the island. Hutton's references to his exploration of Arran in the two volumes of his *Theory of the Earth* that were published in 1795 are limited to a description of the unconformity at Newton Point near Lochranza and to a suggestion that fracturing in 'pudding-stone' conglomerates had been caused by pressure and sedimentation.[11] Hutton's 'Observations on Granite', published in the third volume of *Transactions of the Royal Society of Edinburgh* (1794), summarises his interpretation of intrusive granite veins and lists some of the places where he had found them, including on Arran. Jameson quotes from this paper in *Mineralogy of the Scottish Isles*:

> Dr Hutton maintains, 'that all the solid strata of the earth have been consolidated by means of subterraneous heat; softening the hard materials of these bodies; and that in many places these consolidated strata have been invaded by huge masses of fluid matter similar to lava, but for the most part perfectly distinguishable from it'. Granite he considers as a body which has been transfused in a liquid state from the subterranean regions, and made to break and invade the strata in the manner of basalt. His evidence for this opinion is as follows: He observed in the bed of the river Tilt, near to Blair in Athol, that the granite and shistus were much intermixed at their junction; and in the shire of Galloway and the island of Arran, veins of granite seemed to issue from the strata of granite and traverse the shistus; from this he concluded, as all veins are of a posterior origin to the strata which they traverse, that the veins of granite which traverse the shistus, being continuous with the granite, make the whole after formation to the shistus. (II, pp. 165–6)[12]

It is notable, however, that Hutton does not specify in his 'Observations on Granite' the precise locations on Arran of the granite-schistus junctions that he found there and announces instead that he intended to publish 'a particular account of the construction of Arran, or a mineralogical history of it' (*TRSE*, 3.2, 80–1). And, as we saw in the previous chapter, Hutton's 'An Examination of the Mineral History of the Island of Arran', intended for a projected third volume of *Theory of the Earth*, was not published until 1899.[13] Yet Nicholas and Pearson suggest that while 'It is clear from Jameson's 1797 journal that he had not seen Hutton's *Mineralogical History of the Island of Arran*', he may at least have heard about it: 'It is possible that Playfair may have mentioned the Arran chapter or work previously done by Hutton on the island to Walker. Another possibility is that Walker or Jameson heard of it through one of Edinburgh's many scientific or social clubs' ('Robert Jameson on the Isle of Arran', p. 33). In fact, as we will see, there is some evidence in Jameson's journals and published accounts of Arran that he knew about or read Hutton's 'Mineral History of the Island of Arran' prior to his own explorations of the island.

One of the central aims of the present chapter is to examine the way Jameson visits, revisits and writes about the main Huttonian geological sites on Arran in order to refute Hutton's geotheory. A comparative reading of Jameson's unpublished travel journals and published tours, along with Hutton's accounts of his findings on Arran, will help us to see how the island's geomorphology was successively interpreted and reinterpreted in support of competing theories of the earth in ways that made particular places and formations on the island into essentially contested 'hot spots' in the terrain of Scotland and in the history of geology. This approach will also reveal the way Jameson rewrote, reinterpreted and reorganised his findings and experiences on Arran in order to produce published texts that employ fiction, rhetoric and epiphanic moments in order to discredit Hutton's geological analysis of the island. The approach will also highlight the implications of the stylistic and generic choices that Jameson made in recasting his two journals into the two published books, highlighting significant interconnections between styles, genres and geological theories and the interplay between Enlightenment and Romantic geological travel writing acted out in Jameson's texts.

Jameson's Wernerian Assumptions

Both of Jameson's published tours of Scotland are dedicated to Walker, but their theoretical assumptions are mostly derived from Werner. *An Outline* begins with a preface which celebrates 'the labours of the great Werner' (p. i), while the introduction to *Mineralogy of the Scottish Isles* includes the first summary in English of Werner's mineralogical system in the form of 'An Abstract of the Wernerian Account of the different Kinds of Mountain Rocks; with Geognostic Observations on the Strata of the Scottish Isles, and such parts of the Mainland as are mentioned in this Work' (pp. xiii–xxvi). It is worth looking at this Abstract here because it will help us understand the presuppositions that lie behind Jameson's analysis of geological formations in the Scottish Highlands and Islands and his attempt to refute Hutton.

According to Jameson, the fundamental organising assumption of Werner's mineralogical system is that 'all the strata, of which our globe is composed, may be arranged under the following classes: The Primary, (Urgeburge); the Transition, (Ubergangsgeburge); the Stratified, which comprehends what are called the secondary strata, (Flotzgeburge); and the Volcanic, Alluvial, (Aufgeschwemmte)' (*Mineralogy of the Scottish Isles*, p. xiv).[14] For Werner, all rocks, except the local products of volcanoes or floodplains, were precipitated or sedimented in a primeval ocean in a sequence that is indicated by their position relative to the other strata and by the number of organic fossils they contain. The primary or primitive strata 'are characterised by their never containing the remains of animals or vegetables, nor alternating with such strata as contain these relics' (p. xiv). Primary or primitive strata include granite, gneiss, micaceous schistus, porphyry, primitive limestone and pitchstone (p. xv). Werner's assumptions about granite are especially noteworthy: 'Granite is considered by Werner as the fundamental rock, or that upon which all others are laid, and it is but very rarely that it alternates with other rocks. It is disposed in layers or strata, which are often enormously thick, and frequently horizontal, and extend thus for many miles through a whole chain of mountains' (p. xv). Transition rocks 'seem to have been formed after the primitive, and earlier than the stratified (flotzgeburge) rock' and they 'comprehend all those rocks, the lowermost strata of which contain few or no petrifactions; in the higher they are more abundant; but only petrifactions, the originals of which no longer exist' (p. xvi). Transition rocks include grawacken slate, sandstone, limestone and perhaps some species of porphyry (p. xvi). Stratified rocks 'appear to have been formed after the transition rocks. They consist of sandstone, limestone, argillite, with numerous petrifactions; also, basalt, schistose porphyry, . . . and the various coal strata' (pp. xvi–xvii). Basalt, then, is not a volcanic rock but is included among the stratified sedimentary rocks that were formed in the third and final phase of rock formation in the primeval ocean. The volcanic category 'comprehends the various stony substances altered by action of fire: these are, lava, pumice, volcanic ashes, and volcanic tuff' (p. xvii).

Jameson goes on to relate Werner's classification of rocks to his own observations in the Highlands and Islands of Scotland, which, by 1800, were much more extensive than when he first toured Arran in 1797. The following comments are the most pertinent to an understanding of Jameson's interpretation of Scotland's geomorphology and contest with Hutton:

> GRANITE. This rock forms but a small portion of the Scottish isles, it being found only in the isle of Arran, and in the low part of Mull called Ross, and in the Shetland islands. Upon the Mainland, however, I observed it forming mountains in Sutherlandshire, a considerable part of the county of Aberdeenshire seems to be formed of it, and also the lofty mountain of Cruachan upon the west coast. Granite veins are pretty frequent in several of the islands, as in Arran where they traverse the common granite, and in Coll, Tiree, Rona, the Orkney and Shetland islands, &c. where they traverse micaceous shistus, gneiss, or hornblende slate. Upon the mainland, in the route from Bernera to Perth, the granite veins are extremely common. (p. xviii)

For Jameson, then, granite is more widespread in mainland Scotland than Hutton had recognised, though it is far from ubiquitous. More importantly, Jameson notes that granite veins in 'micaceous shistus, gneiss, or hornblende slate' are extremely common in the Highlands and Islands. This observation is especially interesting, given that such granite intrusions were regarded by Hutton as crucial evidence in support of his theory of the earth and given that Jameson, as we will see, implied that one of Hutton's key examples of this on Arran did not exist. While Hutton saw intrusive granite veins as decisive proof of his geotheory, they would appear to be incompatible with the Neptunist belief that granite is the fundamental primitive rock. If granite was the first of the primitive rocks to be laid down in the primeval ocean, it is difficult to see how it could be precipitated into cracks in other rocks. By contrast, Werner's classification of basalt as a third-phase sedimentary rock meant that the presence of colossal numbers of basalt veins all over Scotland was apparently unproblematic for Jameson (pp. xxiii–xxiv). Having scornfully dismissed the Vulcanist interpretation of basalt in one of the papers that he read to the Royal Medical Society, Jameson insists once again in the preface to *Mineralogy of the Scottish Isles* that 'VOLCANIC ROCKS have never been discovered in Scotland' (p. xxvi).

The Method of a Journal: Genre, Style, Aesthetics, Geology

After its brief mention of Werner, Jameson's preface to *An Outline of the Mineralogy of . . . Arran* presents some reflections on the book's style and genre and their relationship with its scientific aims:

> The outline which I now lay before the public may be thought tedious: it is true I have not followed the usual plan of a *medley*, having adhered entirely to mineralogical observation, without deviating, in any instance, to general subjects, which only distract our attention, and please the fancy, without any real advantage. What I here aim at is to be a faithful narrator of the appearances which nature presented to my view. This may appear to some an easy business: to me it has peculiar difficulties. The observance of nature in a cabinet, and among the mountains of a wild country, are very different employments: in this last, not only the multiplicity of the appearances, the wonderful and tremendous scenery, but the frequent occurrence of storms, and the obscurity which nature, by these means, throws over the most interesting productions, make us liable to error, notwithstanding our greatest care and attention. (*Outline*, pp. iv–v)

While his reference to 'general subjects' is a little vague, it is clear that Jameson seeks to limit his writing to the objective, synchronic description of natural objects without deviating, for example, into the historical and theoretical speculations of geology, which tend to produce general but fanciful theories of the earth. Yet the objective observation of nature is not easy 'among the mountains of a wild country'. Those aspects of a wild mountainous country that produce the Burkean sublime and that the Romantic traveller seeks out – 'the wonderful and tremendous scenery, . . . the frequent occurrence of storms, and the obscurity which nature, by these means, throws over the most interesting productions' – make mineralogical observers 'liable to error, notwithstanding our greatest care and attention'.[15] Yet despite suggesting that mineralogical observation and the aesthetic impact of wild mountainous country are incompatible, Jameson quite frequently celebrates the aesthetic qualities of Arran's terrain. Sometimes, indeed, he challenges Hutton's supposedly atheistical geotheory by claiming that the geology and aesthetic effects of particular places on Arran stimulate epiphanies that confirm the existence and omnipotent power of God. Rather than introducing error, the aesthetic experience of wild mountainous country reveals higher truths about the divine origins of the earth's geomorphology. Jameson's *Outline*, then, hesitates or oscillates between mineralogical observation and aesthetic response, between neutral description of natural appearances and Romantic travel writing, between the Enlightenment and Romanticism, between mineralogy and geology.

Jameson's reflections on the interrelationship between genre, style and geological methodology are further developed in the second chapter of the opening section on the Shetlands:

> In writing the mineral history of any country, various plans have been followed; but these usually depend more upon the degree of information the author is possessed of, than a predilection for any peculiar species of writing. Thus a thorough examination of all the strata of a certain district, their peculiarity of form, situation and composition, is best detailed in the form of a history; whereas a superficial and less satisfactory examination is usually related in the form of a journal. Of mineralogical histories, however, there are but few, excepting some disquisitions by German authors; nor is this to be wondered at, considering the infant state of the science, and the great labour attending investigations of this kind. It is not sufficient that we observe a stratum as we pass along, and remark its appearance again in some distant quarter; but we must trace it from its commencement, through all its various turns to its termination, ascertaining at the same time its connection with others, their mutual gradations, with many other general and particular observations, which require a long and careful observation. On the other hand, Mineralogists, in travelling through undescribed countries, have given much useful and interesting information in the form of a journal; thus Saussure, Charpentier, Ferber and others have in this way detailed a great number of facts, and diffused a very considerable taste for enquiries of this kind.
>
> In the Outline I am now to give of the Shetland islands, and the island of Arran, I find it convenient to follow nearly the method of a journal, as best suited to the general view I am to take. (*Outline*, pp. 11–12)[16]

The kind of 'history' of a place or country referred to here is not, of course, a sequential, diachronic narrative of the events that have happened in that place but a systematic, non-narrative, synchronic description and classification of its mineralogy in the mode of natural history. But the great labour involved in constructing such histories, the relatively undeveloped state of the science, and the fact that Jameson is reporting the observations made on a tour induce him to adopt the 'method of a journal' instead. This method does not dwell on dates and details about the journey and accommodation that we might expect in a travel journal. Instead, it consists largely of observations of mineralogy, geology, landscape, way of life and so on, that are minimally framed within the narrative of a journey. First-person pronouns are used quite sparsely, and the journal is much more focused on mineralogy and geology than on Jameson's experience. The journal form also regularly gives way to a more straightforward mineralogical analysis in which the minerals observed in particular places are listed and described in terms of their colour, lustre, transparency, mode of fracturing, hardness and so on, with occasional comments on the chemical analysis of similar minerals made by mineralogists such as Kirwan. Indeed, the general tendency of the book is to treat each area of the Shetlands and Arran in pairs of chapters, the first consisting of a narrative account of the process of exploring the area and the second presenting a systematic mineralogical 'Description of the Fossils, Mentioned in the Preceding Chapter', thus establishing a formal distinction between mineralogical travel journal and systematic mineralogical analysis.

The bulk of Jameson's *Outline of the Mineralogy of . . . Arran* is devoted to an account of his mineralogical and geological exploration of Arran in the summer of 1797. A close analysis of this part of the book, along with a comparative reading of the journal that Jameson wrote on that tour, will yield particularly revealing insights about the interconnections in the period between written style, genre, geological theory and aesthetic responses to geomorphology. This mode of proceeding will also reveal how the public face of natural history or mineralogy edits out many of the personal and aesthetic experiences of geological travel. Nicholas and Pearson claim that the text for the Arran chapters of Jameson's *Outline* 'follows closely his handwritten journal, minus the more personal observations made during the tour' ('Robert Jameson on the Isle of Arran', p. 34). Given that the generic conventions of natural history travel writing involved playing down personal experiences of all kinds, the natural history tour becomes a construct shaped by rhetorical and scientific conventions as much as by the experiences of the writer. By contrast, the 'Romantic' geological travel writing of the period (such as that of Faujas or Hutton), which is just as much a construct as that of natural history, foregrounds the dangers and hardships of the journey and emphasises the sublime experiences afforded by overcoming those dangers and hardships and by encountering wild mountain landscapes and astonishing geological discoveries. Yet despite Jameson's aspiration to exclude the aesthetic effects of wild mountain country from his natural history writing, he often dwells on them and sometimes modulates into what we might call the geological sublime in order to fashion moments of spiritual epiphany designed to refute the apparently atheistic geotheories of writers such as Hutton. Focusing on these moments will reveal that Jameson's rewriting of his 1797 journal in the 1798 *Outline* was much more extensive than Nicholas and Pearson suggest.

Jameson's First Tour of Arran: Journal into Book

Although Jameson describes *An Outline* as a 'journal', it is actually a carefully rewritten version of his 'Journal of my Tour in 1797', a real journal which 'consists of 116 pages of ink notes and occasional sketches' (Nicholas and Pearson, 'Robert Jameson on the Isle of Arran', p. 34). This journal begins by recording that Jameson sailed to Arran on 20 June 1797 in the company of 'Miss Fullerton' (a daughter of his host on Arran) and Mrs Ballantyne. It goes on to say that

> The approach to Arran is extremely grand and terrific bringing to my recollection all the majestic scenery of Foula or Noss [islands in the Shetlands], but upon a nearer approach, how diminutive do they appear, with what rugged majesty does Goatfield tower above all the other alpine heights, like Mont Blanc amidst the sublime scenery of Switzerland. Having landed we walked towards Kilmichael, (the seat of the ancient family of the Fullertons) where we soon arrived, found all in good health, was introduced to Mrs Fullerton and their young ladies, and soon found myself as happy as I could wish. (Jameson, 'Journal of my Tour in 1797', no pagination)

The comparison between Goatfell (874 metres) and Mont Blanc (4,810 metres) may seem slightly ludicrous, even when we note that Jameson is using 'alpine' as a general term for mountains and suggesting that these two mountains are similar not in height but in the way they soar above the mountains that surround them (Jameson had not visited the Alps). Yet the comparison can be read as an indication of Jameson's emotional and aesthetic experience of approaching

Arran and contemplating the looming heights of Goatfell. Jameson, then, used his 1797 journal to record the details and impressions of his journey as well as his mineralogical findings. This modulation between natural history and a more Romantic response to Arran's natural features is quite typical of Jameson's 'Journal of my Tour in 1797'. But if Jameson emerges as something of a Romantic geological traveller in the journal, we will see that this self-fashioning is significantly refashioned in the published version of his first Arran tour.

Jameson's *Outline of the Mineralogy of ... Arran* was 'the first book-length attempt to controvert [Hutton's] theory on the basis of field evidence' (Dean, *James Hutton and the History of Geology*, p. 99) and offers 'the first published account of the geology of Arran' (Nicholas and Pearson, 'Robert Jameson on the Isle of Arran', p. 34).[17] The section on Arran (pp. 49–144) contains footnotes that reject Hutton's theory at intervals of roughly every ten pages. It begins with a topographical map of the island (Figure 7.1; the place-name boxes

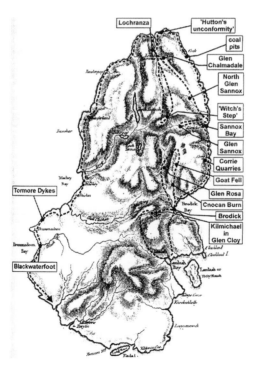

Figure 7.1 Map of Arran in Robert Jameson, *An Outline of the Mineralogy of ... Arran* (between pp. 49 and 50), with additions by Nicholas and Pearson, 'Robert Jameson on the Isle of Arran'.

and the marking of Jameson's main walking routes in 1797 and 1799 were added by Nicholas and Pearson). The opening paragraphs of *An Outline* are very different from those of the journal:

> This island is about thirty-two miles long and twelve broad, situated in the mouth of the Frith of Clyde, about eight miles from Bute, and sixteen from Saltcoats in Ayrshire. Its shape is irregular, but not so much so as many of the Western Islands, which are more exposed to the Atlantic Ocean; here the vicinity of the Scottish and Irish shores prevents any great destruction of land, as is evident from the lowness of the cliffs round the Island, which have not the precipitous, rugged, and bold aspect of the Shetland Islands. (*Outline*, pp. 49–50)

Separate headed paragraphs then describe the island's cliffs, mountains and surface in a manner that echoes the conventions of natural history travel writing that were established in the second half of the seventeenth century. The book, then, edits out the personal details and impressions of Jameson's arrival on Arran that he recorded in his journal, and focuses instead on geography and geology. Arran is located in the abstract dimensions of geometrical space that characterised Enlightenment geography and that contrasted so markedly with the Romantic valorisation of the affective qualities of particular places.[18]

On 21 June 1797, the day after his arrival on the island, Jameson climbed Goatfell, the highest mountain on Arran. His account in 'Journal of my Tour in 1797' includes an epiphany triggered on the summit by Arran's mountainous landscape glimpsed through clouds and rain:

> Set out this morning about 11 oclock for Goatfield in ascending the hills I found all to be sandstone for a considerable height, this was succeeded by Glimmer Schiefer, Granite which last forms the summit of this hill. Having left the sandstone far behind we now began the most rugged part of the ascent composed of immense piles of loose granite rocks, some of the masses columns 16 or 18 feet long. Having gained the summit after considerable fatigue we had the misfortune to be surrounded with clouds which prevented us having an enchanting prospect of the whole island, the west of Scotland, Ireland & the paps of Jura. The view however of the horrible glens underneath throw which the rain & clouds drove with fury, was inconceivably grand & stirring; what human being after witnessing such majestic works can refrain from declaring the existence of a deity, can any one attribute such to chance; if so truth is out of the question &

vanity the most deceitful of human passions leads to conclusions which have had their <u>own</u> influence on mankind. Having contemplated this scene for some time we descended which was extremely tiresome from the immense number of loose masses of granite. – We arrived at Kilmichael about 5 oclock, tired enough and very hungry. (Jameson, 'Journal of my Tour in 1797', no pagination)

This passage is predominantly focused on Jameson's personal experience of climbing Goatfell, making frequent use of first-person pronouns, reporting what he saw and felt, and stressing the fatigue he experienced while ascending and descending the mountain. Description of the geological make-up of Goatfell quickly gives way to the kind of sublime experience generated by wild mountainous scenery and the obscurity of clouds and rain that, according to the preface of Jameson's published account, leads to error. Here, however, the aesthetic experience of the Burkean sublime, generated in part as a pay-off for enduring the dangers and effort of climbing a mountain in challenging conditions and in part through the way that weather conditions both conceal and reveal mountain grandeur, allows the geologist to glimpse the higher truth of the divine agency behind the formation of mountains. This modulation from the natural sublime into religious epiphany is ubiquitous in the poetry of the Romantic period.[19] For Jameson, geology is not incompatible with such epiphanies but intensifies them. His view from Goatfell's summit is 'inconceivably grand and stirring', revealing 'majestic works' that induce the spectator, and ought to stir most truthful human beings, to declare the existence of a deity. Those natural historians, such as Hutton, who supposedly attribute such majestic forms and the geological processes that produced them to chance must be deceitful and vain and their views have a detrimental effect on mankind.

It is notable, therefore, that Jameson omits this epiphany from the published description of his ascent of Goatfell in *An Outline of the Mineralogy of . . . Arran*, which is more extended, more focused on geology and its effects on terrain, more attentive to the view from the summit, equally concerned with aesthetic experience, but omits religious reflections:

GOATFIELD. This mountain, according to Professor Playfair, is about 2945 feet above the level of the sea, and is reckoned the highest in the Island. It rises pretty rapidly from the south side of Brodick bay, until we arrive at the region, where the micaceous shistus disappears. There is a kind of irregular plain, from which the mountain rises in the form of an obtuse pyramid, and is very precipitous, being entirely formed of granite.

. . .

The pyramidal part of the mountain has a very steril [*sic*] and wild aspect, being completely covered with loose blocks of granite, and destitute of all vegetation, excepting a few lichens, which only add to its rude appearance. These blocks differ very much in size, some being about twenty feet long, and generally of a quadrangular shape, and are so heaped upon each other, as to render the ascent very difficult. Having, however, gained the summit, we are well repaid for our labour, by a most extensive view of a wonderful diversity of country. To the northward we look down upon the peaked summits, and deep glens in the neighbourhood of Goatfield, whose arid and reddish appearance, suggest fresh to our minds the effects of a dreadful conflagration. Beyond these, the isthmus of Cantyre, the island of Isla, the lofty and dreary paps of Jura, the long mountainous ridges of Argyleshire, and the far distant mountains of Mull, which are faintly descried, present a view, rather to be felt than described. On the east, the well cultivated island of Bute, the firth of Clyde, the Cumbray islands backed with the beautiful coasts of Renfrewshire, form a most picturesque scene. Towards the south we have below us the lower part of the island spread out like a map, forming a singular appearance, of heath covered mountains, and cultivated glens: further distant, the charming coasts of Ayrshire, the shores and mountains of Galloway, as far as the Mull, the stupendous craig of Ailsa, rising from the bottom of the ocean; all delight the eye, and ravish the imagination. Lastly, on the west, the coast of Ireland, from Fairhead, to Belfast Loch, conclude the amazing view from this interesting height. (pp. 64–7)

There are several notable differences between this passage and the journal version of Jameson's ascent of Goatfell. The journal is mostly concerned with Jameson's subjective experience: first-person pronouns are prominent and the focus is on what he saw and felt on the mountain and afterwards. Although the published account also uses first-person pronouns, they are less prominent and less personal. The suggestion that the features of the landscape seen from the summit 'delight the eye, and ravish the imagination' depersonalises the aesthetic experience: 'the eye' is a general, disembodied eye, not the eye of the narrating 'I'. And while the journal reports that 'Having gained the summit after considerable fatigue we had the misfortune to be surrounded with clouds', the published version describes a panoramic view unimpeded by clouds. In addition, the incidents of personal experience, induced by the accidents of weather in wild mountainous country, are edited out of the 1798 *Outline*. These differences suggest that the published description is not a faithful record of Jameson's actual experience but a fictional reconstruction which exemplifies the clarity of vision of natural history. In the panoramic view from the summit of Goatfell, which was perhaps put together by spreading out a map that delineated the view that anyone might see on a clear day, the eye masters the landscape in what James Thomson had called 'an equal, wide survey'.[20] Furthermore, although both accounts suggest that the labour of climbing Goatfell is repaid with a sublime experience that ravishes the imagination, the published version reveals the way the landforms have been shaped by geology rather than the presence and handiwork of their creator.

Yet, as we will see below, Jameson did not discard the religious epiphany recorded in his journal but redeployed it later in *An Outline* to represent the experience supposedly generated by another, less well-known geological formation that he discovered in the mountains to the north of Goatfell. Jameson's journal also indicates that he did indeed experience a panoramic vision from the top of one of Arran's mountains, though it was not Goatfell. In *An Outline*, then, Jameson reshuffles the experiences on Arran recorded in his journal in the service of his larger rhetorical and geotheoretical aims. Jameson's first published account of Arran therefore begins to seem more like a literary construct than a faithful record of his experiences and findings.

Jameson's 'Journal of my Tour in 1797' reveals that, on 24 June, after only four days on Arran, he set out on an expedition to Ireland. The main objects of this trip were to meet Richard Kirwan in Dublin, with whom he 'had a great deal of interesting conversation' (1 July), and to view the mineralogical collection of the Leskean Cabinet.[21] As Dean points out, Kirwan was 'Hutton's most vociferous opponent' who, in his conversation with Jameson, 'proposed several examples of natural phenomena that would apparently refute the Huttonian theory' (*James Hutton and the History of Geology*, p. 99).[22] Jameson arrived back on Arran on 18 July and set about interpreting the island's geology in ways that would disprove Hutton's theory of the earth in general and his reading of the island's geomorphology in particular.

Jameson began his exploration of Arran's mineralogy and geology by concentrating on the area around Brodick. From 20 to 26 July, like Hutton ten years earlier, he walked the hills around Glen Cloy and attempted to trace junctions between sandstone, basalt and porphyry. Jameson's journal records that on 25 July he was joined on Arran by a 'Mr Walker', thus indicating that part of his first geological field trip to Arran was carried out in the company of the university professor who had helped to form his geological worldview. Jameson and Walker, like Hutton before them, spent several days investigating the geology of Glen Rosa and Goatfell. Then, on 11 August, they set out on an anticlockwise walking tour of the island's coast, heading northward on the first day along the east coast from Brodick to Lochranza. According to 'Journal of my Tour in 1797', when Jameson and Walker reached Sannox Bay they took the coastal route to Lochranza, thus seemingly bypassing Glen Sannox and North Glen Sannox. Yet Jameson claims in *An Outline* that he and Walker did enter Glen Sannox, though he gives no hint that he knew that Hutton had been there ten years before, and that they observed 'several veins of basalt traversing the granite, and in some places we can trace the perpendicular veins, from the bottom to the top of the mountains' (*Outline*, pp. 98–9). Jameson, then, goes out of his way in his published tour to note that the granite sides of Glen Sannox are penetrated by basaltic veins. The implied directionality – from bottom to top – conforms to the Neptunist assumption that veins had been filled from above by material sedimented or precipitated out of the primordial ocean.

Whether or not Jameson and Walker explored Glen Sannox in 1797, there is no suggestion in 'Journal of my Tour in 1797' or in *An Outline* that they entered North Glen Sannox, where, ten years earlier, Hutton had found decisive granite veins intruding into adjacent schistus. Instead, they continued northwards along the coast to the Cock of Arran and then round to Newton Point and Lochranza, where Hutton had discovered his first unconformity, as described in his unpublished 'Mineral History of the Island of Arran' (*Theory of the Earth*, III, pp. 235–7) and in the first volume of *Theory of the Earth* (I, pp. 429–30). The conclusion of the long entry for 11 August in 'Journal of my Tour in 1797' reveals that Jameson, after walking about twenty miles on difficult ground from Brodick to Lochranza, was too tired and hungry to examine Hutton's unconformity. On the following day, 12 August,

Jameson and Walker headed back round the coast toward the Cock of Arran, but ignored Hutton's unconformity in favour of examining 'what Dr Hutton calls the junction of the schistus & Whin' ('Journal of my Tour in 1797', no pagination). In *An Outline*, however, rather than simply ignoring Hutton's unconformity, Jameson says that he found an exposure which revealed strata of micaceous schistus, limestone and sandstone 'all running at the same angle':

> A few hundred yards from the entrance of . . . Loch [Ranza], the sea has formed an interesting section of the strata, which demonstrates, in a satisfactory manner, the relative position of the sandstone, limestone, and micaceous shistus. A large basalt vein, between ten and twelve feet, is to be observed traversing the micaceous shistus, with a slight degree of curvature. At the extremity of the vein, visible at low water, we observe the basalt covered with micaceous shistus. Immediately above this is a stratum of limestone, which contains rounded fragments of a kind of hornblende, and above this is the sandstone, all running at the same angle. (*Outline*, p. 104)

As Nicholas and Pearson suggest, by paying attention 'to the cross-cutting of the schistus and sandstones by basalt "veins" . . . Jameson is stamping a Wernerian seal on what would have been seen as very much a key Huttonian locality' ('Robert Jameson on the Isle of Arran', p. 42). And by saying that the strata of schistus, limestone and sandstone were all running at the same angle, Jameson implies that Hutton had been wrong to claim that the schistus and sandstone met together like the ridge of a house. For Jameson in 1797, then, Hutton's unconformity was no unconformity at all.

Jameson's 'Journal of my Tour in 1797' records that, on 14 August, he, Walker and a Mr Saunders, who had joined them from Brodick, set out early in order to explore 'Glen es na'birach' (Gleann Easan Biorach) and the 'celebrated height of Cairne-na-calleach' (the Witch's Step) in the heart of Arran's granite mountains. It is worth quoting at length from Jameson's journal entry because it will allow us to see further examples of the way *An Outline* creatively reworks the experiences recorded in the journal:

> Having passed thro Glen es na'birach, we now began to ascend and after a pretty fatiguing walk arrived at the North side of Garif hodie . . . here we had a most wonderful & tremendous prospect, an immense glen

of many hundred feet deep dreadfully rugged & broken, rising on its S side forming the lofty Cairne-na-calliach. On this side I observed some specimens of Porphry but could not determine from whence they came all in the neighbourhood was Granite of the same nature as Goatfield. Having rested for some time we began again to ascend, in our ascent observed more of the Porphry & in one place some masses of Pitchstone porphyry. The occurrence of this fossil in the most elevated region of the island and amongst Granite surprised me very much and as I observed but two or three small pieces I concluded them to be accidental. Having gained the summit of the Cairne, which is also of Granite, I now set out to examine the rocks all around and to my great astonishment again found a number of masses of Pit. Porphry. . . . Walking along the top of this awful Glen, I was wonderful struck with a most astonishing appearance, a small Dyke running fairly in granite. I at first could not believe my eyes. I therefore descended I found I was right and that this was most certainly the astonishing phenomena of a Whin Dyke running fairly and decidedly in Granite. This Dyke or stratum is only to be seen running for a few feet, is about a foot broad, a little curved as is the granite in which it runs and both are nearly vertical. The Dyke is a little diffuse [?] in the edges as it approaches the granite having the same appearance with a Whin Dyke in Sandstone. Having collected specimens to demonstrate to my friends this very astonishing fact, I now ascended again to Cairne-na-calliach to have a general view of the Island &c. From this we see almost the whole island. The Coast of Irland, Cantyre, Ila, the lofty paps of Jura, the distant mountains of Mull, the entrance to Loch Fyne, the distant mountains of Inverary, Cowal, island of Bute, Inch Marnock, up the whole Firth of Clyde the Cumbray islands, the coast of Scotland to nearly the Mull of Galloway & the tremendous Craig of Ailsa. . . . NB. There appears to be no regular ridge of hills in Arran, and this may be owing to the vast corpus of mountains that form its central & Northern parts, taking their rise from the lofty Goatfield. These mountains are all composed of Granite, with some schistus admixture, & by this height the rain has torn [worn?] them in a terrible manner, so as to show us a most horrific picture of wild grandeur at the same time it shows that the rain has been the cause of the formation of vallies &c. NB. The top of Cairne-na-caliach has a most singular appearance, looking like an immense corpus [cairn?] of stones piled above each other by some monstrous giant who in former times may have waged war with the gods. These appearances show a peculiarity in the mode in which granite decomposes, how first by exposure to the action of the air or other causes it splits into immense irregular shaped masses, these in time fall down & then by disintegration forms Granitic sand. ('Journal of my Tour in 1797', no pagination)

The leitmotiv here is astonishment – stimulated by geological discoveries as well as the mountainous terrain. As well as giving us a vivid impression of Jameson's exploration of this fairly remote part of Arran, this passage can be revealingly correlated with key passages in *An Outline*. The journal account of the panoramic view from the summit of Cairne-na-calliach is clearly an early draft of the view that, according to *An Outline*, Jameson supposedly experienced earlier in the tour from the summit of Goatfell. And although Jameson describes his wonder and astonishment at seeing 'Garif hodie', there is no religious epiphany. In *An Outline*, however, as we will see in a moment, this feature is said to have prompted the aesthetic and religious epiphany which, according to 'Journal of my Tour in 1797', actually occurred on Goatfell. In other words, when he came to write *An Outline*, Jameson redeployed the aesthetic experiences recorded in 'Journal of my Tour in 1797' for reasons which will soon become clear.

The above passage from 'Journal of my Tour in 1797' also records Jameson's initial surprise and increasing astonishment at discovering 'some masses of Pitchstone porphyry . . . in the most elevated region of the island and amongst Granite' and 'the astonishing phenomena of a [nearly vertical] Whin Dyke running fairly and decidedly in Granite'. Nicholas and Pearson attempt to explain why Jameson might have been so astonished by finding a Whin Dyke (or basalt vein) penetrating granite in this location:

> If it is assumed, as we would today, that the basalt had been intruded into the granite whilst molten, then this observation . . . is unremarkable. However, to a Wernerian, this outcrop juxtaposed the oldest rock on Earth with one of the youngest. Using Neptunian principles, there might be two possible explanations for what Jameson saw. Firstly, that in the last stages of the 'primeval ocean's' retreat, a fissure had opened up that was so deep it had penetrated through all previous strata and into the underlying granite. Basalt had then precipitated into this fissure as a vein. The second possibility would be that in this locality none of the intervening strata had precipitated within the fissure, thus leaving the young basalt to lie directly against granite. ('Robert Jameson on the Isle of Arran', p. 41)

Yet, as we have seen, Jameson had already noticed basalt veins in granite in Glen Sannox without registering surprise. Part of the astonishment here appears to arise from the fact that these materials had been laid down 'in the most elevated region of the island'.

The standard geotheoretical model accounted for the elevation of granite mountains by supposing that layers of granite had been deposited on elevated areas of an uneven sea-bed and that the sea level had subsequently fallen, thus preventing other kinds of rocks from being laid on top of the granite mounds (Rudwick, *Bursting the Limits of Time*, pp. 176–7). Jameson says that he was so surprised at finding pitchstone porphyry and basalt at the most elevated region of the island that he 'collected specimens to demonstrate to my friends this very astonishing fact'. Notably, however, as we will see, his astonishment at discovering field evidence that was not entirely congruous with Werner's theory more or less disappears from the published account of his ascent of Cairne-na-calliach and is replaced by religious epiphany.

The above passage also makes a notable observation about the effects of weathering on Arran's granite mountains, suggesting that rain has torn (or worn) the mountains in 'a terrible manner', producing 'a most horrific picture of wild grandeur' and demonstrating 'that the rain has been the cause of the formation of vallies &c'. This suggestion, however, along with the description of the gradual erosion of granite on the summits, would seem to play into the hands of the Huttonians in that it suggests that erosion takes place over enormous periods of time and is ongoing. As we will see, Jameson was careful to prevent this conclusion in the published version of this passage.

Jameson's published account of his discoveries and experience on the Witch's Step in *An Outline* is significantly different to that in his journal in several respects. His astonishment at discovering loose masses of porphyry and pitchstone among the granite and basalt veins in the granite is entirely edited out. Instead, he merely says that 'After considerable fatigue I was so fortunate as to discover two veins of basalt, upon the side of Cairn-na-cailigh, looking into the Garife-hodie; and, between these, there appeared a perpendicular vein of pitchstone, all running in the common granite' (p. 108). The suggestion that rain is the cause of valleys is omitted, and when he describes the decomposition of granite blocks into sand that either remains on the summits or is washed down into the glens and on to the sea-shore, he adds a footnote that criticises Hutton's claim that the rocks of the present world must have been formed out of the eroded debris of rocks that existed in a former 'world' that had been washed down into the oceans:

Dr Hutton remarks, that the stony matter of this globe has been formed by the decay of a former world, whose debris has been collected by various means, at the bottom of a former ocean. This part of the Huttonian theory differs but little from that of Count Buffon: it includes, however, the question concerning the divinity of the world; a speculation, fit only for fanciful metaphysicians. Leaving, therefore, such abstruse and useless quiblings, let us examine matter of fact. Here, however, we are disappointed; not a shadow of proof is brought of the debris being carried to the bottom of the ocean; on the contrary, we observe the decomposing materials of mountains filling up hollows, or forming plains. In the other instances, the debris is carried to the sea shores . . . where it is mixed with the waters of the ocean, and latterly thrown back upon the same or other shores, forming great tracts of land. (*Outline*, p. 110)[23]

As well as having recourse to 'matter of fact' in refuting abstruse, useless and fanciful metaphysical speculation that brings into question the divinity of the world, Jameson rewrites his journal account of 'Garife-hodie' in order to assert, once more, that an authentic response to geological wonders inevitably reveals the divine origin of the natural world:

Upon ascending, we first stop at the edge of what is called the Garife-hodie. Here a wonderful and most tremendous scene presents itself to our view. An immense hollow, many hundred feet deep, dreadfully rugged and broken, almost entirely surrounded with mountains, whose serrated summits are covered with immense tumuli of granite, exhibits to us, in very legible characters, the vast operations of nature, in the formation and decomposition of our globe. What man, possessed of reason, contemplating this awful scene, could doubt of the existence of that BEING, whose power and wisdom are far beyond the reach of human comprehension? If such a man exists, vanity, not soundness of judgment, is the distinguishing feature of his character. Few, indeed, of those who deny, or even doubt, the existence of Deity, have ever beheld, far less studied, the stupendous and awful works of nature. It is not, then, to be much wondered at, that the pride and arrogance, which so often characterise the closet philosopher, should find their way to mix with the most daring and impious speculations; speculations, which have for their end the propagation of the worst principles, the dissolving of all the bonds, and destroying the sweetest endearments of human society. (*Outline*, p. 107)[24]

The rational geologist who encounters such sublime geological formations in the field is necessarily inspired with religious enthusiasm of
a similar kind to that which the Romantic poets in the same period
claimed to experience in their encounters with the natural sublime.
Here, the geomorphology of a remote place in the recesses of Arran's
glens is represented as exhibiting 'to us, in very legible characters, the
vast operations of nature, in the formation and decomposition of our
globe'. Jameson's rhetorical question – 'What man, possessed of reason,
contemplating this awful scene, could doubt of the existence of that
BEING, whose power and wisdom are far beyond the reach of human
comprehension?' – emphasises the correct interpretation of those 'very
legible characters' and indicates that any man who reads them differently must be mad as well as impious. Again, we can surmise that Hutton is one of the vain men who misread the book of nature. Although
Hutton was characterised by some of his opponents as a 'closet philosopher', Jameson knew that he had explored Arran ten years before.
But for Jameson this would make Hutton's case all the more damning:
it is more rare and perverse that those who *have* 'beheld . . . [and]
studied, the stupendous and awful works of nature' should 'deny, or
even doubt, the existence of Deity'. Yet although Jameson presents
this epiphany as his personal response to the geomorphology of this
remarkable place in the heart of Arran's mountains, and suggests that
it is the inevitable response of all but the most perverse of travellers,
a comparison with 'Journal of my Tour in 1797' indicates that this
epiphany was not stimulated by 'Garife-hodie' but by misty mountains glimpsed earlier in the tour from the summit of Goatfell. In other
words, the crucial epiphany in *An Outline* is a rhetorical construct
designed to counter Hutton's supposedly atheistic geotheory. Jameson
did not have the epiphany that all rational men ought to have.

Arran Revisited: *Mineralogy of the Scottish Isles* (1800)

Jameson's two-volume *Mineralogy of the Scottish Isles; with Mineralogical Observations Made in a Tour through Different Parts of
the Mainland of Scotland* is a composite text made up of accounts
of several different tours in various parts of Scotland between 1794
and 1799. The bulk of the two volumes is devoted to an account of

Jameson's fairly extensive tour, by ship and on foot, of the Highlands and Islands of Scotland in 1798 in the company of Charles Bell, an Edinburgh physiologist, surgeon and anatomical illustrator.[25] Jameson returned to Arran in 1799 and inserted an amalgam of his two tours of the island into *Mineralogy of the Scottish Isles* in a way that makes it appear to be part of the 1798 tour. The first volume begins with two chapters on the mineralogy Jameson encountered between Edinburgh and Glasgow and en route to Ailsa Craig in 1798, followed by six chapters on Arran (derived from the 1797 and 1799 tours) and six chapters devoted to his exploration in 1798 of Bute, Islay, Jura, the Slate Islands and Mull. The second volume contains Jameson's accounts of Iona, Staffa, Coll and Tiree, Eigg, Rum and Canna, Skye, Raasay, Rona and Scalpay. It then describes Jameson and Bell's cross-country hike across the Highlands 'from Bernera . . . to the Firth of Forth' (II, pp. 158–81). This is followed by a two-chapter account of Jameson's 1794 exploration of the mineralogy of the Shetland Islands, first published in *An Outline of the Mineralogy of the Shetland Islands, and of the Island of Arran* (1798), a new chapter on the mineralogy of the Orkney Islands (which Jameson explored in 1799), and a chapter on his return from Orkney down the east coast of Scotland to Edinburgh.

Mineralogy of the Scottish Isles is more ambitious than *An Outline*, not only in terms of the ground (and sea) covered, but also in terms of relating its findings to the growing body of mineralogical and geological travel writing about Scotland, referring en route to travel accounts by figures such as John Walker, Thomas Pennant, Joseph Banks, Barthélemy Faujas de Saint-Fond, John Williams, Thomas Garnett and James Hutton.[26] Throughout the book, Jameson signals his awareness that his path follows and criss-crosses the journeys of these natural historians and geologists, that his interpretation of the mineralogy and geology of the Highlands and Islands is in dialogue with theirs, and that this dialogue is part of an intertextual struggle about the geological history of the earth itself. In addition to Jameson's continued critique of Hutton, *Mineralogy of the Scottish Isles* seeks to discredit Faujas's Vulcanist reading of Scotland's geology and to question several of Pennant's responses to Scotland's geomorphology. In some instances, as we have seen in previous chapters, Jameson dismisses or belittles his precursors' findings or claims to have discovered alternative geological formations that overtop them.

Although the various tours of Scotland that are stitched together in *Mineralogy of the Scottish Isles* retain a number of features of the tour genre, Jameson sought to distance his text from some of the conventions that readers of tours had come to expect. As in *An Outline* two years earlier, Jameson begins with a preface which reflects on the mutually constitutive relationships between literary and scientific styles, the tensions between aesthetic and mineralogical responses to Scotland's terrain, the impact of examining and writing about geomorphology as a traveller, and the implications of employing the genre of the journal:

> I have chosen the form of a journal, because I wished to convey the information I had gleaned in the stile of detailed observation, and in that order which the appearance of the country naturally suggested. But, in adopting this form, I am anxious to caution the reader against expecting that entertainment, and kind of information, which form the groundwork of the many journals through the more interesting parts of our island. If any one shall find this Outline of the mineralogy of these countries deficient in incident, in episodes and stories, and in descriptions of picturesque and romantic scenery; let him recollect, that to indulge in such descriptions was incompatible with the design of this work. I do not despise those ornaments; and I hope that I have not been insensible to the emotions which naturally arise from the retired and striking scenes which often burst upon me in the unfrequented tracts which my pursuits led me to explore: but I have thought it foreign to my purpose to obtrude these things upon the public. (I, pp. v–vi)

Despite these pronouncements, Jameson does include episodes, stories, descriptions and emotional responses to retired and striking scenes in *Mineralogy of the Scottish Isles*. But if aesthetic responses to wild and sublime landscape are supposedly foreign to the mineralogical journal, so too is geotheoretical speculation:

> Another resolution I had formed to myself, and which partly indeed led me to choose the form of a journal, was, to shun the fascinating evil of speculation and hypothesis, which mars all faithful observation. It would ill suit my talents to venture upon deep speculation, were I inclined; and perhaps the state of mineralogical knowledge forbids it. It is a fitter task for me to record faithfully what I have myself examined, and to give a fair report of the materials which were collected, than to

expose myself, by the form or arrangement of the work, to the danger of having the facts twisted and perverted by hypothesis, the rage for which is as remarkable in this as in the other sciences.

While, in mineralogical pursuits, there is much to interest a philosophical mind, the object of true value is its application to economical purposes. I fear that the theories of the formation of the earth, interesting as they are, often mislead the mind, and pervert the understanding; and those who yield to them, become so involved in delusive speculations, so blind to fact and experience, that, like Archimedes, they find but one thing wanting to raise worlds. (I, pp. vi–vii)

This passage reiterates the assumptions of natural history examined in earlier chapters and registers the influence of John Walker. Mineralogy, as a branch of natural history, is an empirical, utilitarian science that can contribute to Scotland's economic improvement by aiding mining, agriculture and manufacturing. The journal is the appropriate genre for faithfully recording what the travelling mineralogist saw and collected and helps him to avoid geological speculation, which distorts observation, twists the facts, misleads the mind, and perverts the understanding. Although the attempt to raise worlds by imaginatively reconstructing the formation of the earth is fascinating, it is also evil because it tends towards atheism, as the examples of Buffon and Hutton were thought to demonstrate. Jameson, then, attempts to exclude from his journal precisely those features – aesthetic response to mountainous terrain and geological speculation – that were the hallmark of Romantic geological travel writing. But the fact that Jameson tells us that he chose the journal form because it helped him 'to shun' the fascinating evil of geotheory perhaps reveals that he was trying to ward off an evil that he found strongly enticing.

Indeed, Jameson is drawn into geotheory when he visits places and formations in the Highlands and Islands that previous geological travel writers such as Hutton and Faujas had interpreted according to theories of the earth that Jameson regarded as untenable and morally dangerous. Jameson does not, of course, regard his own geotheory – a version of the standard Neptunist model indebted to Walker and Werner – as theoretical or speculative but as a natural and neutral interpretation of the earth's geomorphology. As Jameson later insisted in *Elements of Geognosy* (1808), an extended account of Werner's system, 'We should form a very false conception of the Wernesian

Geognosy, were we to believe it to have any resemblance to those *monstrosities* known under the name of *Theories of the Earth*.'

Nicholas and Pearson point out that on his second tour of Arran, which lasted only ten days, Jameson

> targeted three main localities, all of which were crucial to the argument between Neptunism and Plutonism: the granite-schist contact in Glen Sannox, Hutton's unconformity at Lochranza and the Tormore dykes on the west coast. There can be little doubt that this second tour of Jameson's was specifically intended to visit those localities that could topple Huttonian arguments. ('Robert Jameson on the Isle of Arran', p. 34)[27]

In what follows, I concentrate on Jameson's accounts of the granite-schist contact in Glen Sannox and of Hutton's unconformity at Lochranza.

As we saw in Chapter 6, in 1787, having failed to locate granite-schistus junctions in Glen Rosa or on Goatfell, Hutton explored Glen Sannox and North Glen Sannox on his way back from Lochranza. His 'Mineral History of the Island of Arran' reveals that he found what he was looking for in North Glen Sannox:

> in returning [from Lochranza] I quitted my horse, and went over the mosses and muir towards the heads of that North Sanox river which there divides into two streams. Here I had the satisfaction to find the immediate junction of the schistus with the granite, in the solid rock, exposed perfectly to view, and that in both of these rivulets, a little way above their junction.
>
> Nothing can be more evident than that here the schistus had been broken and invaded by the granite; as in this place the regular stratification of the vertical schistus is broken obliquely by the other rock, and parts of the schistus involved or almost insulated in the mass of granite, which from this junction enters and traverses the body of the schistus in little veins terminating in capillaries. (*Theory of the Earth*, III, pp. 220–1)

Jameson's 'Journal of a Tour to Arran in 1799' reveals that he and his 'old guide Ronald' visited both granite-schistus junctions that Hutton found in North Glen Sannox, but it makes no mention of the granitic intrusive veins that were so decisive for Hutton. In his published account in *Mineralogy of the Scottish Isles* Jameson explicitly denies that there were any such veins in these exposures. After having examined Glen Sannox, he tells us, he was 'proceeding toward the sea-shore when I thought it might be interesting to examine the junction of the granite and shistus in some of the neighbouring glens. I therefore changed my course . . . and . . . crossed over a hill . . . to North Glen-Sanicks' (I, p. 73). Jameson thus represents his decision to examine this key Huttonian site as a sudden impulse rather than part of a predetermined plan to refute Hutton. This may well have been the case since there is no firm evidence that Jameson had read Hutton's 'Mineral History of the Island of Arran'. Yet it is striking that Jameson headed unerringly to Hutton's junctions and describes them in ways that contradict Hutton's observations:

> Here we observed a stream running through the glen, and in it I found the schistus in immediate contact with the granite. The schistus appeared to be very compact micaceous rock; but the granite was not intermixed with it at the junction, nor were there any veins to be observed shooting from the granite into the micaceous rock. We now crossed over the hills into another glen, where I observed another junction of the granite and schistus, but it presented nothing remarkable. (I, pp. 73–4)[28]

Nicholas and Pearson point out that 'In North Sannox Burn the thin granite veins described by Hutton can still be seen at the contact and it is remarkable that even though he had stood at the same outcrop, Jameson went out of his way to deny their existence' ('Robert Jameson on the Isle of Arran', p. 42). Given that he was highly alert to the significance of granite veins for Hutton's theory, we are left to conclude either that Jameson deliberately misrepresented the North Glen Sannox junctions in order to defend the Wernerian-Neptunist paradigm or that his commitment to that paradigm made him unable to see physical evidence that contradicted it.

From North Glen Sannox, Jameson and his guide walked on to Lochranza, where he was much more concerned than he had been in 1797 to examine and reinterpret Hutton's unconformity at Newton Point. On the inside back page of his 'Journal of a Tour to Arran in

1799' he copied out, presumably before leaving Edinburgh, a slightly truncated and garbled version of the crucial passage from Hutton's *Theory of the Earth*:

> At L.Ranza – here the shistus & sandstone rise both inclined at an angle of 45°. but these primary and secondary strata were inclined in almost opposite directions, a[nd] thus met like 2 sides of a lambda being . . . a little disordered at the angle of their junction. From the situation of these 2 different masses of strata, it is evidently impossible that either of these could have been formed originally that position.

Jameson's own description of the Lochranza unconformity in *Mineralogy of the Scottish Isles* echoes Hutton's (and contradicts his earlier description of different strata 'all running at the same angle'):

> A few hundred yards from the entrance of the Loch, the sea has formed an interesting section of the strata, which demonstrates, in a satisfactory manner, the relative position of the sandstone, limestone, and micaceous shistus. The micaceous shistus which forms the shore, is inclined at an angle of 45° and dips to the S.E.; the secondary strata, are inclined at an angle of 45°, but dip to the N.W. so that the two kinds of strata meet together, similar, as Hutton remarks, to the two sides of a lambda, or the roof of a house. (*Mineralogy of the Scottish Isles*, I, pp. 77–8)

But although Jameson acknowledges the accuracy of Hutton's description of this unconformity, he sidesteps entirely Hutton's interpretation of the formation of such unconformities. As Nicholas and Pearson suggest, while Hutton saw the unconformity 'as evidence of two different cycles of deposition and uplift', this explanation 'is lost in a Wernerian interpretation. The fact that the younger sandstones irregularly overlie the older "schistus" would be expected in a Neptunist succession and consequently Jameson seems to attach little significance to this stretch of coast' ('Robert Jameson on the Isle of Arran', p. 42). The Neptunist account of the formation of successive strata of different kinds of rock makes it entirely unremarkable that the secondary strata of sandstone and limestone would overlie the schistus. The fact that they dip in different directions and meet at an angle of 90° is equally unremarkable in a theory which assumed, oddly, that strata could be sedimented or precipitated in the primeval ocean at various angles to the horizontal. But it is not convincing to say that Jameson attaches little significance to Hutton's unconformity. Instead, he attempts to render it insignificant from a Neptunist perspective precisely because Hutton's interpretation of it was so challenging for Neptunism.

Religious Epiphanies/Geological Revelations

This chapter has traced a complex series of textual representations and interpretations of some of Arran's key geological features. Hutton's published description and interpretation of his findings on Arran were limited to a few paragraphs of his 1795 *Theory of the Earth*, and Jameson had clearly read those paragraphs prior to embarking on his trips to the island in 1797 and 1799. Whether or not Jameson had read Hutton's much more extensive account of Arran in his 'Mineral History of the Island of Arran', which still lay in manuscript, it is notable that he homed in on two of Hutton's critical findings on Arran. A comparative reading of Jameson's four accounts of his geological explorations of the island (in two handwritten journals and two published books) reveals that his critique of Hutton was not based entirely on objective observation of empirical evidence in the field but sometimes involved distorting or overlooking that evidence. As Nicholas and Pearson suggest, in his journals Jameson 'made observations that were not always easy to explain using a strict Neptunian scheme', but when he came to write up his observations for publication, he 'took a far more hard-line Wernerian view . . . The public politics of the Neptunist-Plutonist debate appears to have overridden any ambiguity in the field evidence' ('Robert Jameson on the Isle of Arran', p. 45). Hutton's two accounts of Arran and Jameson's four accounts can thus be seen as a series of interpretations and reinterpretations of the geological meaning of specific formations in particular places on Arran. The intertextual contest between Hutton and Jameson was also enacted through invoking the aesthetic impact of the sublime. As we saw in Chapter 6, Hutton's 'Mineral History of the Island of Arran' extrapolated from his reading of the geological implications of particular places and formations on the island in order to generate a conjectural vision of Arran's origins in deep time and its eventual destruction in the distant future. Particular hot spots on Arran, then, opened up visions of deep time that revealed the geological origins and eventual fate of all the earth's present land masses. Whether or not Jameson had read Hutton's awesome conjectural narrative, he also deployed sublime responses to Arran's geomorphology in order to reveal not the abyss of deep time but the reassuring, if awesome, presence and handiwork of the creator. Although he set out by suggesting that misty mountains were liable to lead the mineralogist into error, Jameson responded to, or exploited, those features and conditions in ways that produced, or fabricated, religious epiphanies that explicitly condemned geotheories such as Hutton's that appeared to leave no role for God in forming and maintaining the earth. Nicholas and Pearson conclude that 'For a brief period at the end of the eighteenth century, the Isle of Arran played an important role in the debate between Neptunists and Plutonists' (p. 45). It is perhaps more accurate to say that a number of specific places and formations on Arran were made into classic sites in the history of geology because Hutton and Jameson visited them and produced competing interpretations. Thereafter, the island's enduring place in the history of geology was recognised and reinforced in the nineteenth century by a further sequence of written accounts.[29]

Notes

1. See Walker, *Lectures on Geology*.
2. See Sweet and Waterston, 'Robert Jameson's Approach to the Wernerian Theory of the Earth'.
3. See Sweet, 'The Wernerian Natural History Society in Edinburgh'.
4. See Dean, 'Jameson, Robert (1774–1854)', *ODNB*.
5. On the controversy between Jameson and Hutton, see Flinn, 'James Hutton and Robert Jameson'.
6. Quoting Jameson, 'Is the Volcanic Opinion of the Formation of Basaltes Founded on Truth?'. For Dean's discussion of Jameson, see pp. 97–101.
7. Werner's most important publications prior to 1796 were *Von den äusserlichen Kennzeichen der Fossilien* (1774), *Kurze Klassifikation und Beschreibung der verschiedenen Gebirgsarten* (1787) and *Neue Theorie von den Entstehung der Gänge* (1791).

8. Werner, 'Werners Bekanntmachung einer von ihm am Scheibenberger Hügel über die Entstehung des Basaltes gemachten Entdeckung'. Also see Oldroyd, 'The Vulcanist-Neptunist Dispute Reconsidered'.

9. For an account of all Jameson's mineralogical tours in Scotland, see Hartley, 'Robert Jameson, Geology and Polite Culture', pp. 116–38.

10. Jameson's journals of his Scottish tours are held in the Centre for Research Collections in Edinburgh University Library. See Jameson, 'Journal of my Tour in 1797'; 'Journal of a Tour to Arran in 1799'; 'Journal of a Tour Through the Hebrides begun the 22nd of May 1798, volume 1'; 'Journal of a Tour Through the Hebrides begun the 22nd of May 1798, volume 2'; 'Journal of a Tour to Orkney in 1799'.

11. See Hutton, *Theory of the Earth*, I, pp. 467–8, 429–30.

12. Jameson slightly misquotes Hutton, 'Observations on Granite', p. 77. Hutton summarises his argument in 'Theory of the Earth', which was expanded to form the second section of chapter 1 of *Theory of the Earth*, I, pp. 3–200.

13. Hutton's 'An Examination of the Mineral History of the Island of Arran', written in 1787, was first published by the Geological Society in 1899 as James Hutton, *Theory of the Earth, with Proofs and Illustrations*, vol. 3.

14. For a useful account of Werner's geology, see Laudan, *From Mineralogy to Geology*, pp. 87–102.

15. On the potential of obscurity to generate the sublime, and of clarity to deflate it, see Burke, *A Philosophical Enquiry* (1759), II, iii–iv, pp. 99–110.

16. See de Saussure, *Voyages dans les Alpes*.

17. Although both Martin and Pennant visited Arran before Jameson, they did not present a sustained account of its geology; Hutton's 'Mineral History of the Island of Arran' remained in manuscript.

18. See Cresswell, *Place*, pp. 18–24.

19. Wordsworth's description in *The Excursion* (1814) of the Wanderer's early experiences in the Grampian Mountains around Blair Atholl in central Scotland is one example among many. See Wordsworth, *The Excursion*, I, ll. 198–219, in *The Poems: Volume Two*, pp. 46–7.

20. See Thomson, 'Summer' (l. 1617), in *Poetical Works*, p. 112. For an exploration of the phrase in eighteenth-century literature, see Barrell, *English Literature in History*.

21. See Sweet, 'Robert Jameson's Irish Journal'. The revised edition of Kirwan's *Elements of Mineralogy* 'was aided by his negotiated purchase, for the Royal Dublin Society, of the Leskean collections (about 7000 specimens assembled by N. G. Leske, professor of natural history at Leipzig)' (Scott, 'Kirwan, Richard (1733–1812)').

22. See Sweet, 'Robert Jameson's Irish Journal'.
23. This footnote is greatly extended in *Mineralogy of the Scottish Isles*, I, pp. 83–5.
24. The same passage appears in *Mineralogy of the Scottish Isles*, I, pp. 80–1.
25. See Jacyna, 'Bell, Sir Charles (1774–1842)', *ODNB*.
26. Williams's place in the history of geology is usually limited to the fact that the preface to his two-volume *Natural History of the Mineral Kingdom* (1789) contains one of the earliest published reactions to Hutton's 'Theory of the Earth' article which had recently appeared in the first volume of the *TRSE*. Unfortunately, there is no room here to explore its fascinating account of Scotland's mineralogy and geology.
27. There is not space here to discuss Hutton's and Jameson's interpretations of the Tormore dykes on Arran's west coast (see Hutton's 'An Examination of the Mineral History of the Island of Arran' in *Theory of the Earth*, III, pp. 191–267 (pp. 253–6), and Jameson, *Outline*, pp. 125–30, and *Mineralogy*, I, pp. 101–7); for a good discussion, see Nicholas and Pearson, 'Robert Jameson on the Isle of Arran', pp. 42–5.
28. When Jameson visited Glen Tilt in September 1813 he persisted in denying the existence of veins that were so decisive for Hutton and his followers, making the following note in his tour journal: 'Again viewed the great bed of syenite which Dr Hutton, Prof Playfair and Sir James Hall maintain to be veins – one fact is decisive again that [opinion] is that this does not rise through the faults as is the case with veins – on the contrary it has nearly the same level all along and is everywhere covered' (quoted by Hartley, 'Robert Jameson, Geology and Polite Culture', p. 137); Jameson's mineralogical diary of his 1813 tour is held in Edinburgh University Library Special Collections (Dc.7.133).
29. See Headrick, *View of the Mineralogy, Agriculture, Manufactures and Fisheries of the Island of Arran* (1807); MacCulloch, *A Description of the Western Islands of Scotland* (1819), vol. 2; Ramsay, *The Geology of the Island of Arran* (1841); and Bryce, *Geology of Arran and Clydesdale* (1855).

Chapter 8

The End of Romantic Geology in Scotland? John MacCulloch's *A Description of the Western Islands of Scotland* (1819)

A Revolution in Geology

The second half of Martin Rudwick's *Bursting the Limits of Time* and the bulk of its companion volume, *Worlds Before Adam*, trace in great detail the revolution in geology that took place in the first three decades of the nineteenth century. For Rudwick, this reorientation of the earth sciences entailed the formation of geology per se and involved a number of interrelated shifts that marginalised the debates and issues we have traced in the present book: from geotheory and earth physics to geohistory; from attention to 'primary' or 'primitive' rocks to 'secondary' and 'tertiary' rocks and strata; from mountains and volcanoes to lowland plains; from questions about the creation and uplift of rocks to the palaeontological analysis of the organic fossil record; from speculations about the early earth to an investigation of fossil remains which indicated that the earth had undergone a series of catastrophic transformations throughout its history, including a relatively recent event, characterised by a mass extinction of species, which separated the period of human existence from the period immediately preceding it. The major architects of this revolution in geology, such as Georges Cuvier, were Continental savants whose evidence came from lowland areas such as the Paris basin. In Britain, this revolution involved a switch of focus from the geotheoretical struggles of Edinburgh to the empirical project of the Geological Society of London, and from Scotland's mountains to the fossil-rich formations of England's plains.[1]

The founding of the Geological Society of London in 1807 had a decisive impact on the outlook and agenda of early nineteenth-century British geology.[2] Under the leadership of its first president, George Bellas Greenough, the Geological Society attempted to steer geology away from speculative theories of the earth in favour of empirical fieldwork.[3] The Geological Society established networks of co-workers across the United Kingdom from all classes, and soon attracted the leading geologists of the day. The preface to the first volume of the Society's *Transactions* (1811) stressed that it had been formed to encourage and enable the collaborative gathering of empirical facts through travel and local observation. The aim of the *Transactions* was to publish 'a series of inquiries, calculated . . . to excite a greater degree of attention to this important study, than it had yet received in this country; and to serve as a guide to the geological traveller, by pointing out some of the various objects, which it is his province to examine'. The 'present imperfect state of this science' meant that 'it cannot be supposed that the Society should attempt to decide upon the merits of the different theories of the earth that have been proposed'. One of the aims was to produce 'a general geological map of the British territory' (preface to *TGSL*, I, v, viii–ix).

But while many historians of geology, such as Rudwick and Porter, have seen these developments as marking the emergence of geology proper and as shifting attention from outmoded theoretical debates in Edinburgh, Dennis Dean has emphasised the ongoing influence of Hutton's geotheory on geological debate in Britain and on the Continent in the early nineteenth century.[4] John Playfair's *Illustrations of the Huttonian Theory of the Earth* (1802), which included evidence derived from his extensive geological exploration of the mountains, coasts and rivers of northern England, Wales and Scotland, and his 'Biographical Account of the Late Dr James Hutton' (1805) influenced some of the leading members of the Geological Society and led to him being made an Honorary Member at its first meeting in December 1807.

Geological Tours of Scotland in the Early Nineteenth Century

Geologists continued to tour Scotland in the early decades of the nineteenth century. Louis Albert Necker, grandson of Horace-Bénédict de Saussure, arrived in Scotland in 1806 in order to study at the University of Edinburgh, where he imbibed Werner's geotheory from Jameson and Hutton's from leading Huttonians such as Playfair and Sir James Hall. His tours of Scotland in 1806–7 helped him to produce the earliest known geological map of the whole of Scotland, based on both Huttonian and Wernerian principles, which he presented to the Geological Society in November 1808.[5] Several leading players in the Geological Society, including Greenough, William Buckland and Humphry Davy, visited Scotland and were usually conducted by Huttonians such as Playfair and Hall to sites in and around Edinburgh (Arthur's Seat, Salisbury Crags and Siccar Point) that had been important for Hutton.[6] The lectures on geology that Davy gave at the Royal Institution of London between 1805 and 1815 were partly based on first-hand experience and specimens gleaned from his geological tour of Scotland in the summer of 1804.[7] Although Charles Lyell carried out most of his geological fieldwork in England and on the Continent, he made a field excursion to the Inner Hebrides in 1817 which included a visit to Staffa.[8]

But the most comprehensive and systematic account of the geology and landscapes of a particular area of Scotland that appeared during the period examined in this book was John MacCulloch's *A Description of the Western Islands of Scotland, Including the Isle of Man: Comprising an Account of their Geological Structure; with Remarks on their Agriculture, Scenery, and Antiquities* (1819).[9] MacCulloch published his *Description of the Western Islands of Scotland* at a moment when geology in Britain and on the Continent was undergoing the radical self-transformation described above, which served to downplay and marginalise the concerns which had lured Romantic-period geologists into Scotland's Highlands and Islands. Simultaneously, while travel in Scotland's remote areas remained difficult in the early decades of the nineteenth century, increasing tourism and the gradual development of a tourist infrastructure reduced the possibility of representing the Highlands and Islands as locations for Romantic adventure. Walter Scott's poems and novels, like James Macpherson's Ossian poems fifty years earlier, located Romantic Scotland firmly in the past, and the crowds of tourists who ventured into the Highlands and Islands with volumes of Scott in their hands found it increasingly difficult to discover the Scotland of their imagination.[10] The combination of these developments in geology and tourism had a significant impact on the phase or mode of geological travel writing about Scotland examined in the present book. The following discussion of *A Description of the Western Islands* examines whether its empiricism, downplaying of personal experience, avoidance of the travel genre, and relative lack of interest in aesthetic landscape allow us to see it as a transitional text in which Romantic travel and geology had begun to go their separate ways.

John MacCulloch (1773–1835)

The changing fortunes of MacCulloch's geological career were closely related to the revolution in geology described above. He was born in Guernsey in 1773 and from 1790 to 1794 studied medicine at Edinburgh University, where he attended the lectures of John Walker and Joseph Black and became friends with Jameson. In the early decades of the nineteenth century his work as a professional geologist gave him an extensive practical knowledge of Scotland's geology. David A. Cumming, the leading expert on MacCulloch, notes that 'Between 1809 and 1813 he conducted geological surveys in Wessex, Wales, and Scotland, searching for silica-free limestone for millwheels' ('MacCulloch, John', *ODNB*). From 1814 to 1821 he spent his summers working as a geologist on the Trigonometrical Survey of Scotland: 'In eight seasons he examined the geology of hundreds of Scottish peaks, [and] completed a geological map of west Scotland' (*ODNB*). Alan J. Bowden points out that 'MacCulloch spent a total of 15 seasons in the field between 1814 and 1830' and calculates that 'On average, [he] was in the field for 154 days a year covering around 2530 miles in each season on foot or horseback' ('Geology at the Crossroads', p. 260). MacCulloch must therefore have traversed about 38,000 miles of Scotland's land surface, but 'What is not recorded are the thousands of miles he sailed, surveying from small open boats, often taking the helm himself in some of the most treacherous waters, weather conditions and in areas that were heretofore unsurveyed with any pretence to accuracy' (p. 260).

MacCulloch joined the Geological Society of London in 1808 and published some of the findings from his Scottish field trips in its *Transactions*, including papers on Staffa, Skye, Glen Tilt and the Parallel Roads of Glen Roy.[11] Cumming suggests that these 'closely reasoned and well illustrated papers epitomized the Baconian skills advocated by the society' (*ODNB*). Bowden describes MacCulloch as 'a leading light and one of the driving forces' of the Geological Society (he was elected vice-president in 1815 and president in 1816), and notes that he was 'increasingly looked upon as the expert in Scottish geology' ('Geology at the Crossroads', p. 265).

The publication of MacCulloch's 'highly acclaimed' *Description of the Western Islands* in 1819 was the high point of his career and led to his election as a Fellow of the Royal Society (p. 257). For Archibald Geikie, this book

> marks a notable epoch in British geology. . . . So laborious a collection of facts, and so courageous a resolution to avoid theorizing about them, gave to his volumes an altogether unique character. His descriptions were at once adopted as part of the familiar literature of geology. His sections and sketches were reproduced in endless treatises and text-books. Few single works of descriptive geology have ever done so much to advance the progress of the science in this country. (*The Ancient Volcanoes of Great Britain*, II, p. 111)

As we will see, the geological outlook and fieldwork in *A Description of the Western Islands* chimed in with the Geological Society's empirical outlook, its belief that the formation of a geotheory should be deferred until enough empirical facts had been gathered, and its project of synthesising empirical observations into geological maps. MacCulloch's third volume includes landscape views of the Western Islands, made by himself, perhaps using a camera lucida, together with plans, sections and maps that eventually became part of his *Geological Map of Scotland* of 1836.[12] The overwhelming majority of the plates in the third volume illustrate structural geology, focusing on the patterns and effects of intrusive veins, unconformities and so on, and their impact on topography. This focus, which is virtually the same as Hutton's thirty years earlier, indicates the degree to which MacCulloch was out of touch with new developments.

MacCulloch's fortunes were quick to turn. From about 1820 onwards he became increasingly estranged from the Geological Society, precisely at the time 'when the full force of palaeontological stratigraphy swept through the geological brotherhood' (Bowden, 'Geology at the Crossroads', p. 273). In a letter to Leonard Horner in June 1820, MacCulloch referred to the practitioners of palaeontological geology as 'namby pamby cockleologists and formation men'.[13] The gender stereotyping of this put-down is revealing. According to the *OED*, 'namby pamby' used as an adjective means 'inclined to weak sentimentality, affectedly dainty; lacking vigour or drive; effeminate in expression or behaviour'. MacCulloch's newly coined portmanteau word 'cockleologists' (packing in 'cock' and 'cockle' as well as 'conchologists') diminished the new science still further. He contrasts this effeminate cockle-gathering in the plains of southern England with the heroic manliness of those geologists, like himself, who explore the difficult and dangerous mountains of northern Scotland: 'Indeed, [MacCulloch] asked whether the proponents and practitioners of "fossil conchology" brought up on the soft, southern, relatively unaltered, highly fossiliferous young sediments would be able to unravel the complexities of the regions in which he worked' (Bowden, 'Geology at the Crossroads', p. 273). Hard rocks in hard country required hard men.

The Geological Survey of a Country So Often Visited by Travellers

A Description of the Western Islands is not presented as the account of a tour of the Western Islands, or as a series of tours, but is organised instead into sections that group together MacCulloch's analytical descriptions of islands on the basis of their shared geological make-up: 'These are distinguished by the names of the Gneiss, the Trap, the Sandstone, the Schistose, and the Clyde islands' (I, p. 1). Presenting a synthesis of observations gathered on numerous journeys over many years, *A Description of the Western Islands* constitutes a shift away from geological travel narrative about Scotland towards a systematic survey of its geology. Although MacCulloch reveals that, for variety's sake, he has added 'miscellaneous' material from the journal he kept on his travels, he stresses that

> it was no part of the plan to introduce a personal narrative into the description of a country so often visited by travellers. Those travellers have, with various powers and with different success, related much of that which might otherwise have fallen to the lot of the author to describe; but they have not related all, as no one of them has made such wide excursions. (I, p. ix)

MacCulloch not only downplays his personal experience of travelling in the area but also indicates that, by the second decade of the nineteenth century, the western and northern islands of Scotland had lost their aura of novelty and remoteness. But if his belatedness often prevents MacCulloch from representing himself as a Romantic traveller exploring an untrodden wilderness, it adds to the sense that he is treading on classic geological ground. Yet MacCulloch barely mentions the names of any forerunners. Prominent figures such as Martin Martin, Thomas Pennant and Samuel Johnson are referred to only occasionally and in passing, and he stresses that none of them has made such wide excursions as he has. The only geological predecessor that MacCulloch mentions in the preface is Jameson, whom he refers to in distinctly ambiguous ways:

> I must not terminate this part of the subject without noticing Professor Jameson's work on the same tract of country. I would willingly have shortened my own labour by being indebted to it, and am glad to bear testimony to the accuracy of his account, as far as the facts have been described. The difference of the plan on which this survey was conducted, rendered it necessary to examine every thing, and deprived me of the assistance which I might otherwise have derived from that work; which includes, moreover, but a small portion of the territory which has here been investigated. (I, p. xiii)[14]

MacCulloch here asserts his status as a geological pioneer in Scotland by belittling the achievement of his most important forerunner. Although Jameson's account is accurate as far as it goes, it is limited in several respects, forcing MacCulloch to examine everything for himself. Bowden points out that MacCulloch and Jameson 'had been very friendly during their student days when attending the inspirational lectures of Rev. John Walker', but that their 'friendship became progressively more strained from 1809 as MacCulloch's work led him to adopt a more Huttonian stance' ('Geology at the Crossroads', p. 261). After the appearance of *A Description of the Western Islands*, Jameson accused MacCulloch of plagiarising his work, and thereafter they became increasingly estranged.

MacCulloch generally accepts the Huttonian analysis of most geological phenomena, but he never endorses Hutton's overall theory of the earth. Echoing the outlook of the Geological Society, MacCulloch presents *A Description of the Western Islands* as a collection of empirical facts that will contribute to the formation of a science of geology that 'remains yet to be created' (I, p. xiii). While he claims that 'The recent light thrown on geology by the minute circumstances which attend the junctions of different classes of rock and the passage of veins, are too well known to require to be pointed out among the latest improvements in the mode of observation' (I, p. xiv), thus implying that some aspects of Huttonian geology may now be taken for granted, MacCulloch stresses that his own non-theoretical approach was unavoidable given that geology has still not formulated an adequate theory of the earth (I, pp. xiv–xv). MacCulloch's empiricism does not, however, prevent him from making speculative reconstructions of the formative processes that may have produced particular geological features, though he does so only after examining local evidence on various islands and gathering it together into larger generalisations. Ironically, however, the theoretical orientation that was already being formed in Paris, London and Oxford would render irrelevant many of the 'facts' assembled by MacCulloch, precisely because the 'light' in which he places them, and which perhaps helped him see them, was often derived from Hutton.

MacCulloch's commitment to the empirical outlook of the Geological Society has not prevented scholars from regarding him as a Romantic writer. Adelene Buckland has recently claimed that MacCulloch's writing in *A Description of the Western Islands* is 'imbued with the visionary and the romantic at every turn' and that visionary Romanticism 'imbues MacCulloch's geological method too' (*Novel Science*, p. 79). These claims are not wholly convincing. MacCulloch's descriptions of places and landscapes can only occasionally be said to exhibit Romantic sensibility, while his commitment to empiricism and tendency to avoid speculation about causal processes in deep time mean that the geological analysis in *A Description of the Western Islands* only rarely generates Romantic sublimity. Indeed, although MacCulloch can be alert to the sublimity of Scotland's mountains and glens, he suggests, like Jameson, that Romantic responses to landscape are potentially incompatible with geological analysis:

> The geologist whose business it is to seek his amusements and pursue his studies among the more minute details of the surface, if unfortunately he is too sensible to these allurements, is apt to suffer his eye

to wander from his proper subject, and, in the contemplation of the variety around him, to lose the order of the objects of which he is in search. (II, p. 314)

MacCulloch does not say whether he is one of those unfortunate geologists whose sensibility distracts them from scientific exploration, but it is notable that his account of the Western Islands carefully separates geological analysis from aesthetic responses to landscape by locating them in discrete sections.

While the whole of *A Description of the Western Islands* is of great interest, the following discussion is limited to MacCulloch's accounts of Skye and Staffa. Examining MacCulloch's analysis of Staffa will allow us to explore his response to a location that had already been made into classic ground by several of the geological writer-travellers looked at in previous chapters. Although Skye had already been visited and written about by several of the geological travel writers discussed in this book, much of it remained unexplored, allowing MacCulloch to represent himself as a pioneering explorer of its landscape and geology. As we will see, the geology and terrain of these iconic places lured him into geological speculations and aesthetic responses that went against the grain of his overall project.

The Trap Islands

The final section of MacCulloch's analysis of Arran's geology in *A Description of the Western Islands* focuses on the igneous beds and veins that overlie and penetrate the sandstone in the southern portion of the island. These rocks are commonly called 'varieties of trap' and 'are well known by the several names of basalt, greenstone, syenite, claystone, clinkstone, compact felspar, and porphyry' (II, pp. 398, 394).[15] Like Hutton, MacCulloch suggests that the trap beds and veins on Arran may have originated as subterraneous igneous material, and that although they are evidently more recent than the rocks they penetrate or cover, it is not possible to date them (II, p. 410). While trap is just one aspect of Arran's complex geology, Mac-Culloch treats Skye, Mull and their satellite islands as a single group of 'trap islands' because significant portions of their stratified rocks are overlain with beds of trap.

In his 'General Comparison of the Trap Islands', MacCulloch proposes that these islands, along with limited portions of the adjacent western mainland, may once have been connected together at the levels of their primary and secondary strata. But although he surmises that 'a great waste and removal of the strata must have been effected before the present fragments could have been separated as they are now found', and that this process must have taken an enormous time and was completed long before 'the trap rocks were superimposed on their scattered remains', he does not speculate about how that separation may have occurred (II, pp. 66, 67). Towards the end of his account of Mull's geology, however, MacCulloch suggests that 'the absolute horizontality of the trap beds' that overlie folded strata 'shows that these [trap deposits] remain in the position in which they were first formed' (I, p. 574) – an observation which leads to a number of further conclusions:

> The period of this formation is obviously posterior to that of the latest stratified substances with which we are acquainted, since this class of mountains is found covering those substances even to a considerable depth. That no general disturbance and fracture of the earth's surface has taken place since this period, is proved by their freedom from dislocation and change of position. It is difficult to comprehend by what means horizontal deposits of so partial a nature are found occupying positions so elevated. But to whatever causes their formation may be assigned, it is at least evident that their origin, recent as they may appear in comparison with others, is removed to an immense distance, and that the surface of the earth must have undergone material changes, from causes operating quietly through a long space of time, before these extensive strata could have been shaped into distinct mountains by the abrasions of their edges or the loss of extensive portions; before the separation of Staffa from Mull, for example, could have taken place. The true solution of these cases may perhaps never be discovered; but assuredly no theory of the earth can be just which is incapable of being reconciled with the phenomena displayed by the latest rocks of the trap family. (I, pp. 574–5)

If MacCulloch is not committed to any particular geotheory, then, he does point out some of the problems that a geotheory would have to account for. While he uses the empirical evidence of the trap islands to indicate the vastness of geological time and the slow-motion material changes that the surface of the earth must have undergone from causes operating quietly through geological time, he also suggests that they pose an interpretive problem for geology that may never be solved.

MacCulloch's inconsistency with regard to whether the trap was deposited before or after the separation into islands is perhaps indicative of the fact that he assumes that it is impossible to reconstruct an accurate geohistory of the trap islands. He is nonetheless drawn into attempting to reconstruct their 'continuity of structure' by imaginatively replacing 'the portions that seem to have disappeared from among these islands' or removing 'the obstacles which cause the present semblance of discontinuity where, in a geological sense, it may not actually exist' (II, p. 59). Imaginative reconstruction, then, plays an important role in MacCulloch's empirical geology. There is little indication in his account, however, that Pennant and Jameson had published pioneering speculations about the possibility that the igneous rocks and structures on these islands might be parts of a much larger formation whose connections were concealed by the sea. Ignoring his forerunners allows MacCulloch to present his own observations of the possible connectedness of the trap islands as entirely original.

MacCulloch on Skye

MacCulloch's analysis of Skye – the largest, most complex and varied of the trap islands – is divided into separate sections: 'General Description' (I, pp. 262–84), 'Soil and Agriculture' (I, pp. 284–8), 'Antiquities' (I, pp. 288–90), 'Alluvia' (I, pp. 290–5), 'Geology' (I, pp. 295–402) and 'Minerals' (I, pp. 402–19). These sections indicate that while he has not completely divorced the landscape aesthetics of his 'General Description' from 'Geology' (they appear alongside one another), they have begun to go their separate disciplinary ways. MacCulloch's separation of geology and mineralogy into different sections reflects his repeated insistence on the limitations of mineralogy, whose attempt to classify rocks and minerals into stable and wholly distinct species is often exposed as fallacious by the complex, large-scale and site-specific structural geology of Scotland's Western Islands. Because igneous rocks blend into one another, for example, 'we are . . . compelled to acknowledge, in geological description, the necessity of superadding to mineral characters an accurate knowledge of the connexions of the rocks respecting which we are reasoning' (I, p. 371). MacCulloch develops this principle in a footnote in which he suggests that geology, in contrast with mineralogy, needs to take into account a rock's geographical location and its position in a particular sequence of formations and materials, and needs to consider the processes that may have produced or modified it. Although geology may eventually produce a general theory and history of the earth, and thereby establish principles that are universally applicable, in its present state it needs to concentrate on particular locations and situations. In this way, at least, MacCulloch's geology resembles the concern for the particularity and history of specific places that characterised the Romantic literature of the period.[16]

MacCulloch's geological analysis of Skye focuses mostly on the island's structure (composition, sequence, folding, angles of dip, veins). His commitment to the notion that each location has its particular geology leads him to resist the growing tendency of geologists in England to treat organic fossils as an invariable key to dating or sequencing the rocks they appear within. After identifying the limited variety and irregular dispersal of the organic remains in the limestone that begins to appear 'on the north-eastern side of the island at Lucy', MacCulloch goes on to stress the problems in using the palaeontological analysis of organic fossils as a universally valid analytic tool:

> From such remains, geologists have in many cases successfully determined the analogies and relative positions of strata; but they seem at the same time to have expected from them a more perfect demonstration than, in the present state of our knowledge, they are calculated to afford respecting the succession of strata and the different species of animal remains that occur in them. However worthy of confidence these distinctions might be in cases like those of the English strata, where a regular order over an extensive space is found to exist, it is not as yet safe to transfer the same criterion to detached deposits like the present; since the occasional absence of some, and the partial nature of many strata, added to our imperfect knowledge of fossil species, materially interfere with the use of this test. (I, p. 320)

The palaeontological analysis that was being successfully applied to the strata of England's extensive lowland landscapes was thus inadequate for the more fragmented and varied strata of the Scottish Highlands and Islands, where a more locally specific investigation was required and where structural geology remained the main analytic tool. Skye poses interpretive problems to the geologist that cannot be resolved by applying standard strategies or general theories.

MacCulloch's overview of Skye's geology is visually realised in volume III in the form of a fold-out geological map of the island and in diagrams of structural features such as strata, folds and veins. His written analysis of Skye's geology in volume I is divided into sections on 'Gneiss' (I, 295–300), 'Red Sandstone' (I, pp. 300–16), 'Secondary Strata' (I, pp. 316–54), 'Siliceous Schist' (I, pp. 355–60), 'Coal' (I, pp. 360–2), 'Overlying Rocks' (I, pp. 362–93), 'Trap Veins' (I, pp. 393–400) and 'Pitchstone' (I, pp. 401–2). This sequence corresponds to MacCulloch's interpretation of the vertical order of rocks that constitutes the island's geological structure (proceeding from the lowest to the highest rocks and from the south to the north of the island). MacCulloch is quick to note, however, that this apparently straightforward series is frequently disrupted or confused in particular places. Furthermore, he periodically stresses that he uses these rock names as umbrella terms that cover a wide variety of mineral compositions that tend to blend into one another.

MacCulloch also emphasises the problems of tracing the course of formations across a landscape that resists geological exploration. In the Trotternish peninsula, the beds of trap that cover almost the entire surface make the attempt to analyse the underlying strata into a difficult and intrepid interpretive hermeneutics:

> The examination of these strata in Trotternish is a task of no small difficulty; in which, conjecture, or at least analogy, must often supply the place of observation. This difficulty is caused by the trap which covers them more or less completely throughout their whole extent, whence they exhibit on the surface but occasional and slender indications of their nature, or even of their existence; a precipitous rock, or the section afforded by a stream, bringing a small patch or a few scattered fragments to light. It is only from the shore line, where the sections found in the high cliffs are continuously displayed, that a notion can be formed of their extent or dimensions; and even those appearances are so much involved and obscured by the trap connected with them, that they rarely allow the order of the strata to be traced; while their inaccessible state often compels us to judge of their composition by indications which ought never to be trusted where actual contact can be obtained. It may be added to these insuperable causes of obscurity that even the natural order of the strata is inconsistent and uncertain. (I, p. 339)

The difficulty arising from the complexity of Skye's often insuperably obscure geology is compounded by the fact that it is only rarely exposed (I, p. 322). Under such conditions, the geologist is forced to try to 'judge' the composition of underlying strata by using 'conjecture, or at least analogy' and to interpret 'occasional and slender indications', 'scattered fragments' and 'appearances'. Geological analysis thus involves a close reading of subtle signs in the landscape that, on Skye at least, resist interpretation.

MacCulloch's emphasis on complexity and difficulty differentiates geological analysis from the supposedly straightforward procedures of mineralogy; it highlights the problems in analysing an island like Skye; and it perhaps echoes MacCulloch's sense that the geological analysis of Scotland's Highlands and Islands is inherently more difficult, and hence more 'manly', than that of southern England. It also points to the intrinsic complexities of the planet's geology that resist attempts to reduce geology to tidy systems and theories. Furthermore, it correlates with the aesthetic theory of the period, in which difficulty, obscurity and indescribability were conventional markers or triggers of the sublime. Edmund Burke, for example, claimed that the sublime can be caused by 'a surmounting of *difficulties*' and by obscurity: 'It is our ignorance of things that causes all our admiration, and chiefly excites our passions. Knowledge and acquaintance make the most striking causes affect but little' (*A Philosophical Enquiry*, IV, vi, p. 135; II, iv, pp. 60–1). While I suggested earlier that MacCulloch's adherence to the empirical constraints of the Geological Society means that his geological analysis rarely adds geological dimensions to the sublimity of Scotland's Romantic landscape, his foregrounding of the empiricist struggle with geological obscurity and difficulty might serve to endow Skye's landscapes with a new kind of sublime resonance.

The Cuillin, Loch Scavaig and Loch Coruisk

The two most spectacular areas of Skye – geologically and aesthetically – are the Trotternish peninsula in the north and the Cuillin mountains in the south. In his 'General Description of Skye', MacCulloch traces an imagined anticlockwise circuit of the island's coastline, beginning with the southern promontory of Strathaird and proceeding northwards along the east coast, rounding the northern tip of the

Trotternish peninsula to discover columnar formations that ought to rank alongside, and be as well known as, those of Staffa (I, pp. 271, 277–8). For MacCulloch, the geology and landscape of the Trotternish peninsula, which contains the most spectacular stepped trap landscape in Britain and some of the most impressive formations of basaltic columns, is the 'most extraordinary and interesting' part of the island (I, p. 383). But considerations of space require me to leave aside MacCulloch's account of Trotternish in favour of examining his analysis of the geology and aesthetic impact of the Cuillin mountain complex, especially Loch Scavaig and Loch Coruisk. This was the most influential part of his description of Skye and helped to put these places and features on the Romantic map of Scotland.

MacCulloch's imaginary circumnavigation of Skye's coast ends with his encounter with the heights and recesses of the Cuillin mountains in the south:

> The scenes which here occur are as remarkable for their difference of character from the preceding, as for their grandeur; nor must they be passed without notice, though it is impossible to convey any idea of this spot, which before my visit had never been seen by a stranger, and was indeed known to few even of the inhabitants of Sky. Scarcely any but the shepherds had trod these sequestered retreats, the dwelling of clouds and solitude; fit haunts for the poetical dæmons of the storm. (I, pp. 280–1)

Here, MacCulloch represents himself as a pioneering explorer of the Cuillin by deploying elements of the Romantic travel genre and conventional markers of the sublime: these barely known, scarcely trodden and sequestered places are indescribable, remarkable for their 'grandeur', and 'fit haunts for the poetical dæmons of the storm'.

MacCulloch's section on Skye's 'Geology' (I, pp. 295–402) also emphasises the remoteness and inaccessibility of the Cuillin, but he seems at a loss to account for their geology. Indeed, geological analysis of the Cuillin and Loch Coruisk was beyond the scope of early nineteenth-century paradigms. Alan McKirdy et al. note that the Cuillin 'are steeped in the history of geological discovery. They were first studied in earnest in the 1870s, but it was Professor Alfred Harker's classic memoir, published in 1904, that more fully elucidated their geological history' (*Land of Mountain and Flood*, p. 280). Harker's work revealed that the gabbros of the Black Cuillin and the granites of the Red Cuillin 'were formed in the magma chamber of a long extinct volcano . . . [which] was active over 60 million years ago when the North Atlantic was widening apace' (p. 280). Long after subterraneous heat had done its work it was the turn of ice. The Black Cuillin 'are also renowned for their glacial landforms. This is the most spectacular area in Britain for its "alpine" scenery and superb examples of corries, arêtes and ice-moulded bedrock, as well as the glaciated trough of Loch Coruisk' (p. 282).[17] Despite the findings of Pennant and Faujas de Saint-Fond, the possibility that volcanoes had been a major shaping agent of the Highlands and Islands of Scotland in the distant past had not been generally accepted in the early decades of the nineteenth century, while Louis Agassiz's revelation that Scotland's landscape had been sculpted by glaciers would not appear until 1840.[18]

MacCulloch's difficulty with the geology of the Cuillin is indicated by his uncertainty about the origins and nature of the gabbro that is their main building material. He correctly identifies gabbro as a 'hypersthene rock' and wishes to include it among the varieties of overlying trap, but he thinks that it also possesses qualities that make it similar to granite (which he regards as a different 'family' or 'tribe' of rock) (I, p. 388). In addition, the isolation, topography, inaccessibility and climate of the Cuillin make it hard to determine the precise extent of the gabbro (I, pp. 385–6). Such problems of access and interpretation raise the value and power of these places and their geology. Furthermore, the physical qualities of the Cuillin's gabbro play a significant role in generating their aesthetic impact. The gabbro is rough and 'naked' and forms spiry serrated summits and ridges that render them 'inaccessible even to the stags and the wild goats that roam over this region of solitude and rocks' (I, pp. 387, 388). Another distinctive feature of the gabbro is 'its uncommon power in resisting the effects of time and weather' (I, p. 386). Although MacCulloch's geological analysis sometimes reveals that mountain landscapes are dynamic, ever-changing phenomena, he suggests here that the geology of the Cuillin endows them with remarkable durability. Yet both kinds of mountain landscape – that which endures and that which is dynamically changing – generate aesthetic power.

One of the most awesome and inaccessible features of the Cuillin mountain complex is Loch Coruisk, a glacial valley gouged through the volcanic architecture. In his 'General Description', MacCulloch is less concerned with discovering the processes that may have formed the Loch Coruisk glen in the depths of geological time than with emphasising the difficulties that have to be overcome in order to enter it. Given that it is surrounded on all sides by the steep flanks of the Cuillin, the best means of access is via Loch Scavaig, a sea loch that is 'inaccessible by land on the north side and equally so on the south to all but the active and practised mountaineer' (I, p. 282). MacCulloch's account of the traveller's experience of entering Loch Coruisk ramps up the sublimity sentence by sentence, clause by clause:

> On every side the bare rocky acclivities of the mountains rise around, their serrated edges darkly projected on the blue sky or entangled in the clouds which so often hover over this region of silence and repose. At all seasons and at all times of the day darkness seems to rest on its further extremity: a gloom in which the eye, discerning but obscurely the forms of objects, pictures to itself imaginary recesses and a distance still unterminated. . . . Silence and solitude seem for ever to reign amid the fearful stillness and the absolute vacuity around: at every moment the spectator is inclined to hush his footsteps and suspend his breath to listen for some sound which may recall the idea of life or of motion. . . .
>
> The effect of simplicity and proportion in diminishing the magnitude of objects is here distinctly felt, as it is in the greater efforts of architecture: those who have seen the interior of York Cathedral will understand the allusion. The length of the valley is nearly four miles, and its breadth about one; while the mountains that enclose it, rise with an acclivity so great, that the spectator situated at their base views all their summits around him; casting his eye over the continuous plane of their sides, as they extend upwards in solid beds of rock for nearly a mile and present a barrier over which there is no egress. Yet on entering it he will probably imagine it a mile in length, and fancy the lake, which occupies nearly the whole, reduced to the dimension of a few hundred yards. It is not until he has advanced for a mile or more, and finds the boundary still retiring before him unchanged, and his distant companions becoming invisible, that he discovers his error, and the whole force and effect of the scene becomes impressed on his mind. He who would paint Coruisk must combine with the powers of the landscape-painter those of the poet: it is to the imagination, not to the eye that his efforts must be directed. (I, pp. 283–4)

This passage locates the aesthetic and psychological impact of Loch Coruisk in the experience of an impersonal entity (the spectator, the eye) that is referred to using third-person pronouns. Loch Coruisk generates sublimity through the kinds of privation – silence, vacuity,

darkness and solitude – that Burke had identified as effective triggers of the sublime (*A Philosophical Enquiry*, II, vi, p. 71). Initially,
the simplicity, proportion and uniformity of the physical geography misleads and baffles the spectator's imagination, leading him to
fancy that he has entered a rather small valley. But the further the
spectator advances, the more the enormous scale of Loch Coruisk
impresses itself upon him. If 'it is to the imagination, not to the eye'
that a painter's 'efforts must be directed' if he would paint this loch,
the imagination itself is deceived and confounded by the physical
geography of this remote, almost inaccessible glen. The imagination
is also baffled and astonished by the geology of the Loch Coruisk
valley, especially those features (such as erratic boulders) that were
inexplicable to the geology of the period and would only later be
recognised as evidence of glaciation (I, p. 388).[19]

MacCulloch initially published an account of Loch Coruisk in his
'Sketch of the Mineralogy of Skye' in the *Transactions of the Geological
Society* in 1816. But, as Anne MacLeod notes, his claim to be the first
outsider to discover the loch may be disputed:

> Loch Coruisk took on iconic status as a result of two important voyages
> in the summer of 1814: one by John MacCulloch, the other by the emerg-
> ing wizard of the north, Sir Walter Scott. Both men could be credited with
> discovering the loch for the outside world, although it was undoubtedly
> Scott's description in *The Lord of the Isles* (1815) which exerted most
> influence on the popular imagination. (*From an Antique Land*, p. 156)[20]

The Lord of the Isles appeared a year earlier than MacCulloch's
1816 article (and four years before MacCulloch's *Description of the
Western Islands*); its description of Loch Coruisk, one of the most
famous passages in the poem, includes geological imagery:

> For rarely human eye has known
> A scene so stern as that dread lake,
> With its dark ledge of barren stone.
> Seems that primeval earthquake's sway
> Hath rent a strange and shatter'd way
> Through the rude bosom of the hill,
> And that each naked precipice,
> Sable ravine, and dark abyss,
> Tells of the outrage still. (III, xiv)

In these lines, the formation of the glacial valley that contains Loch Coruisk is ascribed to the impact of a 'primeval earthquake'; more interestingly, the geomorphology of the resulting landscape still 'tells' of that 'outrage', suggesting that landforms, when read aright by geologically informed readers, retain the signs of their origins. Scott, of course, misreads Loch Coruisk's geology. As MacCulloch repeatedly stresses, Skye's rocks often resist the geologist's attempt to make them tell the story of their formation in deep time, and they do so here by speaking a geological language that had not yet been invented or discovered. As in Wordsworth's 'The Solitary Reaper', a poem partly stimulated by his 1803 tour of Scotland, the fact that no one can tell what the reaper or the rocks sing adds to their sublimity and gives the imagination room to roam. These rocks resonate with sublime imaginative power precisely because their geological origins appeared unknowable.

Landscape painters soon followed MacCulloch and Scott into the sublime recesses of the Cuillin. William Daniell's prints of Loch Scavaig and Loch Coruisk in his *Voyage Round Great Britain* (1820) were 'accompanied by extensive quotations from Scott's journal' (MacLeod, *From an Antique Land*, p. 158).[21] Charlotte Klonk claims that Daniell's 'Loch Coruisg near Loch Scavig' (Figure 8.1) was both influenced by and 'best matches MacCulloch's geological description' (*Science*

Loch Coruisg near Loch Scavig

Figure 8.1 William Daniell, 'Loch Coruisg near Loch Scavig', from *A Voyage Round Great Britain* (1814–26). By permission of University of Glasgow Library, Special Collections.

and the Perception of Nature, p. 90). But the most famous painting of
Loch Coruisk was by MacCulloch's friend J. M. W. Turner, who toured
Scotland in 1831 in order to produce illustrations – including sketches
of Fingal's Cave and Loch Coruisk – for Robert Cadell's complete edition of *The Poetical Works of Sir Walter Scott* (1834).[22] Yet despite
his interest in geology, Turner's watercolour sketch of Loch Coruisk
(Fig. 8.2) appears to be aesthetically impressionistic rather than geologically informed. Although, as Klonk points out, this watercolour
'was esteemed for its geological accuracy after John Ruskin . . . claimed
that he would prefer it to a geological drawing as a means of explaining
structure' (p. 93), Ruskin's claim that Turner's watercolour marks the
mountain's strata 'stone by stone' is not convincing.[23] As Hugh Miller
suggested, Turner's painting offers 'a kind of transcendental or transfig-
ured geology' ('Landscape Geology', p. 150). Whereas MacLeod suggests that the presence of the two human witnesses in the foreground
of the painting 'gives the contrast between human transience and the
endurance of the landscape a geological significance' (*From an Antique
Land*, p. 161), Klonk more convincingly suggests that 'Turner shows
the atmosphere as indicative of nature in a constant process of change'
(*Science and the Perception of Nature*, p. 95). While both readings
are feasible, we might note that Turner's witnesses, who seem to be
detached from the awesome scene they gaze upon, are significantly
different in this respect from the spectator fashioned in MacCulloch's

Figure 8.2 J. M. W. Turner, *Loch Coruisk, Skye* (1831), National Galleries
of Scotland.

prose account, whose discombobulating experience of Loch Coruisk is only produced when he enters into it.

Although MacCulloch seems to have been wholly committed to the empiricist agenda of the Geological Society, and although he generally edits out his own internal experience on his geological tours of Scotland, he dramatises the hermeneutical difficulties presented by the geological puzzles and aesthetic dynamism of the Cuillin and Loch Coruisk by focusing on the subjective experience of an imagined spectator making his bemused way into a vast landscape that appears solid and timeless but which shifts its shape according to the position from which he views it and resists geological interpretation. While the Geological Society insisted that geology should be limited to gathering facts, MacCulloch's *Description of the Western Islands* suggests that it is impossible to read the geology of these islands without attempting to discern what their rocks tell about their origins in deep time. The fact that the rocks resist this attempt in various ways challenges the belief that geology might be a straightforward empirical science and generates a new kind of geological sublimity.

Staffa and Fingal's Cave

I want to conclude this book by examining MacCulloch's account of Staffa and Fingal's Cave. As we have seen, Staffa had been a magnetic lure since the publication of Joseph Banks's account in the first volume of Pennant's *A Tour in Scotland and Voyage to the Hebrides, MDCCLXXII* (1774). Staffa and Fingal's Cave were visited by most of the geological travel writers examined in the present book (except Jameson), the high point of Romantic enthusiasm and geological analysis coming in Faujas Saint-Fond's *Travels in England, Scotland, and the Hebrides* (1799). By the second decade of the nineteenth century, however, so many accounts of Staffa had been published that it was in danger of losing its aura of aesthetic and geological wonder.[24] But while MacCulloch notes that visitors 'crowd to this far-famed spot' in the summer and that 'Few objects in the Western islands are better known', he also insists that 'few perhaps are more deserving of notice than this celebrated spot, no less the admiration of the geologist than of the painter and the general traveller' (II, pp. 2, 1). In what follows, I will explore MacCulloch's complex and ambivalent response to the problem of Staffa's overfamiliarity and his own belatedness in order to suggest that it signals the end of the era of geological travel writing about Scotland examined in the present book.

MacCulloch's account of Staffa in *A Description of the Western Islands* appears almost at the end of the section on the trap islands but is given pride of place at the opening of the second volume. Following his usual procedure, MacCulloch separates his general description of Staffa from his geological analysis. The general description is shaped by his complex engagement with the fact that he and his contemporaries were belated visitors to this classic ground and engages in revealing ways with the accounts of earlier writers. He suggests at the outset that previous travellers have exaggerated the dangers of the sea voyage to Staffa and that the Highland boatmen have encouraged this because they 'find an interest in exciting alarm' (II, p. 2). While MacCulloch insists that the voyage to Staffa is safe in almost any weather, thus deflating its sublime potential, he also represents himself as a heroic adventurer who has landed and embarked on the island in the most difficult conditions. And whereas Faujas had given the Highland boatmen an Ossianic aura, MacCulloch describes them as dangerously inept and given to encouraging and exploiting travellers' fears because they have been corrupted by the commercial spirit of modernity (II, pp. 4–5, note).

MacCulloch admits that 'Description has long since been exhausted on the cave of Fingal' and that so 'much admiration has been lavished on it by some' that subsequent visitors may well be disappointed because it cannot live up to such hyper-inflated descriptions. He urges such visitors to 'return to this cave again, and again view it, regardless of the descriptions of others and their own ill-founded anticipations'. If they do so, 'after every visit this object will progressively rise in estimation' (II, pp. 15–16). MacCulloch nonetheless offers his own description of the cave's subjective aesthetic impact:

> It would be no less presumptuous than useless to attempt a description of the picturesque effect of that to which the pencil itself is inadequate. But if this cave were even destitute of that order and symmetry, that richness arising from multiplicity of parts combined with greatness of dimension and simplicity of style, which it possesses; still, the prolonged length, the twilight gloom half concealing the playful and varying effects of reflected light, the echo of the measured surge as it

rises and falls, the transparent green of the water, and the profound and fairy solitude of the whole scene, could not fail strongly to impress a mind gifted with any sense of beauty in art or in nature. If to these be added, as in viewing the Scuir of Egg, that peculiar sentiment with which Nature perhaps most impresses us when she allows us to draw comparisons between her works and those of art, we shall be compelled to own it is not without cause that celebrity has been conferred on the cave of Fingal. (II, p. 18)

This passage foregrounds the fact that it presents not an objective description but an account of the cave's subjective impact on a mind gifted with a sense of beauty in art and nature. But while it presses many of the right buttons, MacCulloch's account is perhaps intentionally routine and low-key compared with those of earlier writers. The claim that Fingal's Cave is indescribable and impossible to draw had become a conventional way of indicating an object's sublimity. And the following list of features – 'greatness of dimension', 'simplicity of style', 'prolonged length', 'twilight gloom' and 'solitude' – had long been conventional aspects of sublimity. The comparison with architecture had also become well-worn in the half-century since Banks's visit, though MacCulloch offers a suggestive account of the 'peculiar sentiment' produced by the mind's tendency to compare features like Fingal's Cave or the Sgurr of Eigg with the most impressive productions of architecture:

> The sense of power is a fertile source of the sublime, and as the appearance of power exerted, no less than that of simplicity, is necessary to confer this character on architecture, so the mind, insensibly transferring the operations of nature to the efforts of art where they approximate in character, becomes impressed with a feeling rarely excited by her more ordinary forms, where these are even stupendous. (I, p. 509)

As suggested in Chapter 1, this passage echoes Burke's account in the second edition of his *Enquiry* sixty years earlier of the sublime effects generated by the impression that great force has been required to produce an object. But although MacCulloch's observation might appear to open up the possibility of speculating about the powerful geological forces that had produced Staffa and the Sgurr of Eigg, he avoids this.

MacCulloch's general description of Staffa also includes an extended empirical survey of columns and caves consisting of measurements, dimensions, angles of columns and strata, compass directions and so on. He concludes by saying that he has 'reserved to the last place the geological account, both of the rocks and of foreign substances found in Staffa, which present but little that is interesting' (II, p. 18). This is an extraordinary statement, given Staffa's intrinsic geological interest, but it does reflect the lacklustre character of MacCulloch's attention to the island's basalt columns in his geological account, which is largely restricted to an empirical analysis of their mineralogical make-up which avoids speculation about the processes that might have formed them or the timescale involved.

MacCulloch's general and geological descriptions of Staffa are, then, somewhat underwhelming, especially in comparison with those of some of the earlier writers examined in this book. But he attempts to refresh his otherwise routine and dutifully empirical survey of Staffa's geology by taking note of a feature ignored by other commentators – 'an alluvial deposit consisting of various transported stones, which may be seen on the surface in different parts of the island'. This deposit prompts MacCulloch to make conjectural speculations about its origin:

> The surface of the earth every where presents appearances indicating great changes and revolutions; of which none are perhaps more unquestionable than the existence of transported stones and alluvial substances in countries far removed from those where similar rocks are now found in their natural situations. These are familiar to geologists, and have been subjects of much discussion. The insular position of the example now under consideration, is sufficient to prove that it could not have resulted from the flow of water, whether that flow was gradual, or sudden, without at the same time supposing a state of the surface in which Staffa was continuous, at least, with the neighbouring island of Mull. If we imagine the origin of the alluvial matter to be in that island only, it is sufficient to prove the great changes which the surface must have undergone since the period of this transportation. There is scarcely any other method of explaining the present position of this deposit but by supposing that the island of Staffa had been protruded from below in its present form; a supposition involving changes at least as great, and less consistent with those revolutions of the globe which seem most numerous and most strongly indicated. A contemplation of the map will give the reader a notion of the great waste of land which

must have occurred before the present separation of Staffa from Mull was effected. Whether this loss of surface has resulted from the violent or slow action of destroying forces, we have no means of knowing. Yet perhaps the undisturbed state of the trap strata . . . tends to show that this separation was not effected by dislocations, the consequences of force exerted from below; but that it has been gradual and tranquil, or the result of powers at least which have allowed the neighbouring parts to remain in their original state. (II, pp. 21–2)

Attention to an apparently insignificant detail, unrelated to Staffa's celebrated caves and columns, and unnoticed by all previous geologists, suddenly opens up the geological sublime as MacCulloch imaginatively reconstructs the slow-motion 'revolutions' in the earth's surface that must have led to the deposition of this alluvial matter on the island's surface. Rejecting the possibility that Staffa may have risen from the sea in its present form (therefore rejecting the idea that the island originated in volcanic eruptions or Hutton's subterraneous pressure), MacCulloch envisages the massive forces and the enormous timescale that must have led to the gradual opening up of the gulf that separates Staffa from Mull.

Another way that MacCulloch copes with the sense of belatedness and satiety with Staffa is to alert the world to a more remote and less-trodden island that is more geologically interesting and more sublime. Indeed, MacCulloch had already suggested, towards the end of the first volume of *A Description of the Western Islands*, that Eigg contains columnar structures (of volcanic pitchstone) that are superior, geologically and aesthetically, to those on Staffa:

Although this island [Eigg] is of easy access, and presents one of the most interesting and picturesque spots in the whole circuit of the Western isles, it continues nearly unknown to the southern travellers who for so many years past have made the Highlands the object of their summer excursions. . . .

The columnar ranges so common in the Western islands, present nothing of a character in the least similar to those which occur in Egg; even to him who may have been satiated with the regularity of Staffa or the magnificence of Sky, this island offers both variety and novelty. With that novelty it combines a grandeur and peculiarity of feature yielding to nothing in the whole circuit of Highland scenery; and incapable indeed of being compared with any other elsewhere, since unlike to any thing which has ever yet been delineated by artists. (I, pp. 507–8)

MacCulloch, then, claims to have found a 'nearly unknown' island which contains a unique columnar feature that differs from and outdoes everything else in the 'whole circuit of Highland scenery'. Given that it is 'unlike to any thing which has ever yet been delineated by artists', MacCulloch's illustration in volume III (Figure 8.3), which emphasises its sublime scale by including a diminutive figure who has begun to climb its lower slopes, is also a claim to originality. Yet MacCulloch is able to represent himself as a geological pioneer only by failing to note that Jameson had already identified the Sgurr of Eigg as a superior alternative to Staffa for precisely the same reasons. In the second volume of his *Mineralogy of the Scottish Isles* (1800), Jameson admits that he 'had not an opportunity of landing upon' Staffa. His description of 'this remarkable island' is therefore 'drawn from the accounts of others', including those of Banks, Uno von Troil, Faujas de Saint-Fond and Abraham Mills, though he registers mild scepticism about their enthusiasm for Staffa's wonders and omits or rejects their Vulcanist interpretation of its basaltic pillars (II, p. 7). He compensates for missing Staffa by claiming that he subsequently discovered a formation of porphyry columns on Eigg that was even more impressive than Staffa, thus reclaiming his status as a pioneering geological traveller in the region:

Figure 8.3 John MacCulloch, 'View of the Scuir of Egg', in *A Description of the Western Islands of Scotland* (1819), III, plate v. By permission of University of Glasgow Library, Special Collections.

Staffa, which is the most magnificent assemblage of natural columns that has yet been discovered, is the only one that can bear a comparison with Scure Eigg. Staffa is an object of the greatest beauty and regularity; the pillars are as distinct as if they had been raised by the hand of art; yet it has not the extent or sublimity of Scure Eigg: the one may be compared with the greatest exertion of human power; the other is characteristic of the wildest, and most inimitable works of nature. (II, pp. 46–7)[25]

Jameson's elevation of the Sgurr Eigg over Staffa highlights the difference between Romantic and Enlightenment aesthetic values: Staffa is beautiful because its basaltic pillars are regular and distinct and resemble impressive architecture produced by human power; the Sgurr Eigg is characteristic of nature's power, sublime, wild and inimitable.

MacCulloch's account of the geology and aesthetic qualities of Staffa and Fingal's Cave is thus complex and contradictory. He presents a number of strategies for dealing with the veil of familiarity that had begun to inhibit visitors' responses to Staffa. Visitors could try to erase their knowledge of previous descriptions of the island, though their own descriptions would simply add to the existing superfluity and thereby make it increasingly difficult for future visitors to see the island with fresh eyes. MacCulloch's own description of Staffa's landforms fails to escape the dominant clichés, while his attempt to reassure potential visitors that the crossing to Staffa was not so dangerous as previous writers had claimed would no doubt have encouraged yet more visitors had he not also warned them about the fraud and incompetence of the Highland boatmen. The fact that MacCulloch's geological account of Staffa only comes alive when he attends to a feature not noticed by other observers indicates another way that the satiated visitor might respond to Staffa, though it makes that strategy less possible for future visitors. Another strategy, itself not new, is to push on to more distant islands – such as Eigg or Skye – that are less familiar and more sublime. These strategies potentially prolonged the era of pioneering exploration of the Western Islands of Scotland, but they also anticipate its apparently inevitable end. As the most comprehensive account of the geology of the area, *A Description of the Western Islands of Scotland* both alerted readers to the islands' geological and aesthetic wonders and potentially accelerated their erosion by luring increasing numbers of visitors.

Romantic Staffa

Eric Gidal points out that 'Fingal's Cave came to occupy a privileged space in the popular geological literature of the nineteenth century, as it perfectly combined folkloric romance, sublime aesthetics, and scientific curiosity in a remote and difficult-to-access location at the margins of the British archipelago' (*Ossianic Unconformities*, p. 9). While this is true, I suggest that MacCulloch's account of Staffa marks the end of the pioneering phase of Romantic geology in Scotland. Shortly after the publication of his three volumes, the introduction of steamboats in 1822 removed many of the dangers, real or imagined, of the voyage to the island.[26] It is true that many geologists visited Staffa in the nineteenth century, but it was no longer central to geological debates in the period.[27] Instead, Staffa became the haunt of Romantic poets, writers, painters and composers, including James Hogg, Walter Scott, Sarah Murray, John Keats, William Wordsworth, J. M. W. Turner and Felix Mendelssohn.[28]

But while steamboat travel made it easier to reach Staffa, it made the possibility of experiencing its wonders ever more difficult. Wordsworth visited Staffa on his tour of Scotland in 1833 and included four sonnets about the island and cave in his *Poems Composed or Suggested During a Tour, in the Summer of 1833* (1835). In the first sonnet, the speaker claims that the sheer number of tourists made it difficult even for the most poetic of travellers to experience the cave's sublimity:

> We saw, but surely, in the motley crowd,
> Not One of us has felt the far-famed sight;
> How *could* we feel it? Each the other's blight,
> Hurried and hurrying, volatile and loud. (ll. 1–4)

In the second sonnet, supposedly written 'After the Crowd had departed', Wordsworth rejects the 'presumptuous thoughts' of those who would explain Fingal's Cave according to the 'Mechanic laws' of geology and ascribes its sublimity to the 'Infinite Power' of the creating deity.[29]

The divergence between Romanticism and geology in the early decades of the nineteenth century can also be seen in Turner's artistic response to Staffa and Fingal's Cave on his 1831 tour of Scotland.[30]

Figure 8.4 J. M. W. Turner, *Staffa, Fingal's Cave* (1832). Yale Center for British Art, New Haven, CT.

One of Turner's sketches, from the perspective of a boat just offshore, was the basis for an oil painting that constitutes one of the most powerful Romantic images of Staffa and Fingal's Cave (Figure 8.4). The prominence that this painting gives to the *Maid of Morven*, a steamer which regularly took 'large numbers of tourists to the island from Glasgow' (Shortland, 'Darkness Visible', p. 15), highlights the fact that Staffa had become a destiny of modern tourism. Yet the fact that the steamer adds its storm-blown smoke to the luminous mist, turbulent sky and rough sea conditions in order virtually to obliterate Fingal's Cave and its geological structure suggests that Romantic aesthetic impressions have entirely displaced geological analysis.[31] In Turner's and Wordsworth's responses to Fingal's Cave, despite the fact that they were both keenly interested in geology, Romanticism and geology have gone their separate ways.[32]

A Parting of the Ways

MacCulloch was not, of course, the last geologist to tour Scotland, nor was his *Description of the Western Islands of Scotland* the last published account of the results of such travels.[33] Some of the most prominent British and European geologists of the nineteenth century made geological tours of Scotland, including those, such as Archibald

Geikie, who contributed to the Survey of the Highlands as part of the Geological Survey of Great Britain.[34] But the focus of attention had shifted, along with the mode of writing. Most geological tours of Scotland in the nineteenth century were concerned with the palae-ontological analysis of sedimentary rock formations, and the results of such tours, with notable exceptions, were written up as scientific articles and books rather than as geological travel writing.

Charles Darwin, who from 1825 to 1827 studied medicine at Edinburgh University, where he attended Jameson's lectures in zool-ogy and geology and participated in meetings of the Wernerian Natural History Society,[35] toured the Scottish Highlands in the sum-mer of 1838 and published his 'Observations on the Parallel Roads of Glen Roy' in the *Philosophical Transactions of the Royal Society* (1839). He later admitted to Charles Lyell in a letter of 6 September 1861 that his paper was 'one long gigantic blunder' because it had taken no account of the effects of glaciation.[36] William Buckland, perhaps the most important palaeontological geologist in nineteenth-century Britain, made several tours of Scotland, including with Lyell in 1824 (visiting Glen Tilt and Siccar Point) and with Louis Agassiz in 1840 (finding evidence that Scotland's Highlands had been shaped by glaciation in the distant past, which Agassiz first communicated to the world in a letter from Fort Augustus published in *The Scotsman* on 7 October 1840).[37]

Two of the most influential Scottish geologists who explored the Highlands and Islands in the nineteenth century were Hugh Miller and Archibald Geikie. Miller's *The Old Red Sandstone* (1841) originated in his discovery of 'remarkable fossil fishes in the Old Red Sandstone at Cromarty' in north-east Scotland and made him 'the leading popu-lar expounder of geology in the 1840s and 1850s' (Taylor, 'Miller, Hugh', *ODNB*). His *The Cruise of the Betsey* (1858), which narrates *A Summer Ramble among the Fossiliferous Deposits of the Hebrides*, includes a palaeontological analysis of the organic remains in Eigg's secondary and tertiary formations but more or less ignores its basaltic structures.[38] Geikie's 'earliest work, as a self-taught teenage geolo-gist, was undertaken in Skye', and his early work for the Geological Survey, which began in 1855 in the Lothians near Edinburgh, allowed him to become 'an acknowledged authority on igneous rocks', culmi-nating in his 1897 work *Ancient Volcanoes of Great Britain* (Oldroyd and Hamilton, 'Themes in the Early History of Scottish Geology',

p. 40).[39] In addition to his work for the survey, 'he continued to visit the Hebrides. He visited Eigg in 1864 and published an interesting section in his *Scenery of Scotland* (1865, frontispiece), illustrating his ideas on the origin of the island's famous Sgurr' (p. 40). As we saw in Chapter 4, he suggested 'that the basaltic lavas of the Hebrides, parts of the mainland, and also across in Northern Ireland, might be mere fragments of what was formerly one vast tract of basaltic lavas' (p. 40). In addition, however, 'his most important investigations' included a 'study of the Scottish deposits of Old Red Sandstone' (Oldroyd, 'Geikie, Sir Archibald', *ODNB*).

The centrality of the palaeontological analysis of sedimentary rocks in nineteenth-century British geology can be seen in the work of Sir Roderick Murchison, who made a series of Scottish tours from the 1820s onwards. In 1827, he 'made an extensive tour with the Cambridge geologist Adam Sedgwick ... travelling ... round the northern part of the country' (Oldroyd and Hamilton, 'Themes in the Early History of Scottish Geology', p. 30).[40] As Oldroyd and Hamilton note, 'given that much of Sedgwick and Murchison's journey was made round the coast by sea, they naturally gave attention to the sedimentary deposits as they appeared in the coastal regions, and they were on the lookout for fossils in what they took to be Secondary strata' (p. 30). Murchison was centrally involved in the three major geological controversies that dominated nineteenth-century British geology. Martin Rudwick's *The Great Devonian Controversy* (1985) reconstructs the debate between Murchison and Sir Henry de la Beche about the sedimentary rocks of Devon in the 1830s and 1840s. James Secord's *Controversy in Victorian Geology: The Cambrian-Silurian Dispute* (1986) attends to the contest between Murchison and Sedgwick about the ancient sedimentary rocks in the mountains of northern Wales. And David Oldroyd's *The Highlands Controversy: Constructing Geological Knowledge through Fieldwork in Nineteenth-Century Britain* (1990) explores the disagreement in the second half of the nineteenth century between Murchison and James Nicol concerning the interpretation of the rock sequence of the Northwest Highlands of Scotland.[41] As Oldroyd shows, the Highlands Controversy built on MacCulloch's geological survey of the region and involved extensive fieldwork and tours. But these tours – such as Murchison's tour of the Northwest Highlands with Nicol in 1855, with Andrew Crosbie Ramsay in 1859, and with

Geikie in 1860 – resulted in scientific papers and books rather than the kind of geological travel writing that has been the subject of the present book.[42] Geology and Romantic travel literature had gone their separate ways.

Notes

1. See Rudwick, *Bursting the Limits of Time*, chapters 4 to 10, and the whole of his *Worlds Before Adam*. Also see O'Connor, *The Earth on Show*, chapters 1 to 3 (pp. 31–161). Scotland is not, of course, bereft of fossils, as Hugh Miller went on to demonstrate in books such as *The Old Red Sandstone* (1841), *The Testament of the Rocks* (1857) and *The Cruise of the Betsey* (1858). On Scotland's fossils, see Trewin, *Scottish Fossils*.
2. On the founding and outlook of the Geological Society, see Lewis and Knell (eds), *The Making of the Geological Society of London*, pp. 255–78; Davies, *Whatever Is Under the Earth*; Porter, *The Making of Geology*, pp. 146–9; and Rudwick, *Bursting the Limits of Time*, pp. 463–8, 495–8.
3. See Kölbl-Ebert, 'George Bellas Greenough's "Theory of the Earth" and its Impact on the Early Geological Society'.
4. See Dean, *James Hutton and the History of Geology*.
5. See Eyles, 'Louis Albert Necker, of Geneva, and his Geological Map of Scotland'. Necker's *Voyage to the Hebrides* (1822) is more concerned with landscape than geology.
6. On Greenough's 1805 tour of Scotland, see Rudwick, 'Hutton and Werner Compared'; MacLeod, *From an Antique Land*, pp. 144–5; and Wyatt, 'George Bellas Greenough: A Romantic Geologist', p. 64. On Buckland's travels in Scotland, see Davies, *The Earth in Decay*, pp. 272–80.
7. See Siegfried and Dott (eds), *Humphry Davy on Geology*, pp. xiv, xvi–xvii.
8. See Oldroyd and Hamilton, 'Themes in the Early History of Scottish Geology', pp. 29–30. Lyell's 1817 tour of Scotland, made when he was twenty years old in the company of his father, is traced in Wilson, *Charles Lyell*, pp. 49–56.
9. For discussions of MacCulloch, see Cumming, 'A Description of the Western Islands of Scotland: John MacCulloch's Successful Failure', 'John MacCulloch, F.R.S., at Addiscombe', 'John MacCulloch, Pioneer of "Precambrian" Geology', 'John MacCulloch, Blackguard, Thief and High Priest' and 'MacCulloch, John (1773–1835)', *ODNB*. Also see Buckland, *Novel Science*, pp. 78–88.

10. See Smout, 'Tours in the Scottish Highlands'; Glendening, *The High Road*; Durie, *Scotland for the Holidays*; Grenier, *Tourism and Identity in Scotland*; and Brown (ed.), *Literary Tourism, the Trossachs and Walter Scott*.

11. See MacCulloch, 'On Staffa', 'Sketch of the Mineralogy of Skye', 'A Geological Description of Glen Tilt' and 'On the Parallel Roads of Glen Roy'.

12. For suggestions that MacCulloch may have used a camera lucida, see Rudwick, 'The Emergence of a Visual Language for Geological Science', p. 175, and MacLeod, *From an Antique Land*, p. 146. On MacCulloch's *Geological Map of Scotland*, see Eyles, 'John MacCulloch, F.R.S., and his Geological Map'; Boud, 'Aaron Arrowsmith's Topographical Map of Scotland and John MacCulloch's Geological Survey'; Flinn, 'John MacCulloch M.D., F.R.S., and his Geological Map of Scotland'; and Cumming, 'Geological Maps in Preparation: John MacCulloch on the Western Islands'. Also see 'Mapping the Unseen: Scotland's Geological Landscapes', in Fleet et al., *Scotland: Mapping the Nation*, pp. 235–9.

13. MacCulloch to Horner, 2 June 1820, quoted by Davies, *Whatever Is Under the Earth*, p. 71.

14. See Jameson, *An Outline of the Mineralogy of the Shetland Islands, and of the Island of Arran* (1798) and *Mineralogy of the Scottish Isles* (1800).

15. Whittow points out that 'trap' 'is derived from the Swedish *trappa* meaning "step" and is used internationally to describe the way in which differential erosion of successive lava flows gives a stepped character to the landscape' (*Geology and Scenery in Scotland*, p. 236).

16. On the importance of 'locality' in geological history, especially at the end of the eighteenth century, see Oldroyd, 'Non-written Sources in the Study of the History of Geology'. Regarding the importance of local places in Romantic poetry, see Bate, *The Song of the Earth*, pp. 205–42; Lamont and Rossington (eds), *Romanticism's Debatable Lands*; Stafford, *Local Attachments*; and Fielding, *Scotland and the Fictions of Geography*, pp. 4–11.

17. See Harker, *The Tertiary Igneous Rocks of Skye*. The effects of glaciation on Loch Coruisk and the Cuillin were first identified by the Scottish geologist James David Forbes during his 1845 tour of the West Highlands (see Cunningham, *James David Forbes: Pioneer Scottish Glaciologist*, pp. 191–4).

18. See Agassiz, 'Discovery of the Former Existence of Glaciers in Scotland'.

19. On the puzzle and aesthetic impact of erratic boulders in the period, see Heringman, *Romantic Rocks*, pp. 30–53.

20. According to Klonk, 'although Scott had been a friend of MacCulloch since the 1790s, the two seem not to have met when Scott arrived on

Skye on 23 August 1814' (*Science and the Perception of Nature*, p. 90). For Scott's journal impressions of Loch Coruisk, see Osborne (ed.), *The Voyage of the 'Pharos'*, pp. 83–6.

21. See Daniell, *A Voyage Round Great Britain* and *Illustrations of the Island of Staffa*.

22. See Campbell, *A Complete Catalogue of Works by Turner in the National Gallery of Scotland*, plate 15 and p. 77. Also see Finley, 'J. M. W. Turner and Sir Walter Scott' and *Landscapes of Memory*. On Turner's knowledge of geology, see Hamilton, *Turner and the Scientists*.

23. See Ruskin, *Modern Painters*, vol. I, in Cook and Wedderburn (eds), *The Complete Works of John Ruskin*, vol. III, p. 453, and *Modern Painters*, vol. IV, in Cook and Wedderburn (eds), *Complete Works of John Ruskin*, vol. VI, p. 268.

24. As noted above, MacCulloch's first account of Staffa was published in *TGSL*, 2 (1814), 501–9. Other geological visitors in the first two decades of the nineteenth century included William Buckland, Dawson Turner, Christian Leopold von Buch and Charles Lyell. For Buckland's travels in Scotland (including with Agassiz), see Davies, *The Earth in Decay*, pp. 272–80. For Lyell's correspondence about Staffa, see Wilson, *Charles Lyell*, pp. 53–4.

25. Martin Martin offers a short description of Eigg in *A Description of the Western Islands of Scotland*, pp. 276–9, and Walker includes a short chapter on the island in his *Report on the Hebrides* devoted almost entirely to a statistical account of its people and natural resources (see McKay (ed.), *The Rev. Dr. John Walker's Report on the Hebrides*, pp. 223–6).

26. See Anon, *The Steam Boat Companion; and Stranger's Guide to the Western Islands and Highlands of Scotland*; Donald MacCulloch, *The Wondrous Isle of Staffa*, pp. 23–30; and Klonk, *Science and the Perception of Nature*, p. 89. On the way that Romantic travel in the Highlands and Islands turned into nineteenth-century tourism, see Smout, 'Tours in the Scottish Highlands'.

27. Staffa and Fingal's Cave are not mentioned in Geikie's *The Scenery of Scotland* of 1865, except in an illustration (fig. 48), or in Rudwick's *Worlds Before Adam*, and do not figure significantly in O'Connor's *The Earth on Show*.

28. See Jenkins and Visocchi, *Mendelssohn in Scotland*, pp. 68–79; Osborne (ed.), *The Voyage of the 'Pharos'*, pp. 94–7; and Walker, *Walking North with Keats*, pp. 198–201.

29. See Wordsworth, *The Poems: Volume Two*, pp. 762–3. For an account of the sonnets that Wordsworth wrote about his 1833 tour of the west of Scotland, see Gidal, *Ossianic Unconformities*, pp. 161–8.

30. Turner's sketch of Fingal's Cave looking outwards to the sea became an engraving for *The Lord of the Isles* in volume 10 of Cadell's *Poetical Works of Sir Walter Scott* (1834). See Campbell, *A Complete Catalogue of Works by Turner in the National Gallery of Scotland*, plate 15 and p. 77, and Finley, *Landscapes of Memory*.

31. For an alternative interpretation of Turner's painting of Staffa, see Bunting, *Love of Country*, pp. 120–4.

32. For Wordsworth's interest in geology, see Wyatt, *Wordsworth and the Geologists*; on Turner's knowledge of geology, see Hamilton, *Turner and the Scientists*.

33. For a useful account, see Oldroyd and Hamilton, 'Themes in the Early History of Scottish Geology'.

34. On the geological survey of the Highlands, see Oldroyd, *The Highlands Controversy*, pp. 266–99; R. B. Wilson, *A History of the Geological Survey of Scotland*; and Harry Wilson, *Down to Earth*.

35. See Desmond et al., 'Darwin, Charles Robert (1809–1882)', *ODNB*; also see Ashworth, 'Charles Darwin as a Student in Edinburgh', and Shepperson, 'The Intellectual Background of Charles Darwin's Student Years at Edinburgh'. For an exaggerated account of the impact of Darwin's experiences in Scotland on his later theory of evolution, see Derry, *Darwin in Scotland*. The most succinct account of Darwin's time in Edinburgh is in Desmond and Moore, *Darwin*, pp. 21–44, 254–5.

36. Letter no. 3246, Darwin Correspondence Project, <http://www.darwinproject.ac.uk/DCP-LETT-3246> (last accessed 26 June 2017). See Rudwick, 'Darwin and Glen Roy: A "Great Failure" in Scientific Method?'.

37. For Buckland's tour with Lyell, see Wilson, *Charles Lyell*, pp. 129–34; Oldroyd and Hamilton, 'Themes in the Early History of Scottish Geology', p. 29; and Davies, *The Earth in Decay*, pp. 272–80. Rupke's *The Great Chain of History: William Buckland and the English School of Geology* does not concern itself with Buckland's Scottish tours. See Agassiz, 'Discovery of the Former Existence of Glaciers in Scotland'.

38. See chapters 2 to 5, pp. 16–87. Miller was, of course, an expert on sedimentary rocks, as indicated in *The Old Red Sandstone*. On Miller's poetic geology, see the final chapter of O'Connor, *The Earth on Show*, pp. 391–432. For essays on Miller, see Shortland (ed.), *Hugh Miller and the Controversies of Victorian Science*.

39. See Oldroyd, 'Geikie, Sir Archibald (1835–1924)', *ODNB*.

40. See Sedgwick and Murchison, 'On the Geological Relations of the Secondary Strata in the Isle of Arran', 'On the Old Conglomerates and Other Secondary Deposits on the North Coasts of Scotland' and 'On the Structure and Relations of the Deposits Contained between the Primary Rocks and the Oolitic Series in the North of Scotland'.

41. Also see Oldroyd and Hamilton, 'Themes in the Early History of Scottish Geology', pp. 34–7. For Nicol's side of the argument, see Nicol, *The Geology and Scenery of the North of Scotland.*
42. For accounts of these tours, see Oldroyd, *The Highlands Controversy*, chapters 3 to 5, pp. 48–121.

Bibliography

Abrams, M. H., *The Mirror and the Lamp* (Oxford and New York: Oxford University Press, [1953] 1971).

Adamson, Sylvia, 'From Empathetic Deixis to Empathetic Narrative: Stylisation and (De)subjectivisation as Processes of Language Change', in Dieter Stein and Susan Wright (eds), *Subjectivity and Subjectivisation: Linguistic Perspectives* (Cambridge: Cambridge University Press, 1995), pp. 195–224.

Adamson, Sylvia, 'Literary Language', in Suzanne Romaine (ed.), *The Cambridge History of the English Language, 4, 1776–1997* (Cambridge: Cambridge University Press, 1998), pp. 589–692.

Adamson, Sylvia, 'Subjectivity in Narration: Empathy and Echo', in Marina Yaguello (ed.), *Subjecthood and Subjectivity: The Status of the Subject in Linguistic Theory* (Paris: Ophrys, 1994), pp. 193–208.

Addison, Joseph and Richard Steele, *The Spectator*, ed. Donald F. Bond, 5 vols (Oxford: Clarendon, 1965).

Agassiz, Louis, 'Discovery of the Former Existence of Glaciers in Scotland, Especially in the Highlands', *The Scotsman*, 7 October 1840, p. v.

Allan, David, 'Moray, Sir Robert (1608/9?–1673)', *ODNB*, Oxford University Press, 2004; online edn, October 2007, <http://www.oxforddnb.com/view/article/19645> (last accessed 12 May 2017).

Allen, David Elliston, *The Naturalist in Britain: A Social History* (Harmondsworth: Penguin, 1978).

Anderson, John G. T., *Deep Things out of Darkness: A History of Natural History* (Berkeley and London: University of California Press, 2013).

Andrews, Malcolm, *The Search for the Picturesque: Landscape Aesthetics and Tourism in Britain, 1760–1800* (Aldershot: Scholar, 1989).

Ang, Tom and Michael Pollard, *Walking the Scottish Highlands: General Wade's Military Roads* (London: Andre Deutsch, 1984).

Anon, *The Scottish Tourist, and Itinerary; or, A Guide to the Scenery and Antiquities of Scotland and the Western Islands, With a Description of the Principal Steam-boat Tours* (Edinburgh, 1838).

Anon, *The Steam Boat Companion; and Stranger's Guide to the Western Islands and Highlands of Scotland* (Glasgow, 1820).

Anon, 'Travels of Citizen B. Faujas Saint-Fond', in *An Historical Miscellany of the Curiosities and Rarities in Nature and Art, Comprising New and Entertaining Descriptions of the most Surprising Volcanos, Caverns, Cataracts, Whirlpools, Waterfalls, Earthquakes, Thunder, Lightning, and Other Wonderful and Stupendous Phenomena of Nature. Forming a Rich and Comprehensive View of All that Is Interesting and Curious in every Part of the Habitable World* (London, 1794–1800), vol. 4, pp. 369–79.

Ashfield, Andrew and Peter de Bolla (eds), *The Sublime: A Reader in British Eighteenth-Century Aesthetic Theory* (Cambridge and New York: Cambridge University Press, 1996).

Ashworth, J. H., 'Charles Darwin as a Student in Edinburgh, 1825–1827', *Proceedings of the Royal Society of Edinburgh*, 55 (1934–5), pp. 97–113.

Ashworth, William B., Jr, *Vulcan's Forge and Fingal's Cave: Volcanoes, Basalt, and the Discovery of Geological Time* (Kansas City: Linda Hall Library of Science, Engineering and Technology, 2004).

Axelsson, Karl, *The Sublime: Precursors and British Eighteenth-Century Conceptions* (Bern: Verlag Peter Lang, 2007).

Bacon, Francis, *The Advancement of Learning*, ed. Stephen Jay Gould (New York: The Modern Library, [1605] 2001).

Bacon, Francis, 'Advice to the Earl of Rutland on his Travels', in *Francis Bacon: A Critical Edition of his Major Works*, ed. Brian Vickers (Oxford and New York: Oxford University Press, 1996), pp. 69–80.

Bacon, Francis, *Francis Bacon: A Critical Edition of his Major Works*, ed. Brian Vickers (Oxford and New York: Oxford University Press, 1996).

Bacon, Francis, *The New Organon*, ed. Lisa Jardine and Michael Silverthorne (Cambridge and New York: Cambridge University Press, [1620] 2000).

Bacon, Francis, 'Of Travaile', in *Essays or Counsels Civil and Moral* (London, 1625), pp. 100–4.

Bailey, Edward Battersby, *James Hutton – The Founder of Modern Geology* (New York: Elsevier, 1967).

Baillie, John, *Essay on the Sublime* (London, 1747).

Baines, Paul, *The House of Forgery in Eighteenth-Century Britain* (Aldershot: Ashgate, 1999).

Baines, Paul, *The Long 18th Century* (London: Hodder Arnold, 2004).

Baines, Paul, 'Ossianic Geographies: Fingalian Figures on the Scottish Tour, 1760–1830', *Scotlands*, 4.1 (1997), 44–61.

Baker, Matt and John E. Gordon, 'Unconformities, Schisms and Sutures: Geology and Mythology in Scotland', in Elizabeth Ellsworth and Jamie Kruse (eds), *Making the Geologic Now* (New York: Punctum Books, 2012), pp. 163–9.

Barrell, John, *English Literature in History, 1730–80: An Equal, Wide Survey* (Basingstoke: Palgrave Macmillan, 1984).

Barrell, John, *The Idea of Landscape and the Sense of Place, 1730–1840: An Approach to the Poetry of John Clare* (Cambridge: Cambridge University Press, 1972).

Bate, David G., 'Sir Henry Thomas De la Beche and the Founding of the British Geological Survey', *Mercian Geologist*, 17.3 (2010), 149–65.

Bate, Jonathan, *Romantic Ecology* (London: Routledge, 1991).

Bate, Jonathan, *The Song of the Earth* (London: Picador, 2000).

Batten, Charles, *Pleasurable Instruction: Form and Convention in Eighteenth-Century Travel Literature* (Berkeley, Los Angeles and London: University of California Press, 1978).

Baxter, Stephen, *Revolutions in the Earth: James Hutton and the True Age of the World* (London: Phoenix, 2004).

Beattie, James, *Dissertations Moral and Critical* (London, 1783).

Beer, G. R. de (ed.), *Tour on the Continent, 1765, by Thomas Pennant, esq.* (London: Ray Society, 1948).

Berry, Christopher J., *The Idea of Commercial Society in the Scottish Enlightenment* (Edinburgh: Edinburgh University Press, 2015).

Bewell, Alan, *Wordsworth and the Enlightenment: Nature, Man, and Society in the Experimental Poetry* (New Haven and London: Yale University Press, 1989).

Blair, Hugh, 'A Critical Dissertation on the Poems of Ossian' (1763), in James Macpherson, *The Poems of Ossian and Related Works*, ed. Howard Gaskill, intr. Fiona Stafford (Edinburgh: Edinburgh University Press, 1996).

Blair, Hugh, *Lectures on Rhetoric and Belles Lettres* (Dublin, 1783).

Blundell, D. J. and A. C. Scott, *Lyell: The Past Is the Key to the Present* (London: The Geological Society, 1998).

Bohls, Elizabeth, *Women Travel Writers and the Language of Aesthetics, 1716–1818* (Cambridge: Cambridge University Press, 1995).

Bolla, Peter de, *The Discourse of the Sublime: Readings in History, Aesthetics, and the Subject* (Oxford: Blackwell, 1989).

Boswell, James, *The Life of Samuel Johnson*, ed. David Womersley (London and New York: Penguin, [1791] 2008).

Boud, R. C., 'Aaron Arrowsmith's Topographical Map of Scotland and John MacCulloch's Geological Survey', *The Canadian Cartographer*, 11.1 (1974), 24–34, 114–29.

Bowden, Alan J., 'Geology at the Crossroads: Aspects of the Career of Dr John MacCulloch', in C. L. E. Lewis and S. J. Knell (eds), *The Making of the Geological Society of London* (London: The Geological Society, 2009), pp. 255–78.

Bowen, Margarita, *Empiricism and Geographical Thought: From Francis Bacon to Alexander von Humboldt* (Cambridge: Cambridge University Press, 1981).

Boyle, Robert, *General Heads for the Natural History of a Country, Great or Small; Drawn out for the Use of Travellers and Navigators. Imparted by the late Honourable Robert Boyle, Esq., Fellow of the Royal Society . . . To which is added, other Directions for Navigators, &c. with particular Observations of the most noted Countries in the World: By another Hand* (London, 1762).

Brady, Emily, *The Sublime in Modern Philosophy: Aesthetics, Ethics, and Nature* (New York: Cambridge University Press, 2013).

Bray, Elizabeth, *The Discovery of the Hebrides: Voyagers to the Western Isles 1745–1883* (London: Collins, 1986).

Brennan, Matthew Cannon, *Wordsworth, Turner, and Romantic Landscape: A Study of the Traditions of the Picturesque and the Sublime* (Columbia, SC: Camden House, 1987).

Brown, Ian (ed.), *Literary Tourism, the Trossachs and Walter Scott* (Glasgow: Scottish Literature International, 2012).

Bryce, James, *Geology of Arran and Clydesdale: With an Account of the Flora and Marine Fauna of Arran* (British Association for the Advancement of Science, 1855; Cambridge: Cambridge University Press, 2011).

Bryce, James, *The Geology of Arran and the Other Clyde Islands with an Account of the Botany, Natural History, and Antiquities, Notices of the Scenery and an Itinerary of the Routes* (Glasgow and London: William Collins, 1872).

Brydone, Patrick, *A Tour through Sicily and Malta* (London, 1773).

Bryson, Bill (ed.), *Seeing Further: The Story of Science and the Royal Society* (London: Harper, 2010).

Buchanan, George, *The History of Scotland*, trans. unknown (London, 1790).

Buckland, Adelene, *Novel Science: Fiction and the Invention of Nineteenth-Century Geology* (Chicago and London: University of Chicago Press, 2013).

Buffon, Georges Louis Leclerc, *Les époques de la nature* (1778), in *Histoire naturelle, générale et particulière*, vol. 5 (Paris, 1749–1804).

Buffon, Georges Louis Leclerc, *Théorie de la terre* (1749), vol. 1 of *Natural History, General and Particular*, trans. William Smellie, 2nd edn (London, 1785), chapter 1, pp. 1–58.

Bunting, Madeleine, *Love of Country: A Hebridean Journey* (London: Granta, 2016).

Bunyan, John, *Grace Abounding, with Other Spiritual Autobiographies*, ed. John Stachniewski with Anita Pacheco (Oxford and New York: Oxford University Press, [1666] 1998).

Burke, Edmund, *A Philosophical Enquiry into the Origin of our Ideas of the Sublime and Beautiful*, 2nd edn (London, 1759).

Burke, Edmund, *A Philosophical Enquiry into the Origin of our Ideas of the Sublime and Beautiful* (1757/1759), ed. James T. Boulton (London: Routledge & Kegan Paul, 1958; Oxford: Basil Blackwell, 1987).

Burnet, Thomas, *The Theory of the Earth: Containing an Account of the Original of the Earth and of all the General Changes Which it hath already undergone, or is to undergo, Till the Consummation of all Things*, 2 vols (London, [1684] 1691).

Burnett, Linda Andersson, 'Northern Noble Savages? Edward Daniel Clarke and British Primitivist Narratives on Scotland and Scandinavia, c. 1760–1822', PhD thesis, Edinburgh University, 2012.

Butcher, Norman E., 'Necker, Louis Albert (1786–1861)', *ODNB*, Oxford University Press, 2004, <http://www.oxforddnb.com/view/article/49478> (last accessed 12 May 2017).

Byrne, Angela, *Geographies of the Romantic North: Science, Antiquarianism, and Travel, 1790–1830* (Basingstoke: Palgrave Macmillan, 2013).

Camden, William, *Camden's Britannia, Newly Translated into English: With Large Additions and Improvements, published by Edmund Gibson* (London, 1695).

Campbell, Mungo, *A Complete Catalogue of Works by Turner in the National Gallery of Scotland* (Edinburgh: National Galleries of Scotland, 1993).

Campbell, N. and R. Martin S. Smellie, *The Royal Society of Edinburgh (1783–1983): The First Two Hundred Years* (Edinburgh: Royal Society of Edinburgh, 1983).

Carboni, Pierre, 'Ossian and Belles Lettres: Scottish Influences on J.-B.-A. Suard and Late-Eighteenth-Century French Taste and Criticism', in Deidre Dawson and Pierre Morère (eds), *Scotland and France in the Enlightenment* (London: Associated University Presses, 2004), pp. 74–89.

Cardinal, Roger, 'Romantic Travel', in Roy Porter (ed.), *Rewriting the Self: Histories from the Renaissance to the Present* (London and New York: Routledge, 1997), pp. 135–55.

Carozzi, Albert V., 'Rudolf Erich Raspe and the Basalt Controversy', *Studies in Romanticism*, 8.4 (Summer 1969), 235–50.

Challinor, John, *The History of British Geology: A Bibliographical Study* (Newton Abbot: David & Charles, 1971).

Chalmers, Alan, 'Scottish Prospects: Thomas Pennant, Samuel Johnson, and the Possibilities of Travel Narrative', in Lorna Clymer and Robert Mayer (eds), *Historical Boundaries, Narrative Forms: Essays on British Literature in the Long Eighteenth Century in Honor of Everett Zimmerman* (Newark: University of Delaware Press, 2007), pp. 199–214.

Chard, Chloe and Helen Langdon (eds), *Transports: Travel, Pleasure, and Imaginative Geography, 1600–1830* (New Haven: Yale University Press, 1996).

Chitnis, A., 'The University of Edinburgh's Natural History Museum and the Huttonian-Wernerian Debate', *Annals of Science*, 26.2 (1970), 85–94.

Clark, William, 'Narratology and the History of Science', *Studies in History and Philosophy of Science*, 26 (1995), 1–71.

Class, Monika, *Coleridge and Kantian Ideas in England, 1796–1817: Coleridge's Responses to German Philosophy* (London: Bloomsbury, 2012).

Clery, E. J., *The Rise of Supernatural Fiction, 1762–1800* (Cambridge and New York: Cambridge University Press, 1995).

Constantine, Mary-Ann and Nigel Leask (eds), *Enlightenment Travel and British Identities: Thomas Pennant's Tours in Scotland and Wales* (London and New York: Anthem, 2017).

Conybeare, William Daniel, 'On the Geological Features of the North-Eastern Counties of Ireland', *TGSL*, 3 (1816), 121–235.

Cook, E. T. and Alexander Wedderburn (eds), *The Complete Works of John Ruskin*, 39 vols (London: George Allen; New York: Longman, 1903–12); online edition at the Ruskin Library and Research Centre, Lancaster University, <http://www.lancaster.ac.uk/users/ruskinlib/Pages/Works.html> (last accessed 23 June 2017).

Cooper, Derek, *Road to the Isles: Travellers in the Hebrides, 1770–1914* (Routledge & Kegan Paul, 1979; London: Macmillan, 2002).

Cordiner, Charles, *Antiquities and Scenery of the North of Scotland in a Series of Letters to Thomas Pennant, Esqr. By the Revd. Charles Cordiner, Minister of St. Andrew's Chapel Bamff* (London, 1780).

Cordiner, Charles, *Remarkable Ruins and Romantic Prospects of North Britain, with Ancient Monuments and Singular Subjects of Natural History*, 2 vols (London, 1795).

Costelloe, Timothy M. (ed.), *The Sublime: From Antiquity to the Present* (Cambridge: Cambridge University Press, 2012).

Craig, G. Y. (intr.), *The 1785 Abstract of James Hutton's Theory of the Earth* (Edinburgh: Scottish Academic Press, 1987).

Craig, G. Y. (ed.), *James Hutton's Theory of the Earth: The Lost Drawings* (Edinburgh: Scottish Academic Press, 1978).

Crane, Nicholas, 'Thomas Pennant: 1772: Highlands and Islands', *Great British Journeys* (London: Phoenix, 2008), pp. 155–88.

Cresswell, Tim, *Place: A Short Introduction* (Oxford: Blackwell, 2004).

Cronstedt, Alex Frederic, *Essay Towards a System of Mineralogy*, trans. Gustav von Engerström (London, 1770).

Cumming, David A., 'A Description of the Western Islands of Scotland: John MacCulloch's Successful Failure', *Journal of the Society for the Bibliography of Natural History*, 8 (1977), 270–85.

Cumming, David A., 'Geological Maps in Preparation: John MacCulloch on the Western Islands', *Archives of Natural History*, 10.2 (1981), 255–71.

Cumming, David A., 'John MacCulloch, Blackguard, Thief and High Priest, Reassessed', in A. Wheeler and J. H. Price (eds), *From Linnaeus to Darwin: Commentaries on the History of Biology and Geology* (London: Society for the History of Natural History, 1985), pp. 77–88.

Cumming, David A., 'John MacCulloch, F.R.S., at Addiscombe: The Lectureships in Chemistry and Geology', *Notes and Records of the Royal Society of London*, 34 (1980), 155–83.

Cumming, David A., 'John MacCulloch, Pioneer of "Precambrian" Geology', PhD thesis, University of Glasgow, 1983.

Cumming, David A., 'MacCulloch, John (1773–1835)', *ODNB*, Oxford University Press, 2004, <http://www.oxforddnb.com/view/article/17412> (last accessed 12 May 2017).

Cunningham, Andrew and Nicholas Jardine (eds), *Romanticism and the Sciences* (Cambridge: Cambridge University Press, 1990).

Cunningham, Frank F., *James David Forbes: Pioneer Scottish Glaciologist* (Edinburgh: Scottish Academic Press, 1990).

Cunningham, Robert James May, *Essay on the Geology of the Lothians* (Edinburgh, 1838).

Cutler, Alan, *The Seashell on the Mountaintop: A Story of Science, Sainthood, and the Humble Genius Who Discovered a New History of the Earth* (New York: Dutton, 2003).

Dampier, William, *A New Voyage Round the World*, 5th edn (London, 1703).

Daniell, William, *Illustrations of the Island of Staffa, in a Series of Views, Accompanied by Topographical and Geological Descriptions* (London, 1818).

Daniell, William, *A Voyage Round Great Britain, Undertaken in the Summer of the Year 1813, and Commencing from the Land's End, Cornwall, with a Series of Views, Illustrative of the Character and Prominent Features of the Coast*, 8 vols (London, 1814–26).

Darwin, Charles, '"Parallel Roads of Glen Roy": Observations on the parallel roads of Glen Roy, and of other parts of Lochaber in Scotland, with an attempt to prove that they are of marine origin', *PTRS*, 129 (1839), 39–81.

Darwin Correspondence Project, University of Cambridge, 2016, <https://www.darwinproject.ac.uk/> (last accessed 23 June 2017).

Davies, G. H., 'Robert Hooke and his Conception of Earth-History', *Proceedings of the Geologists' Association*, 75 (1964), 493–8.

Davies, Gordon L. Herries, *The Earth in Decay: A History of British Geomorphology, 1578–1878* (London: Macdonald Technical and Scientific, 1969).

Davies, Gordon L. Herries, *Whatever Is Under the Earth: The Geological Society of London 1807 to 2007* (London: The Geological Society, 2007).

Davis, Leith, Ian Duncan and Jane Sorensen (eds), *Scotland and the Borders of Romanticism* (Cambridge: Cambridge University Press, 2004).

Davy, Humphry, 'A Discourse Introductory to a Course of Lectures on Chemistry' (1802), in *The Collected Works of Sir Humphry Davy*, ed. John Davy, 9 vols (London, 1839), vol. 2, pp. 311–26.

Davy, Humphry, *Humphry Davy on Geology: The 1805 Lectures for the General Audience*, ed. Robert Siegfried and Robert Dott (Madison: University of Wisconsin Press, 1980).

Davy, Humphry, *Six Discourses Delivered before the Royal Society* (London, 1827).

De Quincey, Thomas, 'Letters to a Young Man Whose Education Had Been Neglected', in *Collected Writings of Thomas De Quincey*, ed. David Masson, 14 vols (Edinburgh: Adam and Charles Black, 1889–90), vol. 10, pp. 33–52.

Dean, Dennis R. (ed.), *Coleridge and Geology* (Ann Arbor: Scholars' Facsimiles and Reprints, 2004).

Dean, Dennis R., *James Hutton and the History of Geology* (Ithaca and London: Cornell University Press, 1992).

Dean, Dennis R. (ed.), *James Hutton in the Field and in the Study: A Bicentenary Tribute to the Father of Modern Geology* (Delmar, NY: Scholars' Facsimiles and Reprints, 1997).

Dean, Dennis R., 'Jameson, Robert (1774–1854)', *ODNB*, Oxford University Press, 2004, <http://www.oxforddnb.com/view/article/14633> (last accessed 12 May 2017).

Dean, Dennis R., *Romantic Landscapes: Geology and its Cultural Influence in Britain, 1765–1835* (Ann Arbor: Scholars' Facsimiles and Reprints, 2007).

Dear, Peter (ed.), *The Literary Structure of Scientific Argument: Historical Studies* (Philadelphia: University of Pennsylvania Press, 1991).

Defoe, Daniel, *A Tour through the Whole Island of Great Britain*, ed. Pat Rogers (Harmondsworth: Penguin, [1724–6] 1971).

Demarest, Nicolas, 'Mémoire sur l'origin et la nature du basalte', *Mémoires de l'Académie royale des sciences* (1774), 705–75.

Derry, J. F., *Darwin in Scotland: Edinburgh, Evolution and Enlightenment* (Dunbeath: Whittles, 2010).

Desmond, Adrian and James Moore, *Darwin* (London and New York: Penguin, [1992] 2009).

Desmond, Adrian, James Moore and Janet Browne, 'Darwin, Charles Robert (1809–1882)', *ODNB*, Oxford University Press, 2004; online edn, May 2015, <http://www.oxforddnb.com/view/article/7176> (accessed 12 May 2017).

Drake, E. T., 'The Geological Observations of Robert Hooke (1635–1703) on the Isle of Wight', in Patrick N. Wyse Jackson (ed.), *Four Centuries of Geological Travel: The Search for Knowledge on Foot, Bicycle, Sledge and Camel* (London: The Geological Society, 2007), pp. 19–30.

Drake, E. T., 'Hooke's Concepts of the Earth in Space', in Paul Kent and Allan Chapman (eds), *Robert Hooke and the English Renaissance* (Leominster: Gracewing, 2005), pp. 75–94.

Drake, E. T., 'Hooke's Ideas of the Terraqueous Globe and a Theory of Evolution', in M. Cooper and M. Hunter (eds), *Robert Hooke Tercentennial Studies* (Aldershot: Ashgate, 2006), pp. 135–49.

Drake, E. T., 'The Hooke Imprint on the Huttonian Theory', *American Journal of Science*, 281 (1981), 963–73.

Drake, E. T., *Restless Genius: Robert Hooke and his Earthly Thoughts* (New York: Oxford University Press, 1996).

Drake, E. T. and P. D. Komar, 'A Comparison of the Geological Contributions of Nicolaus Steno and Robert Hooke', *Journal of Geological Education*, 29 (1981), 127–34.

Duffy, Cian, *The Landscapes of the Sublime 1700–1830: Classic Ground* (Basingstoke: Palgrave Macmillan, 2013).

Duffy, Cian and Peter Howell (eds), *Cultures of the Sublime: Selected Readings, 1750–1830* (Basingstoke: Palgrave Macmillan, 2011).

Durie, Alastair J., *Scotland for the Holidays: Tourism in Scotland, c. 1780–1939* (East Linton: Tuckwell Press, 2003).

Eddy, Matthew D., *The Language of Mineralogy: John Walker, Chemistry and the Edinburgh Medical School* (Aldershot: Ashgate, 2008).

Eddy, Matthew D., 'The University of Edinburgh Natural History Class Lists', *Archives of Natural History*, 30 (2003), 97–117.

Elsner, Jaś and Joan-Pau Rubiés (eds), *Voyages and Visions: Towards a Cultural History of Travel* (London: Reaktion, 1999).

Emeleus, C. H. and B. R. Bell, *The Palaeogene Volcanic Districts of Scotland*, 4th edn (Nottingham: British Geological Survey, 2005).

Emerson, R. L., 'Sir Robert Sibbald, Kt, the Royal Society of Scotland and the Origins of the Scottish Enlightenment', *Annals of Science*, 45 (1988), 41–72.

Engell, James, *The Creative Imagination: Enlightenment to Romanticism* (Cambridge, MA, and London: Harvard University Press, 1981).

Eyles, Victor A., 'John Macculloch, F.R.S., and his Geological Map: An Account of the First Geological Survey of Scotland', *Annals of Science*, 2 (1939), 114–29.

Eyles, Victor A., 'Louis Albert Necker, of Geneva, and his Geological Map of Scotland', *Transactions of the Geological Society of Edinburgh*, 14 (1948), 93–127.

Fabricant, Carole, 'The Aesthetics and Politics of Landscape in the Eighteenth Century', in Ralph Cohen (ed.), *Studies in Eighteenth-Century British Art and Aesthetics* (Berkeley: University of California Press, 1985), pp. 49–81.

Farber, Paul, *Finding Order in Nature: The Naturalist Tradition from Linnaeus to E. O. Wilson* (Baltimore: Johns Hopkins University Press, 2000).

Faujas de Saint-Fond, Barthélemy, *Minéralogie des volcans ou description de toutes les substances produites ou rejetées par les feux souterrains* (Paris, 1784).

Faujas de Saint-Fond, Barthélemy, *Recherches sur les volcans éteints du Vivarais et du Velay* (Paris, 1778).

Faujas Saint-Fond, Barthélemy, *Travels in England, Scotland, and the Hebrides; Undertaken for the Purpose of Examining the State of the Arts, the Sciences, Natural History and Manners, in Great Britain*, trans. unknown, 2 vols (London: James Ridgeway, 1799).

Faujas de Saint-Fond, Barthélemy, *Voyage en Angleterre, en Ecosse et aux Iles Hebrides; ayant pour objet les sciences, les arts, l'histoire naturelle et les moeurs; avec la description mineralogique du pays de Newcastle, des montagnes du Derbyshire, des environs d'Edinburgh, de Glasgow, de Perth, de St Andrews, du duche d'Inverary et de la grotte de Fingal* (Paris, 1797).

Ferguson, Frances, *Solitude and the Sublime: Romanticism and the Aesthetics of Individuation* (London and New York: Routledge, 1992).

Fielding, Penny, *Scotland and the Fictions of Geography: North Britain 1760–1830* (Cambridge and New York: Cambridge University Press, 2008).

Findlen, Paula, 'Natural History', in Katharine Park and Lorraine Daston (eds), *The Cambridge History of Science, Volume 3: Early Modern Science* (Cambridge and New York: Cambridge University Press, 2006), pp. 435–68.

Finley, Gerald, 'J. M. W. Turner and Sir Walter Scott: Iconography of a Tour', *Journal of the Warburg and Courtauld Institutes*, 35 (1972), 359–85.

Finley, Gerald, *Landscapes of Memory: Turner as Illustrator to Scott* (London: Scolar Press, 1980).

Fleet, Christopher, Margaret Wilkes and Charles W. J. Withers, *Scotland: Mapping the Nation* (Edinburgh: Birlinn, 2012).

Flinn, Derek, 'James Hutton and Robert Jameson', *Scottish Journal of Geology*, 16 (1980), 251–78.

Flinn, Derek, 'John MacCulloch M.D., F.R.S., and his Geological Map of Scotland: His Years in the Ordnance 1795–1826', *Notes and Records of the Royal Society*, 36.1 (1981), 83–101.

Fortey, Richard, *The Hidden Landscape: A Journey into the Geological Past* (London: Bodley Head, 2010).

Foucault, Michel, *The Order of Things* (London and New York: Routledge, 1989).

Friend, Peter, *Scotland: Looking at the Natural Landscapes* (London: Harper-Collins, 2012).

Frye, Northrop, *Anatomy of Criticism: Four Essays* (Princeton: Princeton University Press; London and New York: Penguin, [1957] 1990).

Fulford, Tim (ed.), *Romanticism and Science: Subcultures and Subversions, 1750–1850* (London and New York: Routledge, 2002).

Fulford, Tim, Debbie Lee and Peter J. Kitson, *Literature, Science and Exploration in the Romantic Era: Bodies of Knowledge* (Cambridge and New York: Cambridge University Press, 2004).

Furniss, Tom, '"As if created by fusion of matter after some intense heat": Pioneering Geological Observations in Thomas Pennant's Tours of Scotland (1769, 1772)', in Mary-Ann Constantine and Nigel Leask (eds), *Enlightenment Travel and British Identities: Thomas Pennant's Tours in Scotland and Wales* (London and New York: Anthem, 2017), pp. 163–81.

Furniss, Tom, *Edmund Burke's Aesthetic Ideology* (Cambridge and New York: Cambridge University Press, 1993).

Furniss, Tom, 'James Hutton's Geological Tours of Scotland: Romanticism, Literary Strategies, and the Scientific Quest', *Science and Education*, 23.3 (2014), 565–88.

Furniss, Tom, 'Joseph Addison', in *The Encyclopedia of Aesthetics*, ed. Michael Kelly, 2nd edn (Oxford: Oxford University Press, 2014), vol. 1, pp. 26–31.

Furniss, Tom, '"Plumb-Pudding Stone" and the Romantic Sublime: The Landscape and Geology of the Trossachs in *The Statistical Account of Scotland* (1791–99)', in Christoph Bode and Jacqueline Labbe (eds), *Romantic Localities: Europe Writes Place* (London: Pickering & Chatto, 2010), pp. 51–65.

Furniss, Tom, 'A Romantic Geology: James Hutton's 1788 "Theory of the Earth"', *Romanticism*, 16.3 (2010), 305–21.

Gabbey, Alan, 'Newton, Active Powers, and the Mechanical Philosophy', in I. Bernard Cohen and George E. Smith (eds), *The Cambridge Companion to Newton* (Cambridge and New York: Cambridge University Press, 2002), pp. 329–57.

Garnett, Thomas, *Observations on a Tour through the Highlands and Part of the Western Isles of Scotland, Particularly Staffa and Icolmkill*, 2 vols (London, 1800).

Gascoigne, John, *Joseph Banks and the English Enlightenment: Useful Knowledge and Polite Culture* (Cambridge: Cambridge University Press, 1994).

Gaull, Marilyn, *English Romanticism: The Human Context* (New York and London: Norton, 1988).

Geikie, Archibald, *The Ancient Volcanoes of Great Britain*, 2 vols (London: Macmillan, 1897).

Geikie, Archibald, *The Founders of Geology* (London: Macmillan, 1897).

Geikie, Archibald, *Geological Sketches at Home and Abroad* (London: Macmillan, 1882).

Geikie, Archibald, *The Scenery of Scotland Viewed in Connection with its Physical Geology*, 3rd edn (London: Macmillan, [1865] 1901).

Geoffrey of Monmouth, *The History of the Kings of Britain*, trans. and ed. Lewis Thorpe (London and New York: Penguin, [1136] 1966).

Gerard, Alexander, *An Essay on Taste* (London, 1759).

Gidal, Eric, *Ossianic Unconformities: Bardic Poetry in the Industrial Age* (Charlottesville and London: University of Virginia Press, 2015).

Gillen, Con, *Geology and Landscapes of Scotland* (Harpenden: Terra Publishing, 2003).

Gilpin, William, *An Essay upon Prints, Containing Remarks upon the Principles of Picturesque Beauty* (London, 1768).

Gilpin, William, *Observations on the River Wye, and Several Parts of South Wales, &c. Relative Chiefly to Picturesque Beauty, Made in the Summer of the Year 1770* (London, 1782).

Gilpin, William, *Observations, Relative Chiefly to Picturesque Beauty, Made in the Year 1776, On several Parts of Great Britain; Particularly the High-Lands of Scotland*, 2 vols (London, 1789).

Gilpin, William, *Three Essays: - On Picturesque Beauty; - on Picturesque Travel; and, on Sketching Landscape* (London, 1792).

Glendening, John, *The High Road: Romantic Tourism, Scotland, and Literature, 1720–1820* (New York: St. Martin's Press, 1997).

Gold, John R. and Margaret M. Gold, *Imagining Scotland: Tradition, Representation and Promotion in Scottish Tourism since 1750* (London: Scolar Press, 1995).

Golinski, Jan, 'Humphry Davy: The Experimental Self', *Eighteenth-Century Studies*, 45.1 (Fall 2011), 15–28.

Golinski, Jan, 'Humphry Davy's Sexual Chemistry', *Configurations*, 7.1 (1999), 15–41.

Golinski, Jan, *Making Natural Knowledge: Constructivism and the History of Science*, 2nd edn (Chicago and London: University of Chicago Press, [1998] 2005).

Gordon, John E., 'Rediscovering a Sense of Wonder: Geoheritage, Geotourism and Cultural Landscape Experiences', *Geoheritage*, 4.1–2 (April 2012), 65–77.

Gordon, John E. and Matt Baker, 'Appreciating Geology and the Physical Landscape in Scotland: From Tourism of Awe to Experimental Re-engagement', in T. A. Hose (ed.), *Appreciating Physical Landscape: Three Hundred Years of Geotourism* (London: The Geological Society, 2016), pp. 25–40.

Gould, Stephen Jay, *Time's Arrow, Time's Cycle: Myth and Metaphor in the Discovery of Geological Time* (Cambridge, MA, and London: Harvard University Press, 1987).

Grenier, Katherine Haldane, *Tourism and Identity in Scotland: Creating Caledonia* (Aldershot and Burlington: Ashgate, 2005).

Gribbin, John, *The Fellowship: The Story of the Royal Society and a Scientific Revolution* (London: Penguin, 2006).

Guettard, J.-É., 'Mémoire sur la minéralogie de l'Auvergne', *Mémoires de l'Académie des sciences* (1759), 538–76.

Hall, Sir James, 'Experiments on Whinstone and Lava', *TRSE*, 5 (1805), 43–74.

Hallam, Anthony, *Great Geological Controversies* (Oxford: Oxford University Press, 1983).

Hamblyn, Richard, 'Landscape and the Contours of Knowledge: The Literature of Travel and the Sciences of the Earth in Eighteenth-Century Britain', PhD thesis, Cambridge University, 1994.

Hamblyn, Richard, 'Private Cabinets and Popular Geology: The British Audiences for Volcanoes in the Eighteenth Century', in Chloe Chard and Helen Langdon (eds), *Transports: Travel, Pleasure, and Imaginative Geography, 1600–1830* (New Haven: Yale University Press, 1996), pp. 179–205.

Hamilton, James, *Turner and the Scientists* (London: Tate Publishing, 1998).

Hamilton, William, *Observations on Mount Vesuvius, Mount Etna, and other Volcanos: In a Series of Letters, Addressed to the Royal Society* (London, 1772).

Harker, Alfred, *The Tertiary Igneous Rocks of Skye* (Glasgow, 1904).

Hartley, Stuart David, 'Robert Jameson, Geology and Polite Culture, 1796–1826: Natural Knowledge Enquiry and Civic Sensibility in Late Enlightenment Scotland', PhD thesis, Edinburgh University, 2001.

Headrick, James, *View of the Mineralogy, Agriculture, Manufactures and Fisheries of the Island of Arran, with Notices of Antiquities and Suggestions for Improving the Agriculture and Fisheries of the Highlands and Isles of Scotland* (Edinburgh: Constable; London: John Murray, 1807).

Henderson, D. M. and J. H. Dickson (eds), *A Naturalist in the Highlands: James Robertson – His Life and Travels in Scotland, 1767–71* (Edinburgh: Scottish Academic Press, 1994).

Heringman, Noah, *Romantic Rocks, Aesthetic Geology* (Ithaca and London: Cornell University Press, 2004).

Heringman, Noah (ed.), *Romantic Science: The Literary Forms of Natural History* (Albany: SUNY Press, 2003).

Hill, Christopher, *The World Turned Upside Down: Radical Ideas during the English Revolution* (London and New York: Penguin, [1972] 1975).

Hipple, Walter John, *The Beautiful, the Sublime, and the Picturesque, in Eighteenth-Century British Aesthetic Theory* (Carbondale: Southern Illinois University Press, 1957).

Holloway, James and Lindsay Errington, *The Discovery of Scotland: The Appreciation of Scottish Scenery through Two Centuries of Painting* (Edinburgh: National Gallery of Scotland, 1978).

Holmes, Richard, *The Age of Wonder: How the Romantic Generation Discovered the Beauty and Terror of Science* (London: Harper, 2008).

Home, Henry (Lord Kames), *Elements of Criticism*, 5th edn (Edinburgh, 1785), ed. Peter Jones, 2 vols (Indianapolis: Liberty Fund, 2005).

Home, Henry (Lord Kames), *Sketches of the History of Man*, 2 vols (Edinburgh, 1774).

Hook, Andrew, 'The French Taste for Scottish Literary Romanticism', in Deidre Dawson and Pierre Morère (eds), *Scotland and France in the Enlightenment* (London: Associated University Presses, 2004), pp. 90–107.

Hooke, Robert, *Micrographia: or, Some Physiological Descriptions of Minute Bodies made by Magnifying Glasses with Observations and Inquiries thereupon* (London: The Royal Society, 1665).

Hooke, Robert, *The Posthumous Works of D. Robert Hooke . . . Containing his Cutlerian Lectures, and Other Discourses, Read at the Meetings of the Illustrious Royal Society*, ed. Richard Waller (London, 1705).

Hose, T. A. (ed.), *Appreciating Physical Landscape: Three Hundred Years of Geotourism* (London: The Geological Society, 2016).

Hoskins, W. G., *The Making of the English Landscape* (Harmondsworth: Penguin, 1970).

Hulme, Peter and Ludmilla Jordanova (eds), *The Enlightenment and its Shadows* (London: Routledge, 1990).

Humboldt, Alexander von, *Personal Narrative of a Journey to the Equinoctial Regions of the New Continent*, ed. Malcolm Nicholson and Jason Wilson (London: Penguin, [1814–25] 1995).

Hume, David, *A Treatise of Human Nature*, ed. Ernest C. Mossner (London: Penguin, [1739–40] 1969).

[Hutton, James], *Abstract of a Dissertation Read in the Royal Society of Edinburgh, upon the Seventh of March, and Fourth of April, M,DCC,LXXXV, Concerning the System of the Earth, its Duration, and Stability* (Edinburgh, 1785).

Hutton, James, 'Observations on Granite', *TRSE*, 3.2 (1794), 77–85.

Hutton, James, 'Of Certain Natural Appearances of the Ground on the Hill of Arthur's Seat', *TRSE*, 2.2 (1790), 3–11.

Hutton, James, 'Theory of the Earth; or an Investigation of the Laws Observable in the Composition, Dissolution, and Restoration of Land upon the Globe', *TRSE*, 1 (1788), 209–304.

Hutton, James, *Theory of the Earth, with Proofs and Illustrations*, 2 vols (Edinburgh: William Creech; London: Cadell and Davies, 1795).

Hutton, James, *Theory of the Earth, with Proofs and Illustrations*, vol. 3, ed. Sir Archibald Geikie (London: The Geological Society, [1899] 1997).

Iliffe, Rob, 'Science and Voyages of Discovery', in Roy Porter (ed.), *The Cambridge History of Science, Volume 4: Eighteenth-Century Science* (Cambridge and New York: Cambridge University Press, 2003), pp. 618–45.

Jacyna, L. S., 'Bell, Sir Charles (1774–1842)', *ODNB*, Oxford University Press, 2004; online edn, January 2008, <http://www.oxforddnb.com/view/article/1999> (last accessed 22 June 2017).

Jameson, Robert, *Elements of Geognosy, Being Vol. III. and Part II. of the System of Mineralogy* (Edinburgh, 1808).

Jameson, Robert, 'Is the Huttonian Theory of the Earth Consistent with Fact?', in *Dissertations by Eminent Members of the Royal Medical Society* (Edinburgh, 1892), pp. 32–9.

Jameson, Robert, 'Is the Volcanic Opinion of the Formation of Basaltes Founded on Truth?', in Jessie M. Sweet and C. D. Waterston, 'Robert Jameson's Approach to the Wernerian Theory of the Earth, 1796', *Annals of Science*, 23 (1967), 81–95 (93–5).

Jameson, Robert, 'Journal of a Tour Through the Hebrides begun the 22nd of May 1798, volume 1' (Edinburgh University Library, GB 237 Coll-1373/3; Dc.7.127).

Jameson, Robert, 'Journal of a Tour Through the Hebrides begun the 22nd of May 1798, volume 2' (Edinburgh University Library, GB 237 Coll-1373/4; Dc.7.128).

Jameson, Robert, 'Journal of a Tour to Arran in 1799' (Edinburgh University Library, GB 237 Coll-1373/5; Dc.7.129).

Jameson, Robert, 'Journal of a Tour to Orkney in 1799' (Edinburgh University Library, GB 237 Coll-1373/6; Dc.7.130).

Jameson, Robert, 'Journal of my Tour in 1797' (Edinburgh University Library, GB 237 Coll-1373/2; Dc.7.126).

Jameson, Robert, 'Mineralogical Notes, and an Account of Cuvier's Geological Discoveries', in Georges Cuvier, *Essay on the Theory of the Earth*, trans. Robert Kerr, 2nd edn (Edinburgh, 1818), pp. 195–332.

Jameson, Robert, *Mineralogy of the Scottish Isles; with Mineralogical Observations Made in a Tour through Different Parts of the Mainland of Scotland*, 2 vols (Edinburgh and London, 1800).

Jameson, Robert, 'On Granite', *A Journal of Natural Philosophy, Chemistry, and the Arts*, 2 (August 1802), 225–33.

Jameson, Robert, *An Outline of the Mineralogy of the Shetland Islands, and of the Island of Arran* (Edinburgh: William Creech, 1798).

Jardine, Lisa, *Ingenious Pursuits: Building the Scientific Revolution* (London: Little, Brown and Company, 1999).

Jardine, Nicholas, James Secord and E. C. Spary (eds), *Cultures of Natural History* (Cambridge: Cambridge University Press, 1996).

Jemielity, Thomas, 'Thomas Pennant's Scottish Tours and *A Journey to the Western Islands of Scotland*', in Prem Nath (ed.), *Fresh Reflections on Samuel Johnson: Essays in Criticism* (Troy: Whitston, 1987), pp. 312–27.

Jenkins, David and Mark Visocchi, *Mendelssohn in Scotland* (London: Chappell, 1978).

Jenkins, Ralph E., '"And I travelled after him": Johnson and Pennant in Scotland', *Texas Studies in Literature and Language: A Journal of the Humanities*, 14 (1972), 445–62.

Johnson, Samuel, *A Journey to the Western Islands of Scotland* (London, 1775).

Jones, Jean, 'The Geological Collection of James Hutton', *Annals of Science*, 41.3 (1984), 223–44.

Jones, Jean, 'Hall, Sir James, of Dunglass, fourth baronet (1761–1832)', *ODNB*, Oxford University Press, 2004; online edn, October 2006, <http://www.oxforddnb.com/view/article/11965> (last accessed 12 May 2017).

Jones, Jean, 'Hutton, James (1726–1797)', *ODNB*, Oxford University Press, 2004; online edn, September 2013, <http://www.oxforddnb.com/view/article/14304> (last accessed 12 May 2017).

Jonsson, Fredrik Albritton, *Enlightenment's Frontier: The Scottish Highlands and the Origins of Environmentalism* (New Haven and London: Yale University Press, 2013).

Jordanova, Ludmilla, *Sexual Visions: Images of Gender in Science and Medicine between the Eighteenth and Twentieth Centuries* (New York: Harvester Wheatsheaf, 1989).

Jordanova, Ludmilla and Roy Porter (eds), *Images of the Earth: Essays in the History of the Environmental Sciences* (Chalfont St Giles: British Society for the History of Science, 1978).

Kant, Immanuel, *Critique of the Power of Judgment*, ed. Paul Guyer and trans. Paul Guyer and Eric Matthews (Cambridge and New York: Cambridge University Press, [1790/1793] 2000).

Kelley, Theresa M., *Wordsworth's Revisionary Aesthetics* (Cambridge and New York: Cambridge University Press, 1988).

Kirwan, Richard, *Elements of Mineralogy*, 2nd edn, 2 vols (London, 1794).

Kirwan, Richard, 'Examination of the Supposed Igneous Origin of Stony Substances', *Transactions of the Royal Irish Academy*, 5 (1793), 51–87.

Kirwan, Richard, *Geological Essays* (London, 1799).

Kirwan, Richard, 'On the Huttonian Theory of the Earth', in *Geological Essays* (London, 1799), pp. 433–99.

Klemun, M., 'Writing, "Inscription" and Fact: Eighteenth Century Mineralogical Books Based on Travels in the Habsburg Regions, the Carpathian Mountains', in Patrick N. Wyse Jackson (ed.), *Four Centuries of Geological Travel: The Search for Knowledge on Foot, Bicycle, Sledge and Camel* (London: The Geological Society, 2007), pp. 49–61.

Klonk, Charlotte, 'From Picturesque Travel to Scientific Observation: Artists' and Geologists' Voyages to Staffa', in Michael Rosenthal, Christiana Payne and Scott Wilcox (eds), *Prospects for the Nation: Recent Essays in British Landscape, 1750–1880* (New Haven: Yale University Press, 1997), pp. 205–29.

Klonk, Charlotte, *Science and the Perception of Nature: British Landscape Art in the Late Eighteenth and Early Nineteenth Centuries* (New Haven and London: Paul Mellon Centre for Studies in British Art and Yale University Press, 1996).

Klonk, Charlotte, 'Science, Art, and the Representation of the Natural World', in Roy Porter (ed.), *The Cambridge History of Science, Volume 4: Eighteenth-Century Science* (Cambridge and New York: Cambridge University Press, 2003), pp. 584–617.

Knellwolf, Christa and Jane Goodall (eds), *Frankenstein's Science: Experimentation and Discovery in Romantic Culture, 1780–1830* (Aldershot: Ashgate, 2008).

Knox, John, *A Tour through the Highlands of Scotland and the Hebrides Isles in 1786* (London, 1787).

Kölbl-Ebert, Martina, 'George Bellas Greenough's "Theory of the Earth" and its Impact on the Early Geological Society', in C. L. E. Lewis and S. J. Knell (eds), *The Making of the Geological Society of London* (London: The Geological Society, 2009), pp. 115–28.

Koprowski, Elizabeth, 'Searching for Salvation, Scenery and Self: Pilgrimage and Tourism in Northern Britain, c. 1500–1800', PhD thesis, University of Strathclyde, 2014.

Ksiazkiewicz, Allison, 'Geological Landscape as Antiquarian Ruin: Banks, Pennant, and the Isle of Staffa', in Mary-Ann Constantine and Nigel Leask (eds), *Enlightenment Travel and British Identities: Thomas Pennant's Tours in Scotland and Wales* (London and New York: Anthem, 2017), pp. 183–201.

Kuhn, Thomas S., *The Essential Tension: Selected Studies in Scientific Tradition and Change* (Chicago: University of Chicago Press, 1977).

Kuhn, Thomas S., *The Structure of Scientific Revolutions* (Chicago: University of Chicago Press, [1962] 1970).

Lamont, Claire and Michael Rossington (eds), *Romanticism's Debatable Lands* (Basingstoke: Palgrave Macmillan, 2005).

Laudan, Rachel, *From Mineralogy to Geology: The Foundations of a Science, 1680–1830* (Chicago and London: University of Chicago Press, 1987).

Leask, Nigel, *Curiosity and the Aesthetics of Travel Writing 1770–1840: 'From an Antique Land'* (Oxford and New York: Oxford University Press, 2002).

Leask, Nigel, 'Mont Blanc's Mysterious Voice: Shelley and Huttonian Earth Science', in Elinor S. Shaffer (ed.), *The Third Culture: Literature and Science* (Berlin and New York: de Gruyter, 1997), pp. 182–202.

Leddra, Michael, *Time Matters: Geology's Legacy to Scientific Thought* (Chichester: Wiley-Blackwell, 2010).

Leeder, Mike and Joy Lawlor, *Geobritannica: Geological Landscapes and the British Peoples* (Edinburgh and London: Dunedin, 2017).

Levere, Trevor H., *Poetry Realized in Nature: Samuel Taylor Coleridge and Early Nineteenth-Century Science* (Cambridge and New York: Cambridge University Press, 1981).

Leveson, D. J., 'What Was James Hutton's Methodology?', *Archives of Natural History*, 23 (1996), 61–77.

Lewis, C. L. E. and S. J. Knell (eds), *The Making of the Geological Society of London* (London: The Geological Society, 2009).

Leyden, John, *Journal of a Tour in the Highlands and Western Islands of Scotland in 1800*, ed. James Sinton (Edinburgh: Blackwood, 1903).

Lightfoot, John, *Flora Scotica: or, a Systematic Arrangement, in the Linnaean Method, of the Native Plants of Scotland and the Hebrides*, 2 vols (London, 1777).

Lindsay, Maurice, *The Discovery of Scotland: Based on Accounts of Foreign Travellers from the Thirteenth to the Eighteenth Centuries* (London: Robert Hale, 1964).

Lindsay, Maurice, *The Eye Is Delighted: Some Romantic Travellers in Scotland* (London: Frederick Muller, 1971).

The Linnaean Correspondence, <http://linnaeus.c18.net/Letters/display_bio.php?id_person=1193> (last accessed 15 May 2017).

Linnaeus, Carl, 'Oration Concerning the Necessity of Travelling in One's Own Country' (1741), in Benjamin Stillingfleet (trans.), *Miscellaneous Tracts Relating to Natural History, Husbandry and Physick* (London, 1759), pp. 1–30.

Lochranza Field Study and Activity Centre, <https://www.lochranzacentre.co.uk/> (last accessed 5 June 2017).

Locke, John, *An Essay Concerning Human Understanding*, ed. Roger Woolhouse (London and New York: Penguin, [1689] 1997).

Lovejoy, Arthur O., *The Great Chain of Being: A Study of the History of an Idea* (Cambridge, MA: Harvard University Press, 1936).

Luc, Jean André de, 'Geological Letters Addressed to Prof. Blumenbach', *British Critic*, 2 (1793), 231–9, 351–8; 3 (1794), 110–20, 226–37, 467–78, 589–98.

Luc, Jean André de, 'To Dr. James Hutton, F.R.S. Edinburgh, on his Theory of the Earth', *The Monthly Review; or, Literary Journal, Enlarged*, 2 (May–August 1790), 206–27, 582–601; 3 (September–December 1790), 573–86; and 5 (May–August 1791), 564–85.

Lyell, Charles, *Principles of Geology, Being an Attempt to Explain the Former Changes of the Earth's Surface, by Reference to Causes now in Operation*, ed. James A. Secord (London and New York, [1830–3] 1997).

Lyle, Paul, *The Abyss of Time: A Study in Geological Time and Earth History* (Edinburgh and London: Dunedin, 2015).

Lythe, S. G. E., 'Thomas Garnett: A Doctor on Tour in the Highlands', in Graeme Cruickshank (ed.), *A Sense of Place: Studies in Scottish Local History* (Edinburgh: Scotland's Cultural Heritage Unit, 1988), pp. 100–8.

MacCulloch, Donald B., *The Wondrous Isle of Staffa* (Edinburgh and London: Oliver and Boyd, 1957).

MacCulloch, John, *A Description of the Western Islands of Scotland, Including the Isle of Man: Comprising an Account of their Geological Structure; with Remarks on their Agriculture, Scenery, and Antiquities*, 3 vols (London and Edinburgh, 1819).

MacCulloch, John, 'A Geological Description of Glen Tilt', *TGSL*, 3 (1816), 259–337.

MacCulloch, John, *The Highlands and Western Isles of Scotland, Containing Descriptions of their Scenery and Antiquities, with an Account of the Political History and Ancient Manners, and of the Origin, Language, Agriculture, Economy, Music, Present Condition of the People, &c. &c. &c. founded on a Series of Annual Journeys between the Years 1811 and 1821, and Forming an Universal Guide to that Country, in Letters to Sir Walter Scott, Bart.*, 4 vols (London, 1824).

MacCulloch, John, 'On the Parallel Roads of Glen Roy', *TGSL*, 4 (1817), 314–92.

MacCulloch, John, 'On Staffa', *TGSL*, 2 (1814), 501–9.

MacCulloch, John, 'Sketch of the Mineralogy of Skye', *TGSL*, 3 (1816), 1–111.

Macfarlane, Robert, *Mountains of the Mind: A History of a Fascination* (London: Granta, 2003).

McIntyre, Donald B. and Alan McKirdy, *James Hutton: The Founder of Modern Geology* (Edinburgh: National Museums of Scotland, [1997] 2001).

McKay, Margaret M., 'Introduction', in *The Rev. Dr. John Walker's Report on the Hebrides of 1764 and 1771* (Edinburgh: John Donald, 1980), pp. 1–30.

McKay, Margaret M. (ed.), *The Rev. Dr. John Walker's Report on the Hebrides of 1764 and 1771* (Edinburgh: John Donald, 1980).

McKirdy, Alan, *Set in Stone: The Geology and Landforms of Scotland* (Edinburgh: Birlinn, 2015).

McKirdy, Alan and Roger Crofts, *Scotland: The Creation of its Natural Landscape: A Landscape Fashioned by Geology* (Edinburgh: Scottish Natural Heritage, 1999).

McKirdy, Alan, John Gordon and Roger Crofts, *Land of Mountain and Flood: The Geology and Landforms of Scotland* (Edinburgh: Birlinn and Scottish Natural Heritage, 2009).

McKusick, James C., '"Kubla Khan" and the Theory of the Earth', in Nicholas Roe (ed.), *Samuel Taylor Coleridge and the Sciences of Life* (Oxford and New York: Oxford University Press, 2001), pp. 134–51.

MacLeod, Anne, *From an Antique Land: Visual Representations of the Highlands and Islands 1700–1880* (Edinburgh: John Donald, 2012).

McMahon, Susan, 'Constructing Natural History in England, 1650–1700', PhD thesis, University of Alberta, 2001.

McNeil, Kenneth, *Scotland, Britain, Empire: Writing the Highlands, 1760–1860* (Columbus: Ohio State University Press, 2007).

Macpherson, James, *The Poems of Ossian and Related Works*, ed. Howard Gaskill, intr. Fiona Stafford (Edinburgh: Edinburgh University Press, 1996).

Mandelbrote, Scott, 'Ray, John (1627–1705)', *ODNB*, Oxford University Press, 2004; online edn, October 2005, <http://www.oxforddnb.com/view/article/23203> (last accessed 12 May 2017).

Marchand, Leslie A. (ed.), *Byron's Letters and Journals, Vol. 3: 1813–1814* (London: John Murray, 1974).

Marren, Peter and Richard Maybey, *Bugs Britannica* (London: Chatto & Windus, 2010).

Martin, Martin, *A Description of the Western Islands of Scotland* (London, 1703).

Martin, Martin, '*A Description of the Western Islands of Scotland Circa 1695*' and '*A Late Voyage to St Kilda*', with '*A Description of the Occidental i.e.*

Western Islands of Scotland, by Mr Donald Monro who travelled through many of them in Anno 1549', ed. Charles W. J. Withers and R. W. Munro (Edinburgh: Birlinn, 1999).

Martin, Martin, *A Late Voyage to St. Kilda, the Remotest of all the Hebrides, or Western Isles of Scotland. With a History of the Island, Natural, Moral, and Topographical* (London, 1698).

Mastroianni, Guido, 'Joseph Addison's Pleasures of the Imagination: The Aesthetics of Nature', in Michele Bottalico, Maria Teresa Chialant and Eleonora Rao (eds), *Literary Landscapes, Landscape in Literature* (Rome: Edizioni Carocci, 2007), pp. 73–9.

Michael, Jennifer Davis, 'Ocean meets Ossian: Staffa as Romantic Symbol', *Romanticism*, 13.1 (April 2007), 1–14.

Miller, Hugh, *The Cruise of the Betsey; or, A Summer Ramble among the Fossiliferous Deposits of the Hebrides*, ed. Michael A. Taylor (Edinburgh: National Museums of Scotland, [1858] 2003).

Miller, Hugh, 'Landscape Geology: A Plea for the Study of Geology by Landscape Painters', *Transactions of the Edinburgh Geology Society*, 6 (1892), 129–54.

Miller, Hugh, *The Old Red Sandstone; or, New Walks in an Old Field* (Edinburgh, 1841).

Miller, Hugh, *The Testament of the Rocks; or, Geology in its Bearings on the Two Theologies, Natural and Revealed* (Edinburgh, 1857).

Mills, Abraham, 'Some Account of the Strata and Volcanic Appearances in the North of Ireland and Western Islands of Scotland. In Two Letters from Abraham Mills, Esq. to John Lloyd, Esq. F. R. S.', *PTRS*, 80 (January 1790), 73–100.

Mitchell, Ian, *Scotland's Mountains Before the Mountaineers* (Edinburgh: Luath Press, 1988).

Mitchell, John, 'Loch Lomondside Depicted and Described: 5. Early Natural Historians', *Glasgow Naturalist*, 24.1 (2000), 65–8.

Mitchell, John, 'The Reverend John Stuart D. D. (1743–1821) and his Contribution to the Discovery of Britain's Mountain Flowers', *Glasgow Naturalist*, 21.2 (1986), 119–25.

Mitchell, Peta, '"The stratified record upon which we set our feet": The Spatial Turn and the Multilayering of History, Geography, and Geology', in Michael Dear, Jim Ketchum, Sarah Luria and Douglas Richardson (eds), *GeoHumanities: Art, History, Text at the Edge of Place* (London: Routledge, 2011), pp. 71–83.

Moir, D. G. (ed.), *The Early Maps of Scotland to 1850*, 3rd edn, 2 vols (Edinburgh: Royal Scottish Geographical Society, [1973] 1983).

Moir, Ester, *The Discovery of Britain: The English Travellers 1540–1840* (London: Routledge, [1964] 2012).

Monk, Samuel H., *The Sublime: A Study of Critical Theories in Eighteenth-Century England* (Michigan: University of Michigan Press, [1935] 1960).

The Monthly Epitome and Catalogue of New Publications (London, 1797–1802), vol. 3, pp. 60–7.

Moore, Donald, *Moses Griffith, 1747–1819: Artist and Illustrator in the Service of Thomas Pennant* (Caernarfon: Welsh Arts Council, 1979).

Morson, Geoffrey V., 'Hamilton, Sir William (1731–1803)', *ODNB*, Oxford University Press, 2004; online edn, September 2014, <http://www.oxforddnb.com/view/article/12142> (last accessed 15 May 2017).

Murray, John, *A Comparative View of the Huttonian and Neptunian Systems of Geology, in Answer to the Illustrations of the Huttonian Theory of the Earth, by Professor Playfair* (Edinburgh, 1802).

Murray, Sarah, *A Companion, and Useful Guide to the Beauties of Scotland, to the Lakes of Westmoreland, Cumberland, and Lancashire* (London, 1799).

Natural History Collections of the University of Edinburgh, <http://www.nhc.ed.ac.uk/index.php?page=1> (last accessed 15 May 2017).

Necker de Saussure, Louis Albert, *Travels in Scotland; Descriptive of the State of Manners, Literature, and Sciences* (London, 1821).

Necker de Saussure, Louis Albert, *A Voyage to the Hebrides, or Western Isles of Scotland; with Observations on the Manners and Customs of the Highlanders* (London, 1822).

Newte, Thomas, *Prospects and Observations, on a Tour in England and Scotland; Natural, Economical and Literary* (London, 1791).

Newton, Isaac, *Opticks: or, A Treatise of the Reflections, Refractions, Inflections and Colours of Light*, 4th edn, ed. Sir Edmund Whittaker, I. Bernard Cohen and Duane H. D. Roller (New York: Dover, [1730] 1979).

Nicholas, C. J. and P. N. Pearson, 'Robert Jameson on the Isle of Arran, 1797–1799: In Search of Hutton's "Theory of the Earth"', in Patrick N. Wyse Jackson (ed.), *Four Centuries of Geological Travel: The Search for Knowledge on Foot, Bicycle, Sledge and Camel* (London: The Geological Society, 2007), pp. 31–47.

Nichols, Ashton (ed.), *Romantic Natural Histories: William Wordsworth, Charles Darwin, and Others* (Boston and New York: Houghton Mifflin, 2004).

Nicol, James, *The Geology and Scenery of the North of Scotland* (Edinburgh: Oliver and Boyd, 1866).

Nicolson, Marjorie Hope, *Mountain Gloom and Mountain Glory: The Development of the Aesthetics of the Infinite* (Seattle and London: University of Washington Press, [1959] 1997).

O'Connor, Ralph, *The Earth on Show: Fossils and the Poetics of Popular Science, 1801–1856* (Chicago and London: University of Chicago Press, 2007).

Oerlemans, Onno, *Romanticism and the Materiality of Nature* (Toronto: University of Toronto Press, 2002).

O'Gorman, Frank, *The Long Eighteenth Century: British Political and Social History 1688–1832* (London: Bloomsbury, 1997).

Oldroyd, David R., 'Geikie, Sir Archibald (1835–1924)', *ODNB*, Oxford University Press, 2004, <http://www.oxforddnb.com/view/article/33364> (last accessed 15 May 2017).

Oldroyd, David R., *The Highlands Controversy: Constructing Geological Knowledge through Fieldwork in Nineteenth-Century Britain* (Chicago and London: University of Chicago Press, 1990).

Oldroyd, David R., 'Non-written Sources in the Study of the History of Geology: Pros and Cons, in Light of the Views of Collingwood and Foucault', *Annals of Science*, 56 (1999), 395–415.

Oldroyd, David R., 'Robert Hooke's Methodology of Science as Exemplified in his "Discourse of Earthquakes"', *British Journal for the History of Science*, 6 (1972), 109–30.

Oldroyd, David R., *Thinking about the Earth: A History of Ideas in Geology* (Cambridge, MA: Harvard University Press, 1996).

Oldroyd, David R., 'The Vulcanist-Neptunist Dispute Reconsidered', *Journal of Geological Education*, 19 (1971), 124–9.

Oldroyd, D. R. and B. M. Hamilton, 'Themes in the Early History of Scottish Geology', in Nigel H. Trewin (ed.), *The Geology of Scotland* (London: The Geological Society, 2002), pp. 27–43.

Osborne, Brian D., 'Introduction', in Thomas Pennant, *A Tour in Scotland, 1769* (Edinburgh: Birlinn, 2000), pp. ix–xix.

Osborne, Brian D. (ed.), *The Voyage of the 'Pharos': Walter Scott's Cruise around Scotland in 1814* (Edinburgh: Scottish Library Association, 1998).

Osborne, Roger, *The Floating Egg: Episodes in the Making of Geology* (London: Pimlico, 1999).

Otter, W., *The Life and Remains of the Rev. Edward Daniel Clarke, LL.D. Professor of Mineralogy in the University of Cambridge* (London, 1824).

Parks, George B., 'The Turn to the Romantic in the Travel Literature of the Eighteenth Century', *Modern Language Quarterly*, 25.1 (March 1964), 22–33.

Pennant, Thomas, *British Zoology*, 4 vols (London and Chester: Benjamin White, 1768–70).

Pennant, Thomas, *The Literary Life of the Late Thomas Pennant, Esq. By Himself* (Cambridge: Cambridge University Press, [1793] 2013).

Pennant, Thomas, 'To every Gentleman desirous to promote the Publication of an Accurate Account of the Antiquities, Present State, and Natural History of SCOTLAND', *The Scots Magazine*, 34 (April 1772), 173–4.

Pennant, Thomas, *A Tour in Scotland and Voyage to the Hebrides, MDCCLXXII*, 2 vols (Chester: Printed by John Monk, [1774] 1776).

Pennant, Thomas, *A Tour in Scotland, MDCCLXIX* (Chester: Printed by John Monk, 1771).

Pennant, Thomas, *A Tour in Scotland, MDCCLXXII, Part II* (London: Printed for Benj. White, 1776).

Phillipson Nicholas T. and Rosalind Mitchison (eds), *Scotland in the Age of Improvement: Essays in Scottish History in the Eighteenth Century* (Edinburgh: Edinburgh University Press, 1970).

Piper, H. W., *The Active Universe: Pantheism and the Concept of Imagination in the English Romantic Poets* (London: Athlone, 1962).

Playfair, John, 'Biographical Account of the Late Dr James Hutton', *TRSE*, 5 (1805), 39–99.

Playfair, John, *Illustrations of the Huttonian Theory of the Earth* (London and Edinburgh, 1802).

Pococke, Richard, *Tours in Scotland, 1747, 1750, 1760*, ed. Daniel William Kemp (Edinburgh: Edinburgh University Press for the Scottish History Society, 1887).

Porter, Roy, *The Making of Geology: Earth Science in Britain, 1660–1815* (Cambridge and New York: Cambridge University Press, 1977).

Pulteney, Richard, *General View of the Writings of Linnaeus* (London, 1781).

Purrington, Robert D., *The First Professional Scientist: Robert Hooke and the Royal Society of London* (Basel, Boston and Berlin: Birkhäuser, 2009).

Rackwitz, Martin, *Travels to Terra Incognita: The Scottish Highlands and Hebrides in Early Modern Travellers' Accounts c. 1600 to 1800* (Münster, New York, Munich and Berlin: Waxmann, 2007).

Ramsay, Andrew Crombie, *The Geology of the Island of Arran, from Original Survey* (Glasgow, 1841).

Rappaport, Rhoda, 'The Earth Sciences', in Roy Porter (ed.), *The Cambridge History of Science, Volume 4: Eighteenth-Century Science* (Cambridge and New York: Cambridge University Press, 2003), pp. 417–35.

Rappaport, Rhoda, 'Hooke on Earthquakes: Lectures, Strategy and Audience', *British Journal for the History of Science*, 19 (1986), 129–46.

Rappaport, Rhoda, *When Geologists Were Historians, 1665–1750* (Ithaca: Cornell University Press, 1997).

Raspe, Rudolf Erich, *An Introduction to the Natural History of the Terrestrial Sphere*, trans. and ed. A. N. Iversen and A. V. Carozzi (New York: Hafner, [1763] 1970).

Rauschenberg, Roy A., 'The Journals of Joseph Banks's Voyage up Great Britain's West Coast to Iceland and to the Orkney Isles, July to October, 1772', *Proceedings of the American Philosophical Society*, 117 (1973), 186–226.

Raven, Charles, *English Naturalists from Neckham to Ray: A Study of the Making of the Modern World* (Cambridge: Cambridge University Press, 1947).

Raven, Charles, *John Ray, Naturalist: His Life and Works* (Cambridge and New York: Cambridge University Press, 2009).

Ray, John, *Miscellaneous Discourses Concerning the Dissolution and Changes of the World, Wherin the Primitive Chaos and Creation, the General Deluge, Fountains, Formed Stones, Sea-Shells found in the Earth, Subterraneous Trees, Mountains, Earthquakes, Vulcanoes, the Universal Conflagration and Future State, are largely Discussed and Examined* (London, 1692).

Ray, John, *Observations Topographical, Moral, & Physiological; Made in a Journey Through part of the Low-Countries, Germany, Italy, and France* (London, 1673).

Ray, John, *Select Remains of the Learned John Ray, M. A. and F. R. S. . . . Published by George Scott* (London, 1760).

Ray, John, *Three Physico-Theological Discourses, Concerning I The Primitive Chaos, and Creation of the World. II The General Deluge, its Causes and Effects. III The Dissolution of the World, and Future Conflagration. Wherein Are largely Discussed the Production and Use of Mountains; the Original of Fountains, of Formed Stones, and Sea-Fishes Bones and Shells found in the Earth; the Effects of particular Floods and Inundations of the Sea; the Eruptions of Vulcano's; the Nature and Causes of Earthquakes: With an Historical Account of those Two late Remarkable Ones in Jamaica and England* (London, 1693).

Ray, John, *The Wisdom of God Manifested in the Works of the Creation* (London, 1691).

Read, H. H., *The Granite Controversy* (London: Allen & Unwin, 1957).

Repcheck, Jack, *The Man Who Found Time: James Hutton and the Discovery of the Earth's Antiquity* (London: Simon & Schuster, 2003).

Rice, Tony, *Voyages of Discovery: Three Centuries of Natural History Exploration* (London: Natural History Museum, 1999).

Richards, Robert J., *The Romantic Conception of Life: Science and Philosophy in the Age of Goethe* (Chicago and London: University of Chicago Press, 2002).

Rider, Malcolm, *Hutton's Arse: 3 Billion Years of Extraordinary Geology in Scotland's Northern Highlands* (Aberdeen: Rider-French Consulting Limited, 2008).

Ritchie, J., 'Natural History and the Emergence of Geology in the Scottish Universities', *Transactions of the Edinburgh Geological Society*, 15 (1952), 297–316.

Rixon, Denis, *The Hebridean Traveller* (Edinburgh: Birlinn, 2004).

Roberts, John L., *The Highland Geology Trail* (Edinburgh: Luath Press, 1998).

Roe, Nicholas (ed.), *Samuel Taylor Coleridge and the Sciences of Life* (Oxford and New York: Oxford University Press, 2001).

Rossi, Paolo, *The Dark Abyss of Time: The History of the Earth and the History of Nations from Hooke to Vico*, trans. Lydia G. Cochrane (Chicago and London: University of Chicago Press, [1979] 1984).

Rossiter, A. P., 'The First English Geologist', *Durham University Journal*, 29 (1935), 172–81.

Rudwick, Martin J. S., *Bursting the Limits of Time: The Reconstruction of Geohistory in the Age of Revolution* (Chicago and London: University of Chicago Press, 2005).

Rudwick, Martin J. S., 'Darwin and Glen Roy: A "Great Failure" in Scientific Method?', *Studies in History and Philosophy of Science, Part A*, 5.2 (1974), 97–185.

Rudwick, Martin J. S., *Earth's Deep History: How It Was Discovered and Why It Matters* (Chicago and London: University of Chicago Press, 2014).

Rudwick, Martin J. S., 'The Emergence of a Visual Language for Geological Science, 1760–1840', *History of Science*, 14 (September 1976), 149–95.

Rudwick, Martin J. S., 'Geological Travel and Theoretical Innovation: The Role of the "Liminal" Experience', *Social Studies of Science*, 26 (1996), 143–59.

Rudwick, Martin J. S., *Georges Cuvier, Fossil Bones, and Geological Catastrophes* (Chicago: University of Chicago Press, 1997).

Rudwick, Martin J. S., *The Great Devonian Controversy: The Shaping of Scientific Knowledge among Gentlemanly Specialists* (Chicago and London: University of Chicago Press, 1985).

Rudwick, Martin J. S., 'Hutton and Werner Compared: George Greenough's Geological Tour of Scotland in 1805', *British Journal for the History of Science*, 1.2 (1962), 117–35.

Rudwick, Martin J. S., *Scenes from Deep Time: Early Pictorial Representations of the Prehistoric World* (Chicago: University of Chicago Press, 1994).

Rudwick, Martin J. S., *Worlds Before Adam: The Reconstruction of Geohistory in the Age of Reform* (Chicago and London: University of Chicago Press, 2008).

Rupke, Nicolaas A., 'The Apocalyptic Denominator in English Culture of the Early Nineteenth Century', in Martin Pollock (ed.), *Common Denominators in Art and Science* (Aberdeen: Aberdeen University Press, 1983), pp. 30–41.

Rupke, Nicolaas A., *The Great Chain of History: William Buckland and the English School of Geology (1814–1849)* (Oxford: Clarendon Press, 1983).

Russell, D. A. and Michael Winterbottom (eds), *Classical Literary Criticism* (Oxford and New York: Oxford University Press, 1972).

Ruston, Sharon, *Creating Romanticism: Case Studies in the Literature, Science and Medicine of the 1790s* (Basingstoke: Palgrave Macmillan, 2013).

Ruston, Sharon, *Shelley and Vitality* (Basingstoke: Palgrave Macmillan, 2012).

Saussure, Horace-Bénédict de, *Voyages dans les Alpes*, 4 vols (Neuchâtel, 1779–96).

Sawyers, June Skinner (ed.), *The Road North: 300 Years of Classic Scottish Travel Writing* (Glasgow: The In Pinn, 2001).

Schama, Simon, *Landscape and Memory* (New York: Vintage Books, 1995).

Schneer, Cecil J. (ed.), *Toward a History of Geology* (Cambridge, MA: MIT Press, 1969).

Scott, E. L., 'Kirwan, Richard (1733–1812)', *ODNB*, Oxford University Press, 2004, <http://www.oxforddnb.com/view/article/15686> (last accessed 22 June 2017).

Scott, Harold W., 'Biographical Introduction', in John Walker, *Lectures on Geology, Including Hydrography, Mineralogy, and Meteorology, with an Introduction to Biology*, ed. Harold W. Scott (Chicago and London: University of Chicago Press, 1966), pp. xvii–xlvi.

Scott, Walter, *The Lord of the Isles* (Edinburgh, 1815).

Scrope, George Poulet, *Memoir on the Geology of Central France; Including the Volcanic Formations of Auvergne, the Velay, and the Vivarais* (London, 1827).

Secord, James, *Controversy in Victorian Geology: The Cambrian-Silurian Dispute* (Princeton: Princeton University Press, 1986).

Sedgwick, A. and R. I. Murchison, 'On the Geological Relations of the Secondary Strata in the Isle of Arran', *TGSL*, 2nd series, 3 (1828), 21–36.

Sedgwick, A. and R. I. Murchison, 'On the Old Conglomerates and Other Secondary Deposits on the North Coasts of Scotland', *Proceedings of the Geological Society of London*, 1 (1828), 77–88.

Sedgwick, A. and R. I. Murchison, 'On the Structure and Relations of the Deposits Contained between the Primary Rocks and the Oolitic Series in the North of Scotland', *TGSL*, 2nd series, 3 (1828), 125–60.

Seymour, Lord Webb, 'An Account of Observations, Made by Lord Webb Seymour and Professor Playfair, upon some Geological Appearances in Glen Tilt, and the Adjacent Country', *TRSE*, 7.2 (January 1815), 303–75.

Shaffer, Elinor S. (ed.), *The Third Culture: Literature and Science* (Berlin and New York: de Gruyter, 1997).

Shapin, Steven, 'Pump and Circumstance: Robert Boyle's Literary Technology', *Social Studies of Science*, 14.4 (1984), 481–520.

Shapin, Steven, *The Scientific Revolution* (Chicago and London: University of Chicago Press, 1996).

Shaw, Philip, *The Sublime* (London: Routledge, 2005).

Shelley, Mary, *Frankenstein, or the Modern Prometheus*, ed. Maurice Hindle (London and New York: Penguin, [1818/1831] 2003).

Shepperson, G., 'The Intellectual Background of Charles Darwin's Student Years at Edinburgh', in Michael Banton (ed.), *Darwinism and the Study of Society: A Centenary Symposium* (London: Tavistock, 1961), pp. 17–35.

Shortland, Michael, 'Darkness Visible: Underground Culture in the Golden Age of Geology', *History of Science*, 32.1 (1994), 1–61.

Shortland, Michael (ed.), *Hugh Miller and the Controversies of Victorian Science* (Oxford: Clarendon Press, 1996).

Sibbald, Sir Robert, *An Account of the Scottish Atlas; or, A Description of Scotland, Ancient and Modern* (Edinburgh, 1783).

Siegfried, Robert and Robert H. Dott, Jr (eds), *Humphry Davy on Geology: The 1805 Lectures for the General Audience* (Madison and London: University of Wisconsin Press, 1980).

Skouen, Tina and Ryan J. Stark (eds), *Rhetoric and the Early Royal Society: A Sourcebook* (Leiden and Boston: Brill, 2015).

Smethurst, Paul, 'Peripheral Vision, Landscape, and Nation-Building in Thomas Pennant's Tours of Scotland, 1769–72', in Benjamin Colbert (ed.), *Travel Writing and Tourism in Britain and Ireland* (Basingstoke: Palgrave Macmillan, 2011), pp. 13–30.

Smethurst, Paul, *Travel Writing and the Natural World, 1768–1840* (Basingstoke: Palgrave Macmillan, 2012).

Smith, Adam, *Lectures on Jurisprudence*, ed. R. L. Meek, D. D. Raphael and P. G. Stein (Indianapolis: Liberty Fund, [1978] 1982).

Smout, Christopher, *Nature Contested: Environmental History in Scotland and Northern England since 1600* (Edinburgh: Edinburgh University Press, 2000).

Smout, Christopher, 'Tours in the Scottish Highlands from the Eighteenth to the Twentieth Centuries', *Northern Scotland: The Journal of the Centre for Scottish Studies, University of Aberdeen*, 5.2 (1983), 99–121.

Stafford, Barbara Maria, *Voyage into Substance: Art, Science, Nature, and the Illustrated Travel Account 1760–1840* (Cambridge, MA, and London: MIT Press, 1984).

Stafford, Fiona, *Local Attachments: The Province of Poetry* (Oxford and New York: Oxford University Press, 2010).

Stafford, Fiona, *The Sublime Savage: James Macpherson and the Poems of Ossian* (Edinburgh: Edinburgh University Press, 1988).

Stephenson, David, *Mull and Iona: A Landscape Fashioned by Geology* (Perth: Scottish Natural Heritage, 2011).

Strange, John, 'An Account of Two Giants Causeways, or Groups of prismatic basaltine Columns, and other curious volcanic Concretions, in the Venetian State in Italy; with some remarks on the Characters of these and other similar Bodies, and on the physical Geography of the Countries in which they are found', *Philosophical Transactions*, 65 (1775), 5–47.

Sweet, Jessie M., 'Robert Jameson's Irish Journal, 1797: Excerpts from Robert Jameson's "Journal of my Tour in 1797"', *Annals of Science*, 23.2 (1967), 97–126.

Sweet, Jessie M., 'The Wernerian Natural History Society in Edinburgh', *Freiberger Forschungshefte*, 167 (1967), 206–18.

Sweet, Jessie M. and C. D. Waterston, 'Robert Jameson's Approach to the Wernerian Theory of the Earth, 1796', *Annals of Science*, 23 (1967), 81–95.

Taylor, K. L., 'Geological Travellers in Auvergne, 1751–1800', in Patrick N. Wyse Jackson (ed.), *Four Centuries of Geological Travel: The Search for Knowledge on Foot, Bicycle, Sledge and Camel* (London: The Geological Society, 2007), pp. 73–96.

Taylor, Michael A., *Hugh Miller: Stonemason, Geologist, Writer* (Edinburgh: National Museums of Scotland, 2007).

Taylor, Michael A., 'Miller, Hugh (1802–1856)', *ODNB*, Oxford University Press, 2004, <http://www.oxforddnb.com/view/article/18723> (last accessed 15 May 2017).

Thompson, Carl, *The Suffering Traveller and the Romantic Imagination* (Oxford and New York: Clarendon Press, 2007).

Thompson, Carl, *Travel Writing* (London and New York: Routledge, 2011).

Thomson, Derick S., 'Macpherson, James (1736–1796)', *ODNB*, Oxford University Press, 2004; online edn, May 2006, <http://www.oxforddnb.com/view/article/17728> (last accessed 15 May 2017).

Thomson, James, *Poetical Works*, ed. J. Logie Robertson (London: Oxford University Press, 1908).

Tomkeieff, S. I., 'James Hutton and the Philosophy of Geology', *Transactions of the Edinburgh Geological Society*, 14.2 (1948), 253–76.

Trewin, N. H. (ed.), *The Geology of Scotland* (London: The Geological Society, 2002).

Trewin, N. H., *Scottish Fossils* (Edinburgh: Dunedin Academic Press, 2013).

Troil, Uno von, *Letters on Iceland: Containing Observations Made during a Voyage Undertaken in the Year 1772 by Joseph Banks, Esq.* (Cambridge and New York: Cambridge University Press, [1780] 2011).

Tyrrell, G. W., 'Hutton on Arran', *Proceedings of the Royal Society of Edinburgh*, 63.4 (1950), 369–76.

Upton, Brian, *Volcanoes and the Making of Scotland* (Edinburgh: Dunedin Academic Press, 2004).

Vaccari, Ezio, 'The Organized Traveller: Scientific Instructions for Geological Travels in Italy and Europe during the Eighteenth and Nineteenth Centuries', in Patrick N. Wyse Jackson (ed.), *Four Centuries of Geological Travel: The Search for Knowledge on Foot, Bicycle, Sledge and Camel* (London: The Geological Society, 2007), pp. 7–17.

Waddell, Peter Hately, *Ossian and the Clyde, Fingal in Ireland, Oscar in Iceland, or Ossian Historical and Authentic* (Glasgow, 1875).

Walford, Thomas, *The Scientific Tourist through England, Wales and Scotland; by which the Traveller is directed to the Principal Objects of Antiquity, Art, Science, and the Picturesque, including the Minerals, Fossils, rare Plants, and other Subjects of Natural History, arranged by Counties. To which is added an Introduction to the Study of Antiquities, and the Elements of Statistics, Geology, Mineralogy, and Botany*, 2 vols (London, 1818).

Walker, Carol Kyros, *Walking North with Keats* (New Haven and London: Yale University Press, 1992).

Walker, John, 'Dr. John Walker's Report Concerning the State of the Highlands and Islands, to the General Assembly 1772', *The Scots Magazine*, 34 (1772), 288–93.

Walker, John, 'Dr. John Walker's Report to the Assembly 1765, Concerning the State of the Highlands and Islands', *The Scots Magazine*, 28 (December 1766), 680–8.

Walker, John, *An Economical History of the Hebrides and Highlands of Scotland* (Edinburgh: Edinburgh University Press, 1808).

Walker, John, *An Epitome of Natural History* (1797), bound MS, Edinburgh University Library, EUL Gen. 708D f.93 and 87.

Walker, John, *Essays on Natural History and Rural Economy* (London and Edinburgh, 1808).

Walker, John, 'A General View of its Literary History', *Notes and Lectures on Natural History* (1789), bound MS, Edinburgh University Library, EUL Gen 50ff.

Walker, John, *Lectures on Geology, Including Hydrography, Mineralogy, and Meteorology, with an Introduction to Biology*, ed. Harold W. Scott (Chicago and London: University of Chicago Press, 1966).

Walker, John, 'Notice of Mineralogical Journeys, and of a Mineralogical System, by the late Rev. Dr. John Walker', *Edinburgh Philosophical Journal*, 6 (1822), 88–95.

Walker, John, 'Report on the Hebrides', King's MS 105, The British Library.

Walmsley, Peter, *Locke's Essay and the Rhetoric of Science* (Lewisburg: Bucknell University Press; London: Associated University Presses, 2003).

Watson, Nicola J., *The Literary Tourist: Readers and Places in Romantic and Victorian Britain* (New York: Palgrave Macmillan, 2006).

Weiskel, Thomas, *The Romantic Sublime: Studies in the Structure and Psychology of Transcendence* (Baltimore: Johns Hopkins University Press, 1976).

Wellek, René, *Immanuel Kant in England 1793–1838* (Princeton: Princeton University Press, 1931).

Werner, Abraham Gottlob, *Kurze Klassifikation und Beschreibung der verschiedenen Gebirgsarten*, facsimile, trans. with an introduction and notes by Alexander M. Ospovat as *Short Classification and Description of the Various Rocks* (New York: Hafner, 1971).

Werner, Abraham Gottlob, *Neue Theorie von den Entstehung der Gänge, mit Anwendung auf dem Bergbau besonders den Freibergischen* (Freiberg, 1791).

Werner, Abraham Gottlob, *Von den äusserlichen Kennzeichen der Fossilien* (Leipzig, 1774).

Werner, Abraham Gottlob, 'Werners Bekanntmachung einer von ihm am Scheibenberger Hügel über die Entstehung des Basaltes gemachten Entdeckung', *Bergmann Journal*, 2 (1788), 845–55.

West, Thomas, 'An Account of a Volcanic Hill near Inverness', *PTRS*, 67 (1777), 385–7.

Whitehurst, John, *An Inquiry into the Original State and Formation of the Earth*, 2nd edn (London, 1786).

Whitehurst, John, *An Inquiry into the Original State and Formation of the Earth; Deduced from Facts and the Laws of Nature* (London, 1778).

Whittow, J. B., *Geology and Scenery in Scotland* (Harmondsworth and New York: Penguin, 1977/1979).

Wickman, Matthew, *The Ruins of Experience: Scotland's 'Romantick' Highlands and the Birth of the Modern Witness* (Philadelphia: University of Philadelphia Press, 2007).

Widmayer, Anne F., 'Mapping the Landscape in Addison's "Pleasures of the Imagination"', *Rocky Mountain Review of Language and Literature*, 50.1 (1996), 19–29.

Willey, Basil, *The Eighteenth-Century Background: Studies in the Idea of Nature in the Thought of the Period* (London and New York: Arc and Routledge, [1940] 1986).

Williams, John, *An Account of Some Remarkable Ancient Ruins, Lately Discovered in the Highlands, and Northern Parts of Scotland* (Edinburgh: William Creech, 1777).

Williams, John, *The Natural History of the Mineral Kingdom*, 2 vols (Edinburgh, 1789).

Wilson, Harry, *Down to Earth: One Hundred and Fifty Years of the British Geological Survey* (Edinburgh: Scottish Academic Press, 1985).

Wilson, Leonard G., *Charles Lyell: The Years to 1841: The Revolution in Geology* (New Haven and London: Yale University Press, 1972).

Wilson, R. B., *A History of the Geological Survey of Scotland* (Edinburgh: Natural Environment Research Council, Institute of Geological Sciences, 1977).

Winchester, Simon, *The Map that Changed the World: William Smith and the Birth of Modern Geology* (New York: HarperCollins, 2001).

Withers, Charles W. J., '"Both Useful and Ornamental": The Rev. Dr. John Walker's Keepership of Edinburgh University's Natural History Museum, 1779–1803', *Journal of the History of Collections*, 5.1 (1993), 65–77.

Withers, Charles W. J., 'Geography, Natural History and the Eighteenth-Century Enlightenment: Putting the World in Place', *History Workshop Journal*, 39.1 (1995), 137–64.

Withers, Charles W. J., 'Geography, Science and National Identity in Early Modern Britain: The Case of Scotland and the Work of Sir Robert Sibbald, 1641–1722', *Annals of Science*, 53 (1996), 29–73.

Withers, Charles W. J., *Geography, Science and National Identity: Scotland since 1520* (Cambridge: Cambridge University Press, 2001).

Withers, Charles W. J., 'The Historical Creation of the Scottish Highlands', in Ian Donnachie and Christopher Whatley (eds), *The Manufacture of Scottish History* (Edinburgh: Polygon, 1992), pp. 143–56.

Withers, Charles W. J., 'Improvement and Enlightenment: Agriculture and Natural History in the Work of the Rev. Dr. John Walker (1731–1803)', in Peter Jones (ed.), *Philosophy and Science in the Scottish Enlightenment* (Edinburgh: John Donald, 1988), pp. 102–16.

Withers, Charles W. J., 'Introduction', in Martin Martin, *'A Description of the Western Islands of Scotland Circa 1695' and 'A Late Voyage to St Kilda', with 'A Description of the Occidental i.e. Western Islands of Scotland, by Mr Donald Monro who travelled through many of them in Anno 1549'*, ed. Charles W. J. Withers and R. W. Munro (Edinburgh: Birlinn, 1999), pp. 1–11.

Withers, Charles W. J., 'Introduction', in Thomas Pennant, *A Tour in Scotland and Voyage to the Hebrides, 1772*, ed. Andrew Simmons (Edinburgh: Birlinn, 1998), pp. xiii–xxiii.

Withers, Charles W. J., 'Natural Knowledge as Cultural Property Disputes over the "Ownership" of Natural History in Late Eighteenth-Century Edinburgh', *Archives of Natural History*, 19.3 (1992), 289–303.

Withers, Charles W. J., 'Pennant, Thomas (1726–1798)', *ODNB*, Oxford University Press, 2004; online edn, October 2007, <http://www.oxforddnb.com/view/article/21860> (last accessed 15 May 2017).

Withers, Charles W. J., *Placing the Enlightenment: Thinking Geographically about the Age of Reason* (Chicago: University of Chicago Press, 2007).

Withers, Charles W. J., 'Reporting, Mapping, Trusting: Making Geographical Knowledge in the Late Seventeenth Century', *Isis*, 90 (1999), 497–521.

Withers, Charles W. J., 'Sibbald, Sir Robert (1641–1722)', *ODNB*, Oxford University Press, May 2006, <http://www.oxforddnb.com/view/article/25496> (last accessed 15 May 2017).

Withers, Charles W. J., 'Walker, John (1731–1803)', *ODNB*, Oxford University Press, 2004; online edn, April 2016, <http://www.oxforddnb.com/view/article/28498> (last accessed 15 May 2017).

Womack, Peter, *Improvement and Romance: Constructing the Myth of the Highlands* (Basingstoke: Palgrave Macmillan, 1989).

Wood, Paul B., 'Buffon's Reception in Scotland: The Aberdeen Connection', *Annals of Science*, 64 (1987), 169–90.

Woodward, John, *An Essay toward a Natural History of the Earth: and Terrestrial Bodies, Especially Minerals: As also of the Sea, Rivers and Springs. With an Account of the Universal Deluge: and of the Effects that it had upon the Earth* (London, 1695 and 1726).

Wordsworth, William, *The Poems: Volume Two*, ed. John O. Hayden (London and New York: Penguin, 1977).

Wordsworth, William, *The Prelude: The Four Texts (1798, 1799, 1805, 1850)*, ed. Jonathan Wordsworth (London and New York: Penguin, 1995).

Wordsworth, William, *Selected Prose*, ed. John O. Hayden (Harmondsworth: Penguin, 1988).

Wordsworth, William and Samuel Taylor Coleridge, *Lyrical Ballads 1798 and 1802*, ed. Fiona Stafford (Oxford and New York: Oxford University Press, 2013).

Wyatt, John, 'George Bellas Greenough: A Romantic Geologist', *Archives of Natural History*, 22.1 (1995), 61–71.

Wyatt, John, *Wordsworth and the Geologists* (Cambridge and New York: Cambridge University Press, 1995).

Wyse Jackson, Patrick N., *The Chronologers' Quest: Episodes in the Search for the Age of the Earth* (Cambridge and New York: Cambridge University Press, 2006).

Wyse Jackson, Patrick N. (ed.), *Four Centuries of Geological Travel: The Search for Knowledge on Foot, Bicycle, Sledge and Camel* (London: The Geological Society, 2007).

Youngren, William H., 'Addison and the Birth of Eighteenth-Century Aesthetics', *Modern Philology*, 79.3 (1982), 267–83.

Youngson, A. E., *After the Forty-Five: The Economic Impact on the Highlands* (Edinburgh: Edinburgh University Press, 1973).

Zalasiewicz, Jan, *The Planet in a Pebble: A Journey into Earth's Deep History* (Oxford and New York: Oxford University Press, 2010).

Index

abyss of time *see* geological time

Addison, Joseph, 17–18, 22, 30n, 43, 107

aesthetic, aesthetics, 1, 4, 6, 11–12, 13, 16–25, 26, 29n, 30n, 43, 58–9, 85, 88–93, 98, 101, 106–8, 117, 121, 130, 131, 134, 138, 139, 142, 153, 179, 184, 203–6, 209–10, 215, 220, 221, 225, 232, 237, 239, 242, 244–5, 248, 249, 250, 253, 255, 256, 257, 261n

Agassiz, Louis, 244, 258, 262n

age of the Earth *see* geological time

Annexed Estates, Board of, 68–87

architecture, 20–1, 22, 25, 42, 115, 119, 142, 244–5, 251

Arran, 27n, 56, 89, 106, 111, 121, 163, 180–6, 192, 196n, 198–200, 202, 203–26, 227n, 228n, 237, 263n

Arthur's Seat, 107–8, 150–1, 154n, 161, 194n, 231

astonishment, 17–18, 19, 130, 137–8, 144–5, 214–16

Auchnacraig, 144–8

Austen, Jane, 176

Auvergne region, 6, 83, 109–10, 124n, 127

Bacon, Francis, Baconian, 7, 8, 9, 28n, 31–4, 58, 59n, 65, 94n, 98, 166, 174, 232

Banks, Joseph, 8, 67, 77, 80, 98, 111, 113–19, 125n, 130, 131, 141–3, 154n, 219, 249, 251, 254

basalt, basalt columns, basalt controversy, 20, 79, 82–4, 107, 109–10, 113–21, 124n, 127, 142–8, 150–1, 161, 197–9, 201–2, 212–13, 215–16, 237, 252, 254–5, 258, 259

Boyle, Robert, 8, 34–6, 46, 71

Buckland, William, 25, 231, 258, 260n, 262n, 263n

Buffon, Georges Louis Leclerc, 24, 44, 81, 94n, 97, 217, 221

Bunyan, John, 176–7, 179

Burke, Edmund, 2, 18–26, 43, 89, 91–2, 107, 130, 137–8, 203, 209, 227n, 242, 245–6, 251

Burnet, Thomas, 16, 29n, 40–4, 58, 61n, 192

Cairne na calleach (Ceum na Caillich, the Witches' Step) on Caisteal Abhail (Arran), 213–18
Cairnsmore of Fleet, 172–4
Camden, William, 44–5
cause, causation, causality, 10, 31–2, 33, 38, 41–2, 43, 58–9, 65, 79–80, 99, 100, 117, 121, 138–9, 155, 162, 184, 185, 188, 199, 214, 216, 236, 238–9
Clerk, John, 163–4, 166–75, 187, 195n
Cuillin, the, 27n, 84–5, 242–9, 261n
Cuvier, Georges, 9, 229

Dampier, William, 8, 36, 50, 52
danger, 12, 18–19, 26, 49–50, 52–3, 56, 74, 88–9, 95n, 100, 130, 133–5, 140, 153n, 205, 209, 221, 234, 250, 256
Daniell, William, 247
Darwin, Charles, 10, 97, 258, 263n
Davy, Humphry, 25, 39, 60n, 174, 231, 260n
de Luc, Jean André, 10, 194n
deep time *see* geological time
Defoe, Daniel, 1–2, 18, 61n
deictic markers ('was now'), 176–80, 191–3, 195n
Demarest, Nicolas, 83, 109–10, 197

difficulty, 12, 15, 19, 20, 24, 26, 50, 52–3, 88–9, 95n, 100, 130, 131, 134–5, 137, 138, 146, 147, 153n, 165, 203, 210, 231, 234, 238, 241–2, 244, 245, 249, 256
Discovery of Scotland, 1, 8, 27n, 193
dynamic earth, 10, 21, 24, 25, 37, 39, 65, 99–100, 108, 119, 121–2, 129–30, 131, 135, 139, 152, 157, 244

Edinburgh, 27n, 33, 45, 48, 63–4, 84, 104, 107–8, 112–13, 120, 128, 148–51, 152, 156, 158, 159, 161, 163, 165, 194–5n, 197, 200, 229–30, 231, 232, 258, 263n
Eigg, 56, 74, 119, 121, 219, 251, 253–5, 258, 259, 262n
Enlightenment, the, 2, 5, 9, 11, 13, 63, 69–70, 71, 73, 94n, 122, 129, 131, 145, 149, 161, 174, 200, 204, 208, 255
epiphany, 130, 153n, 177, 179, 206, 208–9, 211, 215–16, 218
erosion, 121, 159, 171, 184, 188, 216–17

Faujas de Saint-Fond, Barthelémy, 12, 21, 26, 108, 109, 112, 117, 120, 121, 127–54, 161, 205, 219, 221, 244, 249, 254

Fingal's Cave, 3, 20, 114, 116–17, 118, 121, 124n, 125n, 131, 141–5, 248, 249–55, 256–7, 262n, 263n

fossils, 37, 39, 40, 58, 85–6, 95n, 103, 152, 162, 184, 194n, 201, 240, 259, 260n

French Revolution, 127, 185

Garnett, Thomas, 111, 113, 151, 219

Geikie, Archibald, 119–20, 127–8, 164, 181, 195n, 233, 257–9, 260, 262n

genre, 12–15, 34, 53, 58, 60n, 61n, 72, 92, 130, 141, 155, 200, 203–6, 220–1, 232, 243

geological revolution, 9, 229, 232

Geological Society, the, 24, 26, 229–30, 231, 232–3, 235–6, 242, 249, 260n

geological time, 14, 24, 30n, 39–40, 65, 83, 100, 101, 110, 118, 121–2, 129, 133, 136, 142, 152, 155, 156, 157, 170, 171, 173, 180, 184–5, 188, 190–1, 216, 225–6, 236, 238–9, 245, 247, 249, 252–3

geological travel and travel writing, 5–7, 11, 12, 14–16, 18, 21, 23–4, 27n, 35, 36, 53, 93, 100, 109, 119–20, 127, 157, 169–70, 192–3, 200, 205, 207, 219, 221, 230, 231–2, 234–5, 249–50, 258, 260

geostrophic/geological cycle, 156, 160, 185–6, 188, 193n

geotheory *see* theories of the earth

Giant's Causeway, 73, 82–4, 94, 113–14, 116, 118, 124n

Gilpin, William, 1, 90, 95n, 107

Glen Tilt, 104, 166–71, 186, 195n, 199, 228n, 232, 258

Goatfell, 206–7, 208–11, 212, 215, 218, 222

granite, granite intrusions/veins, 154n, 157–8, 165–75, 181–2, 186, 194n, 199, 201–2, 212, 213–17, 222–3

Greenough, George Bellas, 230, 231, 260n

Griffith, Moses, 103–4, 114–15, 123n

Guettard, Jean-Étienne, 109, 124n, 127

Hakluyt, Richard, 177

Hall, Sir James, 63, 109, 159, 163, 188–90, 228n, 231

Hamilton, Sir William, 109–10, 124n

Highlands and Islands of Scotland, 1, 3–7, 18, 21, 24, 26, 43, 45, 48–59, 63, 67, 68–78, 87, 93, 98, 103, 106–8, 112, 121, 129–33, 161, 163, 166–70, 198, 201–2, 219, 221, 231, 240, 242, 244, 253, 258–9

Home, Henry (Lord Kames), 63, 69, 70–1, 74–5, 81, 95n

Hooke, Robert, 37–9, 40, 44, 60n, 83, 110

Humboldt, Alexander von, 12

Hutton, James, 6, 21, 26, 39, 60n, 104, 121, 122n, 129, 149–51, 154n, 155–96, 197–200, 201, 202, 203, 206, 207, 209, 211, 212–13, 216–17, 218, 219, 221, 222–5, 225–6, 226n, 227n, 228n, 230, 231, 233, 235–6, 237, 253, 260n

imagination, 13–14, 17–18, 21, 23, 24–5, 92, 100, 121, 130, 134–5, 139, 145–7, 152–3, 153n, 190–2, 210–11, 221, 239, 245–6, 247, 252–3

improvement, 2, 35, 66, 68–71, 73, 76–8, 86, 94n, 221

Jameson, Robert, 5–6, 63, 113, 120–1, 129, 139, 147–8, 151–2, 158, 192, 194n, 195n, 197–226, 226n, 227n, 228n, 231, 232, 235, 236, 239, 249, 254–5, 258

Jedburgh, 163, 186–8

Johnson, Samuel, 1, 101, 123n, 235

Jura, 56, 78, 80, 81–2, 86–93, 106, 148, 219

Kant, Immanuel, 17, 20, 30n, 39

Kirwan, Richard, 6, 10, 157, 158, 194n, 198, 205, 211, 227n

Lightfoot, John, 64, 67, 94n, 103, 123n

Linnaeus, Carl, 7, 11, 26, 66–7, 73, 93n, 94n, 97, 99, 111, 122n

literature, literary strategies and techniques, 9, 11–16, 22, 24–5, 28n, 29n, 86–93, 100, 122n, 133–5, 141, 146, 165, 176–80, 192, 211, 220, 240, 260

Loch Coruisk, 243–9, 261n, 261–2n

Lochranza, 183–4, 199, 212–13, 222–5

Locke, John, 13, 22–3, 56

Lyell, Charles, 231, 258, 260n, 262n, 263n

MacCulloch, John, 20–1, 26, 112, 120, 147–8, 229–55, 259, 260n, 261n, 261–2n

Macpherson, James, 3, 69–70, 73, 96n, 98, 107, 130, 136, 231

maps, 46, 50–1, 61n, 68, 104–5, 126n, 128, 163–4, 166–7, 171–2, 181, 207, 210–11, 230, 231, 232, 233, 241, 261n

Martin Martin, 26, 47–59, 61n, 72, 85, 114, 227n, 235, 262n

military roads of Highland Scotland, 2, 68, 104–6, 123n, 132–3, 148

Miller, Hugh, 248, 258, 260n, 263n

Milton, John, 18, 21–3

mineralogy, 10–11, 33, 37, 47,
48, 53, 56–7, 63, 64–6, 79,
99–100, 108, 122, 123n,
149, 162, 197, 204–5,
220–1, 239–40
mountains, 2–4, 11, 15, 16–23,
26, 27n, 30n, 35, 37,
39–44, 46, 58, 64, 65, 66,
67, 74, 80–2, 84–5, 87–93,
94n, 95n, 98, 99, 101–3,
106–8, 121, 129–36, 158,
167–74, 180–9, 200–18,
226, 230, 234, 236–8,
242–5, 248, 259
Mull, 56, 74, 78, 80, 82–3,
106, 114, 120, 139–40,
143–8, 154n, 202, 219,
238–9, 252–3
Murchison, Sir Roderick, 259,
263n
Murray, Sarah, 4, 256

natural history, 2, 7–16, 25, 27n,
28n, 31–6, 38, 43, 44–59,
59n, 61n, 63–4, 64–7, 68,
71–3, 75–86, 86–93, 93n,
97–122, 122n, 123n, 127,
130, 135–6, 137–9, 141–3,
149, 151–2, 154n, 163, 167,
177, 187, 190, 197, 204,
205–6, 206–9, 211, 221
Necker, Louis Albert, 230–1,
260n
Neptunists, Neptunism, 5,
6, 44, 65, 84, 95n, 99,
109–10, 112, 120, 129,
151, 152, 156, 157, 158,
161, 165, 166, 170, 192,
194–5n, 197–8, 202, 212,
221–6, 227n

Newton, Isaac, 9, 81, 157, 178,
194n
North Glen Sannox, 182, 212,
222–3

Oban, 136–9, 152
Ossian, 3, 27n, 69–70, 72–3,
91, 94n, 98, 107, 111,
116–17, 121, 130–1,
133–5, 136, 141, 153n,
231, 250

palaeontological analysis,
palaeontology, 229, 233–4,
240, 258–9
Pennant, Thomas, 1, 26, 47,
59, 71–2, 80, 86–7, 93,
94n, 97–126, 122n, 123n,
124n, 125n, 126n, 128,
131, 140, 148, 219, 227n,
235, 239, 244, 249
picturesque, the, 1, 3, 24, 90,
103, 106–8, 124n, 141,
144, 210, 220, 250, 253
pilgrimage, 15, 169, 179, 183,
189
place, 6, 11, 12, 15, 20, 21,
27n, 33, 34–5, 36, 52, 54,
59n, 66, 73, 76, 87, 91, 98,
100, 104, 115, 137, 144–5,
154n, 157–8, 164, 168,
169, 175, 183, 189, 200,
203, 204, 208, 218, 221,
225–6, 237, 240, 241, 243,
244, 261n
Playfair, John, xiii, 24, 63,
121, 149, 158–63, 165–6,
168–9, 180–1, 182, 186–7,
188–91, 192, 193n, 194n,
200, 209, 228n, 230–1

plutonic, Plutonists, Plutonism,
  5, 6, 21, 26, 129, 150, 156,
  161–2, 188, 191, 193n,
  194–5n, 197–8, 222, 225–6
poetry, 3, 11, 12–14, 16, 18,
  22, 28n, 43, 69–70, 73,
  90–3, 98, 106, 116, 124n,
  130, 133–5, 136, 145, 146,
  153n, 154n, 179, 193n,
  209, 218, 231, 243, 245,
  246–7, 256, 263n

quest, 15, 100, 130, 133,
  139–40, 165–6, 174–6,
  192, 275n

Ray, John, 32–3, 40, 43, 44,
  45, 57, 60n, 61n, 65, 66,
  97, 100
revolution, revolutionary, 4,
  9, 10, 25, 36, 39, 98, 110,
  122, 126n, 129, 136, 152,
  156, 162, 186, 188, 190,
  252, 253
Romantic, Romanticism, 3, 4,
  9–12, 14, 15, 19–20, 23,
  25, 28n, 29n, 36, 53, 59,
  71, 85, 91, 93, 98, 100,
  101–2, 107–8, 115, 121–2,
  123n, 129–32, 134–5, 143,
  145, 146, 153n, 154n, 157,
  165, 175–9, 192, 193n,
  194n, 200, 203–4, 205–6,
  207, 208, 209, 218, 220–1,
  231–2, 236, 240, 242, 243,
  249, 255, 256–7, 260,
  260n, 261n
Romantic geological travel and
  travel writing, 200, 205,
  207, 221

Romantic geology, 93, 121–2,
  143, 157, 165, 193, 256
Romantic travel and travel
  writing, 12, 23, 25, 29n,
  71, 85, 115, 123n, 130,
  135, 179, 203–4
Royal Society of Edinburgh,
  63, 64, 149, 156–7, 158,
  161, 163
Royal Society of London, 7–8,
  13, 23, 25, 26, 28n, 33, 34,
  36, 39, 43, 46, 47, 48–9,
  50, 54–7, 64, 97, 109, 112,
  117, 125n, 131, 233

St Kilda, 48–54, 78
Salisbury Crags, 84, 107–8,
  150–1, 154n, 161, 194n,
  231
Scientific Revolution, the, 7–10,
  28n, 31–4, 54–5, 55n
Scott, Walter, 4, 231, 246–7,
  248, 256
Sedgwick, Adam, 259, 263n
Sibbald, Robert, 45–7, 48, 61n,
  71, 72
Siccar Point, 27n, 188–91, 231,
  258
Skye, 27n, 48, 56–8, 74, 78,
  84–5, 118–20, 126n, 219,
  232, 237, 239–49, 261n
Smith, Adam, 69, 149
Southerness Point, 174–5
stadial theory of history, 69,
  77–8
Staffa, 3, 56, 113–17, 118, 120,
  121, 125n, 126n, 128–43,
  154n, 219, 231–2, 237,
  238, 243, 249–55, 256–7,
  261n, 262n, 263n

Stuart, John, 67, 94n, 103, 123n
sublime, the, 2–4, 11, 16–26, 29n, 30n, 39, 42–3, 89–92, 101, 107–9, 115–16, 121, 129–31, 136–9, 145–6, 157, 160, 185–6, 203–6, 209–11, 218, 225–6, 242–7, 251–5, 256
subterraneous/subterranean fire/heat/pressure, 37, 39, 83, 110, 113, 129, 131, 136–8, 142, 144, 147, 150–1, 154n, 156, 160, 161–2, 165, 171, 174, 184, 188, 199, 237, 244, 253
Surveying the Highlands and Islands, 2, 8, 26, 67, 68, 69–71, 74, 86–7, 91, 181, 211, 232, 234–5, 252, 258–9

temporal sublime, 24, 30
theories of the earth, 5, 6, 11, 13, 15, 16, 18, 29n, 39, 40–4, 58, 60n, 64–5, 81, 83, 99, 100, 109–10, 120, 129, 131, 136, 149–52, 154n, 155–63, 166, 169–70, 171, 186, 191–2, 193n, 194n, 197–8, 200–1, 202, 207, 211, 216, 217, 220–2, 223, 226, 229–31, 233, 235–6, 238, 240, 242
Thomson, James, 90–1, 106, 211
tours and tourism, 1–7, 8, 11–12, 14–16, 18, 25–6, 27n, 32, 40, 41, 43, 44–5,

47–59, 63, 66, 67, 68–71, 73–7, 87, 93, 97–8, 100–2, 104–8, 109, 121–2, 123n, 124n, 128–30, 155, 157, 160–1, 163–6, 171, 192–3, 198, 205–6, 207, 212, 218–20, 222, 230–2, 234–5, 247–50, 256–7, 257–60, 261n
travel and travel writing, 2, 4, 5–12, 14–26, 27n, 28n, 29n, 31–6, 43, 44, 48–59, 64, 65–6, 71–3, 73–5, 75–7, 84–5, 86, 92, 93, 95n, 97, 98–9, 100–4, 109, 112, 115, 121, 127–31, 132–5, 140, 141–2, 158, 168–70, 174–5, 178–9, 192–3, 203–5, 219, 220–1, 230, 231–2, 234–5, 237, 243, 245, 249–55, 256–7, 257–60
Troil, Hugo von, 114, 125n, 141–3, 254
Trotternish peninsula (Skye), 85, 241–3
Turner, J. M. W., 4, 248, 256–7, 262n, 263n

unconformity, 27n, 162–3, 166, 183–4, 186–91, 199, 212–13, 222, 223–5, 233

virtual witness/tourist/traveller, 14, 16, 29n, 165, 179, 191–2
volcanic, volcanism, volcanoes, 3, 5, 6, 11, 21, 26, 37, 65, 80–1, 83, 98, 99, 101, 108, 109–13, 117–22, 124n,

125n, 126n, 127–53, 153n, 154n, 156, 161, 197–8, 201–2, 229, 243–4, 253

Vulcanists, Vulcanism, 5, 6, 65, 95n, 99, 109, 111, 113, 127, 129, 148, 150, 152, 161, 197, 198, 202, 219, 254

Walker, John, 10–11, 47, 59, 63–96, 102, 106, 112–13, 114, 124n, 149, 151–2, 161, 192, 197, 198, 200, 212–13, 219, 221, 232, 235, 262n

Werner, Abraham Gottlob, 44, 99, 194–5n, 197–8, 200–2, 213, 215–16, 221–2, 223–5, 226n, 227n, 231, 258

Whitehurst, John, 44, 120, 131

Woodward, John, 34, 43–4, 59n, 61n, 65, 71

Wordsworth, William, 4, 28n, 89, 129–30, 153n, 157, 227n, 247, 256–7, 262n, 263n

writing style, 8, 11–16, 21–5, 29n, 33–6, 48–50, 53, 55–9, 65, 72–3, 75–6, 87–93, 98, 100, 101–2, 104, 107–8, 115–17, 121, 130, 133–47, 157, 165, 168–70, 174–80, 189–91, 192–3, 200, 203–6, 206–8, 208–11, 213–18, 220–1, 230, 232–3, 234–5, 236–7, 243, 245–6, 249, 250–5, 258